CHINA
PROFILED

Essential facts on society, business and politics
in China

Edited by Barry Turner

ST.MARTIN'S PRESS
NEW YORK

CHINA PROFILED

Copyright © 1999 by Barry Turner

St Martin's Press, Scholarly and Reference Division, 175 Fifth Avenue, New York, N.Y. 10010

First published in the United States of America in 1999

Printed in the United Kingdom

ISBN: 0–312–22725–6

Library of Congress Cataloging-in-Publication number 99–051350

Contents

Colour maps fall between pages 112 and 113

CHINA

Zhonghua Renmin Gonghe Guo
(People's Republic of China)

Capital: **Beijing (Peking)**

Area: **9,572,900 sq. km**

Population estimate, 2000: **1,276·3m.**

Head of State: **Jiang Zemin**

Head of Government: **Zhu Rongji**

TERRITORY AND POPULATION

China is bounded in the north by Russia and Mongolia; east by North Korea, the Yellow Sea and the East China Sea, with Hong Kong and Macao as enclaves on the southeast coast; south by Vietnam, Laos, Myanmar, India, Bhutan and Nepal; west by India, Pakistan, Afghanistan, Tajikistan, Kyrgyzstan and Kazakhstan. The total area (including Taiwan) is estimated at 9,572,900 sq. km (3,696,100 sq. miles). A law of Feb. 1992 claimed the Spratly, Paracel and Diaoyutasi Islands. An agreement of 7 Sept. 1993 at prime ministerial level settled Sino-Indian border disputes which had first emerged in the war of 1962.

At the 1991 census the population was 1,130,510,638 (548,690,231 females). Population estimate, 1996: 1,223·89m. (601·89m. female; 359·5m., or 29·3%, urban); density, 128 per sq. km.

The UN gives a projected population for 2000 of 1,276·3m.

China is set to lose its status as the world's most populous country to India by 2050.

1979 regulations restricting married couples to a single child, a policy enforced by compulsory abortions and economic sanctions, have been widely ignored, and it was admitted in 1988 that the population target of 1,200m. by 2000 would have to be revised to 1,270m. Since 1988 peasant couples have been permitted a second child after 4 years if the first born is a girl, a measure to combat infanticide.

43·2m. persons of Chinese origin lived abroad in 1993.

A number of widely divergent varieties of Chinese are spoken. The official 'Modern Standard Chinese' is based on the dialect of North China. The ideographic writing system of 'characters' is uniform throughout the country, and has undergone systematic simplification. In 1958 a phonetic alphabet (*Pinyin*) was devised to transcribe the characters, and in 1979 this was officially adopted for use in all texts in the Roman alphabet. The previous transcription scheme (Wade) is still used in Taiwan and Hong Kong.

China is administratively divided into 22 provinces, 5 autonomous regions (originally entirely or largely inhabited by ethnic minorities, though in some regions now outnumbered by Han immigrants) and 4 government-controlled municipalities. These are in turn divided into 335 prefectures, 666 cities (of which 218 are at prefecture level and 445 at county level), 2,142 counties and 717 urban districts.

Government-controlled municipalities	Area (in 1,000 sq. km)	Population (1990 census, in 1,000)	Density per sq. km (in 1987)	Population (1996 estimate, in 1,000)	Capital
Beijing	17·8	10,870	644	12,590	–
Tianjin	4·0	8,830	777	9,480	–
Shanghai	5·8	13,510	2,152	14,190	–
Provinces					
Hebei[2]	202·7	60,280	301	64,840	Shijiazhuang
Shanxi	157·1	28,180	183	31,090	Taiyuan
Liaoning[2]	151·0	39,980	261	41,160	Shenyang
Jilin[2]	187·0	25,150	132	26,100	Changchun
Heilongjiang[2]	463·6	34,770	76	37,280	Harbin
Jiangsu	102·2	68,170	654	71,100	Nanjing
Zhejiang[2]	101·8	40,840	407	43,430	Hangzhou
Anhui	139·9	52,290	402	60,700	Hefei
Fujian	123·1	30,610	244	32,610	Fuzhou
Jiangxi	164·8	38,280	229	41,050	Nanchang
Shandong	153·3	83,430	551	87,380	Jinan
Henan	167·0	86,140	512	91,720	Zhengzhou
Hubei[2]	187·5	54,760	288	58,250	Wuhan
Hunan[2]	210·5	60,600	288	64,280	Changsha
Guangdong[2]	197·1	63,210	319	69,610	Guangzhou
Hainan[2]	34·3	6,420	191	7,340	Haikou
Sichuan[2]	569·0	106,370	188	114,300	Chengdu

Guizhou[2]	174·0	32,730	186	35,550	Guiyang
Yunnan[2]	436·2	36,750	85	40,420	Kunming
Shaanxi	195·8	32,470	168	35,430	Xian
Gansu[2]	366·5	22,930	61	24,670	Lanzhou
Qinghai[2]	721·0	4,430	6	4,880	Xining
Autonomous regions					
Inner Mongolia	1,177·5	21,110	18	23,070	Hohhot
Guangxi Zhuang	220·4	42,530	192	45,890	Nanning
Tibet[1]	1,221·6	2,220	2	2,440	Lhasa
Ningxia Hui	170.0	4,660	70	5,210	Yinchuan
Xinjiang Uighur	1,646·8	15,370	9	16,890	Urumqi

[1]See also Tibet below.

[2]Also designated minority nationality autonomous area.

Population of largest cities in 1993: Shanghai, 8·76m.; Beijing (Peking), 6·56m.; Tianjin, 4·97m.; Shenyang, 3·86m.; Wuhan, 3·86m.; Chongqing, 3·78m.; Guangzhou (Canton), 3·56m.; Harbin, 3·1m.; Chengdu, 2·67m.; Zibo (1991), 2·46m.; Nanjing, 2·43m.; Changchun, 2·4m.; Xian, 2·36m.; Dalian, 2·33m.; Qingdao, 2·24m.; Jinan, 2·05m.; Hangzhou, 1·74m.; Taiyuan, 1·68m.; Zhengzhou, 1·53m.; Kunming, 1·45m.; Tangshan (1990), 1·5m.; Changsha, 1·48m.; Nanchang, 1·42m.; Anshan (1991), 1·39m.; Qiqihar (1991), 1·38m.; Fushun (1991), 1·35m.; Lanzhou, 1·32m.; Fuzhou, 1·29m.; Jilin (1991), 1·27m.; Shijiazhuang, 1·21m.; Baotou (1991), 1·2m.; Huainan (1991), 1·2m.; Luoyang (1991), 1·19m.; Urumqi, 1·11m.; Datong (1991), 1·11m.; Handan (1991), 1·11m.; Guiyang, 1·07m.; Ningbo, 1·07m.

The autonomous regions and 14 provinces (*see table above*) have non-Han components in their populations, ranging from 97·2% (in 1994) in Tibet to 9·9% in Zhejiang. Total minority population, 1994, 72,818,100. 55 ethnic minorities are identified. At the 1990 census the largest were: Zhuang, 15,555,820; Manchu, 9,846,776; Hui, 8,612,001; Miao, 7,383,622; Uighur, 7,207,024; Yi, 6,578,524; Tujia, 5,725,049; Mongolian, 4,802,407; Tibetan, 4,593,072.

Li Chengrui, *The Population of China*. Beijing, 1992

The Population Atlas of China. OUP, 1988

Song, J. *et al.*, *Population Control in China*. New York, 1985

Tibet

After the 1959 revolt was suppressed, the Preparatory Committee for
the Autonomous Region of Tibet (set up in 1955) took over the func-
tions of local government, led by its Vice-Chairman, the Banqen
Lama, in the absence of its Chairman, the Dalai Lama, who had fled to
India in 1959. In Dec. 1964 both the Dalai and Banqen Lamas were
removed from their posts and on 9 Sept. 1965 Tibet became an
Autonomous Region. 301 delegates were elected to the first People's
Congress, of whom 226 were Tibetans. The Chief of Government is
Gyaincain Norbu. The senior spiritual leader, the Dalai Lama, is in
exile. He was awarded the Nobel Peace Prize in 1989. The Banqen
Lama died in Jan. 1989. The borders were opened for trade with
neighbouring countries in 1980. In July 1988 Tibetan was reinstated
as a 'major official language', competence in which is required of all
administrative officials. Monasteries and shrines have been renovat-
ed and reopened. There were some 15,000 monks and nuns in 1987.
In 1984 a Buddhist seminary in Lhasa opened with 200 students.
A further softening of Beijing's attitude towards Tibet was shown
during President Bill Clinton's visit to China in June 1998. Jiang
Zemin, China's president, said he was prepared to meet the Dalai
Lama providing he acknowledged Chinese sovereignty over Tibet
and Taiwan.

In 1996 the population was 2·49m. In 1994 there were 2·22m.
Tibetans living in Tibet out of a total population of 2·36m. Birth rate
(per 1,000), 1996, 24·7; death rate, 8·5; growth rate, 16·2. Population
of the capital, Lhasa, in 1992 was 124,000. Expectation of life was 65
years in 1990. 2m. Tibetans live outside Tibet, in China, and in India
and Nepal.

Chinese efforts to modernize Tibet include irrigation, road-building
and the establishment of light industry. In 1991 there were 328 township and 123 village enterprises employing 21,168 persons; 12,000
persons worked in heavy industry, 16,000 in state-owned enterprises.

1990 output included 136,300 metres of woollen fabrics, 1,000 tonnes of salt, 1,900 tonnes of vegetable oil, 208,200 cu. metres of timber and 132,300 tonnes of cement.

Electricity production in 1990 was 330m. kWh, of which 323m. kWh were hydro-electric.

In 1996 there were 953,000 rural labourers, including 886,000 in farming, forestry and fisheries. The total sown area was 220,100 ha, including 52,500 ha sown to wheat, 18,300 ha to rapeseed, 18,300 ha to oil-bearing crops and 14,500 ha to soya beans. Output (in 1,000 tonnes), 1996: Wheat, 261; soya beans, 41; oil-bearing crops, 35; rapeseeds, 35. There were 5·10m. cattle, 1·21m. draught animals, 0·36m. horses, 0·22m. pigs, 11·10m. sheep and 5·83m. goats in 1996.

In 1991 there were 21,842 km of roads, of which 6,240 km were paved. There are airports at Lhasa and Bangda providing external links. 30,000 tourists visited Tibet in 1986.

In 1988 there were 2,437 primary schools, 67 secondary schools, 14 technical schools and 3 higher education institutes. The total number of primary school pupils in 1990–91 was 101,000. A university was established in 1985.

In 1990 there were some 9,000 medical personnel and 1,006 medical institutions, with a total of about 5,000 beds.

Barnett, R. and Akiner, S. (eds.) *Resistance and Reform in Tibet.* Farnborough, 1994

Batchelor, S., *The Tibet Guide.* London, 1987

The Dalai Lama, *My Land and My People* (ed. D. Howarth). London, 1962: – *Freedom in Exile.* London, 1990

Grunfeld, A. T., *The Making of Modern Tibet.* London, 1987

Levenson, C. B., *The Dalai Lama: A Biography.* London, 1988

Pinfold, John, *Tibet* [Bibliography]. Oxford and Santa Barbara (CA), 1991

Schwartz, R. D., *Circle of Protest: Political Ritual in the Tibetan Uprising.* Farnborough, 1994

Shakabpa, T. W. D., *Tibet: A Political History.* New York, 1984

Sharabati, D., *Tibet and its History.* London, 1986

Smith, W. W., *A History of Tibet: Nationalism and Self-Determination.* Oxford, 1996

TIME ZONE INFORMATION

For political and administrative reasons and despite its size, China in its entirety adheres to Beijing time. Beijing time is 8 hrs ahead of GMT (7 hrs ahead of BST).

REGIONS

Anhui Province
Capital: Hefei

Other major cities: Huainan, Bengbu, Wuhu, Tongling, Anqing, Ma'Anshan, Huaibei and Tunxi. Ethnic groups: Han, Hui and She.

Area: 130,000 sq. km.

Climate: warm-temperate, semi-humid, monsoonal climate north of the Huaihe River with frequent spring droughts and summer floods; subtropical, humid, monsoonal climate in the south; clear-cut seasons; rains between spring and summer, sometimes followed by summer droughts.

Physical features: mainly plains and hills; the alluvial plain of the Huaihe River and its tributaries, 20–40 metres in altitude, makes up half of the province's farmland; hills line both sides of the Yangtze River.

Dabie Mountains in the central west; in the south, the Huangshan and Jiuhua Mountains. Products: rice, wheat, sorghum, corn, millet, potatoes, soybeans, peanuts, sesame, rape, peas, silk cocoons, cotton, ambary hemp, Chinese tallow tree, ramie, tobacco, apples, pears, yangtao gingko, iron, coal and copper. Anhui is a province famous for tea growing, especially Qimenhong, Tunxilu, Huangshan Maofeng, and Liu'an Guapian teas.

Tourist attractions: Huangshan Mountain is famous for its sea of clouds, hot springs, precipitous rocks and pines. Jiuhua Mountain is famous for its Buddhist temples.

Beijing Municipality

Beijing is the capital city of the People's Republic of China. For population and history see city profile of Beijing on page 63.

Ethnic groups: Han, Hui, Manchu and Mongolian.

Area: 16,800 sq. km.

Climate: Beijing has a warm, often humid, monsoonal climate with hot, rainy summers but cold, dry winters.

Physical features: Mountainous in the north and west. Flatlands dominate the southeast. The Yongding River runs through the municipality and is a tributary of the Haihe River.

Products: Wheat, corn, millet, potatoes, rice, peanuts, soybeans, sesame, cotton, silk cocoons, tobacco, pears, grapes, coal, iron, marble and asbestos. Beijing is famous for its Miyun dates, Jingbai pears and Beijing or Peking duck.

Tourist attractions: The Forbidden City, Temple of Heaven, Great Wall and Summer (see city profile of Beijing on page 63).

Fujian Province

Capital: Fuzhou.

Other major cities: Xiamen, Nanping, Sanming, Zhangzhou and Quanzhou.

Ethnic groups: Han, She, Hui, Miao, Manchu and Gaoshan.

Area: 120,000 sq. km.

Climate: subtropical, humid, monsoonal climate. There can be spring droughts, typhoons and rainstorms in summer and autumn.

Physical features: graduated descent from the northwest to the southeastern seaboard. A large portion of Fujian consists of mountains and hills. There are long and narrow plains along the southern coast. The East China Sea lies at its northeast boundary and the South China Sea lies toward the south. Taiwan Province is across the Taiwan Strait.

Products: Fujian is a fertile crop-growing area producing rice, wheat, sweet potatoes, peanuts, sugar cane, rape, soybeans, sesame, tea, longans, oranges, lychees, pineapples, pomelos, bananas, mushrooms, jute, tobacco, medicinal herbs and tea oil. A substantial part of its crops come from the sea.

Tourist attractions: Gulangyu Island, called the 'garden on the sea', is in Xiamen. Wuyishan is a scenic spot in Chong'an County.

Gansu Province

Capital: Lanzhou.

Other major cities: Jiayuguan, Tianshui, Yumen, Dunhuang and Jinchang.

Ethnic groups: Han, Hui, Tibetan, Dongxiang, Yugur, Baonan, Mongolian, Kazak, Tu, Salar and Manchu.

Area: 390,000 sq. km.

Climate: subtropical, humid climate in the east changes to a temperate, dry climate in the west; cold, humid, highland climate in the Oilian Mountains. Temperatures shift greatly from day to night as well as from season to season in the central and western parts of the province.

Physical features: The Qinghai-Tibet and Inner Mongolia Plateaux, mostly above 1,000 metres, adjoin the province. Where the plateaux meet is a narrow, 1,000-km passage, the Hexi or Gansu Corridor, which was part of the ancient Silk Route leading to the Western

Regions, present-day Xinjiang and areas further to the west. The region is a mountainous one with the Oilian Range along the central part of the Gansu-Qinghai border, the Beishan Mountains in the north and the Dieshan Mountains in the southwest.

Products: Wheat, highland barley, millet, broomcorn millet, potatoes, corn, sorghum, rice, rape, soybeans, sugar beet, cotton, sun-cured tobacco, wool, leather. The area is rich in coal, petroleum, nickel, copper, sulphur and zinc.

Tourist attractions: Dunhuang, a post on the former Silk Road, famous for its Mogao Grottoes.

Guangdong Province

Capital: Guangzhou. For population and history see city profile of Guangzhou on page 73.

Other major cities: Shantou, Foshan, Zhanjiang, Shenzhen, Zhuhai and Shaoguan.

Ethnic groups: Han, Yao, Zhuang, Hui, Manchu and She.

Area: 180,000 sq. km.

Climate: Subtropical–tropical with a humid, monsoon climate. The rainy season lasts from April to Sept. and typhoons are to be expected from May to Nov.

Physical features: Much of Guangdong's land is fertile thanks to the Pearl River Delta which covers a large area of the province, providing silt and water for many crops. Guangdong has a coastline 4,300 km long and is situated on the Tropic of Cancer. It is a varied landscape with hills in the north and lowlands in the south. The Leizhou Peninsula extends to the southwest. Mountains run from west to east in an arc. These are the Yunwu, Nanling, Jiulian and Lianhua Mountains.

Products: Guangdong is famous for its rice growing but products include potatoes, corn, millet, wheat, sugar cane, peanuts, soybeans, sesame, tea, silk cocoons, bananas, oranges, lychees, pineapples and other fruit. The province is rich in tin, bismuth, copper, lead, zinc, oil shale, salt and sulphur.

Tourist attraction: Seven Star Crags in Zhaoqing.

Guangxi Zhuang Autonomous Region

Capital: Nanning.

Other major cities: Liuzhou, Guilin, Wuzhou, Beihai, Pingxiang and Bose.

Ethnic groups: Over 90% of the people that inhabit this region are Zhuang. Others include Han, Yao, Miao, Tong, Mulam, Maonan, Hui, Jing, Yi, Shui and Gelo.

Area: 230,000 sq. km.

Climate: The region has a subtropical and humid, monsoon climate with long, hot summers and warm, short winters. It is one of China's most rainy regions with an average rainfall of 1,500 mm per year, with 80% of that falling between April and Sept.

Physical features: Guangxi's southwestern border joins Vietnam. It has a southern coastline of 1,500 km facing the Beibu bay. It is protected on 3 sides by mountains, high in the northwest and low in the southeast, and is drained by western branches of the Pearl River.

Products: The central plains and low hills of Guanxi support rice, wheat, corn, potatoes, millet, rape, cassava, peanuts, sugar cane, tea, soybeans, silk cocoons, tobacco and an assortment of fruit. Cash crops grown in the region include rubber, coffee, pepper, tea oil and lemongrass. The region is rich in bauxite, salt, coal, plaster stone, sulphur, tin, phosphorus, iron and gold.

Tourist Attractions: The Karst Peaks provide a strange mountainous landscape.

Guizhou Province

Capital: Guiyang.

Other major cities: Zunyi, Lupanshui, Duyun, Anshun, Kaili and Bijie.

Ethnic groups: Han, Miao, Bouyei, Tong, Yi, Shui, Hui, Gelo, Zhuang and Yao.

Area: 170,000 sq. km.

Climate: Guizhou has a subtropical, humid climate with few seasonal changes. It has frequent cloudy and rainy weather. Rainfall is high with an average of 900–1,500 mm per year with high precipitation in the central and southwestern regions.

Physical features: The province is above 1,000 metres above sea level in most areas, situated on the eastern Yunnan-Guizhou Plateau. Mountains in the west slope down towards the north, east, and south.

Products: The land in Guizhou is fertile allowing the farming of rice, wheat, corn, millet, potatoes, rape, sugar cane, soybeans, peanuts, sesame, tea, cotton, lemongrass, cork, coffee, olives and fruit such as pears, oranges, apples, bananas, pineapples, walnuts and chestnuts. The province is rich in mercury, coal, phosphorus, bauxite and natural gas.

Tourist attractions: The Huangguoshu Falls are 20 metres wide and 60 metres high. There are nearby caves and the famous stone forests are located between the Zhenning and the Guanling Counties.

Hainan Province

Hainan Province is China's newest administrative division. Consisting of Hainan Island and the South China Sea Islands, it is the smallest province.

Capital: Haikou.

Ethnic groups: Han, Li, and Miao.

Area: 34,000 sq. km.

Climate: Hainan Province has a tropical climate with high temperatures all year round, with little distinguishable difference between the seasons. Rainfall is high and evenly distributed throughout the year.

Physical features: Hainan Island, also known as Qiong'ai, is the second largest island in China with an area of 32,000 sq. km. The northern Philippine island of Luzon lies to the east and Vietnam is only 200 miles to the west. The Wuzhi and Limu Mountains dominate the central area, taking up a third of the island. The Qiongzhou Strait separates the Hainan Island from the mainland. Over 20 km wide, the Qiongzhou Strait connects the Beibu Bay to the South China Sea.

Products: Hainan Province is rich in iron, salt and petroleum from the South China Sea. Xisha and its neighbouring areas are a rich fishing ground.

Hebei Province

Capital: Shijiazhuang.

Other major cities: Tangshan, Handan, Zhangjiakou, Chengde, Qinhuangdao and Baoding.

Ethnic groups: Han, Hui, Manchu, Mongolian, and Korean.

Area: 190,000 sq. km.

Climate: Hebei has a temperate climate. It is windy in the spring and has hot, rainy summers with dry winters. Rainfall is low except for the seaward side of the mountains.

Physical features: Hebei has high mountains in the north called the Yanshan Mountains, and the Taihang Range runs along the western border. Land is low in the southeast and faces the Bohai Gulf.

Products: Hebei produces corn, millet, wheat, potatoes, rice, soya beans, peanuts, rape, sesame, mushrooms, cotton, silk cocoons, tobacco, chestnuts, apricots, grapes, walnuts, dates and pears. Its natural resources include iron, coal, petroleum and salt.

Tourist attractions: Shanhaiguan is the eastern pass of the Great Wall, and the Imperial Summer Residence is in Chengde.

Heilongjiang Province

Capital: Harbin.

Other major cities: Qiqihar, Mudanjiang, Jiamusi, Jixi, Hegang, Shuangyashan, Daqing and Heihe.

Ethnic groups: Han, Manchu, Korean, Mongolian, Hui, Daur, Oroqen, Hezhen, Kirgiz and Ewenki.

Area: 460,000 sq. km.

Climate: Heilongjiang is a harsh province which spans the cold-temperate and semi-humid plains of the north. It has short summers and long winters with no summer at all in the cold northwest. It is subjected to spring droughts, summer flooding and autumn frost. Temperatures range between –33°C in the winter and 23°C in summer.

Physical features: Heliongjiang borders Inner Mongolia to the west and Russia to the north. The Emur, Yilehuli and Lesser Hinggan Mountains stretch across the north with plains dominating the east and the west. In some areas there are intermittent volcanic eruptions.

Products: Hunting is an important part of life for the inhabitants of Heilongjiang. Very little is grown on a large scale but there is corn, sorghum, millet, wheat, rice, potatoes, soybeans, sugar beet, sesame and sunflower seeds. Many animals are trapped including squirrel, alpine weasel, sable and otter. Other cash crops include ginseng, antlers, tigerbone, musk and other medicinal materials. There is a large yearly crop of chum salmon, sturgeon and huso sturgeon.

Tourist attractions: The ice festival and Sun Island in Harbin.

Henan Province

Capital: Zhengzhou.

Other major cities: Luoyang, Kaifeng, Pingdingshan, Xinxiang, Anyang and Nanyang.

Ethnic groups: Han, Hui, Mongolian and Manchu.

Area: 160,000 sq. km.

Climate: Henan province ranges from the warm and temperate to the semi-humid and subtropical. It can have dry, windy winters and hot, rainy summers. Temperatures range from –3°C in the winter to 29°C in mid-summer. There is high rainfall in the southern and northern mountains. 50% of the rain falls during the summer.

Physical features: Plains cover the east and mountains dominate the west. Part of the Yangtze River Basin lies in the southwest. Products: Wheat, millet, sorghum, corn, rice, potatoes, peanuts, sesame, soybeans, sugar cane, rape, cotton, flue-cured tobacco, oriental oak, apples, peaches, grapes and walnuts. Natural resources include coal, bauxite, mica and nickel.

Tourist attractions: The Shaolin Monastery was the birthplace of China's most famous martial arts tradition, Shaolin Kung Fu.

Hong Kong Special Administrative Region

Hong Kong is an ex-crown colony of Great Britain. Handed back to The People's Republic of China in 1997, it is now a Special Administrative Region. For population and history see city profile of Hong Kong on page 135.

Hubei Province

Capital: Wuhan.

Other major cities: Huangshi, Yichang, Shashi, Xiangfan, Shiyan, Enshi and Jiangling.

Ethnic groups: Han, Tujia, Hui, Manchu, Miao and Mongolian.

Area: 180,000 sq. km.

Climate: Hubei has a subtropical, humid, monsoonal climate. Summers are hot and winters are dry. Hubei is subject to frequent droughts and floods. Temperatures range from as low as 1°C in the winter months to as high as 30°C in mid-summer.

Physical features: Land is high in the west and low in the east. Most of Hubei is mountainous and hilly except in the south. The Yangtze River and its tributary the Hanshui River run through the province. There are many lakes in Hubei including the Honghu, Liangzi, Futou, Zhangdu, Longgarl, Changhu and Diaocha Lakes.

Products: Rice, wheat, sorghum, millet, potatoes, corn, rape, sesame, tea, soybeans, peanuts, sugar cane, cotton, ramie, silk cocoons, sun-cured tobacco, pearls, peaches, yangtao, oranges, chestnuts and tung oil. The province is rich in iron, copper, rock salt and plaster stone.

Tourist attractions: Gezhouba Dam, or the Three Gorges project, near Yichang and Shennongjia Natural Reserve in western Hubei.

Hunan Province

Capital: Changsha.

Other major cities: Zhuzhou, Hengyang, Xiangtan, Shaoyang and Lengshuijiang.

Ethnic groups: Han, Tujia, Miao, Dong, Yao, Hui, Uighur and Zhuang.

Area: 210,000 sq. km.

Climate: Hunan is subtropical and humid. Hunan has short winters with low temperatures in the south and the northwestern mountains. There are frequent rainstorms between spring and summer and droughts from summer to autumn. Temperatures range from 4°C in the winter to 30°C in mid-summer.

Physical features: Mountains and hills cover 80% of the province and a small plain surrounds Dongting Lake in the central north. There are many mountains in the province. The Luoxiao Mountains in the east became a refuge for the Communist forces in the 1920s. The Yangtze River touches the border near Dongting Lake.

Products: Rice, wheat, potatoes, corn, millet, rape, soybeans, peanuts, sugar cane, sesame, tea, cotton, tea oil, lotus seeds, starfruit, oranges, lily, timber, lead, zinc and other non-ferrous and rare metals.

Tourist attractions: Mount Hengshan, 1,290 metres high, is one of the Five Mountains in eastern China. Dongting Lake, once the biggest fresh water lake in China, has an area of 2,820 sq. km.

Jiangsu Province

Capital: Nanjing.

Other major cities: Wuxi, Suzhou, Xuzhou, Lianyungang, Changzhou, Nantong and Zhenjiang.

Ethnic groups: Han, Hui, and Manchu.

Area: 100,000 sq. km.

Climate: Jiangsu is predominantly hot and humid during the summer months with temperatures reaching 29°C. Winter temperatures can fall to as low as –2°C. The south can see heavy rain during the summer.

Physical features: Jiangsu is a low lying province with over 1,000 km of coastline on the Yellow Sea. Plains cover 95% of the province. The Grand Canal runs through the heart of Jiangsu.

Products: rice, wheat, corn, sorghum, millet, potatoes, soybeans, peanuts, rape, sesame, teal cotton, spearmint, bamboo and medicinal herbs. Fruits grown include apples, pears, peaches and star fruit.

Tourist attractions: The Suzhou Gardens, Lake Taihu in Wuxi and the Grand Canal.

Jiangxi Province

Capital: Nanchang

Other major cities: Jiujiang, Ganzhou, Jingdezhen, Ji'an and Ruijin.

Ethnic groups: Han, Hui, Miao, She and Yao.

Area: 160,000 sq. km.

Climate: Jiangxi is subtropical and humid. It is subject to heavy, monsoonal rainstorms in summer. Average temperatures range from 3°C in the winter to 31°C in the summer.

Physical features: The south is hilly and mountainous. These mountains gradually slope towards Poyang Lake in the north. The Poyang Lake is China's largest freshwater lake at 3,583 sq. km.

Products: Jiangxi has fertile soil, products of which include wheat, corn, potatoes, millet, rape, sugar cane, tea, peanuts, soybeans, sesame, cotton, silk cocoons, oranges and lotus seeds. Jiangxi is also famous for its production of pottery and ceramics.

Tourist attractions: Mount Lushan is a mountain resort by Poyang Lake. Jingdezhen, on the Chang River, is an ancient town well known for its production of ceramics.

Jilin Province

Capital: Changchun.

Other major cities: Jilin, Siping, Tonghua, Baicheng, Yanii, Huniiang, Liaoyuan and Tumen.

Ethnic groups: Han, Korean, Manchu, Hui, Mongolian and Xibe.

Area: 180,000 sq. km.

Climate: Jilin has long cold winters and short, rainy summers. Temperatures can plunge as low as −20°C in the winter but summers can see the temperature rise to 24°C.

Physical features: The Changbai Mountains sit on the southeast border with Korea. The Yalu and Tumen Rivers form the boundary between China and Korea. The vast Songliao Plain dominates the northwest.

Products: Corn, millet, sorghum, rice, wheat, potatoes, soybeans, sugar beet, tobacco, flax, silk, ginseng, sable fur, antlers, timber, coal and oil.

Liaoning Province

Capital: Shenyang.

Other major cities: Anshan, Benxi, Dalian, Fushun, Dandong, Jinzhou and Yingkou.

Ethnic groups: Han, Manchu, Mongolian, Hui, Korean and Xibe.

Area: 150,000 sq. km.

Climate: Liaoning has a humid, monsoonal climate in the coastal regions. It has hot, rainy summers but long, cold winters. Temperatures range from −17°C in winter to 25°C in the summer.

Physical features: The Nuluerhu Mountains in the west and the Qianshan Mountains in the east give way to plains in the southern coastal areas. The Liaodong Peninsula in the south stretches out to enclose the Bohai Gulf.

Products: Corn, millet, sorghum, rice, wheat, potatoes, soybeans, peanuts, sesame, cotton, silk cocoons, flax, tussah, apples, pears, grapes, ginseng and antlers. Sea products include cutlass fish, shrimp and shellfish. The province is rich in iron, coal, manganese, magnesium, talcum, petroleum and salt.

Tourist attractions: The Imperial Palace in Shenyang, which was the Manchurian Capital in the 17th Century, is a Forbidden City in miniature.

Nei Mongol Autonomous Region (Inner Mongolia)

Capital: Hohhot.

Other major cities: Baotou, Wuhai, Hailar, Manzhouli, Tongliao, Chifeng, Jining, Erenhot and Ulanhot.

Ethnic groups: Mongolian, Han, Daur, Ewenki, Oroqen, Hui, Manchu and Korean.

Area: 1,100,000 sq. km.

Climate: Inner Mongolia is subject to cold, long winters with harsh blizzards and warm but short summers. Temperatures range from −23°C to 26°C.

Physical features: Nei Mongol is almost completely over 1,000 ft above sea level. West of the Greater Hinggan Mountain range is the Hulunbuir Plateau. This is a vast grassland plateau. Much of Nei Mongol is dominated by desert and salt and alkali lakes.

Products: Wheat, naked oats, millet, corn, potatoes, rape, sugar beet, soybeans, flax, wool, musk, bezoar, liquorice root, iron, coal, alkali, salt, graphite, mica and sulphur.

Qinghai Province

Capital: Xining.

Other major cities: Golmud, Lenghu, Da Qaidam, Yushu, Gonghe and Delingha.

Ethnic groups: Han, Tibetan, Hui, Tu, Salar, Mongolian and Kazak

Area: 720,000 sq. km.

Climate: Qinghai is predominantly dry and cold. It is subject to long winters and short summers and is prone to sandstorms. The temperature differences between day and night are great. Average temperatures vary from −19°C to 21°C.

Physical features: Qinghai borders the Tibetan Plateau. The Yellow and Huangshui River Valleys are in the mountainous east. The Yangtze River's source is in the southwest.

Products: Qinghai is famous for its Xining Wool. Other products include wheat, highland barley, millet, rice, potatoes, rape, broad beans, peas, leather, musk and antlers. Quinghai's natural resources are petroleum, salt, sylvite, coal, lead and zinc.

Tourist attractions: Ta'er Lamasery, in the town of Huangzhong, 25 km southeast of Xining, is the birthplace of Tsong Khapa, the father of the Yellow Hat Sect of Buddhism.

Ningxia Hui Autonomous Region

Capital: Yinchuan.

Other major cities: Shizuishan, Wuzhong, Guyuan, Zhongwei and Qingtongxia.

Ethnic groups: Hui, Han and Manchu.

Area: 66,000 sq. km.

Climate: Ningxia has long, cold winters and short, hot summers. It is subject to strong winds. Average temperatures range from −10°C to 24°C.

Physical features: Ningxia ranges from 2,000 metres above sea level in the mountains to 1,000 metres on the plains. The Yellow River traverses the region from the northeast to the west.

Products: Ningxia is famous for its argali sheep hide and wool. Other products include wheat, millet, potatoes, corn, rape, soybeans, liquorice root, wolfberry fruit, flax, hemp, plaster stone, salt and iron.

Shaanxi Province

Capital: Xian.

Other major cities: Xianyang, Baoji, Hanzhong, Tongchuan and Yan'an.

Ethnic groups: Han, Hui, Mongolian and Manchu.

Area: 190,000 sq. km.

Climate: Shaanxi is cold and desolate in the north with winter temperatures reaching as low as –15°C. This changes to a humid, monsoonal climate in the south with average temperatures as high as 28°C.

Physical features: A windswept plateau dominates the north of the province. This gives way to plains in central Shaanxi. The south is dominated by the Qinling Range of mountains. The Yellow River runs along the northeastern border of Shaanxi.

Products: Wheat, corn, sorghum, rice, millet, potatoes, soybeans, rape, peanuts, tea, sugar cane, sesame, peas, cotton, peaches, grapes, dates, chestnuts, palm, raw lacquer, bamboo, medicinal herbs, coal, iron, graphite and salt.

Tourist attractions: The world famous terracotta armies, guarding the tomb of Emperor Qin Shihuang, are near Xian.

Shandong Province

Capital: Jinan.

Other major cities: Yantai, Weifang, Qingdao, Zibo, Zaozhuang, Jining, Dongying and Oufu.

Ethnic groups: Han, Hui, and Manchu.

Area: 150,000 sq. km.

Climate: Shandong is predominantly warm and humid with rainy summers and dry winters. Shandong has an average rainfall of 865 mm per year with 60% of this falling during the summer.

Physical features: Shandong is in the Lower Yellow River Valley. It is hilly in the central region and on the eastern peninsula. It faces the Bohai Gulf in the north and the Yellow Sea in the east.

Products: The climate in Shandong lends itself to fruit growing. Specialities include Yantai apples, Leling jujubes, Laiyang pears, Pingdu grapes and Dezhou watermelons. Other products include wheat, corn, millet, potatoes, sweet potatoes, rice, soybeans, peanuts, tea, sesame, cotton, tussah, ambary hemp, flue cured tobacco, walnuts, chestnuts, many sea products, coal, petroleum and salt.

Tourist attractions: Confucius' Temple in Qufu, the birthplace of Confucius, is over 1 km long. Taishan is one of China's most sacred Taoist mountains.

Shanghai Municipality
Shanghai is China's largest industrial and commercial city. For population and history see city profile of Shanghai on page 68.

Ethnic groups: Han, Hui and Manchu.

Area: 5,800 sq. km.

Climate: Shanghai enjoys a subtropical climate with 4 distinct seasons. Typhoons often hit the city during the summer.

Physical features: The area is low-lying and flat. Shanghai is situated on the Yangtze River Delta.

Products: Shanghai is the commercial hub of China. Products include rice, wheat, potatoes, rape, soybeans, peanuts, cotton, silk cocoons, pears and assorted sea products.

Shanxi Province
Capital: Taiyuan.

Other major cities: Datong, Changzhi, Yuci, Yangquan, Linfen, Houma and Jiexiu.

Ethnic groups: Han, Hui, Mongolian and Manchu.

Area: 150,000 sq. km.

Climate: Shanxi has long, cold winters when the temperatures might plummet to under −16°C and mild summers with average temperatures in the 20s.

Physical features: Shanxi is situated on the eastern part of the Loess Plateau. In eastern Shanxi is the Taihang mountain range.

Products: Shanxi is known for its grape and pear growing. Other products include wheat, corn, millet, potatoes, soybeans, sesame, peanuts, rape, cotton, silk cocoons, tobacco, pears, dates and walnuts. Shanxi's natural resources include coal and iron.

Tourist attractions: The Yungang Buddhist grottoes near Datong date back to 5th century. The Jinci Temple near Taiyuan is a magnificent temple compound at the source of the Jin River.

Sichuan Province

Capital: Chengdu.

Other major cities: Chongqing, Dukou, Zigong, Yibin, Neijiang, Wanxian, Nanchong, Leshan, Luzhou and Xichang.

Ethnic groups: Han, Yi, Tibetan, Miao, Hui and Qiang.

Area: 560,000 sq. km.

Climate: The climate of Sichuan is varied with a subtropical, humid climate in the east and a temperate climate in the west with temperatures as low as −9°C. The temperature in the lowlands can reach 29°C in the summer months.

Physical features: Sichuan is one of China's larger provinces so the topography, like the climate, varies. The western plateau is over 3,000 metres above sea level but this gives way to the fertile lowlands with an average height of only 500 metres above sea level. The eastern lowlands are closed off by mountains and plateaux on all sides. The Yangtze River flows along Sichuan's southern and western borders.

Products: Much of Sichuan comprises rich and fertile land. Products include rice, corn, sweet potatoes, wheat, rape, sugar cane, peanuts, tea, silk cocoons, cotton, jute, sun-cured tobacco, tung oil, camphor, raw lacquer, bamboo, oranges, tangerines, pears, star fruit, lychees and bananas. Sichuan's natural resources include iron, coal, manganese, natural gas, petroleum, salt, alluvial gold, copper, nickel, phosphorus, sulphur and mica.

Tourist attractions: Wenshu Temple is a Buddhist temple that dates back to the Tang Dynasty. Carvings and sculptures in Dazu County are considered among the best in China and date back to the 9th century. The Leshan Grand Buddha, carved into a cliff, is, at over 70 metres high, the largest Buddha statue in the world. Sichuan is the home of the endangered giant panda and golden-haired monkey.

Taiwan Province

Capital: Taipei. For population and history of Taipei see city profile of Taipei on page 81.

Other major cities: Jilong, Gaoxiong, Tainan, Taizhong, Xinzhu, Pingdong and Taidong.

Ethnic groups: Han, Gaoshan.

Area: 36,000 sq. km.

Climate Features: Taiwan sits on the Tropic of Cancer and has a humid, tropical, monsoonal climate. It has long summers with plenty of rainfall, as much as 5,000 mm per year, and strong winds. Typhoons often hit the province during the summer months.

Physical features: Taiwan lies in the Pacific Ocean. It is 380 km long and 150 km wide and with a coastline 1,566 km long, it is China's largest island. Taiwan has many volcanoes and is prone to much seismic activity.

Products: Taiwan's lowlands are fertile, producing much rice and sugar cane. Other crops include corn, tubers, peanuts, soybeans and jute. Fruits are produced all year round.

For tourist attractions, see city profile of Taipei on page 81.

Tianjin Municipality

Tianjin is a major port city. Tianjin sits towards the southeast of Beijing. It is to this position, on the shores of the Bohai Sea and the Hai

River, that Tianjin owes its importance. It has been a bustling trading port since the 13th century and more recently an industrial success in the style of Shanghai.

Ethnic groups: Han, Hui, Korean, Manchu and Mongolian.

Area: 11,000 sq. km.

Climate: Tianjin has a predominantly warm, monsoonal climate. There are occasional summer floods and frequent spring droughts. Average temperatures range from –4°C in Jan. to 26°C in July.

Physical features: Tianjin sits on the alluvial plain of the Hai River.

Products: Wheat, corn, potatoes, sorghum, peanuts, soybeans, cotton, ambary hemp, pears, walnuts, sea products, petroleum and salt.

Xinjiang Uighur Autonomous Region

Capital: Urumqi.

Other major cities: Kashi, Yining, Hami, Karamay, Aksu, Shihezi, Holan and Korla.

Ethnic groups: Uygur, Han, Kazak, Hui, Mongolian, Xibe, Kirgiz, Ozbek, Tajik, Russian, Manchu, Daur and Tatar.

Area: 1,600,000 sq. km.

Climate: Xinjiang is a large province so the climate varies from north to south. There are also extreme temperature changes between night and day in much of the region. There is little rainfall with only an average of 150 mm falling per year.

Physical features: Three mountain ranges (the Tianshan Range, the Allay Range and the Karakorum, Kunlun, and Altun Mountains in the south) dissect the region into various sized basins and hilly low-land areas. Xinnjiang, as well as being home to mountains over 8,000 metres high, has the lowest point on the Chinese subcontinent. The Turpan depression is 155 metres below sea level. Xinjiang is home to the Taklimakan Desert, the Gurbantunggut Desert and the Gumtay Desert. Products: Wheat, rice, corn, sorghum, millet, potatoes, rape, sesame, sugar beet, peanuts, peaches, grapes, cotton and silk cocoons. Xianjing's natural resources include iron, coal, petroleum, gold, copper, salt, jade and sulphur.

Tourist attractions: Tianchi Lake (Lake of Heaven) near Urumqi, in the Tianshan Range. Bezeklik Thousand Buddha Caves are on the north side of the Flaming Mountains.

Xizang (Tibet) Autonomous Region

Capital: Lhasa.

Other major towns: Xigaze, Gyangze, Qamdo, Nyingchi, Gar, Nyalam.

Ethnic groups: Tibetan, Han, Moinba, Lhoba and Hui.

Area: 1,200,000 sq. km.

Climate: Tibet has a highland climate with lower temperatures and less rainfall than most of China. Due to its altitude, mostly over 4,000 metres above sea level, Tibet enjoys long hours of sunshine but a thin atmosphere. Temperatures range from an average of −18°C to 4°C in winter to between 7°C and 20°C during summer.

Physical features: Tibet is known as the 'roof of the world' and indeed much of Tibet is a plateau. A small area in the southeast descends to the Brahmaputra River Valley.

The Himalayas in southern Tibet have an average height of 6,000 metres above sea level with Mount Everest (Qomolangma) at 8,848 metres high. Tibet has over 1,000 lakes and countless large rivers within its boundaries.

Rivers: the Yarlung Zangbo River, which is the upper reach of the Brahmaputra River, winds its way through Tibet's southern valleys; the Nujiang, Lancang and Jinsha Rivers, which are respectively the upper reaches of the Salween, Mekong, and Yangtze Rivers, cut through the Hengduan Mountains and enter Yunnan Province.

Products: Wheat, highland barley, buckwheat, iron, coal, chromate, copper, borax and salt.

Neighbouring countries: India, Nepal, Sikkim, Bhutan and Myanmar.

Tourist attraction: The Potala Palace in Lhasa was once the winter residence of the Dalai Lama and the home of the Tibetan Government.

Yunnan Province

Capital: Kunming.

Other major cities: Dongchuan, Gejiu, Dali, Luxi and Jinghong.

Ethnic groups: Han, Yi, Bai, Hani, Zhuang, Dai, Miao, Lisu, Hui, Lahu, Va, Naxi, Yao, Tibetan, Jingpo, Blang, Pumi, Nu, Achang, Deang, Mongolian, Drung and Jino.

Area: 380,000 sq. km

Climate: Yunnan's name means 'South of the Clouds' and although it is known for its mild climate, Yunnan actually spans 3 climactic zones; temperate, subtropical and tropical. Temperatures range from an average of 11°C in winter to 21°C in summer. Rainfall is highest in the south where up to 2,400 mm can fall in a year, with 60% of the rain falling during the monsoonal period between June and Aug.

Physical features: Over 90% of Yunnan is mountainous. High mountains in the north, where Yunnan meets Tibet, gradually diminish as one travels south to Yunnan's borders with The Lao People's Democratic Republic, Myanmar and Vietnam.

Products: Rice, wheat, corn, sorghum, potatoes, sugar cane, peanuts, soybeans, peas, rape, tea, oranges, bananas, pineapples, coconuts, walnuts, cotton, silk cocoons, flue-cured tobacco, timber and tropical plants. Yunnan is rich in tin, copper, zinc, marble and phosphorus.

Tourist attractions: Kunming is known as the 'Spring City'. The Golden Taoist Temple is about 13 km north of Kunming in a pine forest. The Stone Forest, about 75 km east of Kunming, is an interesting rock formation and a picnicking spot for locals and tourists.

Zhejiang Province

Capital: Hangzhou.

Other major cities: Hangzhou, Ningbo, Wenzhou, Shaoxing, Jinhua, Jiaxing and Huzhou.

Ethnic groups: Han, She, Hui, Manchu and Miao.

Area: 100,000 sq. km.

Climate: Zheijiang has a subtropical, monsoonal climate with clearly defined seasons. Droughts can occur in July and Aug. but these give way to typhoons from Aug. to late Sept. Temperatures range between 2°C in the winter to 30°C in July with the highest temperatures being recorded in the central basin. Rainfall is highest in the south with an average of 1,275 mm falling per year.

Physical features: Zhejiang has 2,200 km of coastline on the East China Sea. Lowlands dominate the northeast and mountains dominate the southwest.

Products: Rice, wheat, corn, potatoes, sugar cane, rape, sesame, peanuts, tea, jute, cotton, bamboo, oranges, walnuts, star fruit and peaches. Zhejiang is rich in sea products including cuttlefish, shellfish, laver and kelp. Zhejiang's other natural resources include alum, fluorite and salt.

Tourist attractions: The West Lake in Hangzhou has many islands and causeways criss-crossing it. Zhou Enlai, considered by many as the father of modern China, is commemorated at his ancestral home in Shaoxing.

KEY HISTORICAL EVENTS

In the 1920s, fossilized human remains of Peking Man, believed to date back 400,000 years, were found in the Yunnan and Shaanxi provinces of China. It is known that this man walked upright, made simple tools and knew how to light fires. In recent years, archaeologists have unearthed prehistoric settlements that date from 3,000 BC suggesting that the centre of Chinese culture and civilization was probably in what is now Xian, although very little is known about the intervening period.

Opinions differ as to whether the Xia dynasty (2200–1700 BC) derives from mythology or whether it really existed. But the reign of the Yellow Emperor, Huangdi (2490–2413 BC?) is credited with having laid the foundations of Chinese culture and civilization. Huangdi, who ruled with his wife, is also associated with the invention of early irrigation systems, rice planting, the wagon, the boat and the breeding of silk worms. Under his rule astronomical concepts were incorporated into the first Chinese calendar and pictographic characters and the twelve-tone musical scale emerged.

Chinese written history dates back four or five thousand years but it is hard to tell whether the first chronicled records of the Xian dynasty (21st–16th century BC) are fact or mythology. It is known, however, that the Shang dynasty, which followed, grew out of the plains of Northern China and ruled China from 1554–1045 BC. The Shang was an agricultural society based on a form of ancestor worship. The spiritual side of Chinese life was controlled by a caste system of priests who practised divination using oracle bones. The remains of some 50,000 bones have been found which have allowed scholars to identify more than 3,000 early Chinese characters.

The family was at the heart of Shang's social structure and the populace lived enclosed in small towns surrounded by ramparts with the religious buildings and ruler's residence in the centre. They had already mastered the art of breeding silk worms and now they set about refining their techniques for making and weaving silk. Bronze vessels of very fine quality from this dynasty have been found and their intricate designs and inscriptions have shed much light on contemporary society and religious practices. In 1100 BC, the Shang dynasty was overthrown by the Zhou under the pretext that the Shang rulers had forfeited the gods' mercy by leading corrupt and dissolute lives. The Zhou capital was known as Hao and was near Chang'an (present day Xian) and was to remain the seat of power for many sub-sequent dynasties. The Zhou dynasty is generally regarded as having established some of the most enduring of Chinese political concepts. The 'Mandate of Heaven' endorses the rule of wise and virtuous leaders while withdrawing support from those who are corrupt or evil. This concept was later incorporated into a Taoist theory that natural disasters such as earthquakes, floods and plagues were heaven's way of showing disapproval of bad rulers. Heaven was also thought to express displeasure through rebellion, and thus rebellion formed an integral part of the dynastic cycle with each successive dynasty displacing the one before by exercising this heaven-given 'right to rebellion'.

The first, or Western, half of the Zhou Dynasty (1100–771 BC) lasted until barbarian tribes sacked the capital Hao and the Zhou lost control over their feudal lands. They managed to remain symbolic heads of state of the warring kingdoms until 221 BC when they were displaced by the Qin. The two historical books written during this period gave their names to the traditional Chinese division of the Eastern period into the 'Spring and Autumn' period (722–481 BC) and the 'Warring States' period (453–221 BC). The 'Spring and Autumn Annals' is attributed to Confucius, a wandering scholar who travelled the country in search of the ideal ruler to implement his theories for a perfect state. Confucianism and Taoism emerged from this period as the two strongest and most enduring ideologies among many and their representations of the two opposing streams of Chinese thought have lasted to the present day. Confucianism is pragmatic and socially orientated while Taoism is personal and mystical.

The Zhou was finally ousted from power in the 3rd century BC by the Qin who united the Chinese people in one empire for the first time. The

Qin dynasty left behind a legacy of strong centralized control and administrative systems that are still recognizable in modern China. The Qin divided its territory into provincial units controlled by scholars rather than politicians. A nation-wide system of weights and measures and writing were established and books that were hostile to the laws of the state were burned. Millions of conscripts, countless numbers of whom lost their lives, began work on the beginnings of the Great Wall. The Qin dynasty, weakened by rebellion, eventually fell to an uprising led by Liu Bang. In 206 BC he took the title of Emperor and established the Han dynasty that was to rule China until 220 AD. Present day Chinese take their name from this dynasty and still describe themselves as the people of Han.

The Han dynasty was divided into two parts. The Western Han was a time of military expansionism and was notable for the establishment of the Chinese State. The Eastern Han started out in calm and stability but rapidly succumbed to a process of decentralization and weakening of power. When the last of the Han emperors finally abdicated in 220, the turmoil that ensued was to last for 400 years.

From the end of the Han dynasty to the start of the Sui in 581 AD, China was torn apart by the most terrible wars in the country's history but, despite the chaos, Buddhism spread throughout the country and the arts flourished. The administrative and legal reforms undertaken by Yang Jian, the first Sui Emperor (the 'Cultivated Emperor'), were to form the foundation for the Tang dynasty that followed. The Sui dynasty was ruined by Wendi's son, Yangdi, whose massive expenditure on the Great Wall and the Grand Canal and excursions into Korea bankrupted the country and sparked revolt. Yangdi was assassinated in 618 AD by one of his own officials. The first Tang emperor was another Sui official, Li Yuan (known as Gaozu after his death), and after ten years of defending his newly formed dynasty against rivals, he set up a new system of administration. The new administrative system was pyramidical. Headed by the emperor, two policy forming ministries and a Department of State came next and beneath them were nine courts and six boards dealing with specific administrative areas. Gaozu wanted to discourage local power bases and so he divided the empire into 300 prefectures (zhou) and 1,500 counties (xian), a way of delineating China's regions that exists to this day. Gaozu's son, Taizong, succeeded in 600 AD and he built on earlier successes. He led conquests to establish control of the silk routes and protect and encourage international trade. As a result, many Chinese towns had thriving communities of foreigners, mainly from central Asia, who brought new religions, food, music and artistic tradition into the Chinese culture. Tang's foreign contact extended as far afield as Persia, India, Malaysia, Indonesia and Japan. Buddhism was flourishing and Chinese pilgrims travelled widely. A religious schism divided Buddhist thinking into two schools – the Chan School (known as Zen) and the Pure Land School (which later formed the principle form of Buddhism in China). Agricultural output was growing rapidly, thanks to a new system of irrigation, and the Grand Canal was completed which, together with a network of postal coaches and couriers, greatly improved communication and commerce. Culturally, China flourished under the Tang dynasty, producing art and poetry still regarded as unsurpassed in quality.

After Taizong's death in 649, China was ruled for 20 years by Wu Zetian, China's only enthroned Empress. Her son, Xuanzong, took over and under him the dynasty fell into ruin. Corrupt eunuchs ruled in the Imperial Palace, provincial governors and military officials seized local power and in the chaos of a peasant's revolt, nomadic tribes from the north gained strength. After a period of unrest known as the Five Dynasties and the Ten States, the Song dynasty was established and was responsible for creating one of the most prosperous periods of Chinese history. In addition to impressive developments in agriculture, trade and commerce, silver, gold and iron were all being extensively mined. The monetary system was growing and paper money was seen for the first time. 400 years before Gutenberg's invention in Germany, movable-type printing was invented. Confucianism developed into an enduring political and ethical philosophy. Large, highly civilized urban centres were developing and it is said that when Marco Polo arrived in China in the 12th century, he was amazed to find cities far grander and more prosperous than he was used to in Europe.

Meanwhile, repeated raids by the nomadic tribes from the north were beginning to have an effect on China's stability. By 1206, Ghengis Khan had managed to unite these tribes into a new Mongol nation and had conquered most of central Asia, Russia and even some of Eastern Europe. In 1211 he turned eastwards to China. The Great Wall was all that separated China from the Gobi Desert and the great Asian grasslands and in 1213 Ghengis Khan breached the wall and marched on to Beijing, which fell to him in 1215. The Song Chinese resisted fiercely, particularly in the south, and it was not until 1279 that Ghengis Khan's grandson, Kublai Khan, managed to bring southern China under his control and establish the Yuan dynasty. The China ruled by Kublai Khan was the largest empire the world has ever known and the Yuan dynasty lasted until 1368. The Mongols had two capital cities. In summer they ruled from Shangdu in Inner Mongolia and in winter, from Dadu (or Beijing, as it is now known). Widespread changes were made to the structure of Chinese society. Local administrative bodies were militarized and in a new four tier society, the native Chinese were beaten into third and fourth place by the Mongols who came first, with their central Asian allies second. Despite the harshness of the Yuan rule, commercial and economic growth continued unchecked. Work continued on the roads and canal system, further improving communications and the spread of inter-regional trade. Trade all along the 'Silk Route' thrived. The Mongol rulers remained aloof from their conquered Chinese subjects but they were tolerant of them in religious matters. Under Mongol rule,

Tibet became a part of China – a claim that remains strongly contested today. Taxes were greatly increased for all but the Mongols, who were exempt, and Chinese-owned land was confiscated and redistributed among the Mongol nobility and Lamaist monasteries. Poverty increased and gave rise to widespread insurrection. By 1367, a Buddhist novice, Zhu Yuanzhan (later known as Hongwu), had climbed to the top of the rebel leadership and in 1368 his troops overthrew the Mongol forces, expelled the Mongol nobility from China and established the Ming dynasty. Once again, the Chinese were in control of their own country.

In 1420 the third Ming Emperor founded Beijing as the first, or Northern, capital city of China with Nanjing as the second, or Southern, capital. Taxes were lowered, with some land taxes dropped altogether. The position of the central government strengthened and, for the first time, China began to develop into a strong maritime power with fleets of ships sailing as far afield as the Indian Ocean and the South Pacific. Trade links were secured, the first Chinese colonies abroad were established and in 1516, the first Christian missionaries arrived at Canton in Portuguese trading ships. Much work was done to reinforce the Great Wall in order to protect China from the Mongol tribes in central Asia. By the middle of the 15th century, official corruption and intellectual conservatism had weakened the rulers and intrigue and excessive eunuch power paralyzed the imperial court. The secret police became more and more ruthless in their suppression of opposition and, once again, there was a major peasant uprising. The Manchus, a nomadic people from the north, were waiting in the wings to take advantage of the situation. Their ruler, Nuzhen, had succeeded in uniting the nomadic tribes and in 1616 he had established his own dynasty in northern China. With the help of a Ming general, he had breached the Great Wall and in 1644 he took possession of Beijing and established the Qing dynasty. By the end of the 17th century, the Qing occupied the entire Chinese heartland and began the biggest period of expansion in the entire history of China. During the next 150 years, China's expansion took in Taiwan, Tibet and East Turkestan, while the neighbouring states in the south, Burma, Nepal and Northern Vietnam, were forced to acknowledge China's supremacy. The flagging economy was revitalized with more lenient tax and agricultural policies. Trade was boosted and the production of iron ore and salt increased. The ruling Qing was a minority in China and had to rely on popular and prudent policies to keep themselves in power. The Manchu clans ruled along strictly patriarchal lines and discriminated against the Han Chinese, forcing them, among other things, to wear a distinctive plait.

The Portuguese arrived in China in the mid-16th century and set up a trading mission in Macau but it was not until 1760 that the other European powers – the British, Dutch and Spanish – began to compete in the Chinese market place from bases established at Guangzhou. China controlled their trade by means of a guild known as the Cohong. This meant that although European traders were allowed to buy as much tea, silk and porcelain as they wished, sales of European wool and spices to China were severely limited. By 1773, Britain decided to take matters into her own hands and started to flood the market with opium. The Imperial government declared war against the drug but sales rocketed and with it opium addiction. In March 1839 the government sent Lin Zexiu, an official with a reputation for integrity, to Guangzhou to put a stop to the illegal drug trade. He confiscated 20,000 chests of opium from the British and in 1840, this act combined with various military skirmishes gave the British the excuse they wanted to launch a military action, backed by a naval force assembled in Macau, which started the 'Opium Wars'. These conflicts were a disaster for China. A meaningless treaty was signed very early on but neither side recognized it and British troops attacked positions near Guangzhou. A second treaty ceded Hong Kong to the British. Further skirmishes followed until, in 1842, the

Treaty of Nanking was signed. Although this treaty gave Britain control of Hong Kong, it was not until the Convention of 1898 (after the second opium war) that Hong Kong and the New Territories, together with 235 islands, were leased to Britain for 99 years. Hong Kong was formally handed back to China in 1997 when it became The Hong Kong Special Administrative Region of China (HKSAR).

By the late 19th century, the increase in Chinese population far outweighed advances in technology and agricultural improvements. The Imperial court was ruled over by the Dowager Empress Wu Cixi who resisted all attempts to reform the ancient institutions of the empire. The Western powers were advancing further and further into China, carving it up into 'Spheres of Influence'. A war with France from 1883 to 1885 ended China's rule in Indo-China and allowed the French to gain control of Vietnam and later of Laos and Cambodia. The British occupied Burma and in 1895, Japan forced China out of Korea and made them cede Taiwan. By the end of the 19th century, it was clear that the European powers intended to divide China between them. But the United States objected, proposing instead that China should be allowed to trade with any foreign power.

Rebellion against the Qing was the inevitable result of many defeats and humiliations at foreign hands. The first of these rebellions, the Taiping uprising, was led by a failed scholar who, as a result of his contact with Christian missionaries, had decided he was the younger brother of Jesus Christ. The Taipings commanded an army of about 600,000 men and 500,000 women. They banned opium, gambling, tobacco and alcohol. They advocated agricultural reforms, outlawed foot binding for women, prostitution and slavery. They were quite quickly defeated by a coalition of old adversaries – the Qing and Western powers – who were determined not to see China ruled by the Taiping.

Before long, however, a second rebellion rocked China. In 1898 a sect called the 'Boxers United in Righteousness' emerged from the martial arts schools in Shangdong. The Boxers were fanatically xenophobic, believing that 1900 was the start of a new era in which they alone were invincible to foreign bullets. Their organization was chaotic and they roamed the country in bands, indiscriminately attacking foreigners and Chinese Christians. The Empress Dowager tried to cash in on the rising tide of anti-foreign feeling by declaring war on the Western powers but a well organized coalition of British, US, French, Japanese and Russian troops defeated the Boxers and forced the Empress to flee to Xian. The Qing government realized that reform was the only option left to them but China was greatly weakened. When the Dowager Empress died in 1908, the two-year-old Emperor Puyi succeeded her and so China was effectively leaderless. Two events, the Railway Protection Movement and the Wuchang uprising of 1911, made the collapse of the Qing dynasty inevitable. The newly constructed railways had been financed by foreign investment but the Chinese people felt that the railways should be under Chinese control. Plans to construct lines to provincial centres failed and anti-Qing violence erupted. The unrest was at its worst in Sichuan and, in order to quell the riots, nearly all the troops were taken from the Wuchang garrison in Wuhan. Sun Yatsen and his Tokyo-based Alliance Society took advantage of the empty garrisons and seized control of Wuhan. This led to uprisings all over China. Two months later, representatives from 17 provinces gathered in Nanking to establish the Provisional Republican Government of China. With the collapse of China's last dynasty, a cycle of dynastic power that had lasted for over 4,000 years ended.

10 Oct. 1911 (a date that is still celebrated in Taiwan as 'Double Tenth') marked the establishment of the new Provisional Republic Government by Sun Yatsen and Li Yuanhong, a military commander in Wuchang. They were not sufficiently powerful on their own to force a Manchu abdication so they turned to the man who had previously led the Manchu's suppression of the Republican uprisings – Yuan Shikai.

His support was expensive. He forced Sun Yatsen to resign and took his place at the head of the Republican movement. He immediately dissolved the government, amended the constitution and declared himself president for life. Regional opposition to this move caused him to declare himself Emperor. Yunnan seceded from the main body of China and took Guangxi, Guizhou and most of the southern provinces. During the period of ensuing chaos, Yuan died and China fell into the hands of local warlords with no single power strong enough to unite the country.

The collapse of the new Republican government and the social ruin and decay that followed brought new impetus to scholars and intellectuals. Beijing University soon became the centre of Chinese intellectual life and attracted dissenting scholars from all over China. Orthodox Chinese society was criticized and analyzed without restraint. Other philosophies were explored and discussed; the Communist manifesto was translated into Chinese, becoming the basis for the beliefs of some groups, while others favoured anarchy. Russia, where the revolutionaries had recently taken power, was monitored closely.

In 1918, as part of the Treaty of Versailles, Germany's rights of control in Shandong were handed over to the Japanese. This sparked off a huge public outcry and the student protests that followed combined a new sense of nationalism with demands for modernization. Although this uprising was crushed, the 'May Fourth' incident is now regarded as a key moment in the development of modern Chinese history. Sun Yatsen and the Kuomintang (Nationalist Party or KMT) emerged as the dominant force after the fall of the Qing dynasty and created a power base in southern China. They formed and trained the National Revolutionary Army (NRA) in order to challenge the northern warlords. Meanwhile, leading Chinese Marxists were holding discussions with the Soviet Communist International (Comintern) and their influence resulted in the formation of the Chinese Communist Party

(CCP) in Shanghai in 1921. The Comintern was keen to create a buffer against Japanese expansionism and they persuaded the CCP to form an alliance with the KMT. But, after Sun Yatsen's death in 1925, there was a power struggle within the KMT between those who favoured Communist ideals and those who preferred a capitalist state, run by a wealthy elite and supported by a military dictatorship.

Meanwhile, the NRA, under the command of Chiang Kaishek, was mopping up the remaining warlords in the northern provinces and, after taking Wuhan and Nanchang, moved on to Shanghai. As the NRA marched on the city, striking workers took to the streets and took over key installations. Backed by Shanghai bankers and foreigners, Chiang took this opportunity to try to eliminate Communists and their sympathizers by arming the gangsters and underworld thugs of Shanghai, dressing them in NRA uniforms and letting them loose on the workers' militia. In the ensuing battles, about 5,000 Communists were killed. In the chain reaction that followed, Communists and other anti-Chiang factions were killed in their thousands in cities all over China. By 1928, the northern expedition had reached Beijing and although a national government was established, nearly half of the country was still under the control of local warlords. The Communists were divided in to two factions – those who wanted urban insurrection and those who favoured rural revolt. In the Jinggangshan Mountains, Mao Zedong and Zhu De were leading the latter group and by 1930 the Communist forces numbered around 40,000. Although they limited their activities to guerrilla tactics and avoided pitched battles with the KMT forces, the Communists presented a serious challenge to Chiang who, despite repeated extermination campaigns, suffered successive defeats.

In Oct. 1933, Mao and Zhu, under pressure from dissenting voices within the party, changed their tactics. They challenged Chiang's troops head on with disastrous results. By Oct. 1934 the Communists were forced to retreat from Jiangxi and march north to Shaanxi.

The 'Long March' was in fact a series of marches, during which the Communists covered more than 8,000 km of the world's most inhospitable terrain. Along the way, the Communists confiscated property from officials and redistributed land to the people. These peasants, who were armed with weapons taken from the KMT forces and trained in guerrilla tactics, were left behind to harass the enemy. Although of the 90,000 peasants who set out on the Long March, only 20,000 made it to Shaanxi, their strength and endurance proved that their threat should be taken seriously. The 'Long March' also brought together many of the future leaders of China, including Zhou Enlai, Lin Biao, Deng Xiaoping and Liu Shaoqi and Mao Zedong who quickly emerged as leaders of the Chinese Communist movement.

Internal strife left China vulnerable to foreign invasion and in 1931 Japan occupied Manchuria to create a puppet state with the last Chinese Emperor, Puyi, as symbolic head. In 1936 some of Chiang's generals were persuaded by the Communists to take him hostage and after negotiations with Zhou Enlai, an anti-Japanese alliance was formed with the Communists. But the Japanese were unstoppable and by 1939 they had overrun most of Eastern China. That same year, World War II had started in Europe and in 1941, Japan attacked the United States military base at Pearl Harbour bringing America into the war. The US hoped to hasten the defeat of the Japanese with the support of Chiang's troops but he was still obsessed with eliminating the Communists and refused to commit his troops. By 1941 the alliance between the KMT and the Communists had collapsed and, at the end of World War II in 1945, China was gripped by civil war. The United States armed the KMT forces during the war but the Communists had captured so much of their equipment that by 1948 their strength and numbers more than matched those of the KMT. Three decisive battles were fought in 1948 and 1949, which resulted in thousands of defeated KMT troops joining the Communists. By the end of the year, all the major cities of southern China were under Communist control. On 1 Oct. 1949, Mao Zedong proclaimed the foundation of the People's Republic of China. Chiang Kaishek fled to the island of Formosa (Taiwan) taking with him the entire Chinese gold reserves and what remained of his military forces. President Truman, pursuing US anti-Communist policy, ordered a naval blockade of the island to protect Chiang from attack from mainland China. The US continued to recognise Chiang as the legitimate ruler and did not reopen normal relations with the mainland until 1972.

When Mao Zedong first declared the People's Republic of China, war and civil unrest had bankrupted China. The loss of the country's gold reserves meant that the economy was in tatters. Industrial and agricultural output had plummeted to a fraction of the pre-war period and the roads and railways were run down. However, China's sense of national unity was reinforced by the Korean War and by a need to protect itself from a possible US invasion, and throughout the 1950s the Chinese were driven to regenerate their great nation. By 1953 inflation had been halted and industrial output was back to pre-war levels. A massive programme of land reform completed the redistribution of land to the peasants and, taking a model from the Soviets, the country embarked on a five-year plan to lift production on all fronts. The Communist Party controlled all aspects of Chinese life. The country was divided into 21 provinces, five autonomous regions, two municipalities (Beijing and Shanghai) and 2,200 county governments, which had jurisdiction over approximately one million Party sub-branches.

To begin with, the PRC's economy grew rapidly but there were serious social problems. Many of the intellectuals who had left the country now returned in order to lend their skills and qualifications to the effort of rebuilding China. However, they were regarded with suspicion and made to undergo 're-education' courses in special universities. The arts were also subject to ideological controls and many writers, filmmakers and artists suspected of subversion were persecuted and their work suppressed. Mao, together with Zhou Enlai and other leaders, favoured a more lenient approach and the policy of 'letting a hundred flowers bloom' in the arts and 'a hundred schools of thought contend' in the sciences was born. Within six months of the publication of Mao's ideas in 1957, the party found itself swamped by complaints from intellectuals in every corner of China and they were forced to do a rapid volte-face. Over 300,000 intellectuals were branded as rightists, stripped of their jobs and, in many cases, sent off to labour camps.

The five year plan had been a success but, in order to increase agricultural output to meet the needs of a growing urban population, Mao instigated an enormous programme of agricultural reform, creating communes and drawing large numbers of people both from the country and the urban areas to work on water and irrigation projects. Mao believed that ideology was everything and that mass co-operation would overcome any obstacle. He backed small communal industries whose profits were ploughed directly back into the communes for agricultural development. Efficient management of the communes proved problematic and in reality the agricultural output dropped. Added to this, in 1959 and 1960 floods and droughts ruined the harvests. In 1960 the Soviet Union suddenly withdrew their aid. Mao had disagreed with the Soviet Union on the subject of peaceful coexistence with the United States. Krushchev, the Soviet leader, had gradually improved relations with the USA and after his de-Stalinization speech, Sino-Soviet relations suffered a serious setback. Krushchev reneged on a promise to furnish China with a prototype atomic bomb and sided with India in a border dispute. Some 1,500 Russian technicians had been working in China but when the Russian government withdrew aid they also withdrew the technicians and with them the plans for about 600 major projects.

Between 1960 and 1970, Mao led China in another 'Great Leap Forward' when he masterminded the Cultural Revolution. Together with Lin Biao, leader of the People's Liberation Army (PLA), Mao developed a personality cult to protect his position against increasing dissatisfaction from within the ranks of the Communist party. Early in the 1960s the now famous 'Little Red Book,' a collection of Chairman Mao's thoughts and teachings, were published by Lin and rapidly became an integral part of Chinese ideology and required reading for all school children, PLA troops and party officials. Mao backed loyal university students and staff against dissenting members of the party. Before long the students were sporting red arm bands and parading in front of Mao, chanting and waving copies of the little red book. These 'Red Guards' went on the rampage throughout the country, seeking out, persecuting and even killing so-called subversive intellectuals, writers and artists. By Jan. 1967, the Red Guards' excesses could no longer be ignored and the PLA was mobilized to break them up. But many thousands of Chinese people had lost their lives and by Sept. 1967, Mao and Lin had to condemn 'ultra-left' tendencies and endorse the PLA as the sole agent of 'proletarian dictatorship'. The Red Guards were disbanded and the PLA started its 'Campaign to Purify Class Ranks' which was intended to re-educate anyone with a suspect background. In the aftermath of the disastrous Cultural Revolution, Mao's erstwhile ally, Lin Biao, fell from favour. It is believed that he tried to instigate an assassination plot against Mao and, when it failed, was forced to flee to the USSR with his family. He was branded a renegade and a traitor and died when the plane in which he was escaping crashed in Mongolia in Sept. 1971.

The early 1970s saw China return to a state of relative stability and calm. Zhou Enlai was the most influential of the leaders and he worked towards the restoration of China's trade links and diplomatic relations with the outside world. Britain had recognized Communist China some years before but it was not until President Nixon visited

China in 1972 that relations with the United Sates were normalized. In 1973 Deng Xiaoping, who had fallen from grace during the Cultural Revolution, returned to power. Zhou Enlai died in 1976 leaving behind a divided government. On one side the moderates were led by Deng Xiaoping, on the other the radical left wing 'Maoists' led by Jiang Qing. The Maoists gained the upper hand and Mao's protégé, Hua Guofeng, was appointed Acting Premier. Jiang Qing and her group of supporters (known as the Gang of Four) were unpopular. When Zhou died, public sentiment surfaced and, in March, crowds began to gather in Tian'anmen Square in Beijing, ostensibly to honour Zhou's memory with poems, speeches, wreaths of flowers and banners, but in reality to express criticism of Jiang. On 5 April, with the approval of Mao, the Politburo sent in the troops and fights with the crowds continued all day. During the night, 30,000 militia occupied the square and the remaining protestors were beaten and arrested. This incident was blamed on Deng, who fled to Guangzhou and then vanished from public view. After many years of ill health, Mao was finally diagnosed as having a rare form of motor neuron disorder (Lou Gehrig's disease) and for the last few years of his life he was immobilized, unable to speak or feed himself. He died on 8 Sept. 1976. Mao's chosen successor was the acting premier, Hua Guofeng. When Jiang and her supporters challenged Hua's authority, he had them arrested. China was jubilant when the arrests were announced. When the Gang of Four were brought to trial four years later, they were made the scapegoats for the entire failure of the Cultural Revolution. Jiang refused to repent and stuck to her guns throughout the trial, hurling abuse at the judges and declaring the she had simply followed Mao's orders 'like his dog'. Jiang Qing's death sentence was commuted to a life sentence, served under house arrest until her death in 1991.

Deng Xiaoping returned to power for the third time in 1977. He was appointed to various positions including Vice-Premier, Vice-Chairman of the Party and Chief of Staff of the PLA. His first move was to remove Hua Guofeng from power and replace him with Zhao Ziyang. The real power now passed to a standing committee made up of six members of the CCP including Deng, Hu and Zhao. The committee faced serious problems. The need for modernization and freedom had to be balanced by a need for stability and order. Mao Zedong had become almost deified in the eyes of the people and Deng decided that he needed to reduce his status. In 1981 the CCP issued a declaration that managed to strike a balance between Mao as the great Marxist and saviour of China and Mao as the architect of the disastrous Cultural Revolution, the damaging effects of which were still being felt. The resolution acknowledged that Mao had made gross mistakes during the Cultural Revolution but went on to conclude that if 'we judge his activities as a whole, his contributions to the Chinese revolution far outweigh his mistakes'.

During the 1980s, China began to implement pragmatic economic reforms. Special economic zones were set up and in the following 15 years, China achieved an average annual growth rate of 9%. Even though economic and agricultural reforms were moving ahead successfully, political reform was slower in coming and the Communist party remained firmly in control. This fact and increasing inflation that was running at between 20% and 30% led to social unrest, and in 1989 the death of Hu Yaobang sparked off demonstrations. As the leaders gathered inside the Hall of the People for Hu's official funeral ceremonies, some 150,000 students and other activists clamoured for democratic reform outside in Tian'anmen Square. The crowds grew steadily all through the month of April until by the middle of May there were nearly one million people from all walks of life gathered in the square. 3,000 students staged a pro-democracy hunger strike, a statue called the 'Goddess of Democracy' was erected by art students and speeches were made demanding an end to censorship of the press and to corruption and nepotism in government. Hong Kong, Taiwan and Macau expressed support and by now the foreign press corps had set up positions and were sending reports and pictures all around the world. The climax of this demonstration coincided with the arrival of Mikhail Gorbachev, the Soviet leader, who was attending the first Sino–Soviet summit to be held since 1959. His presence temporarily delayed the use of armed troops to dispel the crowds but the minute his plane took off 350,000 troops were deployed around Beijing. In the early hours of the morning of 4 June 1989, the tanks rolled into the square, armed troops opened fire on the demonstrators and although it is impossible to give exact numbers of casualties, there was considerable injury and loss of life among the demonstrators. Since then, however, China has moved cautiously towards a more open society, with an economy that makes allowance for market principles.

For the background to the handover of Hong Kong in 1997, see p. 135.

CHRONOLOGY

Xia and Shang Dynasties

2200–1040 BC

There is little evidence for the existence of these two dynasties, an agricultural people who practised a form of ancestor worship and lived around the Yellow River Plain.

Zhou Dynasty

1040–221 BC

The Zhou Dynasty displaced the Shang Dynasty and built their capital at Xian but were later driven to Luoyang.

This period incorporates *the Spring and Autumn Period* (722–481 BC) and the *Warring States Period* (453–221 BC).

552 BC

The birth of Confucius.

Qin Dynasty

221–207 BC

The Qin Dynasty brought much needed order to a confused China after the Warring States Period. The Empire was divided into provinces and further divided into prefectures.

By the end of the 3rd century BC, the Qin had built an extensive system of walls along the northern border of their kingdom.

214BC

The first Great Wall of China is completed.

Han Dynasty

207 BC–220 AD

Liu Bang, although a commoner, led an army against the Chang'an and established the Han Dynasty. During this period the Han Dynasty expanded the kingdom's borders.

The Han Dynasty collapsed as a result of the internal canker of an over-stretched and greedy administrative system. With the end of the Han Dynasty, China was thrown into nearly four hundred years of upheaval.

The Three Kingdoms

220–589   The turmoil that enveloped China after the collapse of the Han Dynasty led to a division of China into three areas, each around a strong economic centre. In the north, the Wei State held power over all between the Great Wall and the Yangtze River. Shu Han controlled the Sichuan, much of Guangzhou and part of Yunnan. Wu controlled all of southeast China and part of Indo-China in what is now Vietnam. These three kingdoms, as well as nearly twenty other, lesser-considered kingdoms, jostled for supremacy in a series of long and bloody conflicts.

Sui Dynasty

581–618   Yang Jian, a Tuoba military general of the late Wei Dynasty, seized power in the north and went on to conquer the south of China, establishing the Sui Dynasty. The Dynasty, although short lived, did much to reunify China. Much of the bureaucratic and governmental stability that typified the Han Dynasty was rejuvenated during the Sui Dynasty's short reign.

It was during this period that the Grand Canal was built with the use of forced labour. Millions of workers died working on the canal and in 618 Yang Di, the last of the Sui Emperors, was assassinated.

605   The Yangtze and the Yellow River are linked by the Grand Canal.

The Tang Dynasty

618–907   Li Yuan, the first Tang emperor, spent much of his reign fighting off other would-be rulers. Having done this successfully, the Tang Dynasty set about increasing China's influence in a far wider sphere than ever before. International relations were established with many Asian countries. The Tang Dynasty brought military, economic and cultural expansion to China. Foreign traders brought with them new foods, religions and cultural traditions. During the 8th and 9th centuries, Tang influence diminished, discontent grew and the stage was set for another coup.

668   The Chinese defeat Korea.

751   The Battle of Talas River. Islamic soldiers defeat Central Chinese power.

758   Muslims from Arabia and the Persian Gulf loot and burn Guangzhou.

868   The earliest known printed book in China is made.

The Five Dynasties and the Ten Kingdoms Period

907–959   With the absence of a central ruling force, China fragmented once more and China's neighbours joined in the conflicts that ensued. The period is so called because five dynasties took control of the north of China while over ten kingdoms exercised control over the south and west of the country.

919   Gunpowder begins to be used in China.

The Song Dynasty

959–1279   The Song Dynasty and the reunification of a war-torn China were ushered in by Zhao Kuangyin, a military leader. The Song Dynasty brought commercial stability back to China, introduced paper money and made advances in agricultural practices.

The Yuan Dynasty (Mongol Invaders)

1279–1368   The Mongols had been paid not to invade northern China for nearly a century when, in 1211, a huge and powerful army swept into China under the rule of Ghengis Khan and set about conquering all in its path. By 1279, Kublai Khan, Ghengis's grandson, had established the Yuan Dynasty. The Khans did much to repair the effects of five centuries of upheaval. The capital, Khanbalik or Dadu, was built at the site of modern Beijing. Kublai Khan built the Palace of All Tranquilities, later to be known as the Forbidden Palace.

1271   Marco Polo arrives in China.

1290   The Grand Canal is repaired and extended.

The Ming Dynasty

1368–1644   Zhu Wuanshang was an orphan and a Buddhist novice. Declaring himself Hong Wu, or Prince of Wu, he took control of an existing rebellion in Nanjing and heralded the return of home rule for China – the Ming Dynasty. The Ming Dynasty built and fortified the Great Wall to help keep the Mongols out of China. Internal famine, costly wars and an untimely famine in Shaanxi Province brought Ming domination to an end.

1535   Macao becomes a trading base for the Portuguese.

1592   The Japanese invade Korea.

The Qing Dynasty

1616–1911   The Qing Dynasty held power in Manchuria for many years before turning their attention towards the south. Aware of unrest and rebellion in China, the Manchus invaded China, suppressed the peasant uprising and then marched upon Beijing. The Qing Dynasty brought Mongolia and Tibet into China's borders. The Qing Dynasty was toppled by the Wuchang Uprising after the people of China had become disaffected by it.

1720   The Manchu rulers incorporate Tibet into the Chinese empire.

1729   The selling and use of opium are forbidden.

1839–1842   The first of the infamous Opium Wars between the British and Chinese starts when vast quantities of opium are confiscated and destroyed by Chinese officials. After their defeat, the Chinese are made to sign the Treaty of Nanjing.

1856–1860   Second war breaks out after 'The Arrow', a British ship, is allegedly searched.

1859   British and French troops burn the Imperial Summer Palace in Beijing.

1900   The Fists of Righteous Harmony (or 'Boxers') stage an uprising in an attempt to rid China of the 'grabbing hands of foreign devils'. A Royal Chinese edict encourages the killing of foreigners, the burning of foreign property and the destruction of foreign objects.

The Republic

1911   The Provisional Republican Government is established on 10 Oct. 1911 by Sun Yatsen and Li Yuanhong.

1919   May Fourth Movement. Students protest at the passage of rights in Shandong from Germany to Japan.

1921   The Communist Party of China is established.

1925   The death of Sun Yatsen. Chiang Kaishek takes control of the Kuomintang.

1927   Chiang Kaishek and the Kuomintang massacre Communists in Shanghai.

1928   The Kuomintang reach Beijing and vanquish the remaining warlords in the north. A national government is established.

1931   The Japanese invade and occupy Manchuria.

1934–1935   In order to evade Kuomintang troops, the Long March of the Communists from Jiangxi to Shaanxi takes place. It costs the lives of over 60,000 Communist troops.

1936   The Xi'an Incident. The People's Liberation Army and the Kuomintang unite against Japanese occupation of northern China.

1937   Nanjing is occupied by the Japanese imperial army who begin a huge massacre, killing an estimated 300,000 people.

The People's Republic

1949   On 1 Oct., Mao Zedong announces the formation of a People's Republic of China. The Kuomintang Nationalist Party flees to Taiwan.

1950   United States warships are sent by President Truman to the Taiwan Straits to prevent a Communist invasion of the island.

1951   The PLA takes control of Tibet.

1959   His Holiness the 14th Dalai Lama leaves Tibet and goes into exile.

The Cultural Revolution

1966–1970   Chairman Mao Zedong launches a systematic purgation of China's artistic heritage and any cultural material deemed to be subversive or fundamentally opposed to the ideals of the Communist revolution. Writers, artists and intellectuals are persecuted and a system of class cleansing is carried out by the Red Guards.

1971   The Chinese Nationalists, exiled in Taiwan, lose their seat at the United Nations to the Communist government in Beijing.

1972   President Nixon visits China, doing much to help the Sino-USA relationship.

1976   Zhou Enlai, founding father of the Chinese Communist Party, a capable leader during much of the revolution and Premier since 1949, dies.

Students gather in Tian'anmen Square to mourn the death of Zhou Enlai and to protest at the actions of Jiang Qing. The Tian'anmen Incident ends with hundreds of student protesters beaten and arrested.

On 8 Sept. only months after Zhou Enlai's death, Mao Zedong, beloved leader of the revolution, dies.

Jiang Qing (Mao's widow) and three other senior politicians known as the 'Gang of Four' are arrested.

1977   Deng Xiaoping becomes Vice-Premier, Vice-Chairman of the Party and Chief of the PLA. Deng Xiaoping exacts a series of economic and political reforms that open China to the prospect of free trade with other countries.

1982   Margaret Thatcher holds talks with Deng Xiaoping in Beijing.

1984   Sino-British Agreement is signed which decrees that the United Kingdom will hand Hong Kong, as well as Kowloon and the Northern Territories, back to China in 1997.

1989   On 22 April, government officials gather in the Hall of the People. Outside, crowds gather and student activists hold protests against inflation and corruption. Crowds continue to gather throughout April and for many the demonstration becomes a hunger strike for democracy in China. On 4 June, troops attack the protesters. There is no official figure for the number of deaths but many believe that the death toll rises into thousands.

1997   On 4 Feb., Deng Xiaoping dies.

On 1 July the British Crown Colony of Hong Kong is handed back to the Chinese.

President Jiang Zemin and Premier Zhu Rongji visit the USA on a state visit.

CULTURAL BRIEFING

Calligraphy

For the Chinese, calligraphy is one of the highest forms of artistic creation. Children are trained at an early age to value calligraphy and it can determine the outcome of important examinations. The earliest known examples date back more than 3,000 years to the Emperor Shun who, it is said, devised the first writing brush. The basic tools of the calligrapher are the brush, ink, a stone (on which the ink is mixed) and paper. These are commonly known as the 'four treasures of the scholar's study'. The types of brush strokes are referred to in natural organic terms; for example, 'rolling waves', 'sleeping dragon', 'a dewdrop about to fall', 'a startled snake slithering off into the grass'. The qualities of the brush strokes are described in terms of flesh, muscle, bone and blood – this last, for example, referring to the quality of the ink and varied ink tones. The Chinese alphabet has changed very little over the centuries and calligraphy has come to be known as a personal form of artistic self-expression by which the writer can be identified and understood.

Painting

Until the third century, traditional Chinese painting relied mostly on the use of brush and ink. Ink used alone was thought to provide all the necessary qualities. Between the 3rd and 6th centuries, Buddhist art from Central Asia introduced shading and colour, although, at first, these played a minor symbolic and decorative role.

From the Han Dynasty to the Tang dynasty, the human figure was the most important aspect of Chinese painting. Figures were painted against a background of Confucian thinking, for the most part illustrating moral themes. It was not until the 4th and 5th centuries – when communing with nature first became popular among poets and thinkers – that artists began to paint landscapes. From the 11th century onwards, these idealized landscapes dominated Chinese painting. Unlike Western painting, Chinese landscapes relied on the imagination of the viewer to interpret the painting. Cultured Chinese people were expected to paint, compose music and write poetry as part of their scholarly activities. Confucian thought dictated the qualities most appreciated in painting. Although creativity and individuality were highly valued, any deliberate display of technical skill was considered vulgar. Artists developed their own styles by studying the styles of the ancient masters. When the Communists came to power, the Confucian way of thinking was replaced by Communist thinking – often expressed through the 'Little Red Book' (or the thoughts of Chairman Mao Zedong) – and the country's artistic talent was turned to producing enormous revolutionary works glorifying the people and illustrating political slogans. In recent years, a contemporary art scene has begun to thrive while the works of traditional painters can still be seen all over China. Art collecting is now fashionable among China's new rich and young Chinese contemporary artists have been exhibited all over the world to critical acclaim.

Theatre

Contemporary Chinese theatre is usually referred to as opera, owing to the importance of music in what has become a highly stylized mixture of acrobatics, martial arts, poetry, operatic-style arias and dance over the last 900 years. Operas used to be performed by travelling troupes, occupying a very low position on the social scale and, rather like Western travelling circus families, their children were discriminated against in education and employment. Nevertheless, opera was always a popular form of entertainment and to this day it plays an important part in New Year and marriage celebrations, and even at some funerals and ancestral ceremonies. The story-lines vary and evolve but there are always 4 major stylized roles, instantly recognizable to the audience; the male, the female, the 'painted-face' (representing warriors or gods) and the clown. The most famous of present day Chinese opera companies is the Beijing Opera.

Literature

Chinese literature prior to the 20th century falls into two categories – the classical and the vernacular. Many of the classical works remain impossible to translate and therefore inaccessible to Western scholars. Classical Chinese literature was largely Confucian in nature and the texts were regarded as an essential part of Chinese education, with all aspiring civil servants expected to have mastered them. Early classical Chinese texts were written on strips of bamboo, which were then rolled up like a blind, explaining why Chinese writing runs from bottom to top and from right to left. Perhaps for Westerners, the most famous of these early classical works are the thoughts of Confucius. His students collected his works into a series of volumes – the 'Spring and Autumn Annals', the 'Book of Changes' (a system of divination), the 'Book of Rites' and a history of his native state, Lu. Another important classical text available for Western scholars is 'Shijing' (book of odes or songs). Called the 'monument to the bound language', legend has it that more than 3,000 songs were collected from all over China by a civil servant, Cai Shiguan, and that Confucius selected 300 for inclusion in the volume. Poetry has always played an important role in the literary life of China and the 'Chuzi', a collection of songs by the poet Qwu Yuan, was published as early as 322–295 BC. The Tang Dynasty (618–907) saw the golden age of Chinese poetry and among the many famous poets of that time, Lio Bai (or Li Po) is remembered for having written his best-known poems in a state of total drunkenness. Quan Tangshi is a large and complete collection of Tang poetry, containing 50,000 poems by 2,200 poets. Every child in China is familiar with the famous heroes of the novel 'Journey to the West'. The King of the Apes accompanies the monk Zuanzang from China to west India to collect Holy Scriptures. The version available to readers today is attributed to Wu Cheng'en who lived in the 16th century. The 'Shuihuzhuan' (The Water Margin) is a novel dating from the Ming period and its tale of robbers fighting injustice, rather like Robin Hood and his merry men, is said to have been Mao Zedong's favourite book. By the 17th century, the genre novel was popular in China. 'Jinpingmei' (The Plum Blossom in a Golden Vase) dates from the Ming Dynasty and in contrast to the novels of that period that are largely religious (sometimes fanatically so) in content, it recounts the amorous adventures of Ximen in a realistic way and gives a vivid picture of life in the upper echelons of society at that time. The book was banned in 1687 but it continued to be read and in 1708 it was translated into Manchurian. It has also been on the banned list in modern day China. In the 18th century, Cao Xueqin wrote a novel called 'Hongloumeng' (Dream of the Red Chamber) which many consider to be China's greatest novel. It is the story of the rise and fall in the fortunes of a scholar's family. This story of domestic life in the Qing Dynasty has earned the author a reputation as the Chinese Tolstoy. By the beginning of the 20th century, Western novels were beginning to appear in Chinese translation.

The May Fourth Movement of 1919 was aimed at reforming the language and since then prose literature has been used increasingly as a method for the dissemination of radical social ideas. One of the leaders of the new movement was a poet, essayist and novelist, Lu Xun. Believing that modernization would come through revolution, he was one of the first Chinese authors to write in the vernacular. In his novel 'Ah Q' he describes the attitudes and superstitions of the tradi-tionalist Chinese underlings with sarcasm and irony. Lu Xun was also responsible for introducing the essay into Chinese literature. Another novelist of the period, Lao She, produced an allegorical work, 'Cat City', but is most famous for his novel 'The Rickshaw Boys' – a social critique of living conditions of rickshaw drivers in Beijing that has been translated into English many times.

After 1949, China's literary output was hampered by ideological constraints. Mao Zedong's 'Yan'an Talks on Art and Literature' extolled the virtues of literature as a tool for revolution. In the 1960s, the Cultural Revolution virtually halted all literary creativity and after 1976, most authors were put on salary and became members of state-sponsored literary guilds. Contemporary Chinese writing has produced some interesting writers, among them Zhang Xianliang, whose book 'Half of Man is Woman' was regarded as extremely controversial for its sexual content. The works of Wang Shou are considered by the Chinese authorities as a bad influence. With their stories of youth, gambling, drug addiction and prostitution, they have been widely adapted for the cinema and he is very popular with the younger generation, although his works have yet to be translated into English. Lao Gui's 'Blood Red Dusk' is a fascinating account of the Cultural Revolution and Feng Jicai has enjoyed success with satirical and magical short stories. Feng Jicai has also published a collection of accounts of the Cultural Revolution, at the time anonymously, called 'Voice from a Whirlwind', which has recently been published in English.

Cinema

Most of the films produced in China during the period immediately after 1949 were ideologically motivated and have not been subtitled or dubbed into English. However, several recent productions have received critical acclaim in the West. The turning point for modern Chinese cinema came in 1982 when the first generation of post-Cultural Revolution students graduated from the Beijing Film Academy. The group of directors working at this time came to be known as the 'Fifth Generation' and the first of their films to attract attention in the West was 'Yellow Earth', a simple but powerful story illustrating how strong the traditional age-old customs are in rural China (in this case the Shaanxi province). Zhang Yimou's films have received many awards at Western film festivals including 'Hng Goling' (Red Sorghum) which, controversially for China, portrayed an illicit love affair during the Sino-Japanese War. Perhaps the most satirical of the works released by the Fifth Generation is 'hipo shijn' (The Black Cannon Incident), a tale of bureaucratic suspicion, confusion and accusation. The Tian'anmen Square incident was followed by a pause in film production but, recently, Chinese film directors have started to produce some of the best international films. The joint winners of the Golden Bear Award at the 1993 Berlin Film Festival were both Chinese (one from mainland China and one from Taiwan) and Chang Kaige, who directed 'Yellow Earth', released 'Farewell my Concubine', which took joint honours at the Cannes film festival.

Ceramics

Even though the Chinese invented porcelain in the 7th century, at least a thousand years before the Europeans, the history of Chinese ceramics dates back to Neolithic times. Along the Huang He (Yellow River) and the Chang Jiang (the Yangtze), black and red decorated ceramics vessels 7,000–8,000 years old have been found. During the Yangshao and Longshao eras (5,000–2,000 BC), vessels with a diversity of patterns (semi-human masks, stylized fish), decorated stoneware and glazes made from kaolin and lime feldspar were used. The Han period was famous for its green 'yue' glazes. By the time of the Tang dynasty in the 10th century, China had already become known in Europe and the Middle East as the home of porcelain. The earliest Chinese porcelain was made by blending iron oxide with the glaze which resulted in its characteristic green tones. The Tang dynasty was also famous for producing three-colour glazes, mostly green, yellow and brown. Tang ceramic figurines in the shape of horses, camels, ladies of the court and officials were found in tombs of this period. As early as the Yuan Dynasty (14th century) Chinese potters used a Persian technique of underglazing in cobalt blue and this style of decoration with landscapes, figures and theatrical scenes has come to be known as Ming porcelain. This blue and white china with its many elaborate patterns (including the popular 'Willow Pattern') was much copied in Europe and reproductions of Chinese porcelain were produced by almost all the European manufacturers. At the start of the Quing dynasty (17th–early 20th centuries), blue and white porcelain became more and more refined and reached its highest levels of quality. Jingdezhen has been the centre of porcelain production in China since the 14th century, although today porcelain is made all over China and relatively inexpensive pottery can be bought almost everywhere. Genuine pieces of antique porcelain are hard to come by as it is prohibited to sell any porcelain made in China before the 19th century Opium Wars.

Architecture

Temple Architecture

Temple architecture follows a uniform set of rules whether it is Buddhist, Confucian or Taoist. The roof is the dominant feature, usually green or yellow, decorated with figures of divinities and good luck symbols such as dragons or carp. Entrances to temples are usually guarded by carved stone lions. The whole structure is housed in a compound with a north–south configuration. The dominant colours in Chinese temples are red, gold, yellow and green, each colour signifying a particular quality. When you think of a Chinese temple, it is common to think of the pagoda. These slender elegant towers are an important part of the religious architectural heritage of China and are found close to temples and monasteries. The first pagodas recorded in China date back to the 3rd century AD but as they were constructed of timber, none have survived. The oldest pagoda in China is in the district of Dengfeng near the old imperial city of Luoyang. Made of brick and tiles, this 40-metre high twelve-sided pagoda is 1,400 years old. Near to the Songyue Pagoda is the

Shaolin monastery with a forest of 200 chest-height pagodas. The 'Talin' are stone burial pagodas and mark the last resting-places of the monks and abbots. There are many ancient pagodas that have survived including the 'Great Wild Goose Pagoda' at the monastery of Shaolin that was designed by Zuanzang, a monk who, in the 17th century, travelled to India in search of holy scriptures. His story is immortalized in the trilogy 'Journey to the West' and this pagoda is used to store his writings. Towers have formed a strong element in Chinese architecture since the Han dynasty and these massive structures were used in palace walls and gates, and city walls. Highly decorated timber-frame constructions were topped by roofs that echo the shapes of the pagoda roofs. The style of building reflects the Taoist philosophy that there should be complete harmony between people and nature and the decorations and shapes of the towers are designed to blend harmoniously with their natural settings.

Traditional Chinese architecture followed certain principles, notably a north–south walled compound containing one or more structures and a main entrance on the south wall. This applied to buildings from the humblest village farm or homestead to the Imperial Palaces.

Selected Historical and Political Portraits

Dr Sun Yatsen (1866–1925)

Sun Yatsen is considered by many as the father of modern China, who planned to return China to the 'common people'. Born in or near the city of Guangzhou in Guangdong Province, he travelled to Hawaii in 1897 where he graduated from Oahu College. From Hawaii he returned to China and studied at the College of Medicine in Hong Kong. After a failed attempt at revolution, he travelled to Europe and then to Japan where he founded the 'China Revolutionary League'. The League soon became active in such events as the 1906 rebellion in Hunan Province. In 1911 Sun Yatsen's Revolutionary League was instrumental in an uprising in Wuchang. The League seized control of the government in what was to be called 'Double Ten Day' and proclaimed China a republic. On 1 Jan. 1912, Sun Yatsen was elected provisional president of the new republic. The birth of the republic was by no means that easy and in 1925 Sun Yatsen died having achieved less than he had hoped. His death created a power vacuum in Chinese politics that was filled by Chiang Kaishek.

Mao Zedong (1893–1976)

Mao was a Marxist theoretician, statesman and poet. He was born the son of a poor farmer in the village of Shao Shan in the Hunan Province. A library assistant at Beijing University and a head teacher in Changsha, Mao became head of propaganda under Sun Yatsen, leader of the Nationalist Party. In 1931–34 he established a Communist republic in Jiangxi. With Zhu De, he marshalled the Red Army in the long march. As founder of the Chinese Communist Party in 1921, Mao soon emerged as its natural leader. He set up an alliance with the Guomindang Nationalist Party in an attempt to repel the Japanese invasion but resumed his struggle with them in 1946. After defeating the Nationalist Party and ending the war of liberation from 1936–49, he established a People's Republic and Communist rule in China. He headed the Chinese Communist Party and government until his death.

Mao Zedong's real influence diminished with the failure of his 1958–60 Great Leap Forward, but he emerged dominant again during the 1966–69 Cultural Revolution. Mao adapted communism to Chinese conditions, as set out in his Little Red Book.

Deng Xiaoping (1904–1997)

Deng Xiaoping was known, from 1984 until his death at the age of 92, as the 'paramount leader' of China. Xiaoping was the last of the original members of the Communist Party of China; considered as one of the 'old guard'. Deng was born with the name Deng Xiansheng into a landlord family in the southwestern province of Sichuan on 22 Aug. 1904. Deng joined the China Socialist Youth League in 1922. Deng's progress through the party ranks was swift. Summoned to Beijing by Chairman Mao in 1952, Deng was named vice-premier and a year later became minister of finance. During 1966 Deng was forced to sign a self-criticism. As a result he spent 2 years in solitary confinement before being sent, with members of his family, to a long abandoned military school near Nanchang in Jiangxi. Deng was restored to power in 1976 with the death of Mao Zedong. He is credited with transforming China from rural impoverishment to prosperity by opening channels for better relations between the West and China but he is vilified for his part in the Tian'anmen Square Incident in 1989.

His Holiness the 14th Dalai Lama of Tibet (1935–)

Tenzin Gyatso is the head of state and leader in exile of the Tibetan people. He is believed to be the manifestation of the Bhodhisattva (Buddha.) He was born in Lhamo Dhondrub on 6 July 1935. His enthronement took place on 22 Feb. 1940 in Lhasa. He assumed full political power after the 1950 occupation of Tibet by the People's Liberation Army. After a thwarted attempt to bring about a peaceful solution to the Sino–Tibetan problem which resulted in an uprising in Lhasa, the Dalai Lama found political asylum in India. From his residence, 'Little Lahasa', in Dharamasala, the Dalai Lama has campaigned for a peaceful solution to the Sino–Tibetan problem and liberation from Chinese rule. In 1989 the Dalai Lama was awarded the Nobel Peace Prize for his enduring belief in a non-violent liberation of the Tibetan people.

Mei Lan-Fang (1894–1961)

Mei Lan-Fang was China's best-known Beijing Opera master. Born on 22 Oct. 1894 in Tao Zhao in China's Jiangsu province, Mei began studying opera at the age of eight years old. His father and grandfather, famous actors themselves, urged him on and he played his debut role at 12. He joined Xe Lian Cheng Theatre Company at 14 and performed around China with the troupe. He quickly acquired a national reputation and was regarded as the leader of the Pear Garden (a name that refers to the opera community.) It was through the efforts of Mei Lan-Fang that the Western world came to learn of Peking Opera. He toured Japan twice, visited the United States of America in 1930 and Russia in 1932 and 1935. Lan-Fang rediscovered and rejuvenated many long neglected theatrical masterpieces but he is best remembered for his performances in 'Farewell my Concubine', 'Recommanding the Army' and 'Eternal Regret'. Mei Lan-Fang died on 7 Aug. 1961.

Mei Lan-Fang's son Mei Bao-Jiu is the doyen of Peking theatre.

MAJOR CITIES

BEIJING (PEKING):

Capital City of the People's Republic of China.

(2000 Estimated Population: 14,206,000).

Beijing adjoins the Inner Mongolian Highland to the northwest and the Great Northern Plain to the south. Five rivers run through the city, connecting it to the eastern Bohai Sea.

There is evidence of structured settlement in and around Beijing as early as 1000 BC. Beijing began life as a small trading post for local tribes, Mongols and Koreans. Once called Yanjing, capital of the Yan dynasty, it was sacked in 1215 and razed to the ground by Genghis Khan and called Dadu (Great Capital) or Khanbaliq (The Khan's Town). From here, Genghis's grandson, Kublai Khan, ruled much of Asia. It was during this period that Marco Polo visited China and described the many wonders created by the 'benevolent dictator'.

An uprising in 1368 made way for the Ming Dynasty who renamed the city Beiping (Northern Peace). For a time the administrative hub of China moved south and Nanjing was the capital between 1368–1644. Gradually the capital was moved back to the north and Yong Le renamed the capital Beijing (Northern Capital).

After the Manchu invasion in the mid 17th century, until 1911 Beijing was subjected to a catalogue of power struggles, both internal and with foreign nations. In 1860, during the second Opium War, a joint force of British and French troops sacked and burned the Summer Palace.

The Qing dynasty of the Manchus was finally overthrown in the revolution of 1911 when the Kuomintang Party took power and declared a Republic of China. Struggles for power and land continued in China with warlords holding power in the south and foreign forces controlling many of the important trade routes and ports. The Kuomintang Party's hold on power was tentative. The emerging Communists and the Kuomintang Party forged an uneasy alliance to rid the country of the crippling power struggles. Chiang Kaishek was appointed commander-in-chief of the Kuomintang and in 1928 he established his government at Beijing. The Japanese invasion of Beijing in 1937 sent the Kuomintang to Chonquing in retreat.

After the Japanese defeat and the end of World War II in 1945, the Kuomintang only held power for a few years before the Communist revolution removed the Kuomintang Party from Beijing. In 1949 the People's Liberation Army, led by Mao Zedong, entered Tian'anmen Square to proclaim a People's Republic of China.

It was from Beijing that the post-revolution Communist Party sought to consolidate their hold on power. Mao Zedong's Cultural Revolution was launched from Beijing and many writers, artists and intellectuals were persecuted by the Red Guard. Much of the artistic and cultural heritage of Beijing was destroyed or lost during the years of the Cultural Revolution.

TRANSPORT

Airport

Beijing Capital Airport (Code PEK) is situated about 27 km northeast of the Forbidden City.

General flight information for all airlines can be obtained from Aviation Building. Tel: (0)10 6601 7755 or for international flights, Tel: (0)10 6456 7755 Ext 7100.

Shuttle buses to and from the airport run in front of the terminal building and stop at hotels along Capital Airport Road on its way to Aviation Building.

Trains

Beijing has two major railway stations.

Beijing Zhan services rail traffic from and to the north and east and is situated about 4 km east of Tian'anmen Square and just south of Dongchang'an Jie.

Xi Zhan, on Lianhuachi Dong Lu, is Asia's largest railway station and services rail traffic to and from the south. It will become the north-ernmost tip of the Kowloon–Beijing line.

There are foreigners' Ticket Booking Offices in both stations, sign-posted in English.

General Inquiries and train information (in Chinese), Tel: (0)10 651 28931.

For Trans-Siberian or Trans-Mongolian train services, contact the International Train Booking Office at the International Hotel, 9 Jianguomanwai Dajie.

Buses

Dongzhimen Bus Station for travel to and from Shenyang and Dongbei.

Haihutun for travel to and from Tianjin and southern Hebei.

Local Transport

Beijing has a speedy subway system consisting of two lines, the
Circle Line and the East–West Line. Tickets cost 2 yuan per journey.

Buses are plentiful, with over 140 routes, but cramped. Tickets are
bought from the conductor.

Taxis are plentiful.

For telephone booking: Beijing Municipal Taxi Company,
Tel: (0)10 831 2288. Beijing Taxi, Tel: (0)10 6831 2288. Capital Taxi,
Tel: (0)10 6852 7084. Beijing Tourism Taxi, Tel: (0)10 6436 3452.

TRAVELLERS INFORMATION

Beijing Tourism Administration: 28 Jianguomenwai, Beijing 100022.
Tel: (0)10 6515 8844.

Supervisory Office of Travel Agencies Service Quality of Beijing
Municipality was established to protect the rights and interests of
domestic and overseas tourists: Rm. 1001 Beijing Luyou Building,
28 Jianguomenwai, Beijing 100022. Tel: (0)10 6513 0828.

Information Websites: www.beijingnow.com/index.html
www.surfchina.com www.beijingpage.com

Financial & Currency

American Express: Room 2101, China World Travel Tower, Jiangjuo
Wai Avenue, Beijing. Tel: (0)10 6505 2228.

Currency exchange and bank withdrawals at major banks throughout the city.

Postal Services

Mail can be sent from most hotels and large tourist hotels may have a
post office branch. Private carriers can be used.

DHL, Tel: (0)10 466 2211.
Federal Express, Tel: (0)10 501 1017.

Consulates

UK The British Embassy, 11 Guang Hua Lu, Jian Guo Men Wai, Beijing 100600. Tel: (0)10 6532 1961/2/3/4. Fax: (0)10 6532 1930.
USA 3 Xiu Shui Bei Jie, Beijing, 100600. Tel: (0)10 6532 3431.

Emergency

Ambulance, Tel: 120
Fire Hot Line, Tel: 119
Police Hot Line, Tel: 110
Police – Traffic accidents, Tel: 122
Public Security, Tel: (0)10 6512 2471
Hospitals: Beijing Friendship Hospital, Tel: (0)10 6301-4411.
Beijing Hospital, Tel: (0)10 6513-1363.

Landmarks

The Great Wall was started in the 7th century BC. The vassal states under the Zhou Dynasty in the northern parts of the country each built their own walls for defence purposes. After the state of Qin unified China in 221 BC, it joined the walls to hold off the invaders from the Xiongnu tribes in the north and extended them to more than 5,000 km.

The Forbidden City or former Imperial Palace, standing on the site of Kublai Khan's winter capital, was built during the Ming dynasty and was home to 24 Chinese emperors between 1368 and 1911. The Palace extends over 720,000 sq. metres and is surrounded by a wall that is 35 ft high and extends for 2½ miles.

The Summer Palace and imperial gardens were a summer retreat for emperors of the Qing dynasty. The Summer Palace is about 20 km from Beijing City centre.

Tian'anmen Square is one of the largest public squares in the world. It has played an important role in China's revolutionary past. In 1989, after the death of the student icon and liberal politician Hu Yaobang, students organized meetings in the square. These became demonstrations and were forcibly repressed by the government on 3 and 4 June with the loss of hundreds and possibly thousands of lives.

Beijing Art Museum exhibits examples of calligraphy, painting, weaving and embroideries, porcelain, furniture, ancient coins and overseas art objects. In all, there are about 50,000 pieces which range from the Neolithic age through the Ming and Qing Dynasties, up to modern times. Beijing Art Museum is situated at the site of **Wanshou Temple (Temple of Longevity)**.

Other attractions include **Zhoukoudian** (modern residence of prehistoric Peking Man), **Tian Tan (Temple of Heaven)**, **Di Tan (Temple of Earth)** and **Mao's Mausoleum**.

SHANGHAI:

Estimated Population: 14,173,000.

Shanghai, 'Whore of Asia' or 'Paris of the East', really owes its importance to its location, on the Huangpu River near the mouth of the Yangtze River. Before the Opium Wars in the 19th century, it was little more than a fishing town on the banks of the river. Today it is a bustling city and is the largest city in the People's Republic of China.

Shanghai's history, linked to foreign trade and the many races of people that trade brought to the city, is an unsettled one. It has often been at odds with Beijing and the outside world. In 1874 it was the scene of much rioting and many deaths and the base for the Boxer Rebellion of 1900. Shanghai was the setting for the betrayal and the consequent massacre of the Communists by the Kuomintang, led by Chiang Kaishek. The city was also much involved in the Cultural Revolution (1966–76). After the deaths of Zhou Enlai and Mao Zedong, it became the hiding place of the 'Gang of Four'. Shanghai's history as a major trading post has adorned it with many interesting colonial style buildings. On the **Bund** or 'Waitan' there are beautiful sandstone buildings which once housed colonial hotels, Shanghai's first banks and the offices of the opium traders.

Shanghai's reputation as a den of iniquity, not unfounded, ended in the Communist clean-up of 1947. It was noted that along Hui Le Li (the Lane of Lingering Happiness), were 151 'singsong' houses (the polite name for brothels).

Shanghai today is the business hub of China. It accounts for 6% of all money coming into China.

TRANSPORT

Airport

Hongqiao Airport (Code SHA) is just under 16 km southwest of the Bund.

China Eastern Airlines Office. Domestic, Tel: (0)21 6247 5935. International, Tel: (0)21 6247 2255.

Tickets can be bought from most large hotels in Shanghai. Most major hotels operate a shuttle bus system to and from the airport.

Another airport for Shanghai is under construction. Upon scheduled completion, in Oct. 1999, Shanghai Pudong International Airport will be one of the largest international airports in Asia.

Flight information and schedules can be found on the Web at: www.shanghaiguide.com/shanghai/facts/p-airlines.html

Trains

Shanghai's main railway station is 500 metres west of Chengdu Expressway.

Ticket Office Longmen Hotel, Tel: (0)21 6317 000 ext. 5315.

Railway Inquiries: (0)21 6317 9090.

Local Transport

Shanghai has a single, north to south metro line that runs from the railway station in the north, through Renmin Square to the Jinjiang Park. A new east to west metro is due to open that will link Hongqiao airport with Pudong. Tickets are 2 yuan regardless of distance.

Shanghai buses are plentiful and have been slowly upgraded over the last few years. There are an increasing number of air-conditioned buses servicing the city centre.

TRAVELLERS INFORMATION

The China International Travel Service Office is in the Guanming Building, 2 Jinling Donglu. Tel: (0)21 6321 7200.

Tourist hotline, Tel: (0)21 6439 0630.

Web: www.shanghai-ed.com, www.sh.com/guide.htm
www.shanghabc.com/relocating/basics/index.htm

Financial & Currency

American Express: Tel: (0)21 632 38750.

Currency exchange and bank withdrawals at major banks through-out the city.

Postal Services

Mail can be sent from most hotels and large tourist hotels may have a post office branch.

Express mail and poste restante is located at 276 Bei Suzhou.

Private carriers can be used.

DHL, Tel: (0)21 6536 2900.

Federal Express, Tel: (0)21 6275 0808.

Consulates

UK British Consulate, 244 Yong Fu Rd. Tel: (0)21 6433 0508.

USA 1469 Huai Hai Rd. Tel: (0)21 6433 6888.

Emergency

Police, Tel: 110.

Fire, Tel: 119.

Medical emergency, Tel: 120.

Public Security, Tel: (0)21 6321 5380.

China International Travel Service, Tel: (0)21 6321 8888.

Hospitals: Shanghai People's Hospital No1, Tel: (0)21 6324 0100.

Ruijin Hospital. Tel: (0)21 6437 0045.

Internet Access

Internet Café, 3/f Hao Du Plaza, 400 East Jin Ling Lu.

Tel: (0)21 6355 7070.

Infohighway, 181 Rui Jin Er Lu. Tel: (0)21 6415 5009.

O'Richard's Bar and Restaurant. 2/f Pu Jiang Hotel, 15 Huangpu Lu.

Tel: (0)21 6324 6388.

Landmarks

The '**Bund**' refers to part of the west bank of the Huangpu River. It was once the most famous street in Asia. This is where the major firms of the Far East had their headquarters. To walk along the Bund is to go back in time. Buildings include the residence of the British Consulate General during the 19th Century, the former Hong Kong and Shanghai Bank, which after 1949 was used as the city Communist Party HQ, and the Pujiang Hotel.

The **Shanghai Museum** on Renmin Square is considered to hold the world's finest and most extensive collections of Chinese Art. The building itself is shaped like a giant bronze urn.

Longhua Temple at 2853 Longhua Road is an ancient monastery on the south of the Yangtse River, which houses the magnificent Longhua Evening Bell. According to legend, it was built in the Three Kingdoms Period (242 AD). The Longhua Pagoda standing opposite the monastery is seven storeys high and octagonal in shape. This elegant pagoda is a relic of the Song Dynasty.

Yu Fo Temple (**Jade Buddha Temple**) is located at 170 Anyuan Road. Built in 1918 the temple is famous for its jade Buddha statues which are pure white. The construction of pavilions and halls is in the traditional style of the Song dynasty. It has four halls: Hall of the Heavenly Kings, Grand Hall, Reclining Buddha Hall and Jade Buddha Chamber.

Yuyuan Garden (**Garden of Leisurely Repose**) is located on Yuyuan Road in the Nanshi District and was built in 1559 during the Ming Dynasty. Inside the garden, there are beautiful rockeries, dragon walls and differently shaped pavilions and towers and other tourist attractions like **Cuixiu Tang** (**Hall of Gathering Graces**) and **Dianchun Tang** (**Spring Hall**).

GUANGZHOU (CANTON):

2000 Estimated Population: 15,162,000.

Guangzhou is the capital city of China's southern Guandong province and south China's principal seaport, with rail and hovercraft connections to Hong Kong, 182 km to the south. The present day city of Guangzhou dates back to the days of the Qin Dynasty in the 3rd century BC when the dynasty conquered the semi-independent tribes in the south. Guangzhou, like Shanghai, owes its importance to its location in the Pearl River delta. Its fertile land and sub-tropical climate makes it an important rice growing area. Legend has it that the city gained its nickname of Yang Cheng or 'Goat Town' because five gods riding on five rams brought the first grains of rice to the city. In 1685 Guangzhou saw the arrival of the first British trade ships, spearheaded by the British East India Company and it was near Guangzhou that the British traders were allowed to establish warehouses as a base to export tea and silk. In 1757 an imperial edict restricted all foreign trade to a handful of Cantonese merchants. The series of events that followed, as a direct result of this decree, sparked the Opium Wars and led to China's subsequent loss of Guangzhou as part of the Nanking Treaty of 1842. Conditions for the local population were terrible in comparison to their foreign overlords. It is not surprising that Guangzhou became a hotbed of revolution. A rebellion, led by Huang Chao, seized control of the city. In 1917 Sun Yatsen, leader of the Nationalist forces, made Guangzhou his headquarters while he struggled to rid China of the warlords who had control over the north. Guangzhou was the site of the only Communist regional headquarters that dared to operate openly in China.

Guangzhou's post-revolutionary history has been a successful one. Its continued role as an important trading post has allowed it to expand into a modern, if chaotic, city. Over the past 17 years, since the initiation of reform, Guangzhou has laid a solid material foundation with increasingly strong economic growth.

TRANSPORT

Airport
Baiyun, Guangzhou's international airport, is 6 km north of the city centre. Buses run from the airport to a location near the main railway station.

Trains
The main railway station is in the north of Guangzhou and services routes to Hong Kong, Shenzhen and Beijing as well as international routes.

Local Transport
Buses in Guangzhou are plentiful but cramped.

Taxis are available in Guangzhou and all are equipped with meters.

The initial stage of the Guangzhou metro has been in operation since 1997 but a full metro system is under construction. This will take much of the pressure out of travelling by road. Line 1 is 18·5 km long with 16 stations and runs in an east–west direction. It will link Guang Zhou Dong Zhan Station in the east with Xilang in the southwest of the city.

TRAVELLERS INFORMATION

Supervisory Office of Tourism Quality of Guangdong Province, 185 Huanshixilu. Tel: (0)20 666 5039.

The China International Tourist Office is at 179 Huanshi Donglu. Tel: (0)20 666 6271.

Tourist Hotline. Tel: (0)20 667 7422.

Financial & Currency

American Express. Ground Floor, Guangdong International Hotel, Huangshi Donglu. Tel: (0)20 331 1771.

Postal Services

Linhua Post Office is at the northern end of Huanshi Xilu near the railway station.

Most large hotels have post offices.

Private carriers can be used.

DHL, Tel: (0)20 335 5034.

Federal Express, Tel: (0)20 386 2026.

Consulates

UK British Consulate General, 2nd Floor Guangdong International Hotel, 39 Huanshi Dong Lu. Tel: (0)20 8335 1354. Fax: (0)20 8333 6485. Email: guangbcg@gitic.com.cn

US 1 South Shamian Street. Tel: (0)20 8667 7842 or (0)20 8188 8911. Fax: (0)20 8186 2341.

Emergency

Ambulance, Tel: 120.

Fire, Tel: 119.

Police, Tel: 110.

Medical. Guangzhou Red Cross Hospital, Tel: (0)20 444 6411.

Hospitals. City No1 Hospital, Renmin Bei Lu, Tel: (0)20 333 3090.

Zhongshan Medical College. 58 Zhongshan Er Lu, Tel: (0)20 666 1912.

Landmarks

The **Temple of the Six Banyan Trees**, although no longer standing, and the **Octagonal Flower Pagoda** are situated in the centre of the city on Liurong Lu. The Flower Pagoda is 55 metres high and the largest in the city.

Sacred Heart Church was built in the 19th century entirely of granite. It is an imitation of a European Catholic cathedral and was designed by the French architect, Guillemin. It is located near the Pearl River at the north side of Yanijang Xilu.

Mausoleum of the 72 Martyrs & Memorial of Yellow Flowers is a large complex of pavilions, tombs, ponds and a museum between Dongfeng Donglu and Zhongshan 3-Lu. It commemorates the dead of the 1912 uprising, five months before the declaration of a Chinese Republic.

Memorial Garden to the Martyrs on Honghuagang (Red Flower Hill), which was an execution ground during the Communist uprising of 1927. It commemorates the 5,700 people estimated to have been killed during the unsuccessful uprising.

HONG KONG (HONG KONG SPECIAL ADMINISTRATIVE REGION):

Ex-Crown Colony of Great Britain (see also page 135).

The name Hong Kong is derived from the two Chinese characters 'Heung' and 'Gong' which are usually translated as 'Fragrant Harbour'. Hong Kong is divided into four areas – Hong Kong Island, Kowloon, the New Territories and Outlying Islands.

It is often presumed that Hong Kong's history began as a Crown Colony of Great Britain but evidence of Neolithic settlements on Lantau island has recently emerged. Imperial records state that troops were garrisoned at Tuen Mun and Tai Po long before trade with the outside world commenced.

As a result of tactics employed by British traders operating out of Guangzhou, opium addiction in China rose dramatically during the

18th century, in direct correlation to the drain of silver from the country. In Oct. 1838 Lin Zexu, governor of Guangzhou, was summoned to the Imperial Palace in Peking, where the Emperor ordered him to stamp out opium addiction. The ensuing conflicts which lasted on and off until 1898 were known as the Opium Wars. Hong Kong Island was ceded to the British under the terms of the Treaty of Nanking in 1841. The Convention of Peking in 1860 ceded the Kowloon peninsula. The New Territories were leased to the British for 99 Years in 1898.

Although Hong Kong seemed 'a barren island,' as Lord Palmerston remarked, its history as a Crown Colony has been a success. Settlement in the territory grew slowly at first. During the early part of the century, Hong Kong served as a refuge for exiles from China following the establishment of the Chinese Republic in 1912. Immigration into the colony increased during the Japanese invasion of World War II when hundreds of thousands of Chinese took refuge in Hong Kong. On Christmas Day 1941, the British army surrendered Hong Kong to the Japanese but four years later, following Japan's surrender on 14 Aug. 1945, Britain reclaimed the territory. With few natural resources Hong Kong became an industrial centre for manufacture during the 1950s and quickly became one of the world's largest and most respected industrial and economic zones.

After a century and a half of British administration, Hong Kong became a Special Administrative Region of China on 1 July 1997 under the 1984 Sino-British Joint Declaration.

TRANSPORT

Airport

Hong Kong's new **International Airport** opened at Chek Lap Kok on 6 July 1998, replacing the congested Kai Tak Airport. Tel: 2769 7531.

The Mass Transit Railway's Airport Express train leaves every 8 minutes from Central Station on Hong Kong Island.

Trains

Kowloon-Canton Railway Terminus is in Kowloon near the entrance to the Cross-Harbour Tunnel. A single line snakes out of Hong Kong New Territories via Lo Wu and onto Guangzhou. You will need a special ticket to progress as far as Lo Wu.

KCR inquiries. Tel: 2602 7799.

Local Transport

Buses in Hong Kong are plentiful and cheap and will take you wherever you wish to go. The main bus terminal on Hong Kong Island is under Exchange Square. Hong Kong's bus companies include New World First Bus Ltd, Tel: 2136 8888; Citybus, Tel: 2873 0818; and Kowloon Motor Bus, Tel: 2745 4466.

Hong Kong's MTR (Mass Transit Railway) is the easiest way to get around northern Hong Kong Island, Kowloon and as far north as Tsuen Wan in the New Territories. All MTR trains are air-conditioned.

Passenger Information Hotline, Tel: 2881 8888.

Running east and west along the northern side of Hong Kong Island, along the same tracks they have travelled since 1904, trams are cheap and easy to use.

Hong Kong's ferry services are probably the best way to get across the harbour. There are 3 different services but by far the most popular are the Star Ferries which travel from Central and Wan Chai to Tsim Sha Tsui and Hung Hom.

There are many taxis in Hong Kong. Travelling by taxi is not expensive but you will need to pay for any road or tunnel tolls as they arise. Taxis come in different colours, depending on the area that they are allowed to service; red taxis operate in areas such as Hong Kong Island and Kowloon; green taxis operate in the New Territories; and blue taxis operate on Lantau Island. All three may serve the Chek Lap Kok International Airport.

TRAVELLERS INFORMATION

Hong Kong Tourist Association. No 8, Jardine House, Connaught Place, Central. Hotline Tel: 2807 6177.
Information Website: www.hkta.org

Financial & Currency

American Express. 1st floor, 25 Kimberly Road, Tsim Sha Tsui, Kowloon. Tel: 2732 7327. 24-hour hotline, Tel: 2823 9366.

MasterCard. Dah Sing Financial Centre, Gloucester and Flemming Road, Wan Chai, Hong Kong. Tel: 2598 8038.

Visa. Lippo Tower, Tamar Street, Admiralty, Hong Kong. Tel: 2523 8152.

Currency exchange and bank withdrawals at major banks throughout the territory. Many ATMs will accept cards displaying Visa, Cirrus, Global Access, MasterCard and American Express.

Postal Services

Post Office. Tel: 2921 2222.
Private Carriers can be used.
DHL, Tel: 2765 8111.
Federal Express, Tel: 2730 3333.
TNT Express, Tel: 2331 2663.

Consulates

UK The British Consulate-General, 1 Supreme Court Road. Tel: 2901 3000. Email: consular@britishconsulate.org.hk

US American Consulate-General, 26 Garden Road.
Tel: 2523 9011.

Emergency

Police, fire and ambulance, Tel: 999.
St. John's Free Ambulance Service: Hong Kong Island, Tel: 2576
6555. Kowloon, Tel: 2713 5555. New Territories, Tel: 2639 2555.
Hospitals
Queen Mary Hospital. Pokfulam Road, Hong Kong. Tel: 2855 4111.
Queen Elizabeth Hospital. 30 Gascoigne Road, Kowloon.
Tel: 2958 8888.
Prince of Wales Hospital. 30–32 Ngan Shing Street, New Territories.
Tel: 2632 2211.

Landmarks

Victoria Peak is a must-see for anyone visiting Hong Kong. The
journey by funicular tram and the views from the summit are splendid.
Peak Galleria, at the end of the funicular tram, is a restaurant-cum-
shopping centre. The peak tram can be boarded at Garden Road,
Central.

University Museum & Art Gallery, situated at 94 Bonham Road, is part
of the University of Hong Kong and houses the largest collection of
bronze Nestorian crosses in the world. Also on display are bronzes,
ceramics and furniture from the Warring States Period, the Tang
Dynasty and the Qing Dynasty. Tel: 2975 5600.

Sam Tung Uk (three-beam dwelling) **Museum** in the New Territories is a
restored 200-year-old rural walled village. The museum consists of an
ancestral hall, two rows of side houses, an exhibition hall and a lec-
ture hall. It houses displays of period furniture, handicrafts and agricultural equipment.

Man Mo Temple is one of the most famous landmarks on Hong Kong Island. It is situated at the corner of Hollywood Road and Ladder Street in Chinatown.

Zoological & Botanic Gardens at the top of Garden Road which rises from Connaught Place in Central, houses hundreds of species of rare and endangered birds, flowers, shrubs and trees.

TAIPEI:

Capital City of Taiwan.

2000 Estimated Population: 2,880,000.

Beijing considers Taiwan a renegade province of the Chinese motherland. Taiwan is the headquarters of the governmental offices of the Republic of China. Taiwan lost United Nations recognition in 1979 when the UN formally opened diplomatic discourse with the Communist government of the People's Republic of China.

Taipei literally means 'Northern Taiwan'. It is a large and modern city sitting on the banks of the Tamsui River. The area where Taipei now stands was once a lake which dried up over time leaving lush, fertile and grassy lowlands.

Taiwan became a protectorate of mainland China in 1206. Early immigrants from the mainland province of Fukien settled on the banks of the Tamsui in the 18th century, which brought prosperity, making trade in tea and camphor possible.

In 1895 Japanese forces invaded Taiwan and established their administrative headquarters in Taipei. It was during the Japanese occupation of Taipei that much of its infrastructure was established. At the end of World War II, under the terms of the Alta Agreement, Taiwan was returned to Chinese rule. This was opposed by many

Taiwanese and riots broke out. In 1947 anti-Chinese rioting ended with the death of nearly 30,000 Taiwanese. When the Communists took control of mainland China and declared a People's Republic, Chiang Kaishek and the Kuomintang's 'Republic of China' government retreated to Taiwan.

The expected mainland invasion of Taiwan never happened, probably because of the Korean War, but a political 'tug-of-war' continues to this day. The 'PRC' and the 'ROC' declare that they have the exclusive right to govern all of China.

TRANSPORT

Airport

Chiang Kaishek International Airport (Code TPE) is 40 km south west of Taipei at Taoyuan. An airport shuttle bus leaves from the front of the terminal every 15 to 30 minutes. One route goes to the central train station and the other goes to the Sungshan Domestic Airport.

Metered taxis are available.

Trains

Taiwan has 4 rail routes that service most parts of the island.
Tickets can be purchased and inquiries made at
Web: railway.hinet.net/stn_eng.htm

Local Transport

The 'Metropolitan Rapid Transit' system consists of 6 lines and serves much of Taipei County.

Department of Rapid Transit Systems, Taipei City Government, No7 Lane 48, Sec. 2 Chung-Shan North Road. Tel: (0)2 521 5550.

Web: www.dorts.gov.tw

Buses are plentiful in Taipei and service most parts of the county.

TRAVELLERS INFORMATION

Domestic Tourism Bureau Office. 9/F, 280 Chung Hsiao E. Rd,
Sec. 4,Taipei. Tel: (0)2 349 1635/6. Fax: (0)2 773 5487.
   CKS Tourist Service Centre. CKS International Airport.
Tel: (0)2 383 4631. Fax: (0)2 383 4250.
   Travel Information Service Centre (TISC). 340 Tun Hua N. Rd.
Tel: (0)2 713 8359 Fax: (0)2 717 6875.

Financial & Currency

International Bank of China. 15 Chungshan North Road, Section 2.
Tel: (0)2 511 9231.

Postal Services

There is a General Post Office in Chunghsiao West Road, near the
North Gate.
Private carriers can be used.
DHL. 82 Chien Kuo North Road, Section 2. Tel: (0)2 503 8378.

Consulates

UK British Trade and Cultural Office, 9th Floor, Fu Key Building,
99 Jen Ai Road, Section 2. Tel: (0)2 322 4242.
US American Institute in Taiwan, 7 Lane 134, Hsinyi Road, Section 3.
Tel: (0)2 709 2000.

Emergency

English-speaking police, Tel: 311 9940.
Police, Tel: 110.
Fire, Tel: 119.
Ambulance, Tel: 721 6315.
Hospitals: Adventist Hospital, 424 Pate Road, Section 2,
Tel: (0)2 771 8151. National Taiwan University Hospital,
7 Chungshan South Road, Tel: (0)2 397 0800.

Landmarks

The **National Palace Museum** in the north of the city, near the Keelung River, contains an unrivalled collection of Chinese artefacts. This is partly due to the fact that Taiwan never saw the widespread destruction of art and cultural artefacts during the Cultural Revolution.
221 Chihshan Road, Section 2. Tel: (0)2 881 2021.

The **Chung Cheng (Chiang Kaishek) Memorial Hall** is a large structure – its main entrance is more than 30 metres (100 ft) – set in beautiful gardens.
21 Chungshan South Road. Tel: (0)2 394 3171.

SOCIAL STATISTICS

Births, 1996, 20,780,000 (more than the total population of Australia); deaths, 8,030,000. 1996 birth rate (per 1,000 population), 16·98; death rate, 6·56. There were 9,339,615 marriages and 1,132,215 divorces in 1996. Life expectancy at birth, 1990–95, was 66·7 years for men and 70·5 years for women. Annual growth rate, 1990–95, 1·1%. Infant mortality, 1990–95, 44 per 1,000 live births. The average number of live births per woman (married or otherwise) in 1996 was 1·42. The lowest and highest averages by region were Beijing with 0·84 and Hainan with 1·78. Only Beijing and Shanghai had averages less than 1. In 1996 the average Chinese woman had 1·39 living children.

CLIMATE

Most of China has a temperate climate but, with such a large country, extending far inland and embracing a wide range of latitude as well as containing large areas at high altitude, many parts experience extremes of climate, especially in winter. Most rain falls during the summer, from May to Sept., though amounts decrease inland. Beijing (Peking), Jan. 24°F (−4·4°C), July 79°F (26°C). Annual rainfall 24·9" (623 mm). Chongqing, Jan. 45°F (7·2°C), July 84°F (28·9°C). Annual rainfall 43·7" (1,092 mm). Shanghai, Jan. 39°F (3·9°C), July 82°F (27·8°C). Annual rainfall 45·4" (1,135 mm). Tianjin, Jan. 24°F (−4·4°C), July 81°F (27·2°C). Annual rainfall 21·5" (533·4 mm).

CONSTITUTION AND GOVERNMENT

On 21 Sept. 1949 the *Chinese People's Political Consultative Conference* met in Beijing, convened by the Chinese Communist Party. The Conference adopted a 'Common Programme' of 60 articles and the 'Organic Law of the Central People's Government' (31 articles). Both became the basis of the Constitution adopted on 20 Sept. 1954 by the 1st National People's Congress, the supreme legislative body. The Consultative Conference continued to exist after 1954 as an advisory body. Its 9th session was convened in 1998. It has 2,093 members.

New Constitutions were adopted in 1975, 1978, 1982 and 1993, the latter embodying the principles of a 'Socialist market economy'.

The *National People's Congress* can amend the Constitution and nominally elects and has power to remove from office the highest officers of state. The Congress elects a *Standing Committee* (which supervises the State Council) and the *President* and *Vice-President* for a 5-year term. Congress has 2,978 deputies and is elected for a 5-year term, and meets once a year for 2 or 3 weeks. When not in session, its business is carried on by its *Standing Committee*. It is composed of deputies elected on a constituency basis by direct secret ballot. Any voter, and certain organizations, may nominate candidates. Nominations may exceed seats by 50–100%.

The *State Council* is the supreme executive organ and comprises the Prime Minister, Deputy Prime Ministers and State Councillors.

National Anthem
'March of the Volunteers'; words by Tien Han, tune by Nieh Erh.

RECENT ELECTIONS

The 9th *National People's Congress* was elected in March 1998.

CURRENT ADMINISTRATION

President: Jiang Zemin (b. 1926; elected 27 March 1993 and sworn in April 1993).

Deputy President: Hu Jintao.

In Sept. 1999 the government comprised:

Prime Minister: Zhu Rongji.

Deputy Prime Ministers: Li Lanqing, Qian Qichen, Wu Bangguo, Wen Jiabao.

Minister of Agriculture: Chen Yaobang. *Civil Affairs:* Doje Cering. *Communications:* Huang Zhendong. *Construction:* Yu Zhengsheng. *Culture:* Sun Jiazheng. *Education:* Chen Zhili. *Finance:* Xiang Huaicheng. *Foreign Affairs:* Tang Jiaxuan. *Foreign Trade and Economic Co-operation:* Shi Guangsheng. *Information Industry:* Wu Jichuan. *Justice:* Gao Changli. *Labour and Social Security:* Zhang Zuoji. *Land and Natural Resources:* Zhou Yongkang. *National Defence:* Chi Haotian. *Personnel:* Song Defu. *Public Health:* Zhang

Wenkang. *Public Security:* Jia Chunwang. *Railways:* Fu Zhihuan. *Science and Technology:* Zhu Lilan. *State Security:* Xu Yongyue. *Supervision:* He Yong. *Water Resources:* Wang Shucheng.

Ministers heading State Commissions: *Economics and Trade*, Sheng Huaren. *Family Planning*, Zhang Weiqing. *Nationalities Affairs*, Li Dezhu. *Development Planning*, Zeng Peiyan. *Science, Technology and Industry for National Defence*, Liu Jibin.

De facto power is in the hands of the Communist Party of China, which had 57m. members in 1997. There are 8 other parties, all members of the Chinese People's Political Consultative Conference.

The members of the Standing Committee of the Politburo in March 1998 were Jiang Zemin (*General Secretary*), Li Peng, Zhu Rongji, Hu Jintao, Li Ruihuan, Li Lanqing and Wei Jianxing.

POLITICAL PROFILES

Jiang Zemin (1926–)

Born in Yangzhou, Jiangsu Province, Jiang Zemin is the most powerful man in China. He is the President of the Communist Party, General Secretary and Chairman of the State Central Military Commission. He was recently re-elected as President of the National People's Congress. The NPC is the highest organ of state power in the People's Republic of China.

Jiang graduated from Shanghai Jiatong University in 1947 with an electrical engineering degree. While a student he was active in the Communist Party and was involved in demonstrations against the Chiang Kaishek autocratic regime.

After many years plying his trade as an engineer for the new Communist republic, Jiang turned to a political life. Since 1980 he has had a varied career with positions including Deputy Director of the

State Import and Export Administration and the State Foreign Investment Administration, Vice Minister and Minister of the Electronics Industry, Mayor of Shanghai, Secretary of the CPC Shanghai Municipal Committee and member of the Political Bureau of the CPC Central Committee. In 1997 Jiang presided over the peaceful handover of Hong Kong. In the 8 years that Jiang Zemin has held power in the PRC he has been accredited with stabilizing, along with Zhu Rongji, China's economy through the implementation and furthering of Deng Xioaping's economic reforms and with establishing China's place in the trade economy of the world.

Zhu Rongji (1928–)

Jhu Rongji was named as China's Premier after Li Peng stepped down in March 1998.

Born in 1928 in Changsha, capital of Hunan Province, Zhu Rongji joined the Communist Party of China in 1949 after graduating from Qinghua University where he majored in electrical engineering. His route to power saw him working in the State Planning Commission as group head, deputy director of minister's office and deputy section chief. During the Cultural Revolution, Zhu worked as a teacher at a 'May Seventh Cadre School', a centre for re-education. Like Jiang Zemin, he held the position of Mayor of Shanghai where he earned much respect and acclaim as a focused and tough reformer. In 1991 Zhu became Vice-Premier of the State Council and Director of the State Council Production Office. Between 1993 and 1995 he was a member of the Standing Committee of the Politburo of the CPC Central Committee, Vice Premier of the State Council and Governor of the People's Bank of China. Zhu Rongji has succeeded in streamlining state bureaucracy in China by dissolving and merging ministry departments to leave just 29 ministries. He is also the brains behind the decision to privatize the smaller state-run enterprises and to regroup the bigger ones.

Wu Yi (1938–)

Wu Yi is a State Councillor and Minister responsible for Foreign Trade. As such she is one of the few women in the upper echelons of Chinese politics and considered one of the world's most influential women.

She was born in Wuhan in the Hubei province. She joined the Communist Party in 1962. Upon graduating from Beijing Petroleum College as a senior engineer she worked as a technician in the Ministry of Petroleum Industry's technology department. Her rise to power has seen her as Vice-Mayor of Beijing, Vice-Minister and Deputy Secretary of the Ministry of Foreign Economic Relations and Trade, and Minister and Secretary of the Party Group of the Ministry of Foreign Economic Regulations and Trade. She has been an alternate member of the Politburo of the CPC Central Committee since 1997.

Xiao Yang (1938–)

Xiao Yang is the president of the Supreme People's Court. Born in Feb. 1938 in Heyuan in the Guangdong province, he joined the CPC in 1966. After graduating from the People's University of China, Yang became a teacher of law and politics. Posts held by Xiao Yang before becoming the President of the Supreme People's Court include Secretary of the Wujiang District Communist Party Committee, Deputy Procurator-General of the Guangdong Provincial People's Procuratorate and Deputy Procurator-General of the Supreme People's Procuratorate. The Supreme People's Court is the highest judicial organ in the People's Republic of China.

Han Zhubin (1932–)

Born in Harbin in the Heilongjiang province in 1932, Han Zhubin is the Procurator General of the Supreme People's Procuratorate and the Deputy Secretary of the CPC Central Commission for Discipline Inspection. His rise to power has seen him as a train captain under the Harbin Railways Administration, a director of the Shanghai Railways Administration, Deputy Secretary and Minister of Railways.

The role of the Supreme People's Procuratorate is to suppress all treason against the PRC while safeguarding the unity of the country and maintaining public order. The People's Procuratorate also fulfils the role of educating citizens in observing the constitution and laws of the PRC.

Li Peng (1928–)

Li Peng is Chairman of the National Peoples Congress Standing Committee. Born in Chengdu in the Sichuan province, he was adopted by the respected and popular Zhou Enlai after his father, Li Shouxun, was executed by the Kuomintang in 1930.

Li Peng graduated from the Moscow Power Institute in 1955 where he majored in hydro-electric power. He joined the Communist Party in 1945 and while in Russia was Chairman of the Chinese Students Association in the Soviet Union. Posts held by Li Peng include acting Secretary of the Beijing Power Supply Bureau, Vice Minister and Minister of the Power Industry. In 1982 Peng was elected as a member of the CPC Central Committee and a member of the Politburo. He soon became Vice Premier of the State Council and was given responsibility for energy, communications and raw materials departments. In 1987 Li Peng was appointed Prime Minister when Zhao Ziyang resigned from the post. Li Peng stepped down after serving two 5-year terms. He was replaced by Zhou Rongji in 1998.

In his time as Prime Minister, Peng was regarded as an uncompromising hard-liner who, despite instigating many far reaching economic reforms, is remembered for his part in the 1989 Tian'anmen Square repression.

Hu Jintao (1942–)

Hu Jintao is Vice President of the People's Republic of China.

Born in Jixi, Anhui province. Jintao graduated from Qinghua University with a degree in hydroelectric engineering. In 1975 Jintao was made secretary of the Gansu Provincial Construction Committee.

He soon became its Deputy Director. In 1984 Jintao was promoted to Secretary of the Central Committee of the Chinese Youth League. In 1988 he became Secretary of the CPC Tibet Autonomous Regional Committee where he was credited with contributing much to the region's stability and economic growth. In 1992 he was elected to the Politburo Standing Committee where he took responsibility for the ideological training of key personnel. Many international political observers believe that Hu Jintao is being groomed for the presidency of the PRC when Jiang Zemin steps down in 2003 or before.

LOCAL GOVERNMENT

There are 4 administrative levels: (1) Provinces, Autonomous Regions and the municipalities directly administered by the Government; (2) prefectures and autonomous prefectures (*zhou*); (3) counties, autonomous counties and municipalities; (4) towns. Local government organs ('congresses') exist at provincial, county and township levels; and in national minority autonomous prefectures, but not in ordinary prefectures which are just agencies of the provincial government. Up to county level congresses are elected directly. Elections take place every 3 years. Any person proposed by 10 electors may stand after political vetting. There are quotas for Party members and women. Multiple candidacies are permitted at local elections.

DEFENCE

Budget

Defence expenditure, in yuan:

1995 expenditure	63,672m.	(US$7,625m.)
1996 expenditure	72,006m.	(US$8,650m.)
1997 expenditure	81,257m.	(US$9,800m.)

1998 budget   90,990m. (US$11,000m.)
1999 budget   104,650m. (US$12,600m.)

The above are official figures. Calculating expenditure in Western terms and allowing for purchasing power parity (which requires the US$ figures to be multiplied by a factor of about 4), brings true military expenditure roughly in line (higher for 1999) with France and the United Kingdom. The official figures exclude defence equipment procurement, military research and development and pensions for over 5m. retired Service personnel. The 15% rise in the 1999 budget is partially explained by compensation paid to the People's Liberation Army (PLA) for its withdrawal from commercial activities. Substantial pay increases came into effect on 1 Jan. 1999.

Strength of Armed Forces

The PLA is composed of:

Army	1,965,000
Navy	260,000 (includes Coastal Defence, Naval Air and Marines)
Air Force	470,000 (includes Strategic Forces and Air Defence)
Second Artillery Force	125,000
Total	*2,820,000*

The Second Artillery Force is armed with strategic missiles. PLA Reserves (liable for mobilization) and the militia (local defence) are estimated to number about 1,200,000. In Sept. 1997 the PRC announced a reduction of 500,000 in the active strength of the PLA. The reduction has started and, when complete in late 2000, the size of the PLA should be 2,500,000.

Paramilitary Forces

The PRC recognizes the Chinese People's Armed Police Force as an integral part of its armed forces, to undertake 'the tasks for maintenance of security and social order entrusted by the State'. The Police are roughly divided:

a)	Internal security	730,000
b)	Border defence	200,000
c)	Guards	69,000
	Total	*999,000*

Conscription

Conscription is selective and is for 3 years in the Army and Marines and for 4 years in the Navy and Air Force. Of the PLA strength of 2,820,000, an estimated 1,275,000 (45%) are conscripts. Within the Services approximately 51% of the Army, 15% of the Navy and 34% of the Air Force are conscripts.

Nuclear Capability

The PRC has undertaken 45 nuclear tests since 1964, all at the Lop Nur testing site west of Beijing. The largest test, carried out in 1976, had a yield of about 4 megatons. It is believed that the PLA has 5 types of strategic land and submarine-launched missiles, with a range of over 2,500 km. The total number of strategic nuclear warheads is estimated at between 145 and 220. Two tactical nuclear ballistic missiles are believed to be in service, together with some obsolete bombs, artillery ammunition and atomic demolition ordnance. Total tactical nuclear warhead holdings are estimated at between 80 and 125. There do not appear to have been any significant changes in the nuclear inventory recently. There is, however, considerable progress in launch vehicles where civil and military programmes overlap and which will become apparent as launches into space proceed. It is anticipated that the People's Republic of China will have a manned space station by 2025, to include military surveillance satellites.

Policy

A White Paper entitled *China's National Defense* was published by the Information Office of the State Council of China on 27 July 1998. The White Paper covered:

Foreword

The International Security Situation

National Defence Policy

National Defence Construction

International Security Co-operation

Arms Control and Disarmament.

Having declared that the People's Republic of China was devoting itself to modernization, the White Paper stressed the defensive nature of its defence policy together with active participation in the international arms control and disarmament process. The nuclear arms race started by India in May 1998 was viewed with particular concern.

All territorial and marine rights' disputes with neighbouring countries are to be resolved by consultation in accordance with United Nations criteria. Taiwan is deemed to be 'an inseparable part of Chinese territory' and the issue is hoped to be settled through 'peaceful reunification [ending with] one country, two systems'. Should peaceful means fail, the People's Republic of China 'will not commit itself not to resort to force'.

The Government of the People's Republic of China assumed sovereignty over Hong Kong on 1 July 1997 and stationed a garrison of the PLA in the Hong Kong Special Administrative Region (HKSAR), to take charge of its defence. Garrison troops are required to adhere to the principle of 'one country, two systems' and to contribute to the preservation of the long-term prosperity and stability of Hong Kong.

The People's Republic of China adheres to the principle: 'We will not attack unless we are attacked; if we are attacked, we will certainly counter-attack.' The small number of nuclear weapons held are 'entirely for meeting the needs of self-defence.' The People's

Republic of China has 'solemnly declared' that it will not be the first to use nuclear weapons at any time or under any circumstances. As a country with long land borders the People's Republic of China reserves the right to use anti-personnel mines on its territory.

Resulting from the White Paper, the PLA was ordered to cease its commercial activities. These civil interests had grown into an economic empire of some 15,000 industrial production and service companies, supplementing the defence budget. Both the People's Republic of China's economists and the PLA's commanders appear to have been content with the ending of the PLA's non-military ventures which had been the source of considerable corruption.

The White Paper, 'China's National Defense (1998)', can be found on the Web at:

www.china.org.cn/WhitePapers/NationalDefense/National Defense.html

INTERNATIONAL RELATIONS

The People's Republic of China is a member of UN (and its Security Council).

ECONOMY

Policy

A ninth 5-year plan covers 1996–2000; there is also a 15-year strategic plan 'Long-Term Target for 2010'. These plans envisage a continued opening to the outside world, an enhanced development of agriculture, the reduction of tariff barriers and the development of the poorer regions.

A Communist Party statement of Nov. 1993 declared that public ownership should remain the mainstay of the economy, but alongside a modern enterprise system suited to the demands of a market economy in which government control is separated from management.

The new cabinet appointed in March 1998 was composed of technocrats chosen for their ability to solve problems and push through a series of reforms. The new Prime Minister Zhu Rongji stressed the urgency of reforming the debt-ridden state industrial sector consisting of some 370,000 enterprises, and its central bureaucracy. Zhu Rongji stated that the number of civil servants in the central bureaucracy would be halved in 1998.

Performance

In 1997 GDP growth was 8·8%, with a forecast for 1998 of 8%. Between 1990 and 1996 the average annual real growth in GNP per capita was 11% – the second highest in the world after Equatorial Guinea.

China's GNP per capita in 1996 for purchasing power was $3,330.

Budget

1996 revenue was 740,799m. yuan; expenditure, 793,755m. yuan. Of this, local government revenue accounted for 374,692m. yuan and local government expenditure, 578,628m. yuan. Total debt incurred, 1996, 196,728m. yuan, of which 119,510m. yuan were foreign debts. The current account surplus was running at US$29,718m. in 1997.

Sources of revenue, 1996 (in 1m. yuan): Taxes, 690,982; industrial and commercial taxes, 527,004. Expenditure: Economic construction, 285,578 (1995); culture and education, 175,672 (1995); national defence, 63,672 (1995); government administration, 99,654 (1995); agriculture, 51,007; pensions and social welfare, 12,803; debt payments, 131,191.

On the face of it, China's recent economic performance has been hugely impressive. Growth rates of 8–9% a year have led to a tripling of its GNP in less than two decades. Even if the growth rate falls to 6%, within thirty years the Chinese economy will be twice the size of the current American economy. But Chinese statistics are famous for not telling the whole story. For example, the official budget deficit is a respectable 1·2 to 1·8% of GDP. But then the government counts as budget revenues the money it raises from bond issues that are bought by the state banks and account for over 19% of all revenues. This is, in effect, borrowing by another name. Moreover, there is a heavy cost attached to servicing this debt – possibly as much as 22% of government revenues or, excluding the bond issues from income, as much as 40% of the budget. If this is the case, it seems unlikely that China's current levels of public spending are sustainable.

Other problems include tax collection and the reluctance of the general population to spend their way out of the recession caused by the recent turmoil in Asian markets. Conversely, China's high savings rate (more than 40% of GDP) provides a bedrock of resources for the government to tap. Total public debt, domestic and foreign, is only 32% of GDP, low by international standards.

Currency

The currency is called Renminbi (*i.e.*, People's Currency). The unit of currency is the *yuan* (CNY) which is divided into 10 *jiao*, the *jiao* being divided into 10 *fen*. The yuan was floated to reflect market forces on 1 Jan. 1994 though remaining state-controlled, and the official rate of exchange was abolished. It became convertible for current transactions from 1 Dec. 1996. Total money supply in Dec. 1997 was 3,834bn. yuan. In Feb. 1998 foreign exchange reserves were US$140,333m. (only Japan, with US$209,778m., had more). Gold reserves were 12·7m. troy oz. in Feb. 1998. Annualized inflation was 6·1% in 1996, but was forecast to be less than 1% in 1998.

Banking and Finance

Financial and economic commentators note that despite the recent turbulence amongst South East Asian currencies the yuan is in good shape. China seems certain in the years ahead to exert a major impact on the world economy and on the world's financial markets.

The People's Bank of China is the central bank and bank of issue (*Director:* Dai Xianglong, b. 1945). There are a number of other banks, the largest of which are Agricultural Bank of China, Industrial and Commercial Bank of China, Construction Bank of China, Bank of China, Bank of Communications and Agricultural Development Bank of China. Legislation of 1995 permitted the establishment of commercial banks; credit co-operatives may be transformed into banks, mainly to provide credit to small businesses. Insurance is handled by the People's Insurance Company. There were (1994) 350,813 credit co-operatives. The Bank of China is responsible for foreign banking operations.

Savings bank deposits were 2,151,880m. yuan in 1994.

611,566m. yuan was loaned from State Banks in 1996. It is estimated that up to 20% of outstanding loans are bad debts (about US$145bn. at the end of 1996).

There are stock exchanges in the Shenzhen Special Economic Zone and in Shanghai. A securities trading system linking 6 cities (Securities Automated Quotations System) was inaugurated in 1990 for trading in government bonds.

Stock Exchanges

Stock Exchange Executive Council (SEEC). Formed in 1989 to oversee the development of financial markets in China. Members comprise leading non-bank financial institutions authorized to handle securities. A33 Chengfang Jie, Xicheng Qu, Beijing 100032. Tel: (0)10 6493 5210.

Securities Association of China (SAC). Formed in 1991 this is a non-governmental organization with 122 stock exchange and securities companies and 35 individual members.

Olympic Hotel, 52 Baishiqiao Lu, Beijing 100081.

Tel: (0)10 6831 6688. Fax: (0)10 6831 8390.

Shanghai Stock Exchange. Formed in 1990. Shanghai is the home of China's first and foremost stock exchange.

15 Huangpu Lu, Shanghai 200080. Tel: (0)21 6306 8888.

Fax: (0)21 6306 3076.

China Shenzhen Stock Exchange

203 Shangbu Industrial Area, Shenzhen. Tel: (0)755 320 3431.

Fax: (0)755 320 3505.

Beijing Securities Exchange

5 Anding Lu, Chao Yang Qu, Beijing 100029. Tel: (0)10 6493 9366.

Fax: (0)10 6493 6233.

Beijing Commodity Exchange

BCE 311 Chenyun Building, No. 8 Beichen East Road, Chaoyang District, Beijing. Tel: (0)10 492 4956. Fax: (0)10 499 3365

E-mail: sunli@intra.cnfm.co.cn

Shanghai Cereals and Oils Exchange

199 Shangcheng Road, Pudong New District, Shanghai.

Tel: (0)21 5831 1111. Fax: (0)21 5831 9308.

Email: liangzhu@public.sta.net.cn

China Zhengzhou Commodity Exchange (CZCE)

20 Huanyuan Road, Zhengzhou. Tel: (0)371 594 4454

Fax: (0)371 554 5424.

Wuhan Securities Exchange Centre (WSEC)

2nd Floor, Jianghchen Hotel, Wuhan. Tel: (0)27 588 4115.

Fax: (0)27 588 6038.

China Commodity Futures Exchange, Inc of Hainan (CCFE)
Huaneng Building, 36 Datong Road, Haikou, Hainan Province.
Tel: (0)898 670 0107. Fax: (0)898 670 0099.

Guandong United Futures Exchange
JingXing Hotel, 91 LinHe West Road, Guangzhou.
 Tel: (0)20 8755 2109. Fax: (0)20 8755 1654.

Addresses and contact numbers of Stock exchanges worldwide are
available on the Web at: www.numa.com/ref/exchange.htm

Banks

People's Bank of China. Formed in 1948. The Central Bank of China
controls China's financial policies.
 Sanlihe Lu, Xicheng Qu, Beijing 100800. Tel: (0)10 6601 5522.
Fax: (0)10 6601 6704.

Bank of China. Formed in 1912. Handles foreign exchange and international settlements.
 410 Fuchengmen Nei Dajie, Beijing 100818. Tel: (0)10 6601 6688.
Fax: (0)10 6601 6869. Web: www.bank-of-china.com

Bank of Communications Ltd. Formed in 1908. Commercial
banking.
 18 Xian Xiahu, Shanghai 200335. Tel: (0)21 6275 1738.

China Investment Bank. Formed in 1981. Raises foreign funds for
domestic investment.
 A, Eastern Tower, Sichwan Building, 1 Fu Chen Men Wai, Beijing
100037. Tel: (0)10 6834 9933. Fax: (0)10 6303 1944.

China Merchant's Bank. Formed in 1987.
 2 Shennan Lu, Shenzen 518001. Tel: (0)755 224 3888.
Fax: (0)755 224 3666. Web: www.cmbchina.com

Industrial and Commercial Bank of China. Formed in 1984. Handles international business, specializing in industrial and commercial credit.

15 Cuiwei Lu, Haidan Qu, Beijing 100036. Tel: (0)10 68217601. Fax: (0)10 68217920.

Agricultural Bank of China. Formed in 1951. Provides services for agriculture and industry in agricultural areas.

23 Fuxing Lu, Beijing 100036. Tel: (0)10 6847 5321. Fax: (0)10 6829 7160.

Agricultural Development Bank of China. 23A Dong Jiao Min Xiang, Dongcheng Qu, Beijing 100006.

Tel: (0)10 6524 3311. Fax: (0)10 6523 5059.

Export and Import Bank of China. Formed in 1994. Provides credit for the export of goods, especially large machinery. Based in Beijing.

Tel: (0)10 6762 6688. Fax: (0)10 6763 8940.

China Minsheng Banking Corporation. Formed in 1996. China's first privately-funded banking organization.

2nd Floor, Tower B, Vantone New World Plaza, 2 Fu Cheng Men, Xicheng Qu, Beijing. Tel (0)10 6858 8440. Fax: (0)10 6858 8570.

International and Development Banks

World Bank. The World Bank offers money lending and non-money lending services including advice on national monetary policy and technical assistance. China has been a member of the World Bank since 1981 and has been the bank's largest borrower of investment financing since 1992. During the financial year ending in 1998, the World Bank lent US$2866·4m. to China.

Beijing External Affairs Office, The World Bank Resident Mission in China, Beijing. Tel: (0)10 6554 3361. Fax: (0)10 6554 1686. E-mail: lli2@worldbank.org. Web: www.worldbank.org

Hong Kong & Shanghai Banking Corporation

185 Wuanmingyuan Lu, Shanghai.

Tel: (0)21 6329 8383 Fax: (0)21 2132 91775.

Jardine Flemming (Shanghai JF Investments)

1801–1802 North Tower, Shanghai Stock Exchange Building,

528 Pu Dong Rd (South), Pu Dong, Shanghai 200120.

Tel: (0)21 688 12200. Fax: (0)21 688 125 501.

ING Barings Beijing

Room 1510 Landmark Building, 8 North Dongsanhuan Rd,

Beijing 100004. Tel: (0)10 6590 0955. Fax: (0)10 6590 0957.

Weights and Measures

The metric system is in general use alongside traditional units of
measurement.

ENERGY AND NATURAL RESOURCES

Environmental Policy

The Chinese Government is party to the following international
environmental agreements: Antarctic-Environmental Protocol,
Antarctic Treaty, Biodiversity, Climate Change, Desertification,
Endangered Species, Hazardous Wastes, Law of the Sea, Marine
Dumping, Nuclear Test Ban, Ozone Layer Protection, Ship Pollution,
Tropical Timber 83, Tropical Timber 94, Wetlands.

The White Paper 'Environmental Protection in China' (1996)
implies that although China is committed to a policy of environmental
protection it is 'a developing country' with a large population and as
such must realize that 'developing the economy and protecting the
environment' may not be easily reconcilable. This said, the White

Paper does state that 'China has . . .in the process of promoting its overall modernization program, made environmental protection one of its basic national policies'.

'Environmental Protection in China' promises that the government of the People's Republic of China will put into effect a system of laws and regulations 'improving the statutes concerning the environment, formulating strict law-enforcement procedures and increasing the intensity of law enforcement so as to ensure the effective implementation of the environmental laws and regulations, making the causer of pollution responsible for treating it'.

As to the prevention or control of industrial pollution, the Chinese Government notes that 'China's per capita energy consumption level and the emitted sulphur dioxide are much lower than the world average level . . . and it will remain so by the end of this century'. The capability to treat the 'three wastes' (waste gas, waste water and industrial residue) has been enhanced and the comprehensive utilization rate of these materials has been increased.

Section V of the White Paper states that 'The Chinese government regards ecological environmental protection as the focal point of its environmental protection work'. China is committed to a far-reaching programme of reforestation with 33·79m. ha of artificially 'afforested' areas in June 1996.

In 1995 China had 779 regional nature reserves and 99 national level reserves as well as 710 forest parks. These are designed for the protection of 'typical natural eco-systems with scientific research value as well as rare and endangered species'.

'A comprehensive scientific research system composed of the Chinese Academy of Sciences, colleges and universities, and the environmental protection departments is basically in place.' By the end of 1995, 390 research bodies devoted to the study and implementation of environmental protection had been established. This accounts for more than 20,000 'research and managerial personnel'.

The White Paper 'Environmental Protection in China' (1996) can be viewed on the Web at: www.chinanews.org/WhitePapers/EnvironmentalE.html

Electricity

Installed capacity, 1996, 0·2m. MW. 1996 electricity output was 1,081,310m. kWh. Consumption per capita was an estimated 684 kWh in 1995. Sources of energy in 1996 as percentage of total energy production: Coal, 74·8%; crude oil, 17·1%; hydro-electric power, 6·2%; natural gas, 1·9%. Generating is not centralized; local units range between 30 and 60 MW of output.

Oil and Gas

There are on-shore fields at Daqing, Shengli, Dagang and Karamai, and 10 provinces south of the Yangtze River have been opened for exploration in co-operation with foreign companies. Crude oil production was 157·33m. tonnes in 1996.

Natural gas is available from fields near Canton and Shanghai, and in Sichuan province. Production was 20,114m. cu. metres in 1996.

Minerals

Most provinces contain coal, and there are 70 major production centres, of which the largest are in Hebei, Shanxi, Shandong, Jilin and Anhui. Coal reserves were estimated at 1,000,850m. tonnes in 1996. Coal production was 1,397m. tonnes in 1996.

Iron ore reserves were 47,560m. tonnes in 1996. Deposits are abundant in the anthracite field of Shanxi, in Hebei and in Shandong, and are found in conjunction with coal and worked in the north-east. Production in 1996 was 249·6m. tonnes, making China the world's leading iron ore producer.

Tin ore is plentiful in Yunnan, where the tin-mining industry has long existed. Tin production was 40,000 tonnes in 1989.

China is a major producer of wolfram (tungsten ore). Mining of wolfram is carried on in Hunan, Guangdong and Yunnan.

Salt production was 29·96m. tonnes in 1994; gold production was 110 tonnes in 1992; output of other minerals in 1989 (in 1,000 tonnes): Aluminium, 770; copper, 540; nickel, 30; lead, 270; zinc, 430. Other minerals produced: Barite, bismuth, graphite, gypsum, mercury, molybdenum, silver. Reserves (in tonnes) of phosphate ore, 15,766m.; sylvite, 458m.; salt, 402,400m.

Agriculture

Agriculture accounts for approximately 21% of GDP. In 1996 the sown area was 152·4m. ha comprising (in 1m. ha): rice, 31·41; wheat, 29·61; corn, 24·50; beans, 10·54; tubers, 9·8; oil-bearing crops, 12·56m. Intensive agriculture and horticulture have been practised for millennia. Present-day policy aims to avert the traditional threats from floods and droughts by soil conservancy, afforestation, irrigation and drainage projects, and to increase the 'high stable yields' areas by introducing fertilizers, pesticides and improved crops. In spite of this, 18·1m. ha of land were flooded in 1996 and 20·1m. ha were covered by drought. 50·38m. ha were irrigated in 1996. In Aug. 1998 more than 21m. ha, notably in the Yangtze valley, were under water as China experienced its worst flooding in recent times.

'Township and village enterprises' in agriculture comprise enterprises previously run by the communes of the Maoist era, co-operatives run by rural labourers and individual firms of a certain size. There were 24·95m. such enterprises in 1994, employing 120·18m. persons. There were 2,157 state farms in 1994 with 5·18m. employees. In 1996 there were 234·38m. rural households. The rural workforce was 452·88m., of whom 322·6m. were employed in agriculture, fishing or land management. Net per capita annual peasant income, 1996: 1,926 yuan.

In 1992 there were 25,023 agricultural technical stations. There were 670,848 large and medium-sized tractors in 1996.

Agricultural production (in 1m. tonnes), 1996: Rice, 195·10; wheat, 110·57; corn, 127·47; beans, 17·90; tubers, 35·36; tea, 0·59; cotton, 4·20; oil-bearing crops, 22·11; sugar-cane, 66·88; fruit, 46·53. The gross value of agricultural output in 1996 was 2,342,866m. yuan.

Livestock, 1996: Draught animals, 91,920,000; cattle, 139,813,000 (including 4,470,000 milch cows); goats, 170,680,000; pigs, 457,360,000; sheep, 132,690,000; horses,10,038,000; chickens (1995), 2·8bn.; ducks (1995), 463m. China has more goats, pigs, sheep, horses and chickens than any other country, having overtaken Australia in 1996 as the country with the greatest number of sheep. China also has more than half of the world's ducks. Meat production in 1996 was 59·15m. tonnes; milk, 7·36m. tonnes; eggs, 19·54m. tonnes.

Powell, S. G., *Agricultural Reform in China: from Communes to Commodity Economy, 1978–1990*. Manchester Univ. Press, 1992

Forestry

In 1995 the area under forests was 133·32m. ha, or 14·3% of the total land area (133·76m. ha in 1990). Total roundwood production in 1995 was 300·36m. cu. metres, making China the second largest producer after the USA.

Fisheries

Total catch, 1996: 32·88m. tonnes, of which 12·75m. tonnes were freshwater produce. China's annual catch is the largest in the world, and accounts for more than 20% of the world total every year. In 1986 the annual catch had been just over 8m. tonnes.

INDUSTRY

Cottage industries persist into the 21st century. Modern industrial development began with the manufacture of cotton textiles, and the establishment of silk filatures, steel plants, flour mills and match factories. In 1996 there were 7,986,500 industrial enterprises. 113,800 were state-owned, 1,591,800 were collectives and 6,210,700 were individually owned. A law of 1988 ended direct state control of firms and provided for the possibility of bankruptcy.

Output of major products, 1996 (in tonnes): Cotton yarn, 5·12m.; paper, 26·38m.; sugar, 6·40m.; salt, 29·03m.; steel, 101·24m.; rolled steel, 93·38m.; cement, 491·1m.; chemical fertilizers, 28·09m.; aluminium ware, 159,100; silk, 94,900; woollen fabrics, 459·5m. metres; bicycles, 33·61m. units; TV sets, 35·41m. units; radios, 56·50m. units; cameras, 41·20m. units; refrigerators, 9·79m. units; motor vehicles, 1,470,000 units; locomotives, 1,050 units.

The gross value of industrial output in 1996 was 9,959,500m. yuan.

Labour

The employed population at the 1990 census was 647·2m. (291·1m. female). By 1996 it was estimated to have risen to 688·5m., of whom 490·3m. were in rural areas and 198·2m. in urban areas. There were 329·1m. people working in agriculture, 97·6m. in manufacturing, 45·1m. in commerce, 34·1m. in construction and 20·1m. in communications. 109·4m. worked in state-owned enterprises, 29·5m. in urban collectives, and 50·2m. were self-employed. In 1994 there were 446·54m. working as individual rural labourers or in rural collectives and there were 15·57m. individual urban labourers.

At the 1990 census there was a floating population of 21m. internal migrants who tour the country seeking seasonal employment. There were 5·53m. urban unemployed in 1996 (3% of the urban population). Almost one-third of unemployed people had not worked for a year.

Only a quarter of the unemployed in 1996 were registered at employment services and only 1·7% received unemployment relief payments. In early 1998 the official unemployment rate was 3%, but was thought to be much higher.

The average non-agricultural annual wage in 1996 was 6,210 yuan. 4,302 yuan, urban collectives; 6,280 yuan, state-owned enterprises; 8,261 yuan, other enterprises. There is a 6-day 48-hour working week. Minimum working age was fixed at 16 in 1991. There were 19,098 labour disputes in 1994.

Trade Unions

The All-China Federation of Trade Unions is headed by Wei Jianxing. In 1991 there were 614,000 union branches with a total membership of 103·89m. (39·92m. female).

INTERNATIONAL TRADE

Foreign debt was US$116,275m. in 1996. Actual foreign investment totalled US$33,800m. in 1994. Direct foreign investment (in US$1m.) in 1995 by major countries of origin: Taiwan, 11,600; USA, 10,900; Japan, 10,500; Singapore, 3,900; South Korea, 2,300; UK, 2,200.

There are 6 Special Economic Zones at Shanghai and in the provinces of Guangdong and Fujian, in which concessions are made to foreign businessmen. The Pudong New Area in Shanghai is designated a special development area. Since 1979 joint ventures with foreign firms have been permitted. A law of April 1991 reduced taxation on joint ventures to 33%. There is no maximum limit on the foreign share of the holdings; the minimum limit is 25%. Contracts between Chinese and foreign firms are only legally valid if in writing and approved by the appropriate higher authority.

In June 1998 the US President extended most-favoured-nation status to China for a further year.

Imports and Exports

1996: Imports, US$138,944m.; exports, US$151,197m.

Major exports in 1996 (in 1,000 tonnes): Crude oil, 20,330; silk and satin, 147m. metres; coal, 29,030; cotton cloth, 3,043m. metres; cement, 11,800. Imports: Wheat, 8,250; steel products, 15,840; chemical fertilizers, 18,570; iron ore, 43,870.

Exports to (and imports from) major trade partners in 1995: Hong Kong, 24·2% (6·5%); Japan, 19·1% (22·0%); USA, 16·6% (12·2%); Taiwan, 2·1% (11·2%), South Korea, 4·5% (7·8%); Germany, 3·8% (6·1%); Singapore, 2·4% (2·6%). Customs duties with Taiwan were abolished in 1980.

Lardy, N. R., *Foreign Trade and Economic Reform in China, 1978–1990.* CUP, 1992

Pearson, M. M., *Joint Ventures in the People's Republic of China: the Control of Foreign Direct Investment under Socialism.* Princeton Univ. Press, 1991

Wong, K. and Chu, D. (eds.) *Modernization in China: the Case of the Shenzhen Special Economic Zone.* OUP, 1986

Trade Fair Organizers

MOFTEC, PRC (Ministry of Foreign Trade and Economic Co-operation)
2 Dong Chang'an Avenue, Beijing 100731. Tel: (0)10 6708 1526, 6708 1527. Fax: (0)10 6708 1513.

Hong Kong Trade Development Council
1 Harper Road, Wan Chai, Hong Kong. Tel: 258 44333.

Neway International Trade Fairs Ltd
1204 Kodak House II, 321 Java Road, North Point, Hong Kong. Tel: 2561 5566. Fax: 2811 9156. E-mail: neway@newayfairs.com

Specialize in trade fairs in southern China, especially Hong Kong and Guangzhou.

Taipei Chamber of Commerce

6F, 72 Nan King East Road., Section 2, Taipei. Tel: (0)2 531 8217. Fax: (0)2 542 9461.

COMMUNICATIONS

Roads

The total road length was 1,185,800 km in 1996. In 1994, 998,077 km were hard-surfaced. In 1996 there were 5·75m. trucks and 4·8m. passenger vehicles. 2·89m. vehicles were privately owned. The use of bicycles is very widespread. In 1996, 9,838m. tonnes of freight and 11,221m. persons were transported by road.

There were 253,537 traffic accidents in 1994, with 66,362 fatalities.

Rail

In 1996 there were 56,700 km of railway including 10,100 km electrified. Gauge is standard except for some 600 mm track in Yunnan. In 1996 the railways carried 1,668m. tonnes of freight and 941m. passengers.

Civil Aviation

There are international airports at Beijing and Shanghai (Hongqiao). Altogether there were 142 civil airports in 1996, 106 of which can accommodate Boeing 737s or larger aircraft. The national and major airlines are state-owned, except Shanghai Airlines (75% municipality-owned, 25% private) and Shenzhen Airlines (private). Chinese airlines operating scheduled services in 1998 were China Southern Airlines (10,767,000 passengers carried in 1995), Air China (6,274,000 passengers in 1995), China Eastern Airlines (6,240,000),

China Southwest Airlines (5,071,000), China Northern Airlines (4,442,000), China Northwest Airlines (2,488,000), Xiamen Airlines (2,403,000), China Yunnan Airlines (1,854,000), Xinjiang Airlines (1,159,000), Changan Airlines, China National Aviation, Fujian Airlines, Hainan Airlines, Shandong Airlines, Shanghai Airlines, Shanxi Airlines, Shenzhen Airlines, Sichuan Airlines and Xiamen Airlines.

In 1996 airlines carried 55·55m. passengers (4·40m. international) and 1·15m. tonnes of freight. In 1995 the busiest airport was Beijing, with 15,045,000 passengers (11,804,000 on domestic flights), followed by Guangzhou (Baiyun), with 12,575,000 passengers (12,204,000 on domestic flights) and Shanghai (Hongqiao), with 11,076,000 passengers (9,361,000 on domestic flights).

In 1998 services were also provided by Aeroflot, Air France, Air Kazakhstan, Air Koryo, Air Macau, Air Ukraine, Alitalia, All Nippon Airways, Ansett Australia, Asiana, Austrian Airlines, Belavia, British Airways, Canadian Airlines International, Chita Avia, DRAGONAIR, El Al, Ethiopian Airlines, Finnair, Iran Air, JAL, JAT, KLM, Korean Air, LOT, Lufthansa, Malaysia Airlines, Malév, Mongolian Airlines, Pakistan International Airlines, President Airlines, Qantas Airways, Royal Brunei Airlines, Royal Nepal Airlines, SAS, Singapore Airlines, Swissair, Tarom, Thai Airways International, United Airlines and Uzbekiston Airways.

Shipping

In 1995 the ocean-going fleet consisted of 1,826 vessels totalling 34·27m. DWT, representing 5·18% of the world's total fleet tonnage. 308 vessels (35·22% of tonnage) were registered under foreign flags. Total tonnage registered, 15·83m. GRT, including oil-tankers, 2·28m. GRT, and container ships, 1·35m. GRT.

Cargo handled by the major ports in 1996 (in tonnes): Shanghai, 164m.; Qinhuangdao, 83m.; Ningbo, 76m.; Guangzhou (Canton), 75m.; Dalian, 64m.; Tianjin, 62m.; Qingdao, 60m. In 1993, 125·08m. tonnes of freight were carried.

Inland waterways totalled 110,593 km in 1994. 1,070·91m. tonnes of freight and 261·65m. passengers were carried.

Telecommunications

In 1997 there were 70,310,000 telephone main lines (55·8 per 1,000 persons), and in 1995, 270,000 fax machines. At the end of 1996 there were 6·85m. mobile telephone subscribers (3·62m. at end of 1995). There were approximately 1·5m. Internet users in Dec. 1998, of whom 92·8% were male and 83·2% under 35 years of age. At the beginning of the year there had only been around 500,000 users. In 1996 there were 2·6m. PCs in use (2·1 per 1,000 inhabitants).

Postal Services

There were 72,496 post offices in 1996. The use of *Pinyin* transcription of place names has been requested for mail to addresses in China (*e.g.*, 'Beijing' *not* 'Peking').

SOCIAL INSTITUTIONS

Justice

Six new codes of law (including criminal and electoral) came into force in 1980, to regularize the legal unorthodoxy of previous years. There is no provision for *habeas corpus*. The death penalty has been extended from treason and murder to include rape, embezzlement, smuggling, drug-dealing, bribery and robbery with violence. There were 4,376 reported executions in 1996. 'People's courts' are divided into some 30 higher, 200 intermediate and 2,000 basic-level courts, and headed by the Supreme People's Court. The latter tries cases, hears appeals and supervises the people's courts.

People's courts are composed of a president, vice-presidents, judges and 'people's assessors' who are the equivalent of jurors.

CHINA: PROVINCES AND MUNICIPALITIES

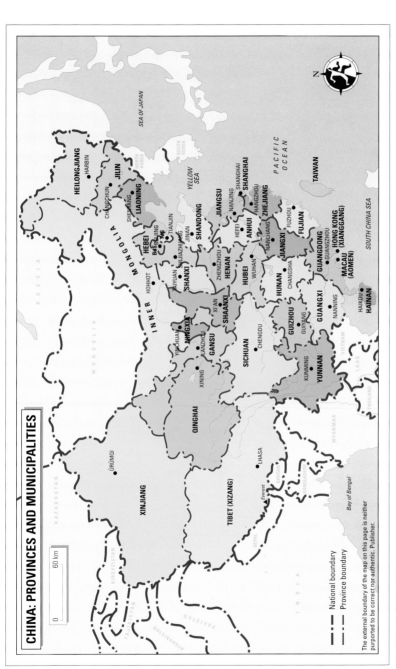

––·––·––	National boundary
–––––––	Province boundary

The external boundary of the map on this page is neither purported to be correct nor authentic. Publisher.

Map © Rough Guides, 1999

The Western Hills

Summer Palace

Yuanmingyuan

Qinghai
University

Beijing
University

HAIDIAN LU

BAISHIQIAO LU

Dazhong
Si

BEISANHUAN XI LU

XISANHUAN BEILU

Zizhuyuan
Park

ZIZHUYUAN LU

KUNMINGHU NAN LU

KUNMINGHU NAN LU

XINJIANG KOU

SANLIHE LU

FUCHENG LU

CCTV
Tower

Gongzhufen

Military
Museum

Muxio

Yuquan Lu

Junshi
Bowuguan

FUXING

LU

Babaoshan

Wukesong

Wanshou Lu

Baiyunguan
Si

LIANHUACHI DONG LU

XISANHUAN ZHONG LU

Xi Zhan

GUANG'ANMEN DAJIE

BEIJING

Map © Rough Guides, 1999

△ The Great Wall

N

Airport △

Asian Games Village

BEISIHUAN ZHONG LU

BEISANHUAN ZHONG LU

Beijiao Bus Station

Hepingli Zhan

BEISANHUAN DONG LU

JINGSHEN LU

LUXIZHIMEN BEI DAJIE

XUEYUAN

ZINJIEKOU DAJIE

DESHENGMEN DAJIE

ANDINGMEN DAJIE

HEPING DONG JIE

Ditan Park

Lufthansa Centre

LIANGMAHE LU

Xizhimen Zhan

XISI BEI DAJIE

ANDINGMEN XI DAJIE

Dongzhimen Bus Station

DONGSANHUAN BEI LU

Exhibition Hall

DI'ANMEN XI DAJIE

DONGZHIMENWAI DAJIE

GONGRENTIYU CHANG BEI LU

SANLITUN LU

Workers' Stadium

Chaoyang Theatre

FUXINGMEN BEI DAJIE

XIDAN BEI DAJIE

DONGDAN BEI DAJIE

CHAOYANGMENWAI DAJIE

CHAOYANG LU

Forbidden City

Silk Market

World Trade Centre

XICHANG AN JIE

DONGCHANG AN JIE

JIANGUOMENWAI DAJIE

TIAN'ANMEN SQUARE

Beijing Zhan

QIANMEN XI DAJIE

QIANMENDONG DAJIE

CHONGWENMEN DAJIE

GUANGQUMENWAI DAJIE

GUANQU LU

QIANMEN DAJIE

Majuan Bus Station

DONGHUASHIXIEJIE LU

Natural History Museum

Tiantan Park

Friendship Hospital

TIYUGUAN LU

Temple of Heaven

CHONGWENMENWAI DAJIE

Taoranting Park

YONGDINGMEN XI JIE

YONGDINGMEN DONG JIE

YONGDINGMENNEI DAJIE

Yongdingmen Train & Bus Station

NANSANHUAN ZHONG LU

NANSANHUAN DONG LU

Haihutun Bus Station

0   4 km

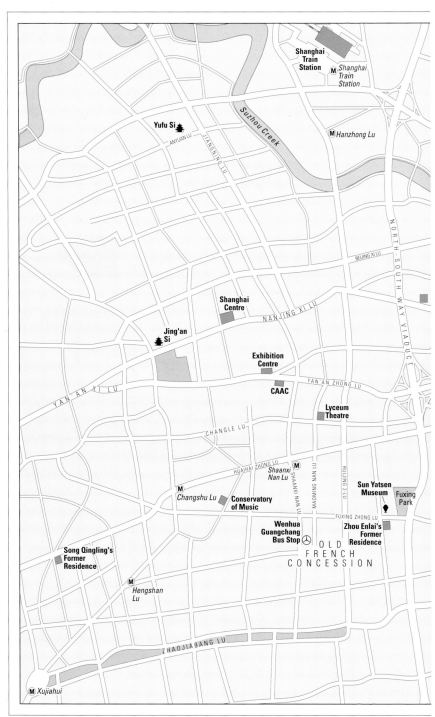

Shanghai
Train
Station

Ⓜ Shanghai
Train
Station

Suzhou Creek

Yufu Si 🏯

ANYUAN LU

JIANGNING LU

Ⓜ Hanzhong Lu

BEIJING XI LU

NORTH-SOUTH WAY VIADUCT

Shanghai
Centre

NANJING XI LU

Jing'an
Si 🏯

Exhibition
Centre

YAN'AN ZHONG LU

CAAC

Lyceum
Theatre

YAN'AN XI LU

CHANGLE LU

HUAIHAI ZHONG LU

Shaanxi
Nan Lu

Ⓜ

SHAANXI NAN LU

MAOMING NAN LU

RUIJIN 2-LU

Sun Yatsen
Museum

Fuxing
Park

Ⓜ
Changshu Lu

Conservatory
of Music

FUXING ZHONG LU

Wenhua
Guangchang
Bus Stop

Zhou Enlai's
Former
Residence

OLD
FRENCH
CONCESSION

Song Qingling's
Former
Residence

Ⓜ
Hengshan
Lu

ZHAOJIABANG LU

Ⓜ Xujiahui

Map © Rough Guides, 1999

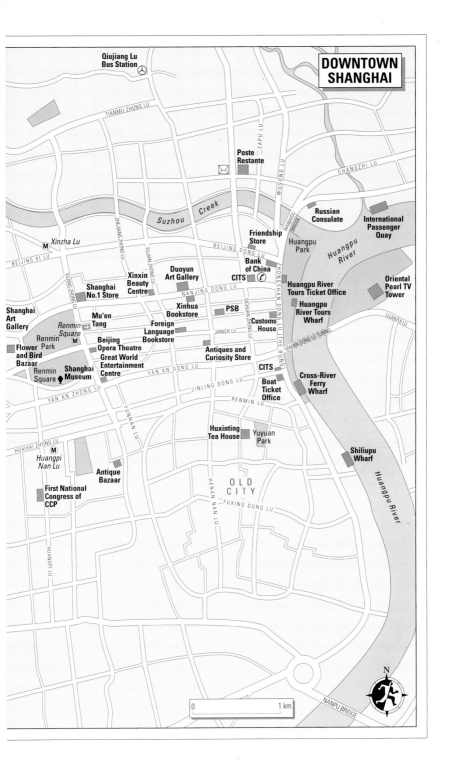

DOWNTOWN SHANGHAI

Qiujiang Lu
Bus Station

TIANMU ZHONG LU

ZAPU LU

WUSONG LU

CHANGZHI LU

Poste
Restante

Suzhou Creek

BEIJING DONG LU

Russian
Consulate

International
Passenger
Quay

Xinzha Lu

Huangpu
Park

Huangpu
River

Friendship
Store

BEIJING XI LU

ZHEJIANG ZHONG LU

FUJIAN ZHONG LU

KXIANG ZHONG LU

Bank
of China
CITS

Oriental
Pearl TV
Tower

Huangpu River
Tours Ticket Office

Xinxin
Beauty
Centre

Duoyun
Art Gallery

Shanghai
No.1 Store

NANJING DONG LU

Shanghai
Art
Gallery

Xinhua
Bookstore

PSB

Huangpu
River Tours
Wharf

LUJIAZUI LU

Mu'en
Tang

Foreign
Language
Bookstore

Customs
House

SICHUAN ZHONG LU

JIANGXI LU

Renmin
Square

Renmin
Park

Beijing
Opera Theatre

Antiques and
Curiosity Store

YAN AN DONG LU TUNNEL

Flower
and Bird
Bazaar

Great World
Entertainment
Centre

YAN AN DONG LU

CITS

ZHONGSHAN DONG LU (THE BUND)

Renmin
Square

Shanghai
Museum

Boat
Ticket
Office

Cross-River
Ferry
Wharf

YAN AN ZHONG LU

YUNNAN LU

JINLING DONG LU

RENMIN LU

HUAIHAI ZHONG LU

Huxinting
Tea House

Yuyuan
Park

Shiliupu
Wharf

Huangpi
Nan Lu

Antique
Bazaar

Huangpu
River

First National
Congress of
CCP

HUANGPI LU

HENAN NAN LU

OLD
CITY

FUXING DONG LU

0   1 km

N

NANPU BRIDGE

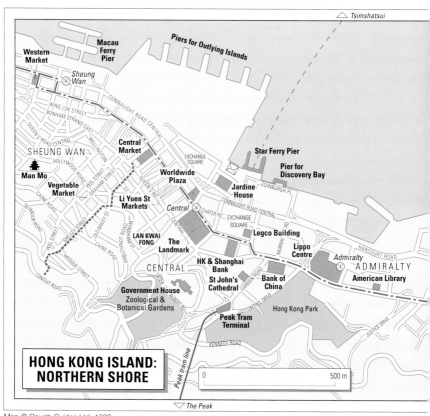

△ Tsimshatsui

Piers for Outlying Islands

Western Market

Macau Ferry Pier

Sheung Wan

WING LOK STREET
BONHAM STRAND EAST
CONNAUGHT ROAD CENTRAL

QUEEN'S ROAD CENTRAL
WELLINGTON

Central Market

EXCHANGE SQUARE

Star Ferry Pier

SHEUNG WAN

HOLLYWOOD ROAD

Worldwide Plaza

Pier for Discovery Bay

Man Mo

Vegetable Market

PEEL STREET
GRAHAM STREET
QUEEN'S RD

Jardine House

EDINBURGH PL

CAINE ROAD

Li Yuen St Markets

EXCHANGE SQUARE

CONNAUGHT ROAD CENTRAL

SEYMOUR ROAD

PEEL STREET
SHELLEY STREET
OLD BAILEY ST

Central

CHATER RD

Legco Building

MURRAY RD

CAINE ROAD

ABERDEEN ROAD
ROBINSON ROAD

LAN KWAI FONG

CENTRAL

The Landmark

Lippo Centre

HARCOURT ROAD

Admiralty

ADMIRALTY

CONDUIT ROAD

MOSQUE STREET

HK & Shanghai Bank

St John's Cathedral

Bank of China

American Library

UPPER ALBERT RD

Government House
Zoological & Botanical Gardens

GARDEN ROAD

COTTON TREE DRIVE

Hong Kong Park

JUSTICE DRIVE

Peak Tram Terminal

Peak tram line

KENNEDY ROAD

HONG KONG ISLAND: NORTHERN SHORE

0   500 m

▽ The Peak

Map © Rough Guides Ltd, 1999

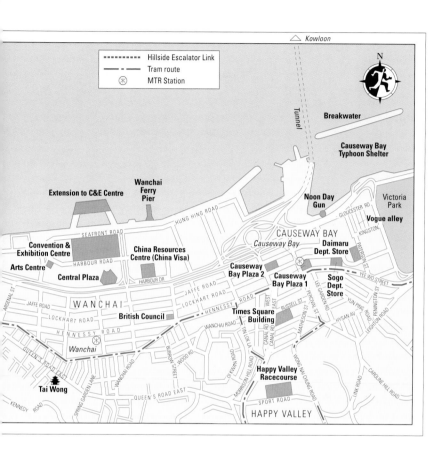

△ *Kowloon*

Legend:
- ---------- Hillside Escalator Link
- —·—·— Tram route
- ⊗ MTR Station

N

Tunnel

Breakwater

Causeway Bay Typhoon Shelter

Extension to C&E Centre

Wanchai Ferry Pier

Noon Day Gun

Victoria Park

HUNG HING ROAD

GLOUCESTER RD

Vogue alley

SEAFRONT ROAD

CAUSEWAY BAY

Causeway Bay

KINGSTON

Convention & Exhibition Centre

China Resources Centre (China Visa)

Daimaru Dept. Store

PATTERSON ST

Arts Centre

HARBOUR ROAD

Causeway Bay Plaza 2

Causeway Bay Plaza 1

YEE WO STREET

Central Plaza

HARBOUR DR

Sogo Dept. Store

JAFFE ROAD

WEST CANAL RD

YUN PING ROAD

PENNINGTON RD

LEIGHTON RD

ARSENAL ST

JAFFE ROAD

LOCKHART ROAD

W A N C H A I

HENNESSY ROAD

CANAL RD EAST

RUSSELL ST

PERCIVAL ST

LEE GARDEN RD

HYSAN AV

LOCKHART ROAD

British Council

WANCHAI ROAD

Times Square Building

MATHESON ST

CAROLINE HILL ROAD

HENNESSY ROAD

TIN LOK LA

Wanchai

BURROWS STREET

WOOD RD

OI KWAN ROAD

WONG NAI CHUNG ROAD

LINK ROAD

QUEEN'S ROAD EAST

MORRISON HILL ROAD

Happy Valley Racecourse

Tai Wong

SPRING GARDEN LANE

WANCHAI ROAD

QUEEN'S ROAD EAST

SPORT ROAD

KENNEDY ROAD

HAPPY VALLEY

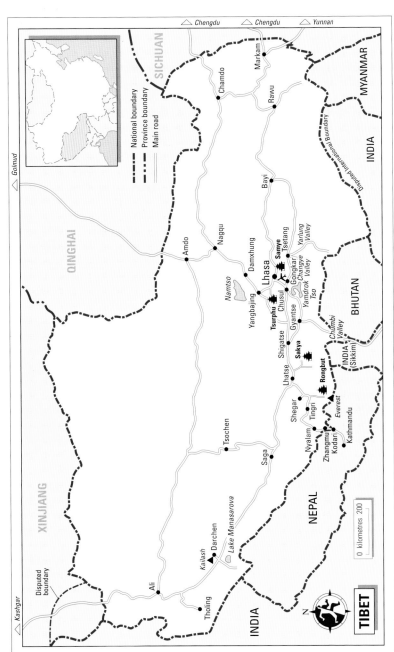

△ Golmud

△ Kashgar

△ Chengdu △ Chengdu △ Yunnan

SICHUAN

Chamdo

Markam

Ravu

MYANMAR

INDIA

Disputed International Boundary

National boundary
Province boundary
Main road

QINGHAI

Amdo

Nagqu

Bayi

Damxhung

Namtso

Lhasa

Yangbajing

Tsurphu Chusul

Samye Tsetang

Gongkar Yarlung

Changye Valley

Valley

Yamdrok

Gyantse Tso

Shigatse

Lhatse

Sakya

Rongbut

BHUTAN

Chumbi

Valley

INDIA

(Sikkim)

Tsochen

Saga

Shegar

Tingri

Everest

Nyalam

Zhangmu

Kodari Kathmandu

XINJIANG

Kailash

Darchen

Lake Manasarova

Ali

NEPAL

Tholing

INDIA

Disputed
boundary

0 kilometres 200

N

TIBET

Map © Rough Guides Ltd, 1999

'People's conciliation committees' are charged with settling minor disputes.

There are also special military courts.

Procuratorial powers and functions are exercised by the Supreme People's Procuracy and local procuracies.

Religion

The government accords legality to 5 religions only: Buddhism, Islam, Protestantism, Roman Catholicism and Taoism. Confucianism, Buddhism and Taoism have long been practised. Confucianism has no ecclesiastical organization and appears rather as a philosophy of ethics and government. Taoism – of Chinese origin – copied Buddhist ceremonial soon after the arrival of Buddhism two millennia ago. Buddhism in return adopted many Taoist beliefs and practices. A more tolerant attitude towards religion had emerged by 1979, and the Government's Bureau of Religious Affairs was reactivated.

Ceremonies of reverence to ancestors have been observed by the whole population regardless of philosophical or religious beliefs.

Moslems are found in every province of China, being most numerous in the Ningxia–Hui Autonomous Region, Yunnan, Shaanxi, Gansu, Hebei, Honan, Shandong, Sichuan, Xinjiang and Shanxi. They totalled 18m. in 1997.

Roman Catholicism has had a footing in China for more than 3 centuries. In 1992 there were about 3·5m. Catholics who are members of the Patriotic Catholic Association, which declared its independence from Rome in 1958. In 1979 there were about 1,000 priests. In 1977 there were 78 bishops and 4 apostolic administrators, not all of whom were permitted to undertake religious activity. This figure included 46 'democratically elected' bishops not recognized by the Vatican. A bishop of Beijing was consecrated in 1979 without the consent of the Vatican and 2 auxiliary bishops of Shanghai in

1984. Archbishop Gong Pinmei, arrested in 1955, was freed in 1988. Protestants are members of the All-China Conference of Protestant Churches. 2 Protestant bishops were installed in 1988, the first for 30 years. In 1997 there were an estimated 73,000,000 Christians in total.

In 1997 there were also estimated to be 247,000,000 Chinese folk-religionists, 147,000,000 atheists, 104,000,000 Buddhists, 1,000,000 advocates of traditional beliefs and 637,000,000 non-religious persons.

Legislation of 1994 prohibits foreign nationals from setting up religious organizations.

Confucianism

The Philosopher Kong Zi or to give him his western name, Confucius, was born in 551 BC in what is now the Shandong Province. He lived during a period known as the Warring States Period when life was made difficult by constant clashes between small kingdoms struggling for power over one another. Confucius noted that with the adherence to some basic codes of conduct or doctrines (what came to be known as Analects), life might become better for 'ruler' and 'ruled' alike. Confucianism is not a recognized religion because, as it appears, it is a philosophical code with no central deities or rituals. Confucianism has, however, touched the lives of the Chinese for generations. As far back as the Han Dynasty, Confucianism became part of the government system.

Taoism

The Tao literally means 'the way', as set out in Taoism's central text, the Dao De Jing. The founding father of Taoism is thought to be a semi-mythical hermit known as Loatse or 'Old One'. Taoism is the unceasing search for harmony with the natural world and even the universe. It is practised all over China and is considered the only truly native religion of the Chinese people.

Buddhism

Buddhism originated in India in the 6th century BC. Its founding father is known as Siddharta Guatama. The central aim of Buddhism is the attainment of enlightenment by the negation of suffering, suffering being the natural end of greed. Contemplation or meditation, it is thought, can achieve enlightenment. Buddhism took root in China during the Ming Dynasty, although Buddhist traders had been visiting China and generating interest in the religion for many generations earlier. It spread rapidly throughout the north of the country. In Tibet a unique form of Buddhism evolved called Lamaist or Tantric Buddhism. In essence this is a combination of Buddhism and an earlier Tibetan religion known as Bon.

Islam

Islam was brought to China by Arab traders who built their mosques in the southern coastal regions. The first mosque to be built was in 650 in Guangzhou. During this period, foreign trade with China was dominated by the Arab states.

Christianity

Although Christian contact with the Chinese world is recorded as far back as the 7th century when a Nestorian monastery was built in Chang'an, Christianity only gained a foothold during and after the Opium Wars in the 19th century.

China has the following national religious organizations: Buddhist Association of China, Taoist Association of China, Islamic Association of China, Chinese Patriotic Catholic Association, Chinese Catholic Bishops' College, Three-Self Patriotic Movement Committee of the Protestant Churches of China, and China Christian Council.

To view the White Paper 'Freedom of Religious Belief in China' visit the Web at:

www.china.org.cn/WhitePapers/FreedomOfReligious.html

Education

In 1996, 82·18% of the adult population were literate (89·88% of men and 74·46% of women). In 1994, 98·4% of school-age children attended school. In 1993 maximum school fees were 10 yuan a term, to which other charges might be added. In 1996 there were 187,324 kindergartens with 26·66m. children and 889,000 teachers. An educational reform of 1985 planned to phase in compulsory 9-year education consisting of 6 years of primary schooling and 3 years of secondary schooling, to replace a previous 5-year system. In 1996 there were 645,983 primary schools with 5,736,000 teachers and 136·15m. pupils; 79,967 secondary schools, with 3,465,000 teachers and 57·39m. pupils; and 10,049 vocational schools with 308,000 teachers and 4·73m. students. There were 1,032 institutes of higher education, including universities, with 403,000 teachers and 3·02m. students. One-third of all higher education students study engineering.

There is an Academy of Sciences with provincial branches. An Academy of Social Sciences was established in 1977.

In 1995–96 in the private sector there were 3 general universities and 9 specialized universities (aeronautics and astronautics; agricultural engineering; agriculture; chemical technology; foreign studies; labour; medicine; traditional Chinese medicine; polytechnic). In the public sector there were 60 general universities, 2 for ethnic minorities and the following specialized universities: Agriculture, 12; agriculture and land reclamation, 1; land reclamation, 1; architecture, 2; architecture and technology, 1; chemical technology, 1; coal and chemical technology, 1; electronic science and technology, 1; engineering, 1; fisheries, 1; foreign languages, 1; forestry, 1; hydraulic and electrical engineering, 1; international business and economics, 1; international studies, 1; iron and steel technology, 1; maritime studies, 1; medicine, 11; traditional Chinese medicine, 2;

mining and technology, 1; petroleum, 1; pharmacology, 1; political science and law, 1; polytechnic, 8; radio and television, 1; science and technology, 5; surveying and mapping, 1; teaching, 4; technology, 6; textiles, 1.

In 1996 there were also 893 teacher training schools. In 1994, 19,000 students were studying abroad. Fees were introduced for university students in 1996–97.

In 1996 total expenditure on education came to 155,611m. yuan (2·3% of GNP), around 11·9% of total government expenditure.

Health

Medical treatment is free only for certain groups of employees, but where costs are incurred they are partly borne by the patient's employing organization. In 1996 there were 1·94m. doctors, of whom 0·35m. practised Chinese medicine, and 1·16m. nurses. About 10% of doctors are in private practice.

In 1996 there were 67,964 hospitals (with 2·87m. beds), 528 sanatoria (with 109,000 beds) and 103,472 clinics. There were 24 beds per 10,000 population in 1996.

Welfare

In 1996 there were 42,821 social welfare institutions with 769,348 inmates. Numbers (in 1,000) of beneficiaries of relief funds: Persons in poor rural households, 30,790; in poor urban households, 2,610; persons in rural households entitled to 'the 5 guarantees' (food, clothing, medical care, housing, education for children or funeral expenses), 2,675; retired, laid-off or disabled workers, 535. The major relief funds (in 1,000 yuan) in 1996 were: Families of deceased or disabled servicemen, 5,187,970; poor households, 712,270; orphaned, disabled, old and young persons, 1,856,680; welfare institutions, 1,551,000.

CULTURE

Millennium Events

There are no official plans for celebrating the Millennium but the government has placed a countdown clock on the Badaling section of the Great Wall where its red digital display exhorts the people to 'seize the moment to build up the motherland'. (Take note, however, that the countdown clock in Tian'anmen Square is nothing to do with the Millennium. It registers the time left to the handover of the Portuguese colony of Macau on 20 Dec. 1999.) There is talk of a fireworks party at the Great Wall and the Hong Kong Cancer Fund has plans to illuminate the Wall with laser beams from space.

There are 4 million officially recognized Catholics in China (and a further 10 million unofficial adherents, according to the Vatican). The Pope has requested permission for them to be allowed to visit Rome during the Great Jubilee Year. More than 20,000 couples have been invited to attend millennium weddings throughout China, kicking off with a ceremony for 2,000 couples on 31 Dec. 1999. The event is supposed to initiate a 'more wholesome, civilized and scientific lifestyle among young couples'.

China's official response to the potential problems of the Millennium Bug in the Chinese aviation industry has been to order all its executives to take a flight on 1 Jan. 2000.

Major Festivals

Lantern Festival, or Yuanxiao Jie, is an important, traditional Chinese festival, which is on the 15th of the first month of the Chinese New Year.

Guanyin's Birthday is on the 19th day of the second month of the Chinese lunar calendar. Guanyin is the Chinese goddess of mercy.

The Lunar New Year, also known as the 'Spring Festival', is a time of great excitement for the Chinese people. The festivities get under way 22 days prior to the New Year date and continue for 15 days after-wards.

Dates of the lunar New Year from 2000–2009

Year of the Dragon.	5 Feb. 2000
Year of the Snake.	24 Jan. 2001
Year of the Horse.	12 Feb. 2002
Year of the Ram.	1 Feb 2003
Year of the Monkey.	22 Jan. 2004
Year of the Rooster.	9 Feb. 2005
Year of the Dog.	29 Jan. 2006
Year of the Pig.	18 Feb. 2007
Year of the Rat.	7 Feb. 2008
Year of the Ox.	26 Jan. 2009

Tomb Sweeping Day, as the name implies, is a day for visiting and cleaning the ancestral tomb and usually falls on 5 April.

Dragon Boat Festival

Dragon Boat Festival is called Duan Wu Jie in Chinese. The festival is celebrated on the 5th of the 5th month of the Chinese lunar calendar.

Moon Festival

The Moon Festival is on the 15th of the 8th lunar month. It is some-times called Mid-Autumn Festival. The Moon Festival is an occasion for family reunion. When the full moon rises, families get together to watch the full moon, eat moon cakes, and sing moon songs.

Public Holidays

In Mainland China

1–2 Jan. – New Year's Day

8 March – International Women's Working Day

1–2 May – International Labour Day

4 May – Youth Day

1 June – Children's Day

1 July – Anniversary of the Founding of the Communist Party

1 Aug. – Anniversary of the Founding of the Chinese PLA

1–2 Oct. – National Day

In Hong Kong

1 Jan. – New Year's Day

6 April – Day after Cheng Ming Festival

1 May – Labour Day

1 July – SAR Establishment Day

1–2 Oct. – National Day

25 Dec. – Christmas Day

26 Dec. – Boxing Day

In Taiwan

1–3 Jan. – Founding Day

29 March – Youth Day

2 Sept. – Mid-Autumn Festival

28 Sept. – Teachers' Day

10 Oct. – National Day

25 Oct. – Taiwan Retrocession Day

31 Oct. – Chiang Kaishek's Birthday

12 Nov. – Sun Yatsen's Birthday

25 Dec. – Constitution Day

ETIQUETTE

Social

The Chinese are extremely hospitable people and if you make friends
they will almost certainly invite you to their home. It would be impolite

to refuse. You will be the object of considerable attention and scrutiny. Invariably, tea followed by a large meal will be served. It is customary to bring a small gift – something Western if possible – not chocolates or flowers and, above all, no watches or clocks (the words for 'to give a clock' sound exactly the same as the words for 'to send someone to their death'). The Chinese people shake hands (usually for much longer than in the West and usually accompanied by a respectful nod) and people of the same sex touch each other more than in the West by taking your hand, patting your arm to emphasize a point, etc. It is quite common to see two men or two women walking along the street hand in hand. Chinese people are more formal than Westerners and you should try and use Mr, Mrs or Miss with a surname if possible. Remember that when you use a person's name in China, the names are presented the opposite way round (for example, Zhang Hua is Mr Zhang, not Mr Hua).

Business

The Chinese are very status conscious and usually seat themselves in order of seniority (including women). Make sure to shake hands with everyone, however, as it is considered very impolite to miss anyone out. Women are treated as equals and you should not give precedence (other than that demanded by her official rank or position) to a woman. Dress should be formal. Although a lot of Chinese women wear smart trouser suits, suits with skirts are still considered more appropriate for business meetings. Punctuality is very important in China and you will not be kept waiting. It is considered the height of bad manners to show up late for a meeting.

Business cards are almost always exchanged at first meetings. It is a good idea to have your business card printed up in Chinese – any good hotel will recommend a printer who will do this inexpensively and quickly – but take care to keep the Chinese version of your name to two or three syllables at the most.

Although some offices close on Saturday afternoons, Chinese companies and organizations work a six-day week.

Most business entertaining is done in restaurants and spouses are not usually invited. Served around 6 p.m., these meals go on for a long time and there are numerous courses. Alcohol (usually beer and wine) and tea are served and many toasts are made in the course of the banquet. Be prepared to use chopsticks – a knife and fork will not be in evidence.

After returning to the West, it is customary to keep in touch with your business contacts, preferably at New Year, by sending a small gift, calendar or card.

BROADCASTING

In 1994 there were 1,107 radio and 766 TV stations. The Central People's Broadcasting Station provides 2 central programmes, regional services, special services, a Taiwan service and external services. China Central Television (colour by PAL) transmits 3 programmes from Beijing, a programme from Shanghai, and an English-language programme. There are 29 regional programmes transmitted from 361 local stations. By 1995 about 600 cable TV systems had been licensed. In 1995 there were 225·5m. radio receivers (only the USA has more) and 250m. TV receivers (the greatest number in any country in the world). In 1980 there had been just 9m., representing an increase of nearly 241m. between 1980 and 1995, or more TV sets than were in use in the USA (the country with the second highest number of sets) in 1995. In urban areas 96%, and in rural areas 48·5%, of households possessed a TV set in 1994. The use of satellite receiving dishes was prohibited in 1993.

Beijing Television, China's first television station, was established in 1958. Its name was changed to China Central Television in 1979.

The state run CCTV has 8 channels, broadcasting 138 hours of programmes daily. CCTV-1 broadcasts a comprehensive range of programmes, with the emphasis on news and current affairs. CCTV-2 focuses on economic, social and educational topics.CCTV-3 airs operas and music. CCTV-4, also known as CCTV international, presents a variety of programming targeted at overseas viewers. CCTV-5 is a sports channel. CCTV-6 is for movies. CCTV-7 is for children's programmes, agriculture, the military and science subjects. CCTV-8 is devoted chiefly to art and entertainment. The coverage of CCTV-1 now reaches over 84% of the total population of China, with the number of regular viewers exceeding 900m.

China now has over 3,000 cable television stations.

China Central Television
Bureau of Broadcasting Affairs of the State Council, Beijing.
Web: www.cctv.com

In 1997 there were 1,244 radio and 744 medium and short-wave relay and transmitting stations in China. The largest of these is the Central People's Broadcasting Station (CPBS).

The CPBS, CCTV, Radio Beijing, China Record Co., Beijing Broadcasting Institute, Broadcasting Research Institute and the China Broadcasting Art Troupe, among others, are all controlled by:

Ministry of Radio, Film and Television
Fu Xing Men Wai Jie 2, POB 4501, Beijing. Tel: (0)10 686 2753.
Fax: (0)10 6801 2174.

China National Radio (CNR). Formed in 1945.
Fu Xing Men Wai Je 2, Beijing 100866.

China Radio International (CRI). Formed in 1941. Radio Beijing Foreign Service. Broadcasts in 38 languages across the world.
2 Fu Xing Men Wai Dajie, Beijing 100866. Tel: (0)10 6609 2274.
Fax: (0)10 6851 3174.

CINEMA

There were 4,639 cinemas in 1995. 148 feature films were made in 1994. In 1992 there were some 10,600m. cinema attendances.

PRESS

In 1994 there were 1,635 newspapers with a combined circulation of 125,200m. and 7,325 periodicals with 2,210m. The Party newspaper is *Renmin Ribao* (People's Daily), which had a daily circulation of 3m. in 1994. 103,836 book titles were produced in 6,007·75m. copies in 1994. There were 2,596 public libraries in 1993.

Newspapers

China had 1,083 newspapers in 1996 and a total impression of 179·5m. copies. As well as newspapers affiliated and controlled by the Communist Party and other large organizations, China has newspapers specializing in economic information, newspapers about science and technology, newspapers for children and teenagers and newspapers for 'peasants'. Newspapers controlled by the CCP and other mass organizations account for a large portion of the circulation.

A selection based on circulation/major conurbation/interest for business and travel:

Guangming Ribao (Brightness Daily) Founded in 1949. Circulation: 6m. Affiliation: Minority Parties.

106 Yongan Lu, Beijing 100050. Tel: (0)10 6301 0636. Fax: (0)10 6301 6716

Web: www.guangmingdaily.com (NB: Website under construction)

Renmin Ribao (People's Daily) Founded in 1948. Circulation: 3m. Affiliation: CCP Official Central Committee.

2 Jin Tai Xi Lu, Beijing. Tel: (0)10 509 2121. Fax: (0)10 6509 1982.
Web: www.peopledaily.com

Quingdao Ribao (Quingdao Daily) circulation: 2·6m. Shandong
Province Publication

Gongren Ribao (Worker's Daily) Founded in 1949. Circulation: 2·4m.
   Affiliation: Trade Union activities and workers' lives.
   Liupukang Andingmen Wai, Beijing. Tel: (0)10 6421 1561
Fax: (0)10 6421 4890.

Nanfang Ribao (South China Daily) Founded in 1949. Circulation: 1m.
Guangdong Province Publication.
   289 Guangzhou Da Lu, Guangzhou, Guangdong 510601.
Tel: (0)20 876 3998. Fax: (0)20 8737 5203.

Jiefang Ribao (Liberation Daily) Founded in 1949. Circulation: 1m.
   Affiliation: Shanghai CCP Municipal Committee
   300 Han Kou Lu, Shanghai 200001. Tel: (0)21 6351 5461.
Fax: (0)21 6351 5461

Beijing Ribao (Beijing Daily) Founded in 1952.
   Affiliation: Beijing Municipal Committee of the CCP.
   34 Xi Biaobei Hutong, Dongdan, Beijing 100734.
Web: www.beijingdaily.com (NB: Website under construction)

Selected Periodicals
Renmin Hubao (China Pictorial.) Founded in 1950.
   Huayuancun, West Suburbs, Beijing100044. Tel: (0)10 6841 1144.
Fax: (0)10 6841 3023.

Liaowang (Outlook) Founded in 1981. Circulation: 400,000.
Sponsored by Xiuha News Agency.
   57 Xuanwumen Xijie, Beijing. Tel: (0)10 6307 3049.

Zhongguo Funu (Women of China) Founded in 1956. Monthly, women's rights, marriage and family issues.

15 Jiang Guo Men Dajie, Beijing 100730. Tel: (0)10 644 4761.

News Agencies

Xinhua News Agency (New China) Formed in 1941. Xinhua is the state news agency of the People's Republic of China and the largest news and information gathering and distribution centre in the country.

57 Xuanwumen Xidajie, Beijing 100803 Tel: (0)10 6307 1114 Fax: (0)10 6307 3735. Web: www.xinhua.org

Zhongghuo Xinwen She (China News Agency) Formed in 1952.

POB 1114, Beijing.

Reuters (UK)

The Beijing Hilton, 4 Bei Dong Shanhuan Lu, Beijing 100027. Tel: (0)10 6532 1921. Web: www.reuters.com

United Press International (USA)

7-1-11 Qia Jia Yuan, Beijing. Tel (0)10 6532 3271. Fax: (0)10 6532 3419. Web: www.upi.com

Associated Press (USA)

8-1-11 Jiang Guo Men Wai, Diplomatic Quarters, Beijing.

Tel: (0)10 6532 6650. Fax: (0)10 6532 3419.

Book Publishers

Beijing Publishing House

Founded 1956. Subjects include English as a second language, fiction (including Western fiction), business, science, education, engineering, history, medicine, philosophy and women's studies.

6 Beisanhuan Zhonglu, Beijing 100011. Tel: (0)10 6201 6699. Fax: (0)10 6201 2339

Foreign Language Press

Founded 1952. Publishes in a wide range of languages, including English, French, German Russian, Spanish, Swahili and Vietnamese.

24 Baiwanzhuang Lu, Beijing 100037. Tel: (0)10 6832 0579. Fax: (0)10 6832 6642.

Higher Education Press

Founded 1954. Publishes academic and textbooks.

55 Shatan Houjie, Beijing 100009. Tel: (0)10 6401 4043. Fax: (0)10 6401 4048.

Kunlun Publishing House

Founded 1951. Subjects include fiction and general non-fiction.

42 Baishiqiaolu, Beijing 100081. Tel: (0)10 6680 1009. Fax: (0)10 6218 3683.

Liaoning People's Publishing House.

Founded 1951. Subjects include economics and history.

108 Beiyi Malu, Heping Dist., Liaoning, Shenyang 110001. Tel: (0)24 386 3316. Fax: (0)24 371 472.

Shandong People's Publishing House

Founded 1951. Subjects include history, economics, political science, sociology and philosophy.

39 Shengli Daljie, Shandong, Jinan 250001. Tel: (0)531 2010 055-5009. Fax: (0)531 610 055.

Shanghai Educational Publishing House

Founded 1958. Academic publishers.

123 Yongfulu, Shanghai 200031. Tel: (0)21 6437 7165. Fax: (0)21 6433 9995.

World Affairs Press

Founded 1934. Subjects include fiction, biography, political science, history and sociology.

A31 Waijiaoobujie, Dongcheng, Beijing 100005.
Tel: (0)10 6523 2695. Fax: (0)10 6526 5961.

TOURISM

51,128,000 tourists visited in 1996, including 44,229,000 from Hong
Kong, Taiwan and Macao, and 155,000 other overseas Chinese.
The World Tourism Organization predicts that China will overtake
France as the world's most visited destination by 2020 and become
the world's 4th most important source of tourists to other countries.
Income from tourists in 1996 was US$10,200m.

Chinese Tourist Offices in the United Kingdom and the United States of America

UK

China National Tourist Office, 4 Glentworth Street, London NW1 5PG.
Tel: 0891 600-188 (for information and brochure orders in UK).
Tel: (0)20 7935-9787 (for administration office).
Fax: (0)20 7487-5842.

USA

China National Tourist Office, 333 West Broadway, Suite 201,
Glendale CA 91204. Tel: 818 545-7505. Fax: 818 545-7506.

Visa Information

There are three types of visa:

Tourist/Business

(For UK nationals) This costs £25 (Single-entry), £50 (Double-entry),
£75 (Multiple-entry, valid 6 months) or £150 (Multiple-entry, valid
12 months).

Tourist

(Other nationals) The cost for this will vary according to nationality. Contact the Chinese Embassy for further information.

Group, Business or Transit

Again, there are variations according to nationality. Apply to the Chinese Embassy for details.

When applying for a visa to visit or travel in China one should leave a minimum of 3–5 working days for applications in person and 2–3 weeks for postal applications. Apply in writing or in person to:

The People's Republic of China Embassy in the UK
Consular Section
31 Portland Place, London W1N 3AG
Tel: (0)20 7631-1430 (telephone enquiries).
Fax: (0)20 7636-9756.
Opening hours: 09.00–12.00 Monday to Friday.

The People's Republic of China Embassy in the USA
2300 Connecticut Avenue, NW, Washington, DC 20008
Tel: (202) 328-2500. Fax: (202) 328-2582.
or
Consulate General of the People's Republic of China
520 12th Avenue, New York, NY 10036
Tel: (212) 330-7400.
Opening hours: 10.00–15.00 Monday to Friday.

For Tourist visas one will need a completed application form, a passport-size photograph, a passport with at least 6 months' validity and one blank page to affix the visa. Payment can be made by cash or postal orders only; cheques will not be accepted. You may be asked if you have sufficient funds for the duration of the intended stay and confirmation of hotel reservations and onward or return tickets. If applying for a Business visa you will need to obtain an official invitation from the Chinese government or a government-approved company. If applying for a Group visa, applications should be accompanied by a confirmation letter or fax from the Chinese travel company concerned. A list of all group members should be presented in triplicate. If you are merely applying for a Transit visa you may be required to show a visa for the next country of destination or an airline ticket.

There are too many hotels in Chinese cities and towns to list in this publication. However, hotel reservations with every price range catered for, can be made and information found through the China International Travel Service (CITS).

For online information about hotels in all major cities and reservation procedures visit the Web at: www.citsusa.com/hotel.html

CITS in the USA: 975 East Green Street, Suite 101, Pasadena, CA 91106, USA.
Tel: (626) 568 8993. Fax: (626) 568 9207
E-mail: info@citsusa.com

CITS in France: 30 Rue de Gramont 75002 Paris, France.
Tel: (1) 42-86-88-66. Fax: (1) 42-86-88-61

For the China National Tourist Office in London see page 128.

Hotel information and reservations in Hong Kong can be made easier by visiting the Hong Kong Tourist Association's Website at: www.hkta.org/uk/hotels.html

Hotel information for Taiwan can be found at: www.tbroc.gov.tw

LIBRARIES

In 1993 there were 2,579 public libraries and 5,000 higher education libraries with a combined 720,571,000 volumes and 11,401,724 registered users.

DIPLOMATIC REPRESENTATIVES

Of China in Great Britain (49-51 Portland Pl., London W1N 4JL)
  Ambassador: Ma Zhengang.

Of Great Britain in China (11 Guang Hua Lu, Jian Guo Men Wai,
Beijing 100600)
  Ambassador: A. C. Galsworthy, CMG.

Of China in the USA (2300 Connecticut Ave., NW, Washington, D.C.,
20008)
  Ambassador: Li Zhao Xing.

Of the USA in China (Xiu Shui Bei Jie 3, 100600 Beijing)
  Ambassador: James Sasser.

Of China to the United Nations
  Ambassador: Qin Huasun.

Of China to the European Union
  Ambassador: Mingjiang Song.

FURTHER READING

State Statistical Bureau. *China Statistical Yearbook*

China Directory [in Pinyin and Chinese]. Tokyo, annual

Adshead, S.A.M., *China in World History.* Macmillan, London, 1999

Baum, R., *Burying Mao: Chinese Politics in the Age of Deng Xiaoping.*
  Princeton Univ. Press, 1994

Beeching, J., *The Chinese Opium Wars.* Harcourt, 1997

Boorman, H. L. and Howard, R. C. (eds.) *Biographical Dictionary of
  Republican China.* 5 vols. Columbia Univ. Press, 1967–79

Brown, Raj, *Overseas Chinese Merchants.* Macmillan, London, 1999

Brugger, B. and Reglar, S., *Politics, Economics and Society in Contemporary
  China.* London, 1994

The Cambridge Encyclopaedia of China. 2nd ed. CUP, 1991

The Cambridge History of China. 14 vols. CUP, 1978 ff.

Chang, David Wen-Wei and Chuang, Richard Y., *The Politics of Hong Kong's Reversion to China.* Macmillan, London, 1999

Cook, Sarah, Yao, Shujie and Zhuang, Juzhong, (eds) *The Chinese Economy Under Transition.* Macmillan, London, 1999

De Crespigny, R., *China This Century.* 2nd ed. OUP, 1993

Deng Xiaoping, *Speeches and Writings.* 2nd ed. Oxford, 1987

Dixin, Xu and Chengming, Wu, (eds) *Chinese Capitalism, 1522–1840.* Macmillan, London, 1999

Dietrich, C., *People's China: a Brief History.* OUP, 1986

Dreyer, J. T., *China's Political System: Modernization and Tradition.* 2nd ed. London, 1996

Evans, R., *Deng Xiaoping and the Making of Modern China.* London, 1993

Fairbank, J. K., *The Great Chinese Revolution 1800–1985.* London, 1987. – *China: a New History.* Harvard Univ. Press, 1992

Fairbank, J. K. and Goldman, M., *China: A New History.* Harvard Uni. Press, 1998

Fathers, M. and Higgins, A., *Tiananmen: the Rape of Peking.* London and New York, 1989

Glassman, R. M., *China in Transition: Communism, Capitalism and Democracy.* New York, 1991

Goldman, M., *Sowing the Seeds of Democracy in China: Political Reform in the Deng Xiaoping Era.* Harvard Univ. Press, 1994

Goodman, D., *Deng Xiaoping and the Chinese Revolution: a Political Biography.* 2nd ed. London, 1994. – and Segal, G., (eds.) *China in the 90s: Crisis Management and Beyond.* Oxford, 1991

Gray, J., *Rebellions and Revolutions: China from the 1800s to the 1980s.* CUP, 1990

Hayford, C. W., *China.* [Bibliography] 2nd ed. Oxford and Santa Barbara (CA), 1997

Hinton, H. C. (ed.) *The People's Republic of China 1949–1979.* 5 vols. Wilmington, 1980

Ho, Samuel P.S. and Kueh, Y. Y., (eds) *Sustainable Economic Development in South China*. Macmillan, London, 1999

Huang, R., *China: a macro History.* 2nd ed. Armonk (NY), 1997

Hunter, A. and Sexton, J., *Contemporary China*. Macmillan, 1999

Jenner, W. J. F., *The Tyranny of History: the Roots of China's Crisis*. London, 1992

Lichtenstein, P. M., *China at the Brink: the Political Economy of Reform and Retrenchment in the Post-Mao Era*. New York, 1991

Lieberthal, K. G., *From Revolution through Reform*. New York, 1995. – and Lampton, D. M. (eds.) *Bureaucracy, Politics and Decision-Making in Post-Mao China*. California Univ. Press, 1992

Lippit, V. D., *The Economic Development of China*. Armonk, 1987

Loewe, M., *The Pride that was China*. London, 1990

Lu, Aiguo, *China and the Global Economy Since 1840*. Macmillan, London, 1999

Ma, Jun, *Chinese Economy in the 1990s*. Macmillan, London, 1999

McCormick, B. L., *Political Reform in Post-Mao China: Democracy and Bureaucracy in a Leninist State*. California Univ. Press, 1990

MacFarquhar, R. (ed.) *The Politics of China: the eras of Mao and Deng*. 2nd ed. CUP, 1997. – *The Origins of the Cultural Revolution*. 3 vols. Columbia University Press, 1998

Mackerras, C. et al., *China since 1978: Reform, Modernization and Socialism with Chinese Characteristics*. New York, 1994. – and Yorke, A., *The Cambridge Handbook of Contemporary China*. CUP, 1991

Mok, Ka-Ho, *Social and Political Development in Post-reform China*. Macmillan, London, 1999

Moise, E. E., *Modern China: A History*. London, 1986

Nathan, A. J., *Chinese Democracy*. London, 1986: – *China's Crisis: Dilemmas of Reform and Prospects for Democracy*. Columbia Univ. Press, 1990

Nolan, P., *State and Market in the Chinese Economy: Essays on Controversial Issues*. London, 1993

Phillips, R. T., *China since 1911*. London, 1996

Riskin, C., *China's Political Economy: The Quest for Development since 1949.* OUP, 1987

Roberts, J.A.G., *A History of China.* Macmillan, London, 1999

Rodzinski, W., *A History of China.* Oxford, 1981–84

Schram, S., (ed.) *Mao's Road to Power: Revolutionary Writings 1912–1949.* 4 vols. Harvard, 1998

Shen, Xiaobai, *The Chinese Road to High Technology.* Macmillan, London, 1999

Sheng Hua, et al., *China: from Revolution to Reform.* London, 1992

Shirk, S. L., *The Political Logic of Economic Reform in China.* Univ. of California Press, 1993

Spence, J. D., *The Chan's Great Continent: China in Western Minds.* Norton, New York, 1998

Spence, J. D., *The Search for Modern China.* London, 1990

Suyin, H. *Eldest Son, Zhou Enlai and The Making of Modern China.* Kodansha Globe, 1995

·Weldon, Elizabeth, Tsui, Anne and Li, Jiatao, (eds) *Management and Organisations in China.* Macmillan, London, 1999

White, G. (ed.) *The Chinese State in the Era of Economic Reform: the Road to Crisis.* London, 1991. – *Riding the Tiger: the Politics of Economic Reform in Post-Mao China.* London, 1993

Womack, B. (ed.) *Contemporary Chinese Politics in Historical Perspective.* CUP, 1992

Yan, Yanni, *International Joint Ventures in China.* Macmillan, London, 1999

Yeung, Henry Wai-Chung and Olds, Kristopher, (eds) *The Globalisation of Chinese Business Firms.* Macmillan, London, 1999

Zhang, Xiao-Guang, *China's Trade Patterns and International Comparative Advantage.* Macmillan, London, 1999

TOURIST AND HOTEL GUIDES

Atiyah, J., Leffman, D. and Lewis, S., *China: The Rough Guide.* Penguin, 1997

Baedeker Guide: China. AA Publishing, 1996

Haw, S. G., *A Traveller's History of China*. Windrush Press, 1998

Mason, C. and Murray, G., *The Simple Guide to China Customs and Etiquette*. Global Books, 1999

Mayhew, B., and Huhti, T., *South-West China*. Lonely Planet Publications, 1998

Storey, R. et al, *China*. Lonely Planet Publications, 1998

Van Itallie, N. *Fodor's China* (1st edition). Fodor's Travel Publications, 1998

Web: www.chinabusiness.com/govern/index.html (Government organizations of The People's Republic of China)

Web: www.chinaindustrynet.com/associate.htm (China Information Provider and e-commerce information)

Web: sun.sino.uni-heidelberg.de/igcs/igpol.htm#polchina *Internet Guide for China Studies*. Ed, Lecher, H. Heidelberg University. (1999.)

Web: Surf China.Com.

Web: chinasite.com/ (Information provider for all aspects of Chinese culture)

Other more specialized titles are listed under TERRITORY AND POPULATION; TIBET; DEFENCE; AGRICULTURE; INTERNATIONAL TRADE.

National statistical office: State Statistical Bureau, 38 Yuetan Nanjie, Beijing.

HONG KONG

KEY HISTORICAL EVENTS

Hong Kong island and the southern tip of the Kowloon peninsula were ceded by China to Britain after the first and second Anglo-Chinese Wars by the Treaty of Nanking 1842 and the Convention of Peking 1860. The New Territories were leased to Britain for 99 years by China in 1898. Talks began in Sept. 1982 between Britain and China over the future of Hong Kong after the lease expiry in 1997. On 19 Dec. 1984, the two countries signed the Joint Declaration of the British and

Chinese Governments on the Question of Hong Kong which entered into force on 27 May 1985. By the terms of this Hong Kong became, with effect from 1 July 1997, a Special Administrative Region of the People's Republic of China enjoying a high degree of autonomy, and vested with executive, legislative and independent judicial power, including that of final adjudication. It was agreed that the laws currently in force in Hong Kong would remain basically unchanged. The existing social and economic systems, and the present lifestyle, were to remain unchanged for another 50 years. This 'one country, two systems' principle, embodied in the Basic Law, which was enacted by the National People's Congress of the People's Republic of China in 1990, became the constitution for the Hong Kong Special Administrative Region.

TERRITORY AND POPULATION

Hong Kong island is situated off the southern coast of the Chinese mainland 32 km east of the mouth of the Pearl River. The area of the island is 79·99 sq. km. It is separated from the mainland by a fine natural harbour. On the opposite side is the peninsula of Kowloon (46·27 sq. km). Total area of the Territory is 1,091 sq. km, a large part of it being steep and unproductive hillside. Country parks and special areas cover over 40% of the land area. Since 1945, the Government has reclaimed over 5,400 ha from the sea, principally from the seafronts of Hong Kong and Kowloon, facing the harbour. The 'New Territories' are on the mainland, north of Kowloon.

The population was 5,674,100 at the 1991 census. 2000 estimated population: 6, 097,000. Some 43,100 persons emigrated in 1995. The British Nationality Scheme enables persons to acquire citizenship without leaving Hong Kong. There were 45,986 legal immigrants from China in 1995. 60% of the population was born in Hong Kong, 34% in

China (1991 census). The population of Vietnamese migrants ('boat people') in Oct. 1996 was 12,710. All remaining 'boat people' were repatriated by Jan. 1997.

The official languages are Chinese and English.

SOCIAL STATISTICS

Annual growth rate, 1998, 2·8%. Vital statistics, 1998 (provisional): Known births, 53,100; known deaths, 32,200; registered marriages, 31,700. Rates (per 1,000): Birth, 7·9 death, 4·8; marriage, 4·7; infant mortality, 3·2 (per 1,000 live births). Life expectancy, 1998: Males, 76·9 years; females, 82·3. The most popular age for marrying was 30 for males and 27 for females. Fertility rate, 1990–95, 1·9 children per woman.

CLIMATE

The climate is sub-tropical, tending towards temperate for nearly half the year, the winter being cool and dry and the summer hot and humid, May to Sept. being the wettest months. Normal temperatures are Jan. 60°F (15·8°C), July 84°F (28·8°C). Annual rainfall 87" (2,214·3 mm).

THE BRITISH ADMINISTRATION

Hong Kong was administered by the Hong Kong Government. The Governor was the head of Government and presided over the *Executive Council*, which advised the Governor on all important matters. The last British Governor was Chris Patten. In Oct. 1996 the

Executive Council consisted of 3 ex-officio members and 10 appointed members, of whom 1 was an official member. The chief functions of the *Legislative Council* were to enact laws, control public expenditure and put questions to the administration on matters of public interest. The Legislative Council elected in Sept. 1995 was, for the first time, constituted solely by election. It comprised 60 members, of whom 20 were elected from geographical constituencies, 30 from functional constituencies encompassing all eligible persons in a workforce of 2·9m., and 10 from an election committee formed by members of 18 district boards. A president was elected from and by the members.

At the elections on 17 Sept. 1995 turn-out for the geographical seats was 35·79%, and for the functional seats (21 of which were contested), 40·42%. The Democratic Party and its allies gained 29 seats, the Liberal Party 10 and the pro-Beijing Democratic Alliance, 6. The remaining seats went to independents.

CONSTITUTION AND GOVERNMENT

In Dec. 1995 the Standing Committee of China's National People's Congress set up a Preparatory Committee of 150 members (including 94 from Hong Kong) to oversee the retrocession of Hong Kong to China on 1 July 1997. In Nov. 1996 the Preparatory Committee nominated a 400-member Selection Committee to select the Chief Executive of Hong Kong and a provisional legislature to replace the Legislative Council. The Selection Committee was composed of Hong Kong residents, with 60 seats reserved for delegates to the National People's Congress and appointees of the People's Political Consultative Conference. On 11 Dec. 1996 Tung Chee-hwa was elected Chief Executive by 80% of the Selection Committee's votes.

On 21 Dec. 1996 the Selection Committee selected a provisional legislature which began its activities in Jan. 1997 while the Legislative Council was still functioning. In Jan. 1997 the provisional legislature began repealing some civil rights legislation.

Hong Kong is a Special Administrative Region of the People's Republic of China. It is supposed to retain a high degree of autonomy, and the legislative, judicial and administrative systems which were previously in operation are to remain in place. The Special Administrative Region Government is also empowered to decide on Hong Kong's monetary and economic policies independent of China.

In July 1997 the first-past-the-post system of electing the Legislative Council was replaced by proportional representation.

RECENT ELECTIONS

In the Legislative Council election held on 25 May 1998 pro-democracy candidates won 63% of the popular vote, compared to 51% in the 1995 election. However, under an electoral system which allows only a third of the seats to be chosen by the entire electorate, the pro-democracy members remained a minority political force. Of the 20 seats elected by universal suffrage, 9 went to the Democratic Party, 3 to Frontier and 1 to Citizens (all pro-democracy), 5 to the Democratic Alliance for the Betterment of HK and 2 to independents. The other 40 seats were elected by committees and professional associations. The make-up of the Legislative Council following the elections was: Democratic Party, 13; DAB (pro-China, populist), 9; Liberals (pro-business), 9; HK Progressive Alliance (pro-China), 5; Frontier, 3; Citizens, 1; Non-affiliates, 20.

CURRENT ADMINISTRATION

Chief Executive: Tung Chee-hwa (b. 1937; elected 11 Dec. 1996).
    Chief Secretary: Anson Chan, CBE, JP.
    Financial Secretary: Donald Tsang, OBE, JP.
    The Chief Executive is aided by the Executive Council, consisting of the Chief Secretary, the Financial Secretary and 12 other members.

Local Government

There are 2 municipal councils, the Urban Council and the Regional Council. With all appointed seats abolished in 1995, 59 of 80 seats were open to direct election in the March 1995 elections. Turn-out was 25·8%. Elections to the 18 Consultative District Boards set up in 1982 were held in Sept. 1994; turn-out was 33·1%.

    At local council elections on 18 Sept. 1994 for 346 council seats, turn-out was 33·1%. The United Democratic Party gained 77 seats; the Alliance for Democracy, 28; the Democratic Alliance for a Better Hong Kong (pro-Beijing), 37; the Liberal Party, 30; the United Democrats of Hong Kong won 11 out of 27 seats; independents 11; the Liberal Democratic Federation 3; and Communists 2.

ECONOMY

Performance

Hong Kong was second behind Singapore in the World Economic Forum's Global Competitiveness Reports, which assesses countries on their potential for economic growth and their income levels, in both 1997 and 1998. Total GDP in 1998 was US$166·4bn. Following real GDP growth of 5·7% in 1997, it was negative in 1998, at –5·1%, representing Hong Kong's most severe recession since the 1970s.

Budget

The total Government revenue and expenditure for financial years
ending 31 March were as follows (in HK$1m.):

	1996	1997	1998
Revenue	180,045	208,400	275,200
Expenditure	191,338	173,600	194,200

Public expenditure, 1998, was divided as follows (HK$1bn.):
Education, 47·0; support, 30·2; health, 28·0; housing, 24·7; security,
23·8; social welfare, 21·7; infrastructure, 21·5; economic, 17·8;
community and external affairs, 13·1; environment, 7·0.

Currency

The unit of currency is the *Hong Kong dollar* (HKD) of 100 *cents*.
Banknotes are issued by the Hongkong and Shanghai Banking
Corporation and the Standard Chartered Bank, and, from May 1994,
the Bank of China. Total money supply was HK$174m. in Jan. 1998.
Fiscal reserves at 31 March 1997 stood at HK$163,000m. In Feb.
1998 gold reserves were 70,000 troy oz. and foreign exchange
reserves US$78,617m. Inflation was 2·6% in 1998.

Banking and Finance

As at Dec. 1995 there were 185 banks licensed under the Banking
Ordinance, of which 31 were locally incorporated, 63 restricted
licence banks and 154 representative offices of foreign banks.
Licensed bank deposits were HK$2,601,971m. in June 1997;
restricted licence bank deposits were HK$62,033m. There were 132
deposit-taking companies registered under the Banking Ordinance
with total deposits of HK$18,419m. as at Nov. 1995.

There is a stock exchange. The summer of 1997 saw record highs
on the Hang Seng index (16,365 in July 1997 compared with 10,681 in
July 1996). In July 1997 the average daily turnover was HK$19,500m.

Weights and Measures

Metric, British Imperial, Chinese and US units are all in current use in Hong Kong. However, Government departments have now effectively adopted metric units; all new legislation uses metric terminology and existing legislation is being progressively metricated. Metrication is also proceeding in the private sector.

ENERGY AND NATURAL RESOURCES

Electricity

Installed capacity was 10·32m. kW in 1994. Production in 1994 was 25·14bn. kWh. Consumption in 1998 was 35·4bn. kWh.

Water

Reservoirs are needed to store the summer rainfall in order to meet supply requirements. There are 17 impounding reservoirs with a total capacity of 586m. cu. metres. Water is also purchased (720m. cu. metres in 1996). Consumption in 1996 was 928m cu. metres.

Agriculture

Agriculture supplies about a quarter of domestic demand. Only 3·4% of the total land area is suitable for crop farming and most produce derives from intensive market gardening: 1,350 ha were under cultivation in 1995. In 1995, 88,000 tonnes of vegetables and 4,820 tonnes of fruit and nuts were produced. Poultry production was 24,921 tonnes; milk, 407 tonnes; eggs, 1,112 tonnes. There were 109,000 pigs in 1996.

Forestry

Timber production in 1995 was 200,000 cu. metres.

Fisheries

The fishing fleet of 4,800 vessels supplies about 62% of fresh marine fish consumed locally. In 1995 the marine fish catch was 203,300 tonnes. Inland freshwater farming and coastal marine farming provided 8,200 tonnes of fish.

INDUSTRY

An economic policy based on free enterprise and free trade, a skilled workforce, an efficient commercial infrastructure, the modern and efficient sea-port (including container shipping terminals) and airport facilities; a geographical position relative to markets in North America and traditional trading links with the UK all contributed to Hong Kong's success as a modern industrial territory. Links with China have been growing increasingly strong in recent years and will remain so.

In 1995 there were 31,114 manufacturing firms employing 386,106 persons. Firms by product type (and persons employed): Textiles and clothing, 7,046 (139,931); plastics, 2,250 (15,997); electronics, 1,109 (44,078); watches and clocks, 1,006 (12,119); electrical appliances, 136 (2,589); shipbuilding, 374 (4,510).

Labour

In 1998 the labour force (economically active population aged 15 and over) totalled 3,434,000 (1,356,000 female). The employed population in 1996 included 1,047,000 people in wholesale, retail, restaurants and hotels, 391,000 in finance, insurance, business and real estate, 327,000 in manufacturing, 184,000 in the civil service and 77,000 manual labourers. In 1990, 3,495,000 working days were lost due to strikes and lockouts. Unemployment in June 1998 was running at a 15-year high of 4·5%.

Top Six Companies

Company name	Industry	Revenue ($m.)	World Ranking
Jardine Matheson	Multi-industry	11·52	210
First Pacific	Multi-industry	8·31	297
Hutchison Whampoa	Multi-industry	5·76	422
Cathay Pacific Airways	Transportation	3·96	606
Sun Hung Kai Properties	Real estate	3·74	637
Swire Pacific	Multi-industry	3·17	731

EXTERNAL ECONOMIC RELATIONS

Imports and Exports

Industry is mainly export-oriented. In 1998, the total value of imports (c.i.f.) was HK$1,429·1bn. and exports (f.o.b.) HK$1,347·6bn. In 1998, 34·4% of exports went to China, 23·4% to the USA, 5·2% to Japan, 3·9% to Germany and also 3·9% to the United Kingdom. The main suppliers of imports were China (40·6%), Japan (12·6%), USA (7·5%), Taiwan (7·3%) and South Korea (4·8%).

In 1996 domestic exports included (in HK$1m.): Clothing and accessories, 69,400; electrical machinery and parts, 30,400; textiles and fabrics, 13,700; watches and clocks, 12,000. The chief import items were consumer goods (573,000), raw materials (540,900), capital goods (324,000) and foodstuffs (65,200).

Visible trade normally carries an adverse balance which is offset by a favourable balance of invisible trade, in particular transactions in connection with air transportation, shipping, tourism and banking services.

Hong Kong has a free exchange market. Foreign merchants may remit profits or repatriate capital. Import and export controls are kept to the minimum, consistent with strategic requirements.

COMMUNICATIONS

Roads

In 1998 there were 1,865 km of roads, more than 900 km of which were in the New Territories. There are 8 major road tunnels, including 2 under Victoria Harbour. In 1998 there were 501,000 licensed motor vehicles, including 318,000 private cars, 115,000 goods vehicles and 23,000 motor cycles. There were 14,790 road accidents in 1995, 259 fatal. A total of 14·8m. tonnes of cargo were transported by road in 1996.

Rail

There is an electric tramway with a total track length of 33 km, and a cable tramway connecting the Peak district with the lower levels in Victoria. The electrified Kowloon-Canton Railway runs for 34 km from the terminus at Hung Hom in Kowloon to the border point at Lo Wu. It carried 232m. passengers in 1995. In 1996, 939,000 tonnes of cargo were transported by rail. A light rail system (32 km) is operated by the Kowloon-Canton Railway Corporation in Tuen Mun, Yuen Long and Tin Shui Wai; it carried 123m. passengers in 1995.

A metro, the Mass Transit Railway system, comprises 43·2 km with 38 stations. It carried 812m. passengers in 1995.

In 1996 a total of 3·9m. passenger journeys were made on public transport (including local railways, buses etc.).

Civil Aviation

The new Chek Lap Kok airport, built on reclaimed land off Lantau Island to the west of Hong Kong, opened in July 1998, replacing Hong Kong International Airport (Kai Tak), which was situated on the north shore of Kowloon Bay. After initial problems following its inauguration, 61 airlines now operate services. British Airways operates 14 flights a week to the UK. Cathay Pacific Airways, one of the 3 Hong

Kong-based airlines, operates more than 365 passenger and cargo services weekly to Europe (including 16 passenger and 5 cargo services a week to the UK), the Far and Middle East, South Africa, Australasia and North America. Hong Kong Dragon Airlines Ltd operates scheduled and non-scheduled services to a number of cities in Asia and the People's Republic of China. Air Hong Kong, an all-cargo operator, provides a scheduled service 5 times a week to Manchester, UK, and operates non-scheduled services around the region. In 1995–96, 150,118 aircraft arrived and departed. In 1996, 23·48m. passengers and 1·56m. tonnes of freight were carried on aircraft. Hong Kong International Airport handled more international freight in 1996 than any other airport.

Shipping

The port of Hong Kong handled 12·6m. 20-ft equivalent units in 1995. The Kwai Chung Container Port has 31 berths with 6,059 metres of quay backed by 228 ha of cargo handling area. Merchant shipping in 1995 totalled 8,795,000 GRT. In 1995, more than 41,000 ocean-going vessels, 108,000 river trading vessels and 64,000 international passenger vessels called at Hong Kong. In 1996, 125·4m. tonnes of freight were handled.

Telecommunications

In 1998 there were 3,708,000 telephones (554 per 1,000 population), of which 1,549,000 were for business use and 2,159,000 were residential lines. There were also over 284,000 fax lines. Basic local telephone services are provided by Hong Kong Telecom, which also offers fax services and value-added telephone services. The company also provides international voice, data and video transmission services, telex and telegram services, international private leased circuits, and shore-to-ship and ground-to-air communications. International facilities are provided through submarine cables, microwave and satellite radio systems. There were approximately 850,000 Internet users in April 1998. There were 798,000 cellular phone subscribers (129 per 1,000 persons) in 1995 and 720,000 PCs (116 per 1,000 persons).

Postal Services

There were 126 post offices in March 1996. In 1998 the postal services handled 1,264m. letters and 1,112,000 parcels.

SOCIAL INSTITUTIONS

Justice

The common law of England and the rules of equity were in force so far as they are applicable to the circumstances of Hong Kong. UK Acts of Parliament, however, were only binding if expressly applied to Hong Kong. By 1997 Hong Kong possessed a comprehensive body of law which owed its authority to its own legislature. The Hong Kong Act of 1985 provided for Hong Kong ordinances to replace English laws in specified fields.

The courts of justice comprise the Supreme Court (which includes the Court of Appeal and the High Court), the District Court (which includes the Family Court), the Magistracies, the Coroner's Court, the Juvenile Court and 4 tribunals. The Court of Appeal hears appeals on all matters, civil and criminal, from the lower courts. Pursuant to the Joint Declaration, the powers of final judgement were to be vested in the Court of Final Appeal, inaugurated in the territory in June 1997 to take over the functions of the UK Privy Council. While the High Court has unlimited jurisdiction in both civil and criminal matters, the District Court has limited jurisdiction. The maximum term of imprisonment it may impose is 7 years. Magistracies exercise criminal jurisdiction over a wide range of indictable and summary offences, and the powers of punishment are generally restricted to a maximum of 2 years' imprisonment. The Lands Tribunal determines on statutory claims for compensation over land and certain landlord and tenant matters. The Labour Tribunal provides a quick and inexpensive method of settling disputes between employers and employees. The Small Claims Tribunal deals with monetary claims involving amounts not exceeding HK$15,000.

After being in abeyance for 25 years, the death penalty was abolished in 1992.

71,962 crimes were reported in 1998, of which 14,682 were violent crimes. 40,422 people were arrested in 1998, of whom 9,207 were for violent crimes. The prison population was 13,117 in 1995.

Religion

In 1997 there were 4,790,000 Buddhists and Taoists, 280,000 Protestants, 270,000 Roman Catholics and 1,150,000 people of other beliefs.

Education

Adult literacy was 92·2% in 1995 (96% among males and 88·2% among females). Free and compulsory education is available to all children aged from 6 to 15 years. In around three-quarters of the schools teaching has been in Cantonese since Hong Kong reverted to Chinese sovereignty in 1997, with only a quarter of schools still using English. In 1995–96 there were 180,317 pupils in 731 kindergartens (all private), 467,718 in 860 primary schools (some 10·1% in private schools) and 459,845 in 38 government, 337 aided and 91 private secondary schools.

There are 7 technical institutes with (in 1995–96) 13,972 full-time and 34,409 part-time students; 2 technical colleges with 9,300 students, and 5 teacher training colleges of education with 2,863 full-time students.

The University of Hong Kong (founded 1911) had 10,325 full-time and 2,618 part-time students in the academic year of 1995–96, the Chinese University of Hong Kong (founded 1963), 10,388 full-time and 2,536 part-time students, the Hong Kong University of Science and Technology (founded 1991), 5,792 full-time and 503 part-time students, the Hong Kong Polytechnic University (founded 1972 as the Hong Kong Polytechnic), 11,157 full-time and 9,289 part-time students, the City University of Hong Kong (founded 1984 as the City Polytechnic of Hong Kong), 10,061 full-time and 6,881 part-time students, the Hong Kong Baptist University (founded 1956 as the Hong Kong Baptist College), 4,146 full-time and 600 part-time students and the Lingnan College (founded 1967), 2,059 full-time and 2 part-time students.

Total government expenditure on education in 1995 was HK$31,398m.

Health
In 1996 there were 9,196 doctors, 1,654 dentists, 36,395 nurses, 1,067 pharmacists and 20 midwives; in 1995 there were 88 hospitals and 29,328 hospital beds.

Welfare
The Government co-ordinates and implements expanding pro-grammes in social welfare, which include social security, family services, child care, services for the elderly, youth and community work, probation and corrections and rehabilitation. 170 non-governmental organizations are subsidized by public funds.

The Government gives non-contributory cash assistance to needy families, unemployed able-bodied adults, the severely disabled and the elderly. Caseload as at 31 Dec. 1995 totalled 623,029. Victims of natural disasters, crimes of violence and traffic accidents are finan-cially assisted.

CULTURE

Broadcasting

Broadcasting is regulated by the Broadcasting Authority, a statutory body comprising 3 government officers and 9 non-official members. There is a government broadcasting station, Radio Television Hong Kong, which broadcasts on 7 channels (4 Chinese, 1 English and 1 bi-lingual service, and 1 dedicated to BBC World Service), 6 of which provide a 24-hour service. Hong Kong Commercial Broadcasting Co. Ltd and Metro Broadcast Co. Ltd transmit commercial sound programmes on 6 channels. Television Broadcasts Ltd and Asia Television Ltd transmit commercial television in English and Chinese on 4 channels, in colour (by PAL). Hutchvision Hong Kong broadcasts by satellite to the entire Asian region on 14 TV and 2 radio channels and also carries the BBC World Service. There is also a cable TV network. In 1994 there were some 3·9m. radio receivers; in 1995 there were over 2·3m. TV receivers.

Cinema

In 1995 there were 184 cinemas; attendance was 27·4m. (57m. in 1990). 315 films were made in 1995.

Press

In 1996 there were 52 daily newspapers, and in 1995, 675 periodicals. Circulation of dailies in 1996 was 5,000,000. At 800 newspapers per 1,000 inhabitants, Hong Kong has one of the highest rates of circulation in the world. A number of news agency bulletins are registered as newspapers.

Tourism

There were about 11·7m. visitor arrivals in 1996 (2,380,000 from Japan, 751,000 from the USA). Receipts totalled US$10·84bn.

Libraries

In 1995 there were 2 public libraries and in 1990 there were 17 higher education libraries. These libraries held 8,336,000 volumes for 2,119,383 registered users.

FURTHER READING

Statistical Information: The Census and Statistics Department is responsible for the preparation and collation of Government statistics. These statistics are published mainly in the *Hong Kong Monthly Digest of Statistics.* The Department also publishes monthly trade statistics, economic indicators and an annual review of overseas trade, etc. *Web:* www.info.gov.hk/cen-statd/

Hong Kong [various years] Hong Kong Government Press

Bonavia, D., *Hong Kong 1997.* London, 1984

Brown, J. M. (ed.) *Hong Kong's Transitions, 1842–1997.* London, 1997

Buckley, R., *Hong Kong: the Road to 1997.* CUP, 1997

Cameron, N., *An Illustrated History of Hong Kong.* OUP, 1991

Chang, David Wen-Wei and Chuang, Richard Y., *The Politics of Hong Kong's Reversion to China.* Macmillan, London, 1999

Chill, H., et al (eds.) *The Future of Hong Kong: Toward 1997 and Beyond.* Westport, 1987

Cottrell, R., *The End of Hong Kong: the Secret Diplomacy of Imperial Retreat.* London, 1993

Courtauld, C. and Holdsworth, M., *The Hong Kong Story.* OUP, 1997

Endacott, G. B., *A History of Hong Kong.* 2nd ed. OUP, 1973. – *Government and People in Hong Kong, 1841–1962: a Constitutional History.* OUP, 1965

Flowerdew, J., *The Final Years of British Hong Kong: the Discourse of Colonial Withdrawal.* Hong Kong, 1997

Keay, J., *Last Post: the End of Empire in the Far East.* London, 1997

Lo, C. P., *Hong Kong*. London, 1992

Lo, S.-H., *The Politics of Democratization in Hong Kong*. London, 1997

Morris, J., *Hong Kong: Epilogue to an Empire*. 2nd ed. [of *Hong Kong: Xianggang*]. London, 1993

Patrikeeff, F., *Mouldering Pearl: Hong Kong at the Crossroads*. London, 1989

Roberti, M., *The Fall of Hong Kong: China's Triumph and Britain's Betrayal*. 2nd ed. Chichester, 1997

Roberts, E. V. et al. *Historical Dictionary of Hong Kong and Macau*. Metuchen (NJ), 1993

Scott, I., *Hong Kong:* [Bibliography]. Oxford and Santa Barbara (CA), 1990

Segal, G., *The Fate of Hong Kong*. London, 1993

Shipp, S., *Hong Kong, China: a Political History of the British Crown Colony's Transfer to Chinese Rule*. Jefferson (NC), 1995

Tsang, S. Y., *Hong Kong: an Appointment with China*. London, 1997

Wang, G. and Wong, S. L. (eds.) *Hong Kong's Transition: a Decade after the Deal*. OUP, 1996

Welsh, F., *A History of Hong Kong*. 3rd ed. London, 1997

Wilson, D., *Hong Kong, Hong Kong*. London, 1991

Yahuda, M., *Hong Kong: China's Challenge*. London, 1996

TOURIST AND HOTEL GUIDES

Baedeker Guide: Hong Kong. AA Publishing, 1999

Fodor's 99 Hong Kong (Fodor's Gold Guides). Fodor's Travel Publications, 1999

Frommer's Hong Kong. Macmillan, 1999

Harper, D., *Hong Kong*. Lonely Planet Publications, 1998

Harper, D. and Storey, R., *Hong Kong, Macau and Guangzhou*. Lonely Planet Publications, 1998

MACAO

KEY HISTORICAL EVENTS

Macao was visited by Portuguese traders from 1513 and became a
Portuguese colony in 1557. It was soon a principal entrepôt for international trade with China and Japan. Initially sovereignty remained
vested in China, with the Portuguese paying an annual rent. In 1848–
49 the Portuguese declared Macao a free port and established
jurisdiction over the territory. A Sino-Portuguese treaty of 1 Dec. 1887
confirmed Portuguese rights to the territory. Diversion of its trade to
Hong Kong, and the opening of the treaty ports by China, left Macao
handling only local distributive trade, although its entrepôt role was
briefly revived during the closure of the Hong Kong/China border in
1939. It was an Overseas Province of Portugal from 1951-74. In 1976
it became a Territory under Portuguese administration. On 6 Jan 1987
Portugal agreed to return Macao to China on 20 Dec. 1999 under a
plan in which it would become a special administrative zone of China,
with considerable autonomy.

TERRITORY AND POPULATION

The territory, which lies at the mouth of the Pearl River, comprises a
peninsula (7·84 sq. km) connected by a narrow isthmus to the
People's Republic of China, on which is built the city of Santa Nome
de Deus de Macao, and the islands of Taipa (5·79 sq. km), linked to
Macao by a 2-km bridge, and Colôane (7·82 sq. km) linked to Taipa
by a 2-km causeway. The total area of Macao is 21·45 sq. km. Land is
being reclaimed from the sea. The population (1991 census) was
339,464 (174,858 females). Population on 31 Dec. 1997, 415,850

(215,700 females); density, 19,387 people per sq, km. An estimated 98·8% of the population lived in urban areas in 1995. The official language is Portuguese but Cantonese is used by virtually the entire population.

In Dec. 1993, 19,305 foreigners were legally registered including 12,731 from Hong Kong.

SOCIAL STATISTICS

1997: Births, 5,468 (13·2 per 1,000 population); marriages, 2,106 (5·1); deaths, 1,413 (3·4); divorces, 320 (0·8). Annual growth rate, 1990–95, 4·4%. Infant mortality, 1990–95, 9 per 1,000 live births; fertility rate, 1·6 births per woman.

CLIMATE

Sub-tropical tending towards temperate. The number of rainy days is more than a third of the year. Average annual rainfall varies from 39–79" (1,000-2,000 mm). It is very humid from May to September.

CONSTITUTION AND GOVERNMENT

By agreement with Beijing in 1974, Macao is a Chinese territory under Portuguese administration. An 'organic statute' was published on 17 Feb. 1976. It defined the territory as a collective entity, *pessoa colectiva,* with internal legislative authority which, while remaining subject to Portuguese constitutional laws, would otherwise enjoy administrative, economic and financial autonomy. The Governor is appointed by the Portuguese President, who also appoints up to 7 Under-Secretaries on the Governor's nomination. The Legislative Assembly of 23 deputies, chosen for a 3-year term, comprises 8 members directly elected by universal suffrage, 8 indirectly elected by economic, cultural and social bodies and 7 appointed by the Governor. In April 1990 the Portuguese parliament unanimously approved laws passed by the Legislative Assembly to widen its powers and those of the governor.

RECENT ELECTIONS

At the elections held on 22 Sept. 1996 there were 62 candidates. The business-orientated pro-integration Associação Promotora para a Economia de Macau (Promoting Association for the Economy of Macao) won 2 seats, with 16·6% of the vote, and the pro-Beijing União Promotora para a Progreso (Promoting Union for Progress) also won 2 seats, with 15·2% of the vote. 4 other parties each gained 1 seat. The next elections are due by Sept. 2000.

CURRENT ADMINISTRATION

Governor: Gen. Vasco Rocha Vieira.

ECONOMY

Performance
Real GDP growth was an estimated 3·85% in 1995 and 3·6% in 1996.

Budget
In 1995, revenue was 11,033·8m. patacas and expenditure 10,314·9m. patacas. Provisional figures for 1996 are revenue, 8,569·3m; expenditure, 8,545·1m.

Currency
The unit of currency is the *pataca* (MOP) of 100 *avos* which is tied to the Hong Kong dollar at parity. Inflation was 8·6% in 1995 and an estimated 6·5% in 1996.

Banking and Finance
The bank of issue is the Banco Nacional Ultramarino. The Monetary and Foreign Exchange Authority functions as a central bank (*Director*, António dos Santos Ramos). Commercial business is handled (1993) by 20 banks with 112 branches in Macao, 6 of which are local and 14 foreign (including 4 offshore banking units). Total banks' deposits, 1993, 53,232·6m. patacas (including 4,679·7m. patacas in current and 15,198·3m. patacas in savings accounts).

ENERGY AND NATURAL RESOURCES

Electricity
Installed capacity was 260,000 kW in 1994. Production in 1994 was 1·2bn. kWh. In 1996 the electricity consumption per capita was 3,250 kWh. The net import was 174·0m. kWh.

Fisheries

The catch in 1995 was 1,604 tonnes.

INDUSTRY

The economy is based on gambling and tourism with a light industrial base of textiles and toy-making. In 1996 the number of firms was 1,265 (509 in textiles and clothing). In 1992, output was valued at 14,301,883 patacas. Number of firms (and value of output in 1m. patacas) per sector: textiles, 237 (2,924·40); clothing, 644 (7,316·18); food products, beverages and tobacco, 133 (214·58); paper, paper products, printing and publishing, 137 (306·91); wood and cork, 36 (20·26).

Labour

In 1995 a total of 180,000 people were in employment. In 1996 there was 66·7% employment of which 30·6% were employed in public, social and private services; 27·5%, restaurants and hotels; 20·6%, manufacturing; 7·5%, construction and public works; 6·6%, banks, insurance and services to companies and 7·2% in other employment. Unemployment stood at 4·3%.

INTERNATIONAL TRADE

Imports and Exports

The trade, mostly transit, is handled by Chinese merchants. Imports in 1997 were US$2,079m.; exports, US$2,145m., around 75% of which were textiles and garments.

In 1995, 29% of imports came from Hong Kong and 22% from China. 42% of exports went to USA, 32% to the EU (mainly Germany, France and UK); clothing accounted for 68·2% of exports, textiles for 10·5% and toys 3·6%.

In 1996 exports were valued at 15,898·5m. patacas of which the main products were: textiles and garments, toys, electronics, footwear, cement, travelling articles, ceramic articles and optical products. The main markets were the EU, USA, China, Japan, Hong Kong and Australia. The total imports were 15,930·7m. patacas of which the main products were: foodstuff, beverage and tobacco, other consumer goods, raw materials and semi-manfactured goods, capital goods, fuels and lubricants. The main origins were: EU, USA, China, Japan and Hong Kong.

COMMUNICATIONS

Roads

In 1994 there were 90 km of roads. There were 6,185 traffic accidents in 1993. In 1996 there were 45,206 registered vehicles of which 41,403 were light load and 3,803 heavy load. There were 5,787 vehicles registered during the year. There are 109 cars per 1,000 inhabitants.

Civil Aviation

An international airport opened in Dec. 1995. In 1998 Air Macau flew to Bangkok, Beijing, Chongqing, Fuzhou, Kaohsiung, Manila, Nanjing, Shanghai, Taipei, Wuhan, Xiamen and Zhengzhou. Services were also provided by Air Koryo, China Northern Airlines, China Northwest Airlines, China Southwest, China Yunnan Airlines, EVA Airways, Pacific Airlines, Shanghai Airlines, Singapore Airlines, TAP, Trans Asia Airways, Trans Pacific Air and Xiamen Airways.

Shipping

Macao is served by Portuguese, British and Dutch steamship lines.
Regular services connect Macao with Hong Kong, 65 km to the northeast. In 1995 merchant shipping totalled 2,000 GRT.

Telecommunications

There were 206,154 telephones in 1996 and 188 telex instruments.
In 1995 there were 37,000 cellular phone subscribers, 40,000 PCs
and 7,300 fax machines.

SOCIAL INSTITUTIONS

Justice

There is a judicial district court, a criminal court and an administrative
court with 13 magistrates in all. Appeals lie to
the Court of Appeal and then the Supreme Court, both in
Lisbon.

In 1996 (1995) there were 8,576 (7,181) cases of crimes known to
the police, of which 5,460 (4,618) were against property. There were
625 persons in prison in 1996 (482 in 1995).

Religion

The majority of the Chinese population is Buddhist. About 6% are
Roman Catholic.

Education

In 1992–93 there were 108 schools and colleges and 3,536 teachers.
Numbers of schools and colleges by category: pre-primary, 16 (7
private); pre-primary and primary, 38 (36); private pre-primary, primary and secondary, 14; primary, 10 (3); primary and secondary,

10 (8); private primary and secondary technical, 2; secondary, 8 (6); secondary and teacher training, 1; secondary and tertiary, 1; private secondary and teacher training, 1; teacher training and tertiary, 1; nurses training, 2 (1); tertiary, 7 (1). There were 9 special schools with 72 teachers and 211 enrolments. The University of East Asia, established in 1981 on Taipa, had 1,647 students and 155 teachers in 1991–92.

	1994–95	1995–96		1994–95	1995–96
Total students	93,587	96,846	teacher training	318	338
pre-primary	20,476	19,770	nurses training	172	177
primary	45,153	46,703	Higher education	5,655	6,418
secondary	20,624	22,277	Special education	349	359
secondary technical	1,189	1,163	Adult education	38,456	38,506

Health

In 1993 there were 2 general hospitals (1 private) and 41 health centres (26 private) with 892 beds. In 1995 there were 467 doctors, 22 dentists, 861 nurses and 41 pharmacists. In 1996 there were 517 inhabitants per doctor and 428 per hospital bed.

CULTURE

Broadcasting

One government and a private commercial radio station are in operation on medium-waves broadcasting in Portuguese and Chinese. Number of receivers (1995), 145,000. Macao receives television broadcasts from Hong Kong and in 1984 a public bilingual TV station began operating. There were (1995) 45,000 receivers (colour by PAL).

Press

In 1993 there were 11 daily newspapers (4 in Portuguese and 7 in Chinese) and 16 periodicals (5 in Portuguese and 11 in Chinese).

Tourism

In 1995 there were 7·8m. visitors, but only 2·2m. spent one night or more. In 1996 there were 8·2m. visitors. Receipts totalled US$3·22bn.

FURTHER READING

Direcção de Serviços de Estatística e Censos. *Anuário Estatístico/Yearbook of Statistics Macau in Figures.* Macao, Annual.

Edmonds, R. L., *Macau.* [Bibliography] Oxford and Santa Barbara (CA), 1989

Porter, J., *Macau, the Imaginary City: Culture and Society, 1557 to the Present.* Oxford, 1996

Roberts, E. V., *Historical Dictionary of Hong Kong and Macau.* Metuchen (NJ), 1993

TOURIST AND HOTEL GUIDES

Brown, J., *Hong Kong and Macau: the Rough Guide.* Rough Guides, 1996

Harper, D. and Storey, R., *Hong Kong, Macau and Guangzhou.* Lonely Planet Publications, 1998

TAIWAN

KEY HISTORICAL EVENTS

Five hundred years ago Taiwan was populated by Malay–Polynesian aborigines. The few contacts with China were through refugees from the mainland. Taiwan was christened Ilha Formosa (beautiful island) by Portuguese sailors. They arrived in 1590, establishing a settlement in the north, near Taipei. Taiwan was ceded to Japan by China by the Treaty of Shimonoseki in 1895. After the Second World War the island was surrendered to Gen. Chiang Kaishek who made it the headquarters for his crumbling Nationalist Government. Chiang Kai-shek used the ideology of eventual Kuomintang victory as an excuse for authoritarian, military backed rule and the maintenance of a large standing army on the island. On Chiang Kaishek's death in 1978 he was succeeded by his son, Chiang Ching-Kuo. Until 1970 the US fully supported Taiwan's claims to represent all of China. Only in 1971 did the government of the People's Republic of China manage to replace that of Chiang Kaishek at the UN. In Jan. 1979 the UN established formal diplomatic relations with the People's Republic of China, breaking off all formal ties with Taiwan. Taiwanese fears that USA recognition of China spelt the end of the island's independence were not realized. The US Congress subsequently authorized continuing economic and social ties with Taiwan. Taiwan itself has continued to reject all attempts at reunification, and although there have been frequent threats from mainland China to precipitate direct action (including military manoeuvres off the Taiwanese coast) the prospect of confrontation with the USA supports the status quo.

A devastating earthquake struck Nantou, in central Taiwan, on 20 Sept. 1999, with heavy casualties and causing widespread damage.

TERRITORY AND POPULATION

Taiwan lies between the East and South China Seas about 100 miles from the coast of Fujian. The territories currently under the control of the Republic of China include Taiwan, Penghu (the Pescadores), Kinmen (Quemoy), and the Matsu Islands, as well as the archipelagos in the South China Sea. Off the Pacific coast of Taiwan are Green Island and Orchid Island. To the north-east of Taiwan are the Tiaoyutai Islets. The total area of Taiwan Island, the Penghu Archipelago and the Kinmen area (including the fortified offshore islands of Quemoy and Matsu) is 13,970 sq. miles (36,182 sq. km). Population (1997), 21,740,000. The indigenous Han Chinese are of Fujian origin. Of the population 15% is Hakka and 15% mainland Chinese who came with the Nationalist forces. There are also 389,900 aboriginals of Malay origin. Population density: 601 per sq. km.

Taiwan's administrative units comprise (with 1997 populations): 2 special municipalities: Taipei, the capital (2·60m.) and Kaohsiung (1·44m.); 5 cities outside the county structure: Chiayi (262,822), Hsinchu (351,800), Keelung (379,370), Taichung (901,961), Tainan (717,811); 16 counties (*hsien*): Changhwa (1,277,744), Chiayi (567,695), Hsinchu (421,721), Hualien (358,007), Ilan (466,603), Kaohsiung (1,227,160), Miaoli (560,344), Nantou (546,707), Penghu (91,169), Pingtung (913,764), Taichung (1,447,761), Tainan (1,096,251), Taipei (3,420,535), Taitung (253,002), Taoyuan (1,614,471), Yunlin (757,913).

SOCIAL STATISTICS

In 1997 the birth rate was 1·01%; death rate, 1·22%; rate of growth, 0·8% per annum (2000 target: 0·72% per annum). Life expectancy, 1996: Males, 71·89 years; females, 77·77 years. The death rate was 5·71 per 1,000 persons; infant mortality per 1,000 live births, 6·66.

CLIMATE

The climate is subtropical in the north and tropical in the south. The typhoon season extends from July to Sept. The average monthly temperatures of Jan. and July in Taipei are 59·5°F (12·9°C) and 83·3°F (33·8°C) respectively, and average annual rainfall is 83·8" (2,080·4 mm). Kaohsiung's average monthly temperatures of Jan. and July are 65·5°F (15°C) and 83·3°F (31·8°C) respectively, and average annual rainfall is 69" (1,732 mm).

CONSTITUTION AND GOVERNMENT

The ROC Constitution is based on the principles formulated by Dr. Sun Yatsen, the founding father of the Republic of China. The ROC government is divided into 3 main levels: central, provincial/munici-pal and county/city each of which has well-defined powers.

The central government consists of the Office of the President, the National Assembly, with 332 seats, and five governing branches called 'yuan', namely the Executive Yuan, the Legislative Yuan (225 seats, increased from 160 for the 1998 elections), the Judicial Yuan, the Examination Yuan and the Control Yuan.

At the provincial level, the provincial governments exercise administrative responsibility. Since the ROC government administers only Taiwan Province and two counties in Fukien Province, only two provincial governments are currently operational – the Taiwan Provincial Government and the Fukien Provincial Government. Taipei and Kaohsiung are special municipalities which are under the direct jurisdiction of the central government. At the local level, under the Taiwan Provincial Government are five city governments: Keelung, Hsinchu, Taichung, Chiayi and Tainan; and 16 county governments with the governments of their subordinate cities. The Fukien Provincial Government oversees the regional affairs of Kinmen County and Lienchiang County. From 5 May to 23 July 1997 the *Additional Articles of the Constitution of the Republic of China* underwent yet another amendment. The roles of the provincial government and the Control Yuan have taken on drastic changes. Under the newest revision:

- The provincial government is to be streamlined and the popular elections of the governor and members of the provincial council are suspended.
- A resolution on the impeachment of the President or Vice President is no longer to be instituted by the Control Yuan but rather by the Legislative Yuan.
- The Legislative Yuan has the power to pass a no-confidence vote against the president of the Executive Yuan, while the president of the Republic has the power to dissolve the Legislative Yuan.
- The president of the Executive Yuan is to be directly appointed by the president of the Republic. Hence the consent of the Legislative Yuan is no longer needed.
- Educational, scientific and cultural budgets, especially the compulsory education budget, will be given priority, but no longer restricted by Article 164 of the Constitution to remain at least 15% of the total national budget.

The governing political party is the Kuomintang (KMT or Nationalist Party) which has its origins in secret societies founded in the late 19th century by Sun Yatsen.

National Anthem

'San Min Chu I'; words by Dr Sun Yatsen, tune by Cheng Mao-yun.

RECENT ELECTIONS

Presidential elections are due in March 2000. Elections to the Legislative Yuan were held on 5 Dec. 1998. The Kuomintang (KMT or Nationalist Party) is in power. It increased its majority in the legislature, winning 124 of the 225 seats. Voter turn-out in the 2 biggest cities, Taipei and Kaohsiung, was over 80%. At the National assembly elections on 23 March 1996 the Kuomintang won 183 of the 332 seats, Min-chu Chin-pu Tang 99, Hsin-Tang 46, Green Party Taiwan 1, and non-partisans and others 3.

CURRENT ADMINISTRATION

President: Lee Teng-hui (b. 1923; sworn in 20 May 1996).

Vice President: Lien Chan (b. 1936).

The cabinet comprised the following in March 1999:

Prime Minister and *President of the Executive Yuan:* Vincent C. Siew. There are 8 ministries under the Executive Yuan: Interior; Foreign Affairs; National Defence; Finance; Education; Justice; Economic Affairs; Transport and Communications.

Vice-President, Executive Yuan: Liu Chao-shiuan.

President, Control Yuan: Wang Tso-yung.

President, Examination Yuan: Hsu Shui-teh.

President, Judicial Yuan: Weng Yueh-sheng.

President, Legislative Yuan: Wang Jin-ping.

Minister of Foreign Affairs: Jason Hu. *National Defence:* Tang Fei. *Interior:* Huang Chu-wen. *Finance:* Paul Chiu. *Education:* Lin Ching-chiang. *Economic Affairs:* Wang Chih-kang. *Justice:* Yeh Chin-fong; *Transport and Communications:* Lin Feng-cheng.

In addition to the Mongolian and Tibetan Affairs Commission and the Overseas Chinese Affairs Commission, a number of commissions and subordinate organizations have been formed with the resolution of the Executive Yuan Council and the Legislature to meet new demands and handle new affairs. Examples include the Environmental Protection Administration, which was set up in 1987 as public awareness of pollution control rose; the Mainland Affairs Council, which was established in 1990 to handle the thawing of relations between Taiwan and the Chinese mainland; the Fair Trade Commission, which was established in 1992 to promote a fair trade system; and the Consumer Protection Commission, which was set up in July 1994 to study and review basic policies on consumer protection. Since 1995 even more commissions have been set up to provide a wider scope of services: the Public Construction Commission was set up in July 1995, the Council of Aboriginal Affairs in Dec. 1996, and the National Sports Council in July 1997.

These commissions and councils are headed by:

Aborigines Commission: Hua Chia-chih. *Agricultural Council:* Peng Tso-kuei. *Atomic Energy Council:* Hu Ching-piao. *Central Election Commission:* Lin Feng-cheng. *Consumers Protection Committee:* Hsu Li-teh. *Cultural Planning and Development Council:* Lin Chung-chih. *Economic Planning and Development Council:* Chiang Pin-kung. *Fair Trade Commission:* Chao Ching-yang. *Labour Affairs Council:* Hsu Shieh-kwei. *Mainland Affairs Council:* Chang King-yuh. *Mongolian and Tibetan Affairs Commission:* Kao Koong-lian. *National Palace Museum:* Chin Hsiao-yi. *National Research, Development and Evaluation Commission:* Huang Ta-chou. *National Science Council:* Huang Chen-tai. *National Youth Commission:* Lee Chi-chu. *Overseas Chinese Affairs Commission:* Chiao Jen-ho. *Physical Education and Sports Commission:* Nancy Chao Li-yun. *Public Construction Commission:* Ou Chin-teh. *Research, Development and Evaluation Commission:* Yang Chou-hsiang. *Vocational Assistance for Retired Servicemen Commission:* Gen. Yang Ting-yung.

DEFENCE

Conscription is for 2 years. Taiwan has more than 4m. soldiers (mostly reserves).

Defence expenditure in 1997 totalled US$13,657m. (US$634 per capita). In 1997 Taiwan spent US$7·3bn. on defence imports (up from US$1·8bn. in 1996), making it the world's second largest buyer of arms, mainly from the USA and France. Only Saudi Arabia spends more on international arms purchases.

Army

The Army numbered about 230,300 in 1998, including 21,000 military police. In 1997 it consisted of 10 infantry divisions, 2 mechanized infantry divisions, 2 airborne brigades, 6 independent armoured brigades, 1 tank group and 2 surface-to-air missile battalions. The aviation element comprises 6 squadrons with about 100 transport and 65 armed helicopters. The primary weapon systems of the ROC ground forces include M48H and M60A3 tanks; M109 and M110 self-propelled artillery; M113, V150, and CM–21 armoured personnel carriers; UH–1H helicoptors; Kung-feng 6A rocket systems; TOW–type anti-tank guided weapons; chapparal SP, Hawk, Tien-kung (Sky Bow), and Tien-chien (Sky Sword) air defence missile systems; and Hsiung-feng I and Hsiung-feng II anti-ship missile systems.

Navy

Active personnel in 1998 totalled 33,000 in the Navy and 30,000 in the Marine Corps. There are over 67,500 naval and marine reservists. The operational and land-based forces consist of destroyer fleets, a frigate fleet, amphibious landing fleet and amphibious landing vessel fleet, anti-submarine helicopter group etc. The Navy's coastal SAM batteries employ Hsiung-feng missiles which resemble US Harpoon missiles. The Knox-class missile frigates are rented from the US Navy, La Fayette (Kang-ting) frigates are imported from France, and the Cheng-kung frigates are built in Taiwan.

The Naval Air Command operates 31 S-2 Tracker aircraft, 12 small anti-submarine helicopters operated from the destroyers, and 12 SH-2F and 10 S-70 Seahawk helicopters based ashore.

The Customs service operates 12 cutters.

Air Force

Units in the operational system are equipped with aircraft that include locally developed IDF, F–16, Mirage 2000–5 and F–5E fighter-interceptors, C–130H and C–119 transporters, AT–3 trainers, and S–70C helicoptors. The ROC Army will spend over US$385m. to deploy 200 fourth-generation Patriot missiles. Patriot missiles are installed in missile batteries around Taiwan. Total strength in 1996, 68,000 personnel.

INTERNATIONAL RELATIONS

By a treaty of 1 Dec. 1954 the USA was pledged to protect Taiwan, but this treaty lapsed 1 year after the USA established diplomatic relations with the People's Republic of China on 1 Jan. 1979. In April 1979 the Taiwan Relations Act was passed by the US Congress to maintain commercial, cultural and other relations between USA and Taiwan through the American Institute on Taiwan and its Taiwan counterpart, the Taipei Economic and Cultural Representative Office in the USA, which were accorded quasi-diplomatic status in 1980.

The People's Republic took over the China seat in the UN from Taiwan on 25 Oct. 1971.

In May 1991 Taiwan ended its formal state of war with the People's Republic.

As of Dec. 1998 the ROC has formal diplomatic ties with 27 countries and maintains substantive relations with over 100 countries and territories around the globe.

In Sept. 1997 at the invitation of the Panamanian government, President Lee participated in the World Congress on the Panama Canal. In the wake of the visit to Panama, President Lee travelled to 3 other nations: Honduras, El Salvador and Paraguay. At a summit meeting with leaders of 6 Latin American nations held in El Salvador, the ROC was invited to join the System of Central American Integration, a regional grouping modelled after the European Union, which is known by its Spanish acronym SICA.

ECONOMY

Policy

As regional economic blocs take shape, Taiwan plans to develop itself into an operations centre for the Asia-Pacific region over the next 10 years. The plan calls for 6 operations centres to handle high value-added manufacturing, air and sea cargo and passenger transportation, and professional services.

Performance

Though Taiwan was less affected by the Asian crisis than many of its neighbours, the forecast for GDP growth in 1999 was just 4·74%, and the government announced that, after the previous year's figure of 4·83%, economic expansion was at its weakest for 16 years. Between 1990 and 1997 growth was around 6% each year.

Budget

There are 2 budgets, the central government's general budget together with some special defence and infrastructure appropriations and the provincial budget for Taiwan proper. For the fiscal year July 1997–June 1998 the central government's general budget was NT$1,253,440m. Expenditure planned: 21·2% on defence; 9·8% on economic development; 12·8% on social security; 15·8% on education, science and culture. Foreign exchange reserves were US$86,558m. in Oct. 1998.

Currency

The unit of currency is the *New Taiwan dollar* (TWD) of 100 *cents*. Gold reserves were 13·57m. oz. in Oct. 1998. Inflation was forecast at 1·65% between Jan. and Nov. 1998.

Banking and Finance

The Central Bank of China (reactivated in 1961) regulates the money supply, manages foreign exchange and issues currency. *Governor:* Perng Fai-nan. The Bank of Taiwan is the largest commercial bank and the fiscal agent of the government. The number of financial institutions totalled 6,257 in Oct. 1998. Banks in Taiwan have the lowest bad-loan ratios in Asia.

There are 2 stock exchanges in Taipei.

ENERGY AND NATURAL RESOURCES

Electricity

Output of electricity in 1997 was 133bn. kWh; total installed capacity was 25,735 MW, comprising 63·4% thermal, 20% nuclear and 16·7% hydro-electric. There are 3 nuclear power stations (capacities 1·72m., 1·97m. and 1·9m. kW) and a fourth is envisaged. Consumption per capita stood at 3,627 litres of oil equivalent in 1997.

Oil and Gas

Refined oil production in 1997 was 37·9m. kilolitres; natural gas, 901m. cu. metres.

Minerals

In 1997 coal production was 0·1m. tonnes.

Agriculture

The cultivated area was 864,817 ha in 1997, of which 364,000 ha were paddy fields. Rice production totalled 1,660,000 tonnes in 1996.

In 1996 livestock production was valued at more than US$3,200m., accounting for 38·18% of Taiwan's total agricultural production value. However, the outbreak of foot and mouth disease in March 1997 posed a major threat to Taiwan's pork industry. A total of 6,147 hog farms in 20 cities and counties along Taiwan's west coast were stricken by the disease. The government soon exterminated all hogs at contaminated farms and imported 21m. doses of vaccine for healthy ones. Pork exports were banned and the outbound shipment of 105 kinds of products from cloven-hoofed animals were also prohibited. The government compensated pig farmers for their slaughtered animals and provided relief to both farmers and pork exporters in the form of US$1,100m. in low-interest loans. The Executive Yuan also allocated a special budget of US$378m. for relevant government agencies to carry forward remedial measures. Accordingly, the disease was soon brought under control and the wholesale price of pork rebounded to the normal level.

Forestry

Forest area, 1996: 2,102,311 ha. Forest reserves: trees, 358,239,000 cu. metres; bamboo, 1,127m. poles. Timber production, 35,603 cu. metres.

Fisheries

By 1997 Taiwan's fishing fleet totalled 28,164 vessels (of which 13,194 were powered craft); the catch was approximately 900,000 tonnes. In 1997 Taiwan produced US$2,800m. worth of fish. Of this, 50% came from deep-sea fishing, 28% from aquaculture, 17% from offshore fishing and 4% from coastal fishing. More than 33% of the catch was exported, with the biggest items being skipjack and eel.

INDUSTRY

Output (in tonnes) in 1997 (and 1996): Steel bars, 7·3m. (6·8m.); sugar, 0·35m. (0·36m.); cement, 21·5m. (21·5m.); pulp, 0·35m. (0·31m.); cotton fabrics, 836,60 sq. metres; computers, 4·6m. portable (3·4m.) and 9·1m. desktop (5·1m.).

Labour

In the third quarter of 1998, the total labour force was 9·6m., of whom 9·3m. were employed. Of the employed population, 8·93% worked in agriculture, forestry and fisheries; 37·63% in industry (including 27·95% in manufacturing and 9·2% in construction); and 53·44% in the service sector (including 21·97% in commerce and 15·83% in social and personal services). The unemployment rate was 2·98%.

INTERNATIONAL TRADE

Restrictions on the repatriation of investment earnings by foreign nationals were removed in 1994.

Taiwan has the world's third-largest foreign reserves and one of the world's lowest foreign debts.

Imports and Exports

Total trade, in US$1m.:

	1992	1993	1994	1995	1996	1997
Imports	72,007	77,061	85,359	103,551	102,371	114,425
Exports	81,470	84,917	93,056	111,659	115,951	122,081

In 1997 the main export markets were the USA (24·2%), Hong Kong (23·5%), Japan (9·6%) and Singapore (4·0%). The main import suppliers were Japan (25·4%), the USA (20·9%), Germany (4·7%) and South Korea (4·4%).

Principal exports in 1997, in US$1bn.: Textiles, 16·66; basic metals and articles, 11·53; machinery, 58·99; plastic and rubber products, 7·71; vehicles and transport equipment, 5·59; footwear, headwear and umbrellas, 1·40; toys, games, sports equipment, 2·38.

Principal imports in 1997, in US$1bn.: Basic metals and articles, 11·67; chemicals, 11·44; machinery, 41·12; minerals, 10·30; vehicles and transport equipment, 5·36; textile products, 3·65; precision instruments, clocks and watches, musical instruments, 6·38.

COMMUNICATIONS

Roads

In 1997 there were 20,144 km of roads. 15·3m. motor vehicles were registered including 4·4m. passenger cars, 22,522 buses, 811,023 trucks and 10m. motor cycles. 1,163m. passengers and 277m. tonnes of freight were transported (including urban buses).

Rail

In Dec. 1997 total route length was 2,363 km. Freight traffic amounted to 16·9m. tonnes and passenger traffic to 165m. in 1997.

Civil Aviation

There are 2 international airports: Chiang Kaishek at Taoyuan near Taipei, and Kaohsiung in the south. In addition there are several domestic airports: Taipei, Hualien, Taitung, Taichung, Tainan, Chiayi, Pingtung, Makung, Chimei, Orchid Island, Green Island, Wangan, Kinmen and Peikan. In Oct. 1997 there were 17 domestic airlines, of which 4 are international carriers: China Airlines (CAL), EVE Airways Corp. (EVA AIR), Mandarin Airlines (MDA; CAL's subsidiary) and Trans Asia Airways (TNA) operate international services to 42 destinations in 27 countries. 35 foreign airlines also operate services. In 1996, 52m. passengers and 1·2m. tonnes of freight were flown. To accommodate this heavier air passenger and cargo traffic a US$800m. expansion project at Chiang Kaishek International Airport began in 1989. The project includes a second passenger terminal, aircraft bays, airport connection roads, car parks and the expansion of air freight facilities. The facilities are designed to allow the airport to handle an additional 14m. passengers annually by the year 2010.

Shipping

Maritime transportation is vital to the trade-oriented economy of Taiwan. As of Dec. 1996 the ROC's shipping industry had a fleet of 255 vessels over 100 gross tons, for a total of 9·14m. dead weight tons. There are 6 international ports: Kaohsiung, Keelung, Hualien, Taichung, Anping and Suao. The first 2 are container centres. Suao port is an auxiliary port to Keelung.

Telecommunications

In 1997 there were 11m. telephones, 1,253,987 mobile phones and 2,496,090 radio pager subscribers. There were approximately 2·8m. Internet users in Sept. 1998. PCs numbered 1,773,000 in 1995 (83 per 1,000 inhabitants).

SOCIAL INSTITUTIONS

Religion

There were 4·51m. Taoists in 1997 with 8,557 temples and 33,200 priests; 4·86m. Buddhists with 3,938 temples and 9,200 priests; 0·42m. Protestants; and 0·3m. Catholics.

Education

Since 1968 there has been compulsory education for 6–15 year olds with free tuition. The illiteracy rate dropped to 5·99% in 1995 and is still falling. In 1997–98 there were 2,540 elementary schools with 92,104 teachers and 1,905,690 pupils; 1,151 secondary schools with 99,411 teachers and 1,874,747 students; 139 schools of higher education, including 38 universities, 40 colleges and 61 junior colleges, with 38,806 teachers and 856,186 students. More than one-quarter of the total population attended an educational institution.

Health

In 1997 there was 1 physician serving every 844 persons, 1 doctor of Chinese medicine per 6,903 persons and 1 dentist per 2,866 persons. Some 126,162 beds were provided by the 97 public and 653 private hospitals, averaging nearly 56 beds per 10,000 persons. In addition to the 497 public and 19,113 private clinics, there were 368 health stations and 502 health rooms serving residents in the sparsely populated areas. Acute infectious diseases were no longer the number one killer. Malignant neoplasms, cerebrovascular diseases, accidents and adverse effects, and heart diseases were the first 4 leading causes of death.

Welfare

A universal health insurance scheme came into force in March 1995 as an extension to the incorporation of 13 social insurance plans which only cover 59% of Taiwan's population. Premium shares among the government, employer and insured are varied according to the insured statuses. By the end of 1997 about 20·49m. people or 96·27% of the population were covered by the National Health Insurance programme. The 7·99m. new beneficiaries are mainly the elderly, children, students and housewives.

CULTURE

Broadcasting

At Dec. 1998 there were 91 radio stations, 4 commercial TV services and 102 cable systems. June 1997 saw the inauguration of a fourth over-the-air television station – The Kaohsiung-based Formosa Television – which is affiliated with the opposition Democratic Progressive Party and telecasts on VHF low-band. A Public Television Law was promulgated on 18 June 1997.

Cinema

In 1998 cinemas numbered 232. In 1997, 29 full-length films were made.

Press

There were 241 domestic news agencies, 354 newspapers and 5,898 periodicals in 1998.

Tourism

In 1997, 2,372,232 tourists visited Taiwan and 6,161,932 Taiwanese made visits abroad.

FURTHER READING

Statistical Yearbook of the Republic of China. Taipei, annual. *The Republic of China Yearbook.* Taipei, annual. *Taiwan Statistical Data Book.* Taipei, annual. *Annual Review of Government Administration, Republic of China.* Taipei, annual.

Arrigo, L. G. et al. *The Other Taiwan: 1945 to the Present Day.* New York, 1994

Cooper, J. F., *Historical Dictionary of Taiwan.* Metuchen (NJ), 1993

Gälli, A., *Taiwan ROC: A Chinese Challenge to the World.* London, 1987

Gold, T. B., *State and Society in the Taiwan Miracle.* Armonk, 1986

Hughes, C., *Taiwan and Chinese Nationalism: National Identity and Status in International Society.* London, 1997

Lee, S.-Y., *Money and Finance in the Economic Development of Taiwan.* London, 1990

Lee, W.-C., *Taiwan* [Bibliography]. Oxford and Santa Barbara (CA), 1990

Liu, A. P. L., *Phoenix and the Lame Lion: Modernization in Taiwan and Mainland China, 1950–1980.* Stanford, 1987

Long, S., *Taiwan: China's Last Frontier.* London, 1991

Moody, P. R., *Political Change in Taiwan: a Study of Ruling Party Adaptability.* New York, 1992

Tsang, S. (ed.) *In the Shadow of China: Political Developments in Taiwan since 1949.* Farnborough, 1994

Tsang, Steve and Tien, Hung-Mao, *Democratisation in Taiwan.* Macmillan, London 1999

TOURIST AND HOTEL GUIDES

Storey, R., *Taiwan.* Lonely Planet Publications, 1998

National library: National Central Library, Taipei (established 1986).

HuA bao

ll Craft Store

The Powerholders

David Kipnis

The Powerholders

The University of Chicago Press
Chicago and London

DAVID KIPNIS is professor of psychology
at Temple University. He is the author of
Character Structure and Impulsiveness
and numerous journal articles.

The University of Chicago Press,
Chicago 60637
The University of Chicago Press,
Ltd., London

© 1976 by The University
of Chicago
All rights reserved.
Published 1976
Printed in the United States
of America

80 79 78 77 76   987654321

Library of Congress Cataloging in Publication Data

Kipnis, David.
    The powerholders.

    Includes bibliographical references and index.
    1. Control (Psychology)   I. Title.
BF632.5.K56   301.15'5'019   75-43230
ISBN 0-226-43731-0

To Andrew and Elliot

Contents

Preface

Modern technology, modern communication systems, and the accumulation by individuals, corporations, and states of enormous amounts of "slack" capital provide a surprisingly large number of people with occupations in which they make decisions that affect the lives of still larger numbers of other people. Moreover, people can make these decisions without once having seen or known personally those whose lives are being influenced.

Thus persons can be hired, fired, placed under surveillance, drafted into the military, moved to new cities, required to learn new skills, or have their tastes and values subtly altered without once meeting those whose interests are served by such changes. Each party then is cushioned from the other by time, space, and technology. For many persons, power appears to be exercised without human feelings being at all important.

It is only when forces of resistance are mobilized in response to some particularly gross act of influence that we obtain firsthand knowledge of the actors who are in positions of power. For instance, the recent articles in the public media reporting the Vietnam War and the political scandals of the second Nixon administration revealed the very human motives underlying the seemingly impersonal decisions that were made.

We can conclude from these brief insights that, despite the fact that modern-day exercises of power appear to be devoid of human content, there is much that psychologists can learn from examining this process. The observations on the use of power that are given in this book are based on the assumption that the exercise of power is an important concern for many people.

There are two themes here; broadly speaking, the first examines how power is used, and the second examines what happens to powerholders as a result of using power. The book is intended to provide a conceptual framework for viewing these events. Wherever possible I have based my conclusions on my own research or on research done by others who deal with these topics. Since empirical research by psychologists is sparse, I have frequently made educated guesses concerning the psychological processes that are involved. In addition I have included materials from other social science disciplines. These sources help show that power is a central concern of all people. Scores of scholars from Thomas Hobbes in the seventeenth century to Harold Lasswell in our times have viewed the question of power as one of the central issues of society. Basically the major question is, Can individuals who have access to resources needed by others be trusted to use these resources without destructive consequences either for themselves or for others? A related concern examined in this book considers what if any alterations take place in the values of powerholders so that their original humanitarian impulses are replaced by selfish and egoistic ones.

In writing this book, I have foraged among the writings of many social scientists. I hope that I have given credit where it is due. Of particular value in forming my thoughts was an integrative review by Dorwin Cartwright (1965) of what is known about the use of social power.

Many of my colleagues and friends have given generously of their time and knowledge in preparing this book. My good friend Richard Petrow instructed me in the art of writing. Both Louise Kidder and Ralph L. Rosnow provided many comments and criticisms which have been incorporated into the book's content. Much of my early laboratory research was done in collaboration with Barry Goodstadt, whose contributions I am happy to acknowledge. Parts of chapter 1 were taken from an unpublished article prepared by Goodstadt and myself. Appreciation is expressed to Carolyn Hegeler, who provided editorial assistance in preparing the manuscript, and to Sondra Candeub, who patiently deciphered my writing while typing the final draft of this book. Last, Temple University provided me with small grants of money to conduct research and, more important, the time to write. My thanks, indeed.

1   Introduction

So long as we need the services of others, we are never far from the world of power. This is as true in our day-to-day exchanges with loved ones, friends, and employers as it is of more remote exchanges reported in the press between political and industrial leaders. At times we are the targets of power-based influence attempts, and at other times we are the sources—trying to influence others to do something they normally would prefer not to do.

This is a book about people who are trying to influence others; that is, people who control and use power. I propose to examine the consequences for the powerholder of controlling resources that are needed by others. In particular, the psychological consequences of using power will be explored, rather than the political or economic consequences. Yet, since all social sciences are interrelated and ultimately derive their content from the problems experienced by society, we shall not be able to avoid reaching conclusions that go beyond those of interest to psychology.

Power is a central concept for any attempt to understand social behavior. Most of us like to feel in control of our actions and outcomes. We avoid with contempt and fear the drunk, the addict, and the psychotic, for the simple reason that they do not appear to us to be in control of their own behavior. Indeed, the control of power is considered by many to be a prerequisite for psychosocial development. Persons who do not control material, social, or intellectual resources are generally found by social scientists to act passively and to believe that luck or chance controls their fate. For instance, Rollo May, in his book *Power and Innocence*, suggests that those who are unwilling to exercise power and influence may be condemned to experience unhappiness throughout their lives. At the level of society, most social issues of our time are readily translated into issues of power. What parties are contending? For what resources? Who has friends with influence? Newspaper columnist James Kilpatrick recently noted this when he wrote: "The name of the game is power. Nothing else. Who has power, how he gets it, how power is delegated, how power is restrained, how power is exercised—these are the questions that absorb us." And these are the questions that absorb the interests of many social scientists as well.

Although at one time or another everyone attempts to influence the behavior of others, explicit references to power are considered in bad taste. At best we use "influence" to get our way— never power. Thus the world of power seems remote from the concerns of ordinary people. We often think of power acts as activities reported in public media that are carried out by actors moved by dark and pernicious forces, unlike the forces that motivate ourselves. How is the man in the street to understand the continued incidents of abuse of power reported in the press and television except by assuming that the actors involved were moved by a lust for power and other corrupting forces not encountered in their own daily lives? In the chapters that follow, I will attempt to show that our own subtle influence attempts can in fact be viewed as power acts, with many of the same psychological consequences for how we see ourselves and others that are reported in the media about remote actors holding high office in some distant land.

When the use of power is spoken about approvingly, it is in the context of using one's natural gifts of intelligence and dexterity to defeat unyielding nature. We speak approvingly of the use of power to overcome natural forces, and by so doing increase the comfort of life. Man's flight to the moon, the discovery of how to use electricity, the attempts to use the hydrogen atom as a source of cheap electric power are described in school texts as representing our finest moments. When we speak about exploiting natural forces, most persons can agree with the conclusions of the political scientist Adolph Berle that the use of power is a refuge from chaos. Without the striving to exercise control over forces impinging on our lives, we would not be able to live in society. Intuitively, people know that to deny the existence and importance of power is to invite personal disaster. Yet still, when we seek to increase the comforts of our lives by directly attempting to cause behaviors in our fellow human beings, we feel uneasy. Hence the substitution of more acceptable words such as "social influence," "leadership," or "persuasion" as a means of signaling that we have caused other persons to do what we want.

In this book I propose to examine the use of power from the perspective of the powerholder. My focus on the powerholder is based on the conviction that he plays a critical dual role in social and behavioral change processes. First, as a result of the power he controls he can shape outcomes for others. Even the most ordinary people can change the course of society if they have access to resources that are needed by others. The politician controls patronage, the banker money, the military officer weapons, the college professor the baccalaureate degree. In all instances, access to these resources increases the individual's potential for controlling the behavior of others, and so for shaping society.

A second reason for studying the psychology of the powerholder is that he himself may change because of the resources at his disposal and his use of these resources to change others. As Sigmund Freud pointed out in his description of "countertransference," therapists are often very much influenced by the role they play in therapy sessions and, as a function of such therapy, come to change their feelings toward patients. A somewhat analogous process may be operative among powerholders, who are themselves affected by the act of influencing others.

In order to understand the role of the powerholder in the process of social and self change, it is essential that some systematic and rational meaning be given in the language of psychology to the problems outlined above. In particular there are two major issues involving the use of power that are of concern to psychologists and that shall be examined in this book. The first issue is: What determines how power is used once it has been obtained? That is, what social-psychological forces can be isolated that determine the powerholder's decisions to change another's behavior? For example, what are the circumstances surrounding a father's decision in one instance to threaten his child as a means of obtaining compliance, and in a second instance to spend long hours teaching his child in order to obtain compliance?

The second major issue deals with the question of how the control and use of power can change the powerholder's view of himself and his view of others who are subject to his influence. That such changes occur have been well documented in literature and in history. Furthermore the kinds of forces that seem to bring about such changes are social-psychological forces. They include the fact that the control of power tends to make people more likely to have the "last word," provides them with greater life-satisfactions, and tends to encourage others to flatter them. Needless to say, these events, if repeated often enough, cannot help but cause profound changes in the powerholder's conscious representation of himself and his world.

Despite the importance of these issues, psychology has had surprisingly little to say about the use of power. Almost several decades ago, Dorwin Cartwright (1959) wrote that psychology was "soft on power." By this he meant that psychology was willing to examine such issues as persuasion, leadership, education, and others that involved changing the lives of people but was unwilling to admit that it was in fact studying some of the many faces of power. As a result, to this day, we find comparatively few mentions of the topic *social power* in reference periodicals that list topics studied in psychology.

Moreover, the mainstream of social-psychological thought and research on power has focused on the target of power. That is, it has been concerned with how individuals and groups respond to social forces designed to change beliefs, cognitions, and behavior. With but few exceptions, social psychologists have tended to ignore the person trying to change these beliefs, cognitions, and behavior. In this regard Harvard psychologist Herbert Kelman has observed that psychologists prefer to study the powerless rather than the powerful. That is, psychologists will study the problems of the black minority but, as many critics have noted, do not study the problems of the white majority that produced the minority's problems in the first place. Considerable time and scientific effort have been expended by social scientists determining the conditions under which individual attitudes can be changed and private compliance obtained. Far less time has been spent studying the person doing the persuading. As a result of this emphasis on the target of power, there are large gaps in our knowledge which pertain to some very practical social questions. Let us examine instances where psychologists must remain silent for lack of information.

Organizational use of power. Within work organizations there are known to be wide variations in how managers use their authority to conduct business. In dealing with subordinates, for example, some managers seem to rely heavily on the use of threats and punishments as a means of exacting conformity, while others rely much less on punishments. Why the differences in use of coercive power? Further, the same manager may use threats with one worker but say nothing to a second worker doing equally poor work. Again, why the selectivity in the use cf coercive power by managers? Perhaps we may obtain some insights by asking the managers to justify their actions. If we do this we are likely to hear managers tell us that the worker he threatened was a born troublemaker, while the second worker had a "good deal of promise." If we pursue the matter further, we might find that the second worker spends a lot of time talking to the manager—that is, apple-polishing, a tactic frequently noted in the literature as a way to gain the esteem of a superior (Kipnis 1960; Kipnis and Vanderveer 1971). Then again, we might find that the manager was emotionally upset because of a fight with his boss the day before he threatened the first worker. Obviously, there are many possible factors that could have determined this particular use of power beyond the stated reason that the worker was a "born troublemaker." Unfortunately, social sciences have few generalizations to offer in this area.

Political office. Another arena of power usage about which psychologists have little to say concerns the use and abuse of power in public office. For instance, a recent presentation to the Philadelphia Court of Common Pleas documented an instance in which the president of a local corporation that provided services to city-controlled transportation facilities paid a city official a large amount of money in exchange for certain guarantees from the city. How do we explain this bribery? Psychologists would tend to first ask questions about the president's moral and ethical development, as these might serve to guide his behavior. However, we would probably find that the president had a strong superego and completely accepted the norms and values of our culture as they related to ethical practices. Perhaps a further examination might find that the president had conducted his business in a climate in which "payoffs" were the norm and were not considered unethical behavior. Thus the president's role demanded that he violate the law, since if he refused to participate in the bribery racket his company would not have survived. In this instance we would have to turn our attention from the individual to the cultural context in which the decision to exercise power was carried out.

Furthermore, in both of the above instances we have very little idea of what was happening to the beliefs and values of the manager and the company president as they pursued their day-to-day exercise of power. Did they enjoy seeing others "dance to their tune"? What did they think of themselves as they threatened and bribed? What did they think of the target persons who had complied with their influence attempts? Will they get along with others better or worse as a result of causing them to carry out their wishes? These and similar questions have not received systematic attention in psychology.

Reasons for Not Studying the Powerholder

Some years ago Marwell and Schmitt (1967) defined social behavior as the manipulation of other people to achieve one's own goals and the study of interactions between people as really, the study of how people control each other. This definition suggests that the use of power and influence should be the central focus of study by social psychologists. The fact that it is not deserves comment.

There are several overlapping explanations, I believe, for psychology's lack of concern with the powerholder.

First of all, persons in positions of power resist being studied. It is far easier to carry out research among the labor force than among top business executives. Since people in positions of power tend to control the funding of research, it is most likely that they will encourage research on topics that are of concern to themselves. These might include, for example, building tests to select persons for social roles, or finding the best means of socializing our children. Rarely will they encourage study of themselves. Historians and political scientists are fully aware of the difficulty of obtaining documents that describe the forces shaping the decisions of political leaders. Most of the time these documents are locked away with the proviso that they cannot be made public for thirty to one hundred years after the actor's death. Thus one block to research in this area is the power-holder's penchant for secrecy. Power, then, tends to preserve itself from scrutiny by directing the efforts of potential examiners elsewhere. In fact, one can make fairly shrewd estimates of a person's or group's status and power from the frequency with which he is placed under systematic surveillance. The more he is studied, the less his power.

A second and related reason for the absence of studies of the powerholder has to do with the cultural context in which research originates. Despite the many wars, scandals, and outrages that periodically erupt, one can still argue that most persons in Western society lead comfortable lives. As a result, the goal of persons in society, including behavioral scientists, is to maintain and improve this state of affairs. We want to know how to eliminate delinquency and criminal behavior. We want to improve methods of education and training so that our children as adults can contribute to society and prosper. The goal of psychotherapy is to increase a person's ability to cope with the world rather than to change the patient's world. In this regard Caplan and Nelson (1973) have pointed out that social science usually attempts to change the deviant's behavior rather than the social conditions producing this behavior. The natural assumption is that whatever is causing the patient's defects are his fault rather than society's. In short, when society provides benefits for most of its citizens, an accepted goal of science becomes the devising of means that will bind the individual to his society. This collective goal tends to exclude examining persons who represent society.

A last reason why psychology has not systematically studied the powerholder is that most persons, at most times, hold normative values that stress the importance of accepting legitimate authority. As a result, the act of studying the powerholder has the unpleasant implication that one is challenging authority. Such emotional feelings are less likely to be experienced by the researcher when investigating the *target* of power. Only when society enters a period of crisis and disorganization are social scientists likely to become interested in the person making the decision. To live in an age where the major collective question is, "What went wrong?" leads inevitably to an examination of authority. To live in an age where most persons feel all is right with the world leads to the study of the target of power.

Definition of Power

Social-psychological descriptions of human behavior are plagued by the fact that there may be no single correct perspective from which to view events. If we consider the act of love, for instance, we find that some social scientists choose an "X-rated" description of what is going on behaviorally or physiologically at the moment (e.g., Masters and Johnson 1966). That is, they are concerned with the process of interaction between the parties making love. Still others are concerned with the outcomes of love and analyze the subsequent quality of married life as a function of the initial attractions between the lovers. Others are concerned with the resources of the lovers, such as beauty, wealth, and status, that may have initially attracted each to the other (Walster et al. 1966); and, finally, still others are concerned with a description of the cultural context which produced the particular interaction in the first place.

While the eventual expectation of all researchers is that their particular perspective will dovetail with other views of the same problem, this hardly ever occurs. Lacking both a common vocabulary and a common conceptual frame of reference, each researcher experiences bafflement when attempting to integrate his findings with those of others.

The problems of perspective and boundaries are particularly troublesome when we consider the power act. Like love, we know that power exists, but we cannot agree on a description of it. Pollard and Mitchell (1973) point out that most theories of power offer explanations that cannot be precisely translated into each other's terms. Yet it is difficult to find direct contradictions between them. In commenting on this state of affairs, Cartwright (1965) has suggested that the literature on social power requires the construction of a theory-map to plot the linkages between the various approaches to social influence and power. The theory-map, as sketched by Cartwright, includes identifying the person who exercises power, the methods used by the powerholder to gain compliance, information about the target of power, the target's motives, and the conditions under which the target will oppose or comply with the powerholder's influence attempts. Since this book covers only part of the range of thinking about social power, it is necessary to first describe on Cartwright's map the major approaches to viewing power, so that the reader can understand which areas have been left out of this book.

The Target's Response to Power

Perhaps the most widely accepted treatment of social power is in terms of the outcome of power acts. From this perspective, the focus is on the interaction between two parties, the powerholder and the target person, in which the target person's behavior is given new direction by the powerholder. That is, power is said to be exercised when changes occur in the target person's behavior that can be attributed to the powerholder's influence and that serve the powerholder's interests or intentions (Dahl 1957). Furthermore, these changes would ordinarily not have been carried out by the target person. Thus the elements of a power act include the facts that person A caused person B to do something that B would not do ordinarily. Research stemming from this view tends to focus on when B will comply and when he will resist influence.

Within this focus on the process and outcomes of influence there is considerable variation as to what kinds of acts can properly be labeled as power acts. Some argue that power acts should be limited to the target person's response to force (Bierstedt, 1950). Bachrach and Baratz (1963) have proposed a stringent view of power in which a distinction is made between exacting compliance from a target person through using appeals based upon (a) one's legitimate role, (b) force, (c) influence that involves simple persuasion, and finally (d) threats. The power act in Bachrach and Baratz's view is reserved for the last instance, in which the powerholder causes compliance by threatening to deprive the target person of things he values.

Perhaps the most influential view of power in social psychology was provided by French and Raven (1959) almost two decades ago. The goal of these investigators was to describe the various ways in which "person A could cause person B to do something which was contrary to B's desire." Furthermore, the authors were concerned with the consequences of using various power tactics on: (a) the target person's subsequent liking for the powerholder and (b) the target person's willingness to obey. A critical distinction offered in this regard by French and Raven was whether the power tactic caused public compliance but not private acceptance by the target person, or private acceptance as well. Private acceptance implies that a relatively permanent change in the target's behavior has taken place that will continue independently of the powerholder's influence. Thus, for instance, teachers hope that they can develop a permanent love for scholarship among students, so that their students will continue to study even when teachers no longer assign books to read. The distinction between public and private compliance is perhaps critical in any analysis of the long-range effects of using power. A failure to cause private compliance requires that the powerholder continually monitor the behavior of the target person, producing a situation of mutual distrust and antipathy (Raven and Kruglanski 1970).

The important elements of French and Raven's conception of power include the resources held by the powerholder and the needs, or "motive bases," of the target person. The use of different resources, or power bases in French and Raven's terms, will result in differing amounts of private acceptance and liking for the powerholder. The following classifications of power stem from use of various resources in the French and Raven taxonomy. The reader may note the wide divergence from Bachrach and Baratz's definition, especially with regard to the use of persuasion, legitimacy, and referent power. These bases of power do not rely upon threats and yet are labeled as power acts.

Reward power. The powerholder may influence behavior because he controls rewards that are wanted by the target person. Over a short range, the use of rewards will engender public, but not private, compliance, and the target may regard favorably the powerholder.

Coercive power. The powerholder may influence behavior because he can control the punishments experienced by the target person. Threats engender public, but not private, compliance. However, the use of threats leads to the target person disliking the powerholder.

Legitimate power. The legitimate power of the powerholder stems from internalized values of the target person which dictate that the powerholder, by virtue of his role, has the right to prescribe behavior. The use of legitimate power tends to produce both public and private compliance. The target person tends to view the powerholder with indifference.

Expert power. Expert power is based upon the target person's belief that the powerholder possesses superior knowledge or ability. In terms of compliance and liking, the outcomes are similar to those believed to occur for legitimate power.

Referent power. The powerholder has power because the target person admires him and identifies with him. Thus power can be exercised because the target person wishes to please the powerholder. Use of this power base leads to the most favorable outcomes for the powerholder, according to French and Raven. The target person readily complies with the powerholder, accepts privately his suggestions, and admires him even more for exerting power.

We see that in this view the powerholder can cause changes in the target's behavior through reliance on a variety of means of influence. Successful influence stems from the fact that the power base used is coordinated with some motive of the target. Person A controls some resource to which person B will respond, be it expert knowledge, rewards, or threats. Thus person A can use these resources in exchange for compliance.

French and Raven's approach has the advantage for psychologists of subsuming a wide variety of social-influence acts under the general rubric of power. Furthermore, it focuses the investigator's attention upon the kinds of resources that are available to the powerholder when attempting to influence others. In addition, it provides very specific predictions about the immediate and long-range effects of invoking various bases of power. For example, the use of coercive power will produce public compliance, but not private compliance, in a target person. Reliance on expert power, however, is likely to produce both public and private compliance. A large variety of ingenious laboratory experiments and field studies have been carried out over the last fifteen years to test these predictions. Basically, this research has examined the target person's response to influence acts, as the power base used by the powerholder has varied.

Power as an Exchange of Influence

The previous approach to power focuses mainly on the responses of the target person. The concern is with the reasons for the target's compliance and how the target feels about himself as a result of this compliance. A second major approach to power examines the interactions between two contending parties who vary in the benefits and costs they may provide each other. This approach has been affiliated with a more general conception of human interactions called "exchange theory." Here interpersonal relations are considered social exchanges in which each party's behavior toward the other yields benefits, although often at some costs. Power is seen in this approach as the ability of one person to affect the balance of rewards and costs of the other party. The more one party can adversely affect this ratio without costs to self, the greater the first party's power over the second (Thibaut and Kelley 1959).

This conception of power leads to study of it in terms of bargaining and negotiations (Swingle 1970), or in terms of how the contending parties evolve norms to regulate the use of power (Thibaut and Faucheux 1965), or in terms of how systems of justice and equity serve to guide the distribution of rewards and costs in a power relationship (Emerson 1962). Whatever the particular focus, the core idea is retained of two or more parties attempting to influence each other in order to get the most for the least cost. Furthermore, the emphasis is on rationality. Both parties, it is assumed, are guided in their negotiations by logically working out how to maximize gains and minimize costs. The literature in this area does not examine in any depth the emotional feelings of the persons contending for control, except as these emotional feelings distort a person's ability to reach logical conclusions (Brown 1970; Tedeschi, Schlenker, and Bonoma 1973). The darker forces that may be generated by the exercise of power (Zimbardo 1970) tend to be left unexamined, or considered simply unnecessary "noise" in the process of conflict negotiation.

An "End-Run" Approach to Power

In terms of Cartwright's theory-map of the terrain of power, we have so far charted the region that deals with the interaction between the powerholder and the target person, or with two parties struggling for control of some desired outcome. Many people think of these kinds of situations when they are asked to define power.

There are several problems, however, in defining power in terms of its outcomes for one or both persons. One basic problem is that it is very difficult, outside of the laboratory, to decide when a target person's behavior was "caused" by the powerholder and when in fact the target person was acting independently of the powerholder but on a parallel course (Dahl 1957; Gamson 1968). For instance, Dahl (1957) provides us with an instance of a Senator X, whose vote on any congressional bill is perfectly correlated with whether or not the bill passes. On the surface it would appear that Senator X exerts considerable influence with his colleagues. However, Dahl points out that Senator X may first informally poll the sentiments of his colleagues and then vote the way he predicts the majority would. Thus rather than exerting influence, he is in fact being influenced by others.

In psychology, a good example of this problem of deciding whether the actions of the powerholder changed the behavior of the target person can be found in attempts to evaluate the outcomes of psychotherapy. The difficulty here is in deciding when the therapist's advice and counsel in fact caused the client to change his behavior and when the observed changes were due to the effects of other influences simultaneously acting on the client.

A second problem with focusing on the process and outcomes of power is that the image of the powerholder is blurred. We don't know what motivated him in the first place, nor do we have a psychological profile of what he is like. All we know is that by using various strategies of influence he was successful in getting the target to do what was wanted.

Because of these two difficulties—the inability to measure satisfactorily the effects of power and the need to bring the powerholder into sharper focus—several investigators (e.g., Cartwright 1965; Mott 1970) have attempted what Gamson (1968) calls an "end run" approach to the study of power. Instead of examining the outcomes of influence, Gamson suggests, examine the behavior of the powerholder in terms of how he attempts to influence others and the kinds of resources he possesses. This shift in emphasis moves the center of study from the behavior of the target to the behavior of the powerholder.

As Gamson points out, it is far easier objectively to determine the capabilities or the resources of the powerholder and the frequency with which he attempts to exert influence, than it is to determine whether or not influence has caused changes in the target's behavior.

It is precisely these sets of questions that are examined in this book. Thus the reader should recognize that when mention is made of the exercise of power, I am referring to the powerholder's attempts to influence others. Whether or not the target person complies is an issue which will not be examined. Discussions pertaining to the circumstances under which target persons comply to power acts may be found in books edited by Dorwin Cartwright (1959) and by James Tedeschi et al. (1973). In terms of Cartwright's map of power, this book will describe the region concerned with the people and the events that set the stage for the moment when the target of power must decide what he is going to do.

2   The Power Act: A Descriptive Model

There is no one theory of power usage but a multitude of overlapping descriptions. Even when we seem to fully understand the forces shaping the decisions of the powerholders, a slight shift in perspective can reveal new and at times even contradictory information about their actions. For example, the political scientist Harold Lasswell has continually pointed out the importance of early childhood experiences of political figures in shaping their adult actions. In his view, powerholders' actions are determined to a fair extent by the kinds of deprivations they experienced as children. Yet C. Wright Mills (1956) in his analysis of powerholders offers equally compelling arguments that we can gain better understanding of the use of power by examining the resources controlled by individual powerholders; still other social scientists (A. Berle 1967; P. Zimbardo 1969) suggest that the use of power cannot be understood without considering the restraints elaborated by society to govern its use.

Cartwright (1965) has provided what may be the most useful clarification of the many views of power. This chapter will present a descriptive model of the power act from the point of view of the powerholder that is a partial adaptation of Cartwright's system, with additions by the present author. The model does not attempt to integrate the various views of power that have been described in the first chapter. It does provide the reader with (in Cartwright's term) a theory-map of the terrain of power, as this terrain is seen by powerholders. The model is summarized in figure 1. It is basically an attempt to describe the chain of events that culminates in the decision of the powerholder to invoke his resources as a means of exercising power.

Power Motivation

We start at Step 1, with the initial motivations of the powerholder to influence others. We can begin by asking why power is exercised. That is, why does a powerholder want to make a target do something he ordinarily would not do? Why does he want to change the behavior of others? The answer originates, of course, in people's dependence on others to mediate important outcomes for themselves. When this dependence on others is combined with the belief that others are unwilling to provide what is wanted, then the powerholder experiences an inclination to influence others, and so gain satisfaction. We designate these inclinations to influence others as power motivations. *Power motivations arise when an individual experiences an aroused need state that can only be satisfied by inducing appropriate behaviors in others.* Power motivations are reduced when the target performs the desired behavior.

This definition of power motivation is an extension of Lewin's definition of power as the "possibility of inducing forces in another person." However, the idea of satisfying personal wants is stressed here, in that the individual is inducing forces in another person in order to achieve some personal goal. Stress is also placed on the term "induction." The definition assumes that the target will not respond appropriately without some urging by the powerholder. As a trivial example, if A's back itches and he is willing to scratch it himself, or others willingly do so, no power motivations are involved. If, however, the itching can only be relieved by having to convince someone else to do the scratching, then power motivation would be involved. (Minton [1972] has also defined power motivation as the need to obtain social compliance and thus achieve intended effects.) Power motives, then, are least likely to arise when the relations are between persons who freely give to each other, without hesitation, and out of

1. Power Motivation
　　Aroused need state satisfied by
　　appropriate behaviors in others.
2. Request for Compliance
3. Resources
4. Region of Inhibition
　　Physiological
　　Values
　　Costs
　　Self-confidence
　　Institutional norms
　　Culture
5. Means of Influence
　　Persuasion
　　Threats
　　Promises
　　Rewards
　　Force
　　Ecological change

Target's Motivations and Resources ► **6. Response of Target**
　　Compliance
　　Private acceptance
　　Self-esteem
　　Esteem for powerholder
7. Consequences for the Powerholder
　　Changes in need state
　　Self-perceptions
　　Perception of target
　　Changes in values

Fig. 1. A Descriptive Model
of the Power Act

mutual affection. (Schermerhorn 1961). They are most likely to arise in the absence of such mutual feelings.

Power motives are also less likely to arise when the individual has reached a point in life when his psychological needs can be satisfied by his own actions rather than by the actions of other people. Maslow (1955) makes this point in his discussions of differences between persons seeking to satisfy higher-order needs and lower-order needs. Maslow points out that the "needs for safety, belongingness, love relations, and respect can only be satisfied by other people, i.e., from outside the person. . . . In contrast, the self-actualizing individual, by definition gratified in his basic needs, is far less dependent, far less beholden, far more autonomous and self-directed. Far from needing other people, growth-motivated people may actually be hampered by them" (p 127).

Maslow goes on to point out that since self-actualizing people depend less on other people, they are less ambivalent about them, less hostile, and less anxious. In short, to the extent persons have extensive needs which require the service of others, stresses and strains occur in interpersonal relations. In our own research, support has been obtained for Maslow's views in that we have found that the process of inducing behaviors in others appears to cause distortions of the powerholder's perceptions of others (Kipnis 1972).

Origins of Power Motives

Power motives can be classified in many ways depending upon the particular personal wants that the individual is seeking to satisfy through influencing other people.

Let us briefly examine some of the more important reasons why power motivations may be aroused. By so doing we can distinguish between different conceptions of power motivation as these are currently emphasized in the literature.

Power motivation as irrational impulse. Power motivation is frequently defined in psychology as gaining satisfaction from manipulating and influencing others. When defined in this way, the act of manipulation is seen as both the means and the end in itself. In essence, the powerholder derives satisfaction from perceiving that he has shaped outcomes for others, either because he derives enjoyment from these activities (Christie and Geis 1970; McClelland 1969) or because such activities allow him to avoid feelings of weakness and loss of control (Adler 1956; Fromm 1959; Veroff and Veroff 1972). Dynamically oriented psychologists have variously ascribed the origins of the need to influence others to either the developing individuals way of responding to an absence of love (Fromm 1959), or to his feeling of inferiority (Adler 1958), or to continual anxiety (Horney 1950). It should come as no surprise that when we talk of power motivations in terms of gaining satisfactions from influencing others many people see power needs as representing the irrational, neurotic, and perverted aspects of man's nature.

Power motivation as role behavior. A second and more pervasive reason why people attempt to influence others' behavior derives from their involvement in their institutional roles. Here, the needs to be satisfied originate in the individual's desire to do his work well. When the powerholder perceives that other persons in his "role set" (Kahn et al. 1964) are behaving in ways that interfere with the goals of the organization, feelings of distress are aroused within the powerholder which subsequently lead to attempts by him to correct this deviant behavior. It is important to note that, under these circumstances, the powerholder may not experience any personal satisfaction from influencing others and indeed may find the act of influencing distasteful (Milgram 1963). In a sense the individual is trapped by his own loyalties to legitimate authority; he discovers that it is almost impossible to ignore the demands of authority.

When power motivations arise as a result of institutional involvement, the individual frequently finds himself forced to deliver noxious stimuli to a target in order to influence his behavior. On the surface, the individual should experience shame and guilt over his own action, and over time he should refuse to continue this kind of influence. Yet, this rarely happens.

What mechanisms allow individuals in their institutional roles to carry out behaviors that they would personally condemn if done outside the institution? The answer appears to be that the individual believes that the institution has granted him absolution for his acts. Since the individual perceives that he has no choice but to obey, he also sees himself as not being responsible for the suffering he causes. He views himself as a "pawn" rather than as an "origin of behavior," to borrow DeCharms' (1968) phraseology. Blame, if placed, is directed toward the institution, the rationalization being that "If I don't do it, someone else will." Thus, the banker who forecloses, the instructor who flunks a student, the supervisor who makes a worker redo his work, the mother who spanks, may all believe themselves absolved from blame because they are "doing their duty".

Power motivation as instrumental behavior. A third and equally important explanation of why people are motivated to use power arises from the fact that the induction of behavior in others can be instrumental in obtaining rewards for oneself. This source of power motives is frequently associated with the view that power motivation is a universal attribute of human beings (e.g., Hobbes and, more recently, Mulder, 1963). When this attribute is viewed as a universal drive, the emphasis is on the pursuit of resources which in turn enhance each individual's ability to influence others and to enjoy the "good life." In contrast, there is a deemphasis on the enjoyment of seeing others "dance to your tune."

Cartwright (1965) describes this version of power motivation as follows: "All men seek to influence others and to strive for positions of influence, because they seek certain objectives whose attainments require the exercise of influence" (p. 7). Both the criminal's need for money and the lonely man's need for affection can only be satisfied by convincing someone else to take appropriate actions, that is, to part with money in the first instance and return affection in the second.

In summary, power motivations arise when people have needs that can be satisfied only by inducing appropriate behavior in others. Three reasons why these motivations arise have been described. It is proper to assume that the three reasons mentioned here can overlap. In addition to his need for money, the criminal may come to enjoy frightening his victims and seeing them grovel. The police officer may use the authority of his office to "finagle" a bribe from a motorist. There are obviously many other reasons for the motivations to arise. Frequently, the mere possession of these resources can instigate new needs, setting up an endless procession of reasons for influencing others. We stress, however, that what is common to all these reasons is the fact that they can be satisfied only by inducing appropriate behaviors in others.

Request for Compliance

Given an aroused need, the next step, as shown in figure 1, is for the individual to induce appropriate behavior in a target that will satisfy this need. In theory, this induction begins with a simple request, for example: "I love you. Will you marry me?" Frequently, of course, this step is omitted since the individual anticipates refusal. The consumer knows that, without money, his request for a new car from the automobile dealer will be refused, and the criminal knows that a polite request for money from passersby will often be ignored. When the target ignores such requests, the individual is tempted to invoke whatever resources are available to him in order to convince the target to comply.

Resources

We cannot understand the action of a powerholder after a target person has refused some request unless we have information about the powerholder's resources. Gamson (1968) whimsically calls resources "influence in repose." This is because resources represent the powerholder's *potential* for successful influence. Stress is placed on the term "potential" because there are many reasons why persons who control resources hesitate to invoke them in order to gain compliance. We shall touch on these reasons in a later section of the chapter which discusses factors inhibiting the use of power.

Let us begin with a definition. Resources are commodities, tangible or intangible, (a) that are possessed by powerholders, (b) that if given to target persons will provide them with positive outcomes, or if withheld will prevent the occurrence of negative outcomes, and (c) that target persons believe cannot be obtained outside of their relation with the powerholder. The powerholder possesses something that target persons want and cannot get elsewhere. The scarcer the commodity and the more it is valued, the greater the powerholder's potential for exercising influence. The dependence of the target person is, fundamentally, the reason why the powerholder has the potential for exercising influence.

Of course, if a target person gives up wanting the resource possessed by the powerholder, then the powerholder no longer has the potential to influence the target person. To illustrate, an acquaintance of mine was bitterly complaining to me that the next week of his life had to be spent in entertaining an elderly couple from out-of-town, whom he detested. When I asked why he bothered, his answer was quite simple: "I have to, I'm in their will." Thus the elderly couple had power over my friend so long as he wanted their money.

Classification of Resources

Figure 1 lists some of the common resources available to individuals in our society. We have found it useful to distinguish between resources that reside within the individual (*personal resources*) and resources available to the individual by reason of his *institutional* role.

Personal resources are fashioned out of each individual's unique endowments and include superior intelligence that can be used to convince the target to comply, superior physical strength to intimidate the target, personal beauty to seduce the target, and the ability to grant or withhold affection and services. The reader may think of many other personal resources that a target person will give weight to and that can, accordingly, be used as a base of influence. What all personal resources have in common is that they go where the person goes, that is, they are part of the person's makeup.

The second grouping of resources available to the individual is derived from his participation in institutional life. These resources detach themselves from the individual at the time when he decides to leave the institution. It can be a shock to a person who has spent years in a position of power to leave his office. The trauma arises from the fact that he can no longer issue orders and that he ceases to receive deference and compliments from his associates. Stripped of his institutional resources, he finds that life has become far less pleasant.

There are several ways of distinguishing between personal and institutional resources. Of central interest is the fact that the control of institutional resources increases the individual's potential for controlling the behavior of others. For example, in my personal relations I have the potential for influencing a few people because they admire or in some way depend on me. Yet, my personal resources are limited and so, too, are the sheer number of people I am liable to influence. In my role as college instructor, however, I exercise my influence over several hundred people a week. I say, "Speak," and people speak. I say, "Write," and people write. What power! Since this compliance never occurs outside of the classroom, it would seem foolish to attribute my success to my personality or other personal attributes. Quite simply, the fact that I can invoke the college's resources (to flunk, grant degrees, and so on) provides the added weight that produces student compliance. The same is true of countless others who find themselves unable to get even the least of what they want in personal relations, despite the fact that they shout and scream and rage, but in their roles of supervisors, managers, military leaders, political officeholders, teachers, and government representatives can easily cause the behavior of many thousands of others by merely whispering. Thus, access to institutional powers transforms insignificant men and women into giants.

Adolph Berle (1967) has pointed out a second distinction between institutional and personal resources. This is that institutional resources can be preserved for longer periods of time. Personal resources soon disappear, because the individual encounters someone who is stronger, more loquacious, or simply because personal bases of power erode with time—beauty fades. Resources controlled by institutions, however, are less dependent upon the vitality of any single person. If one person resigns from an institution he may only take with him his hat and coat and letters of appreciation that were gathered along the way. What he must leave for his successor is the right to use the institution's resources, be they the command of other people, the command of machinery, or the command of money. Nothing can be taken away; even ideas developed while in the service of the institution must remain. In this way institutions preserve their resources against forces of decay which inevitably must reduce all individual powerholders.

The Relation between Available Resources and the Satisfaction of Power Needs

Several points need to be made in connection with the control of resources.

First of all, consider what happens when an individual has few or no resources. It follows that he must cease in his attempts to induce the target to comply. His needs must remain unrequited since he lacks the resources needed to convince others to take appropriate action. Thus, small businessmen may desire to control the pricing strategies of their sources of supplies but cannot even attempt to induce such changes due to their limited monetary resources. Large corporations, however, tend to be more successful in this regard (Galbraith 1967).

Another point is that there are functional relations between the nature of the powerholder's demands from the target and the kinds of resources it is proper to invoke.

For example, in a work context it has been found (Goodstadt and Kipnis 1970; Kipnis 1972) that when they had a choice between invoking personal or institutional resources as a means of influencing the behavior of their subordinates, supervisors overwhelmingly preferred the institutional. That is, attempts to change subordinates' behavior were based almost exclusively upon economic resources (offers of pay raises, and the like) rather than simple persuasive attempts that made no mention of institutional resources.

The most general statement of the relation between available resources and wants of the powerholder is provided in the theory of resource exchange (Foa and Foa 1975). These authors present evidence that particular needs may only be satisfied by a reliance upon particular resources. For example, Foa and Foa's theory suggests that, to obtain love and affection from a target, an individual should invoke his persuasive resources rather than, say, economic resources—at least initially.

Furthermore, the Foas pointed out that some resources are rapidly expended, such as the offer of money in exchange for compliance, while the use of other resources, such as the offer of love and affection, leaves the powerholder as well-off as before. Thus, to the extent a powerholder can achieve his goal of exercising influence through the invoking of nonmaterial resources such as his intelligence, persuasive powers, or the ability to grant or withhold love and companionship, he will not have much concern for exhausting his bases of power. Offering material goods, on the other hand, leaves the powerholder in the position of having to exercise "sharp" bargains so that his power base is not weakened.

Region of Inhibition

So far the potential user of power has proceeded part way along the route to his goal of influencing a target person and thus gaining satisfaction. We began with a person who wanted something that could be gained only by convincing a target to take appropriate action. To the annoyance of the powerholder, the target simply ignored, or worse, refused the request. At this point, it was suggested that the powerholder would be tempted to invoke his resources as a means of reinforcing his demands.

In many instances, the foreplay of first asking and then demanding does not occur. Because of previous experience with the target, the powerholder may realize that the target person will resist a gentle request, and therefore the powerholder may be tempted to invoke his resources without first asking. For example, members of President Nixon's staff, prior to the well-publicized Watergate break-in, did not go to the Democratic party and ask for information. Rather, Nixon's staff was immediately tempted to invoke various resources that might provide this information, despite Democratic party objections.

With the powerholder at the point of invoking his resources, what then remains to be considered? There is one major barrier that must be dealt with by the powerholder. That is, before resources can be involved, there is a region of inhibition, as shown in figure 1, that the powerholder must successfully navigate. We next consider the problems presented to the powerholder by this inhibitory region.

The study of factors inhibiting behavior has been a traditional concern of the social sciences. Hence, the reader should not be surprised to find that factors inhibiting the invocation of resources to satisfy power needs have been analyzed at many different levels of abstraction. For some (Delgado 1969; Moyer 1971), the problem has been stated in physiological terms; here the emphasis is on the inhibition of aggressive behaviors that are instigated by such negative emotional states as frustration, fear, humiliation, pain, and anger. Evidence is now available that these aggressive behaviors may be inhibited through direct brain stimulation or extirpation, through alterations in hormonal balance, or through the use of calming drugs.

The possibility of an emerging psychotechnology capable of inhibiting temptations to invoke resources for coercive means was recently noted by Kenneth B. Clark (1971) in his presidential address to the American Psychological Association. While perhaps speculative, and surely controversial, Clark's address urged that biochemical substances should be developed which rulers and important political figures would be required to take during their terms of office. Noting, how easily individuals with access to great power are tempted to use this power for selfish ends, Clark argued that biochemical interventions could stabilize and make dominant the "moral and ethical propensities of man by *inhibiting his primitive aggressive behaviors*" (p. 1055; emphasis added).

Others think of the region of inhibition of power at a cognitive level in terms of the costs of attempting to influence others (Dahl 1957; Harsanyi 1962; Tedeschi, Schlenker & Bonoma 1973; Thibaut and Kelley 1959; Pollard and Mitchell in press). As Cartwright (1965) points out: "When an agent is deciding whether to exercise influence, it must be assumed that he calculates in some sense the net advantage to him of making an influence attempt" (p. 8). If the results of his calculations indicate that he will lose more than he will gain, presumably the individual does not attempt to influence others. Thus, what inhibits the invoking of resources at this level of abstraction is a hedonistic calculus that yields negative results.

Still others view the problem of inhibition in terms of subjective values and attitudes (Berkowitz and Daniels 1963; Levanthal and Lane 1970; Pepitone 1971; Staub 1971; Walster, Berscheid, and Walster 1973). Despite the fact that the individual may gain substantial advantage by invoking his resources, it frequently happens that he inhibits the invoking of resources because he questions the propriety of the act. Hence, the need to act in an ethical manner overrides the temptation to maximize gains.

To use the example of the Watergate incident, it seems clear that the participants erroneously discounted the possible costs involved in invoking the resources of the office of the president. Notions of the ethics of public office that might have also served to inhibit their actions were missing. Further, there was little public surveillance of how presidential aides used resources. Congressional constraints over activities of members of the executive branch have also lessened in the past two decades thereby minimizing control by other government branches. Such anonymity then, as suggested by Zimbardo (1968), produces a state of affairs in which few means are taboo. In the absence of these forms of restraint on presidential aides, decisions were apparently made to use resources of uncertain legitimacy to get the desired information regarding Democratic party campaign strategies.

Returning to the general question of inhibitions, the decision as to whether to invoke resources can also be related to stable individual differences in personality and values (Christie and Geis 1970; Megaree 1971). For example, in several studies that have directly investigated individual differences in relation to choice of resources (Kipnis and Lane 1962; Goodstadt and Kipnis 1970; Goodstadt and Hjelle 1973), it has been found that appointed leaders who either lacked confidence or believed that external forces such as luck and chance controlled their lives were reluctant to invoke personal resources as a means of inducing behaviors in others. Rather than trying to persuade others to comply, less confident or externally controlled individuals either did nothing or else relied exclusively on institutional resources. Thus, tempermental factors inhibited the use of some resources and favored the invoking of others.

Finally, still other investigators discuss factors inhibiting the invoking of resources in terms of restraints that originate in the norms of groups, institutions, and society (Berle 1967). Powerful guidance is given to when and where resources will be used by these norms, laws, traditions, and values. While not absolute, these written and unwritten norms tend to form a moral climate which serves to restrain the use of resources, even though their use would be considered completely appropriate in a different moral climate. Today, managers of modern corporations are restrained by law from using their vast economic resources to openly intimidate potential business competitors, although in the late nineteenth century, use of economic resources for this purpose was not uncommon (cf. Tarbell 1904). Daniel Elazar (1969), in his book *The Politics of American Federalism,* has discussed how variations in political morality in different regions of the United States directly determines the frequency of corrupt practices in government. In the northeast region of the country, where an individualistic political morality exists, few persons see anything wrong in "dipping into the public till." Such behaviors, however, appear to be restrained in states like Minnesota and Wisconsin where a moralistic orientation toward political office tends to guide an officeholder. Beliefs about public service, rather than personal gain, serve to direct the behaviors in this midwest area.

From these remarks it can be seen that the use of power is not simply a function of the motives of the powerholder and the possession of adequate resources. The burden of our argument is that the description of the power act can be understood more precisely by explicitly taking into account the nature of the restraining forces acting on the powerholder. At all levels one may note the operation or the failure of the operation of these restraining forces. To ignore their presence would drastically simplify our understanding of what is happening when "Person A influences B to do something B would ordinarily prefer not to do." Chapter 6 will explore in greater detail the issues raised in this section.

Means of Influence

If the potential powerwielder has not been restrained by the various means of inhibition mentioned in the previous pages, the next step in the power act, as shown in figure 1, is for him to invoke his resources in order to induce compliance from the target. At this step the question is, How shall the resources be presented to the target—as a promise, as a threat, or what? To answer this question it is suggested that the powerholder must carry out an active cognitive search for the best means to influence the target person. These decision-making steps incorporate an evaluation of the power-holder's own needs, his resources, the presumed responsiveness of the target person, as well as existing social constraints on the power-holder's behavior.

To illustrate this point, let us consider the various contingencies that government planners must consider when deciding on how best to influence the policies of other countries. David Baldwin (1974), a political scientist, provides us with insight into this issue in his discussion of the pros and cons that planners must weigh when deciding whether to exert influence through promise of economic aid or through the threat of military intervention. It is clear that such a decision is not a matter of momentary impulse but rather involves an active cognitive evaluation of the immediate and long-range consequences associated with each of these means of influence.

a) Economic techniques tend to have widespread general effects on another nation's future behavior, while military techniques tend to have limited, specific effects on a nation's present behavior.

b) Economic techniques tend to be slow, continuous, and circuitous, whereas military techniques tend to be fast, intermittent, and direct.

c) A nation provided with economic aid will lose social cohesion, and the aid provided is less visible than military intervention.

This concern with consequences can be found at all levels of usage. Sometimes the concern will be a rather primitive calculation that the target person is too strong to risk directly threatening him. At other times, a more elaborate cognitive search for the best means will be employed, as, for instance, when parents confer on the best means of changing the behavior of their child. Later chapters will examine in detail the various factors influencing this decision-making process. It suffices to say here that the decision as to how to use power is not a simple matter of provocation followed by an instinctive response.

Classification of Means of Influence

Attempts to influence suffer from the same basic ambiguities as attempts to precisely define power. These ambiguities arise from the fact that influence attempts are social acts and, hence, subject to various interpretations as to their intent by each actor involved (Tedeschi, Smith, and Brown, 1972). Thus, a wife's threat to divorce her husband may be viewed by the husband as an appeal to be more accommodating, while the wife, in fact, may be deadly serious. Despite these problems, several writers have discussed various classification schemes for analyzing power strategies. These schemes can be briefly reviewed at this point.

In Chapter 1, we reviewed the classification of means of influence proposed by John French and Bert Raven. A somewhat similar classification has been proposed by Cartwright (1965) who suggests that the powerholder may exploit a base of power by exercising control over: (a) the target's physical movements or his environment; (b) over the gains and costs that the target will actually experience; (c) over the information available to the target; or (d) by making use of the target's attitudes about being influenced. A study by Kipnis and Cosentino (1969) of how supervisors exercise influence over their workers readily illustrates Cartwright's classifications. Some supervisors exercised influence by controlling the workers physical environment, that is, by shifting them to a new job or work location; other supervisors attempted to control the money earned by workers by assigning them to work that allowed overtime pay or higher piece rates; some supervisors attempted to influence their workers by discussing the work with them; while still other supervisors exercised control by means of their legitimate authority and simply ordered their workers to carry out some behaviors. The effectiveness of this last power tactic hinges on the worker's beliefs that supervisors have a legitimate right to exert influence and that he (the worker) is obliged to accept this influence.

The tactical use of power has been approached in yet another way by Michener and Schwertfeger (1972), who view the powerholder as attempting to increase the value of the resources he controls and so gain for himself in an exchange with a target. Michener and Schwertfeger, drawing on the writings of Emerson (1962) and Blau (1964), describe four strategies that powerholders may use to increase their outcomes. *Blocking outcomes* consist of blocking another person's access to valued outcomes. By restricting the access of the United States to their oil reserves, for example, the Arab nations increase their bargaining position with this country on other matters, such as the United States' support of Israel. *Demand creation* is a second power tactic that may be used to influence a target. Here the powerholder attempts to "create a need" for his resources so that a target will pay more for them. Thus, merchants may advertise their product to increase its value in the eyes of the customer. If the demand is increased as a result of the advertisements, then more money can be asked for the product, since it is seemingly worth more to the buyer. *Extension of the power network* is a third strategy that powerholders may use. Here the powerholder develops alternate sources of supply for his wants so that he is not solely dependent on the target. Thus, if two persons who are dating disagree on whether to get married, one of them may threaten to date others if the partner will not comply. *Withdrawal* is the last strategy described by Michener and Schwertfeger. Here the powerholder decides that the price demanded by the target is more than he wishes to pay. Hence, he abandons his needs that gave rise to the influence act in the first place. This is, of course, the extreme case and represents a failure of the act of power.

Still another mode of classifying influence attempts has been offered by Tedeschi and his co-researchers in their book, *Conflict, Power, and Games* (1973). This classification scheme considers the extent to which the powerholder controls adequate resources. Furthermore, Tedeschi et al. considers whether the powerholder wishes openly to manipulate the target or prefers to do so "behind the scenes." These two dimensions of influence result in a classification scheme shown in table 2.1. The particular means of influence used under each of these circumstances are shown as cell entries.

Table 2.1 Classification of Influence Tactics

| | | Powerholder Intends to: | |
		Openly Influence Target	Manipulate Target
Powerholder controls resources	Yes	Threats and promises (A)	Reinforcement control (B)
	No	Persuasion, noncontingent promises, or threats (C)	Information control (D)

Adapted from Tedeschi, Schlenker, Bonoma (1973, p. 88)

It can be seen in cell A that, when a powerholder has available sufficient resources, he can openly attempt to obtain compliance by threatening punishment if the target does not comply or by promising specific rewards if the target does comply.

If the target has a more clandestine bent, as shown in cell B, then he may exert influence without the target being quite aware of what is happening. Studies by Bachrach and Baratz (1963), dealing with what they call "nondecisions," illustrate this clandestine method of exerting influence.

Nondecision-making occurs when a powerholder mobilizes his resources to suppress the demands for change by targets before these demands are made public. University instructors may be unhappy over the amount of "say" they have in running their department affairs. The instructors decide that at the next department meeting they will offer a resolution that faculty be given voting rights on teaching loads, tenure committees, review of salary, and other relevant department issues. The chairman may suppress these demands in three ways before they emerge for public debate. First, he may decide not to call any department meetings. Second, if the meetings are called, he may not recognize the dissident instructors when they request permission to speak. Third, if the instructors are recognized, the chairman may simply rule the motion "out of order," thus stopping debate.

Through these various tactics, the department chairman has exercised power in such a manner that the viewing public has not even been aware that authority has been challenged. This is a tactic of power that can be expected to be continually used in situations where the powerholder suspects that his influence is resisted. It is to his benefit to prevent public debate from even arising.

Bachrach and Baratz suggest that nondecision-making can take several forms, from direct physical harassment of persons liable to demand change, such as the killing of several civil-rights leaders in the South during the early 1960s, to such parlimentary tactics as those described above, which prevent issues from being raised.

When a powerholder does not control the appropriate resources, but still wishes openly to influence a target (the tactic indicated in cell c of table 2.1), then his position is weak. Tedeschi et al. indicate that the powerholder must rely on noncontingent promises or threats, such as are frequently used in advertisements, in order to induce target compliance. An audience is told, for instance, that the use of a particular toothpaste will gain one more friends or prevent the loss of one's teeth. "In this way the powerholder can attempt to tie his own interest to those of the target, so that their interests appear to correspond" (p. 90). However, the advertiser in these instances cannot directly cause the target to buy his product, since he has no direct control over the consumer's behavior.

The last means of influence considered by Tedeschi et al. in table 2.1. concerns instances in which the individual does not possess the appropriate resources needed to influence a target and decides to act in an undercover way in order to get what he wants. To satisfy his wants in these instances, the powerholder must first arouse the fears and credulities of the target without the target fully realizing what has happened. Once these fears and credulities have been aroused, the powerholder can openly offer to reduce them in exchange for compliance. The goal is to make the target falsely believe that he has more to lose than gain by not accepting the advice of the powerholder.

Fear arousal, stealth, and Machiavellian tactics serve the wielder of power very well in these instances, since his real aims must not be publicly revealed at the outset. In *King Lear,* for instance, Edmund, the bastard son of the Earl of Gloucester, seizes his father's wealth and title by first arousing his father's suspicions concerning the loyalty of the legitimate son, Edgar. Once these fears have been falsely aroused, it is a simple matter for Edmund to act as the defender of his father's safety. Similarly, Iago destroys the noble Othello by first convincing him that Desdemona could not really love him. What Shakespeare tells us is that the tactics of bluff and deceit, used covertly, must serve in the absence of real resources by arousing new concerns within the target that can be satisfied by the powerholder. Recent studies of ingratiation (Jones 1964; Kipnis and Vandeveer 1971) provide support for this process of covert influence.

Restraints on Choice of Means

While not shown in figure 1, restraints exist which shape the particular means of influence chosen by a powerholder. For instance, discipline in the armed forces can no longer be maintained by arbitrary threats of loss of leave and furlough, although this means of influence was acceptable prior to revisions in the Uniform Code of Military Justice. Or again, union contracts markedly limit the range of influence companies may use with their employees. While coercive means may still be used, government laws forbid such modes of influence as "yellow dog'" contracts, blacklisting of employees, as well as actual physical force against workers.

How Means of Influence Determine Interpersonal Relations

As could be expected by examining figure 1, there is also a relation between the resources invoked and the means of influence that are attempted. Some resources—guns and knives, for example, are particularly suited for threatening and intimidating targets. Others, such as the possession of superior knowledge, mainly favor the use of persuasion. Money provides the powerholder with a broad spectrum of means of influence, with a particular emphasis on rewards and punishments.

The relation between resources and means of influence has far-reaching consequences for the kinds of social relations that evolve between powerholders and target persons. Etzioni (1968) has classified institutions in terms of the means of influence that are used to exact compliance from their members. Those institutions whose representatives can only rely on coercive means produce, according to Etzioni, hostile and destructive forms of interpersonal relations.

Institutions that provide their members with only coercive means include most prisons, correctional institutions, custodial mental hospitals, and coercive unions. Persons working in such institutions in supervisory roles tend to encounter intensive negative involvement from those under their control. This is because supervisory personnel find that the institution has provided them only with the authority to use threats and punishments as means of influencing others.

An experimental study by Berger (1973), dealing with the control of coercive power, found results that were consistent with Etzioni's views. Managers in a simulated organization, who were delegated only coercive means to influence their workers (pay deductions), generally believed that their workers disliked them. Further, Berger found that the managers who possessed only coercive means directed most of their attention toward the marginal workers who were the potential targets of this means of influence. Satisfactory workers were ignored. These results seem consistent with Etzioni's assumption that the kinds of means available structure both the sort of relations powerholders may enter into with others, as well as the powerholder's feelings about these others.

The Target's Response to the Influence Attempt

Consider now the target's response to the powerholder. This step has received considerable attention from psychologists using the brilliant conceptualization of the problem by French and Raven (1959). Here one asks: Does the target comply with the source of influence? And, if so, under what circumstances does this occur? How long does it last? Is this willing compliance or is it given grudgingly? What are the processes within the target that produce yielding? Further, when will a target person ignore or actively resist the powerholder's influence? These questions and many more like them have, since World War II, been the basis for much social-psychological research dealing with power and related areas such as attitude change and leadership.

Here we ask another question. If the target resists, what happens next to the powerholder? We suggest that the powerholder must recycle through earlier stages (a procedure not shown in figure 1). Depending upon the strength of the original need that aroused the motive to influence others, a reexamination of the resources that are available, and the strength of the restraining forces in the field, the powerholder may decide either to abandon his influence attempt, to modify his original needs, or to persist by invoking different means of influence.

If he persists, then the question of tactics becomes important. What new means of influence are liable to convince the target? While in many instances these new means of influence will take harsher forms (Deutsch and Krauss 1960), or will escalate in intensity (Goldstein, Davis, and Herman, 1975), that will not always be the case. Rather, the new means of influence will be selected to increase pressure for change on the target. Not only may they include threats but also promises of additional rewards, or even greater reliance on informational modes of influence.

Basically, the choice of means depends upon the powerholder's ability to diagnose the causes of the target's resistance. A wrong diagnosis may increase rather than decrease resistance. This cycling through various means of influence in order to induce compliance is well illustrated in the government's attempts to achieve racial balance in public schools during the 1960s and into the early 1970s. Among the means used were threats of economic sanctions against state school systems in the form of withdrawal of federal money; new information on the utility of integration—provided through public information programs; court orders to force the bussing of school children; and in Alabama military force.

This continual pressure to bring about compliance could only be brought to bear on the target because of the wide variety of resources available to the government.

Individuals may also cycle through various influence tactics, although each of these tactics will be considerably weaker than those used by the government. A parent, attempting to make his child improve at school, may promise an extra allowance for better grades or threaten to reduce the child's allowance if the grades remain poor. At the same time, he may have a serious talk with the child on the relation between school performance and the child's adult career; he may appeal to the child's love for his parents, or he may even physically threaten him. And, if all else fails, the parent may consult with the teacher for additional means to apply pressure, such as using the schools' counseling services. This continual pressure will stop only if the parent becomes convinced that his son is not destined to achieve in school, or if the child finally complies and raises his grades.

Consequences for the Powerholder

Up to this point we have described the decision processes of the powerholder in his attempts to induce change in the behavior of others. Still to be reckoned with is the notion that the simple possession and use of power may affect the powerholder himself. If the powerholder's influence attempts are resisted and his needs remain unfulfilled, he should experience frustration and self-doubt. Furthermore, his views of the target will fluctuate in relation to the amount of resistance shown by the target. Will the powerholder like the target more or less if he complies? The last step in the descriptive model of the power act is concerned with the reaction of the powerholder to his own use of power. These reactions can be called the *metamorphic* effects of power and refer to how the exercise of power may transform the powerholder's self-concepts, his values, and his views of the less powerful.

Since Chapter 9 is concerned with a full discussion of the metamorphic effects of power, here I will only briefly indicate the basis for my interest, as a psychologist, in this subject.

Basically, this interest was stimulated by writings of political scientists and philosophers in which persons who control economic and political power are viewed, at best, with mixed emotions. On the one hand, there is admiration for their ability to amass great power and, at times, admiration for the way in which their power is used to influence events in society. On the other hand there is profound suspicion that these powerholders, no matter what their original motives, will use their resources to exploit others and further enrich themselves. This suspicion of the corrupting influence of power has been voiced by political scientists for many centuries. There is fear that power, once consolidated, will become used for despotic ends. Indeed, Hobbes in *Leviathan* maintained that men formed societies as a means of limiting the exploitive consequences of the unequal division of power. The system of checks and balances and the separation of powers between the executive, legislative, and judicial departments contained in the American Constitution are based on the same fears of the consequences of excessive power. Underlying these fears is the assumption that human nature is mean and self-serving. Hobbes viewed all men as moved by a never-ending stream of appetites which could only be satisfied by the control of power. Similarly, James Madison, writing in the

Federalist Papers (no. 14), viewed men as "ambitious," "vindictive," and "rapacious" and believed their access to power had to be limited.

The important question, then, for psychologists is to understand the relation between appetitive drives, the control and use of power, and changes in self-image. Why do we continually find references in the literature to the idea that persons with power become "puffed up with importance," devalue the worth of others, and deny that ordinary morality applies to their acts? What processes underlie these changes? To anticipate the arguments that are presented in Chapter 9, I suggest that individuals take cues as to their own worth from the quality of interaction they have with others. To the extent that these interactions are continually supportive, self-esteem may rise. To the extent that they are less so, self-esteem may fall. Simply put, control of resources gives the powerholders an "edge," so that society tends to act "extra nice" when interacting with them. These kinds of positive feedback gradually allow powerholders to believe that they are more worthy than others and, in fact, deserve more as a simple matter of justice.

Summary

From the point of view of the powerholder, the power act is like a game. Each step flows from the previous one with penalties continually arising to block progress. The contingencies are such that, without a need, an attempt to influence others is unlikely. Without resources, influence is unlikely to be attempted. In the presence of strong inhibition, influence is also unlikely to be attempted. Again, without the proper means of exercising it, influence is unlikely to be attempted. Strong resistance from a target will make the powerholder move back several squares and recycle through all the various steps mentioned. A serious consideration of the use of power must in fact consider all of these points to describe adequately what is happening when influence is exerted.

The initial sequences of the power act can be described in terms of an instrumental view of motivation. The perception that others mediate desirable outcomes for the powerholder provides the incentive to take action. Expectation of successful influence, the second major variable in instrumentality theories, is provided by the kind and amount of resources available. The more that resources can be used without cost to the powerholder, the broader the scope of the resources, the more the resources are given weight by the target —then the higher the powerholder's expectations of successful influence.

As the individual proceeds from step to step in the power-act sequence, expectancies of success and the incentive value of influencing the target take on new values. Further, the region of inhibition adds negative values to the instrumentality act.

Several other investigators (Pollard and Mitchell 1973; Tedeschi, Schlenker, and Bonoma 1973) have also stressed the usefulness of some form of instrumentality theory for explaining the power act. An added value of the present analysis is its consideration of how the availability of resources can shape the initial expectations of the powerholder. In addition, this approach requires the analysis of behavior to begin with a classification of the objective environment in terms of the resources possessed by the person, as well as with some hypothesized psychological state of the person. Both units of information are needed to predict behavior of the powerholder, since the combination of an aroused power need and the possession of resources can be expected to lead to action, while the absence of either will lead to inaction.

3   The Use of Power

Once a person has gained control of resources that are given weight by others he must consider how best to use these resources. Statesmen must decide when to offer to negotiate, and when threats will produce the advantageous outcome. Parents must similarly decide how to convince their children to eat their food, to dress properly, and to study.

And so it goes—for all levels of society the perplexing problem is how to gain compliance without losing the long-term affection of the target person, and yet use one's resources economically. In the face of these uncertainties, it is not surprising that there is a continual demand for books that promise to give advice on these matters. Niccolò Machiavelli in *The Prince* provides extensive advice to rulers on how to extend and consolidate their power. Similarly, books on leadership provide advice to managers on the best way to influence subordinates, and books on child psychology are continual best-sellers among parents groping their way from one "identity crisis" of their children to the next.

In the present chapter, rather than offering advice on how best to exert influence, I shall more prudently limit myself to the question of what influences a powerholder's selection of influence tactics, regardless of whether the consequences of this choice lead to favorable or unfavorable outcomes.

The reader should be aware that I have adopted the perspective of the powerholder in discussing the particular means of influence that are used. That is, if the powerholder believes he is offering to reward the target for compliance, I will accept this belief as valid, even though the target may view the offer as an insult and an outside observer may see the same promise of reward as a threat. This kind of relativity exists in defining power relationships, since they represent social acts rather than processes that are invariant with respect to who is doing the observing (Tedeschi, Smith and Brown, 1972; Bachrach and Baratz 1963). Hence different observers may disagree sharply on the benefit and meaning of any social exchange.

Instincts and Power Usage

One possible answer to the question of what determines the choice of means of influence comes from social philosophers who stress man's inherent enjoyment in exercising power in order to inflict harm on others. Freud, writing in *Civilization and Its Discontent*, described man's destructive impulses this way:

> Men are not gentle, friendly creatures wishing for love, who simply defend themselves if they are attacked . . . a powerful measure of desire for aggression has to be reckoned as part of their intrinsic, instinctual endowment. The result is that their neighbor is to them not only a possible helper or sexual outlet, but also someone who tempts them to satisfy their aggressiveness on him, to exploit his capacity for work without compensation, to use him sexually without his consent, to seize his possessions, to humiliate him, to cause him pain, to torture, and to kill him. Homo homini lupus. Who in the face of all his experience of life and history will have the courage to dispute this assertion?
>
> As a rule this cruel aggressiveness waits for some provocation or puts itself at the service of some other purpose, whose goal might also have been reached by milder methods. In circumstances that are favorable to it, when the mental counterforces which ordinarily inhibit it are out of action, it also manifests itself spontaneously and reveals man as a savage beast to whom consideration to its own kind is something alien. . . . The existence of this inclination to aggression, which we can detect in ourselves and justly presume to be in others, is the factor which disturbs our relations with our neighbors and which makes it necessary for culture to institute its highest demands.

Here we have Freud enumerating various coercive means by which man may harass his neighbor, and for no other reason than to satisfy primitive aggressive instincts that make up his natural endowment. If we are to take Freud seriously on this matter, the decision as to what particular means of influence to use will depend primarily on the presence or absence of societal restraining forces. In their absence, the powerholder will choose the cruellest means available. In this way he may satisfy both the manifest reason for exerting influence and the instinctual reason relating to the gratifications achieved by inflicting harm on others.

Freud's assumptions, however, are not easily verified when we examine the day-to-day behaviors of powerholders in the process of exerting influence. Except under special circumstances of intense anger we find that most powerholders tend to reject the immediate use of coercive means of influence. There is a preference for using less harsh means that will preserve a friendly relationship if possible. And if friendship is impossible, means of influence are sought that will at least allow civil intercourse between the powerholder and the target.

A study by Michener and Schwertfeger (1972) illustrates how the choice of destructive modes of influence are reserved for those persons we dislike to begin with, rather than being used indiscriminately. These investigators reported that, in conflict with a landlord over a rent increase, tenants who liked the landlord either attempted to change his decision through persuasion or by offering to move into a cheaper apartment in the same building complex. Tenants who disliked the landlord, however, appeared to follow the destructive pattern described by Freud, in that their choice of influence tactics were more likely to cause pain to the landlord. That is, tenants who initially disliked the landlord favored either forming a tenant's union to militantly resist the landlord's demands for higher rent or threatened to move elsewhere, thus depriving the landlord of any rent at all. It is mainly when strong antipathy is felt toward a target person that we appear to deliberately make our first choice of influence coercive rather than gentle.

Institutional Settings Guide the Choice of Influence Tactics

Any discussion of decisions concerning how power is used, whether benignly or with malevolent application, properly begins with the setting in which the influence is to be exercised. Each formal grouping in our society possesses some unique repertoire of influence means that are considered proper to use in that setting. This repertoire exists to provide persons directly responsible for goal achievement with the means to coordinate and guide the behavior of other participants, and so to achieve the setting's goals. In business organizations, Pelz (1951) and Godfrey, Fiedler, and Hall (1959) have found that when appointed leaders were deprived of power usually associated with their positions (by superiors not supporting their decisions), the appointed leaders were less able to influence their employees. Few of the employees listened when they realized that their supervisor's opinions about their work no longer counted. Clearly, personal charm may have only limited value for inducing behavior in settings that traditionally rely on institutionally based means of influence.

Table 3.1 shows the kinds of coercive means of influence that were found to be available to powerholders in three different settings—marriage, work, and custodial mental hospitals. These means of influence were gathered by the writer and his colleagues while interviewing marriage partners, first-line supervisors, and psychiatric aides. The targets of influence were the respondent's spouse, the employee, and the mental patient.

One of the first impressions gained from examining these listings is that the coercive power in each of these settings directs itself toward different values and needs within the target person. In marriage the coercive means of influence are based upon the ability of one spouse to withdraw emotional support and services from the other. The threat is to "move away" from the other partner. Further in the marriage setting, one has an impression that the threats used are vague and do not precisely specify exact consequences for noncompliance. In the mental hospitals, however, the threats appear to be quite precise. Also, the coercive means tend to be directed at the physical well-being of the patient. Rather than withdrawing emotional support and "moving away" from the target, psychiatric aides may threaten to "move against" the patient if compliance is not forthcoming. Among first-line supervisors the threats are directed toward withholding economic support or toward reducing the employee's self-esteem.

Another impression that is gained from examining table 3.1 is that the first-line supervisors appear to control a wider range of coercive influence means than do marital partners or psychiatric aides. That is, supervisors appear to control "low keyed" threats for minor forms of resistance and massive threats (firings or suspensions) for strong forms of resistance. Having access to this range of influence means should make the first-line supervisors far more flexible in their attempts to influence employees than either marital partners or psychiatric aides, who may have to choose threats that are inappropriate for the kinds of opposition being encountered from their spouses or patients.

A good deal can be learned about the attempts of powerholders to influence others from simply tabulating the means of influence available to them in each setting. Can rewards be given out freely?

Table 3.1 Coercive Means of Influence Available in Three Settings

Marriage

1. I act cold and say very little to him/her.
2. I make the other person miserable by doing things he or she does not like.
3. I get angry and demand that he/she give in.
4. I threaten to use physical force.
5. I threaten to separate or seek a divorce.

Work

1. I chewed him out.
2. I gave him a verbal warning.
3. I threatened to give him a written warning.
4. I ignored him while being friendly with everyone else.
5. I kept riding him.
6. I scheduled him to work hours he didn't like.
7. I gave him work he didn't like.
8. I put him in a work area he didn't like.
9. I put him in an area of lower premium pay.
10. I gave him a written warning.
11. I took steps to suspend him.
12. I recommended that he be brought before the disciplinary committee.
13. He was suspended from work.
14. He was fired.

Custodial Mental Hospital

1. Warn the patient of loss of privileges (passes, cigarettes).
2. Put the patient in isolation.
3. Scold the patient.
4. Physically control the patient (restraints, etc.).
5. Give medicine to the patient (to sedate).
6. Discipline the patient by removing things or privileges that the patient wants.

What types of punishments may be threatened for noncompliance? Can the target person's environment be altered? If the answer to most of these questions is "no," one can suspect that the influence potential of the individual will be low, regardless of his personality, loquacity, or personal charm.

Suppose we observe two persons attempting to influence target persons. The first adopts a pleasant, democratic style in which mild *requests* for compliance predominate. The second person adopts a brusque, demanding tone with little concern for the feelings of the target person. If asked to explain these differences, we might guess that the first person is rather timid, while the second has an authoritarian personality. However, we would probably alter our interpretation if we were told that the first person was the president of the local Parent-Teacher Association interacting with one of the members, while the second person was a business manager talking with a subordinate. Rather than resulting from personality differences, the two styles of influence can at least in part be attributed to the fact that the PTA president has no formal sanctions available to induce compliance, while the business manager has such sanctions available.

As a general rule, one should look for increased assertiveness in powerholders as the number of ways in which they can influence others increases. Support for this general rule can be found in several studies by psychologists of the relationship between the availability of means of influence and the assertiveness of the powerholder. In one study by Columbia University psychologists Morton Deutsch and Robert Krauss (1960) it was found that persons running a simulated business game who were given the power to threaten their rivals became far more demanding and less willing to compromise with their business rivals. Seemingly, the added power encouraged the development of a belief system: "We're stronger—we deserve more."

Somewhat similar findings were also obtained by the present writer (1972) in an experimental study in which managers ran a simulated business. The job of manager required the supervision of the work of four employees. There were two conditions in the study. In the first, managers were provided with a number of different ways of influencing the employees; that is, the managers were allowed, if they chose to do so, to give pay raises, pay deductions, to shift their employees from one job to another, to train their employees, or to fire them. In a second condition, the managers were not provided with any of these means of influence. Instead they had to rely on their personal ability to persuade their employees, or on their legitimate rights as managers to issue orders.

The results of this study were that managers who controlled a broad range of ways of influencing were far more assertive and demanding in their relations with their employees than were managers who were not provided with this range of influence. Managers with many institutional powers made twice as many demands upon their employees to work harder as did managers with no institutional powers.

It seems clear, then, that as we move individuals into settings that provide additional ways of influencing others, these individuals will respond by making far more demands upon the world.

There is also a hint in the experimental literature that the kinds of demands made upon others will vary with the kinds of means of influence that are available. In a study of how two people make concessions when bargaining with each other, Schlenker, and Tedeschi (1972) provided some participants with the power to reward their opponents if the opponents complied, other participants with the power to punish noncompliance, and still other participants with both the power to reward compliance and to punish noncompliance. The finding of considerable interest was that the type of power available had important effects on the behavior of the powerholders.

Powerholders sent more threats, and actually invoked coercive power more frequently when they possessed *only* coercive power than when they possessed both coercive and reward power. Thus persons acted more aggressively when they could only punish to gain compliance than when they could choose to either punish or reward. Further, powerholders promised fewer rewards when they possessed *only* reward power than when they possessed both reward and coercive power. These findings suggest that users of power will be less benevolent and more coercive in situations where they can only reward, or only punish, as compared to situations where they control the power to both reward and punish. Perhaps the power of prison guards to threaten and coerce should be augmented with the power to provide genuine rewards to prisoners in exchange for compliance. One wonders if by this means we could reduce the number of prison-abuse incidents that occur. For if the only way we have to get our way is to threaten and bully, it seems clear from everyday observation that most of us, sooner or later, will get used to the idea of threatening and bullying.

The Influence of Status on the Choice of Means

So far we have stated that simply tabulating the number and kinds of means of influence available to a powerholder in a given setting will tell us a good deal about how the powerholder is likely to behave. Here we wish to consider the implication of this statement as it relates to a person's status within the setting. To state an obvious fact, persons with high status tend to have available a wide variety of means to influence. There are also few restraints on their use of these means as compared to the restraints on persons of lower status. Children can only beg, ask, plead, or whine in order to influence their parents. Parents can legitimately punish, reward, and train their children—that is, bring strong means of influence to bear on their children.

Within institutional settings individuals with high status and great office may have unlimited access to resources, while those with less status, such as supervisors or teachers, will have only limited access to the institution's resources. A study of role conflict among business managers by Robert Kahn and his associates at the University of Michigan (1964) nicely illustrates how access to influence varies with the person's work status in the organization. In this study managers were asked the extent to which they could use a variety of means to influence various target persons with whom they worked. The respondent was either a superior, peer, or subordinate of the target person.

Table 3.2 shows these responses in terms of average rating by each respondent of his ability to use four means of influence: legitimate power, reward power, coercive power, and expert power. Quite clearly, top supervisors reported that they had greater latitude to use legitimate, reward, and coercive powers than did subordinates. It may also be seen that all persons in the organization, regardless of level, felt that they could use their expert power to influence a target person.

This indicates that powers derived purely from participation in the organization, such as the power to reward and punish, are closely linked with level in the organization. High-status persons have a wider range of influence to choose from than low-status persons. On the other hand, when the means of influence depend upon the individual's own abilities, such as his expert knowledge, we are more likely to find persons at all levels using such means. Thus first-line supervisors can change their superiors' behavior by using professional knowledge. However, first-line supervisors will hardly ever attempt to change this behavior by promising to raise their bosses' pay, that is, by using reward power. This latter power tactic is reserved for those with higher status.

Table 3.2 Ability to Use Various Means of Influence at Differing Organizational Levels

	Top Supervisor	Immediate Supervisor	Peer	Subordinate
Legitimate power	4.6	4.3	2.3	1.6
Reward power	4.0	3.7	2.2	1.5
Coercive power	4.1	3.6	1.3	1.3
Expert power	4.1	4.1	4.1	4.1

NOTE: The higher the score the greater the ability to use the given power.
*Estimated from text's statement that all respondents averaged above 4.0 on a scale of 1 to 5 (Kahn et al. [1964], p. 200).

Calculation and the Choice of Influence

The previous two sections pointed out that powerholders' willingness to assert themselves is closely tied to the kinds and amount of power bases that are available to them. Assume now that a powerholder does possess a suitable position and an array of means of influence that can be freely used. That is, assume the powerholder can choose to do whatever he wants to make the target person comply. In these circumstances, what determines the powerholder's particular choice of influence from this array? Why does he use one particular means of influence in one situation but not in another? Why in one instance does a teacher use flattery to encourage a student to study but flatly order a second student to engage in similar behavior? Why does a supervisor in one instance spend long hours training an incompetent worker to reach acceptable levels of performance but in another instance threaten to fire an equally incompetent worker? Is the answer, as Freud suggests, simply that powerholders select the means liable to do the most harm, so long as they are not punished themselves? Or are more rational processes involved?

All evidence indicates that more rational processes are almost always involved in decisions concerning tactics of influence. As Raven (1974) points out: "On the assumption that man is rational we would expect him to use the base of power which would most likely lead to successful influence" (p. 192). Raven goes on to point out that if the goal of the powerholder was to produce long-lasting changes in the behavior of the target person, then the powerholder would probably avoid coercive means of influence and perhaps attempt to influence through providing the target person with new information. If long-lasting compliance was not an issue, however, then the powerholder might decide to obtain immediate satisfaction by invoking strong sanctions.

Planning and rationality can almost always be found when powerholders are deciding which of several means of influence should be used in a given situation. This does not mean of course that emotions and feelings do not affect the powerholder's decisions. Such emotional feelings, however, appear to act by narrowing or expanding the range of influence means that the powerholder is likely to believe effective in that situation.

Gamson (1968) illustrates how emotions serve to guide the powerholder's choice of influence means. When the powerholder trusts the target person, persuasion is most likely to be used to convince the target person. Because of this trusting relationship, the powerholder is willing to allow the target person the freedom to make up his own mind, confident that the target person will freely do what the powerholder has requested. If the powerholder does not trust the target person, then it is quite likely that he will decide to invoke threats and punishments. The assumption here is that one cannot rely on influence means that allow the target person freedom of choice (such as persuasion), because with freedom the distrusted target person will probably do exactly the opposite of what the powerholder wants him to do. As Gamson notes: "Since the probability of favorable outcomes is already very low . . . , it is hardly necessary to worry about [the target's feelings]. The attitude then that 'the only thing they understand is force' is a perfect manifestation of this trust orientation" (p. 169).

Choice of Influence—A Two-Stage Process

If we assume that powerholders act rationally when choosing how best to influence a target person, then it follows that there must be at least two stages involved in the choice of a particular means of influence. First the powerholder must diagnose the reasons for the target's refusal to comply with his request. Is the reason for the target's refusal due to the target's dislike of the powerholder, or is it because the target person does not possess the ability to do what the powerholder wants? Perhaps it is because a lack of trust exists between the two parties so that the target person will refuse any suggestion made by the poweholder, no matter how beneficial the suggestion is to both parties. Clearly, there is no end to the number of possible reasons why the target person has offered resistance.

Yet if the powerholder does not understand the reason for this resistance, he will be forced to flail about until by chance he discovers the one influence means that will produce compliance. Given this time-consuming alternative, the rational powerholder, before taking further action, prefers to spend some time analyzing why the target person has refused his request.

Frequently this stage in the decision-making process is complicated by the lack of open communication between the powerholder and the target person. The target person may lie about his reasons or sullenly refuse to talk, since once the causes of resistance have been discovered the powerholder may attempt to overcome the resistance.

Further, the powerholder can make mistakes in his diagnosis. He is in the position of the sixteenth-century physician who possessed only the crudest of diagnostic tools with which to decide what was bothering his patient. As mistakes were common then among physicians, so too are they today among powerholders. The history of modern international negotiations contains many examples where signals of one nation were misperceived by another nation, which saw hostility where in fact peace overtures were intended. We have no X-ray devices available to peer into the mind of the target person and discern there the reasons for his refusal to comply with our request. Our closest approach to such a device is perhaps the consumer surveys that seek to discover the cause of citizen antipathy toward consumer products, or toward politicians, so that precise campaigns can be planned to overcome these resistances. For most powerholders, however, diagnosing the causes of the target persons' resistance remains a subtle art based upon past encounters with the target person, hunches, and the powerholder's own perceptiveness.

Once the diagnosis is reached, regardless of whether it is correct, we reach the second stage of the decision-making process, which involves the actual choice of means of influence. Assuming that the powerholder is acting rationally, this stage is almost completely dependent upon the powerholder's initial diagnosis of the cause of the target's resistance. As the powerholder's diagnosis of the reasons for the target's lack of cooperation varies, so too will his choice of tactics vary.

This two-stage process has an analogy in the practice of medical diagnosis and treatment. When a patient appears at a physician's office and complains of feeling sick, the physician must first decide what is causing these complaints. It is only after the diagnosis has been made that the physician can select a particular mode of treatment. Furthermore, the treatment that is selected must be the one that holds the highest promise of cure. If the physician ignores this treatment in favor of another, his action tends to be viewed as a breach of medical ethics. The concept of "treatment of choice" in medicine refers to this general rule that the treatment with the highest probability of cure must be used before any other is tried. Once the diagnosis has been made, one can predict with almost complete certainty the kinds of treatments the physician will use.

There is also a "treatment of choice" rule associated with the selection of means of influence. We have found that if powerholders agree on the reason for a target person's resistance to their influence, they will also agree on the proper means of influence to use. This two-stage process can be illustrated by studies done by myself and my colleagues William Lane and Joseph Cosentino (1962; 1969) among Navy and industrial supervisors.

The purpose of these studies was to determine how appointed leaders used their delegated powers to influence the performance of their subordinates. At the beginning of the studies we had no particular preconceived ideas as to how power would be used. Rather it was hoped to catalogue the range of means of influence that were relied upon, and to get some idea of when each means was used.

Our procedure consisted of asking supervisors in both the Navy and in various business organizations to describe a recent incident in which they had to correct the behavior of one of their subordinates. We asked the supervisors to describe the problem they faced and what they or someone else did about it. In telling us what they did, the supervisors were in effect telling us about the kinds of influence they had the authority to use.

In terms of the model of the power act given in Chapter 2, we note that the reason for these influence attempts did not arise from any particularly sinister motives. Rather they arose from the supervisors' involvement in their work. As part of this work there were obligations to make sure that employees performed at acceptable levels and to force changes if this level was not reached.

The nature of the employee problems that disturbed the supervisors in the first place was also tabulated. Basically the problems could be diagnosed as those caused by an inability of the employee to do his work or by a lack of motivation to do the work or by problems of discipline, in which company rules were violated (such as the problem of habitual lateness). Sometimes a supervisor would describe a subordinate whose poor performance was due to a combination of these problems. These employees were described as manifesting "complex" problems.

Next we looked at the ways in which the supervisors said they attempted to correct their employees' performance. Their attempts involved the use of a variety of institutional means of influence, which we classified as follows: (*a*) coercive power—threatening or actually demoting the subordinate or assigning him to less pleasant or lower-paying work, or reducing his responsibilities, or sending him an official letter of warning, or suspending or firing him; (*b*) ecological control, in which the subordinate was shifted to a new job, work shift, or a new job location but not for the purpose of punishment; (*c*) expert power, in which new information or new skills were shown the worker; (*d*) legitimate power expressed in terms of direct requests or orders for change.

In addition to these institutional means of influence, supervisors also relied upon their personal powers of persuasion convincing subordinates to change by praising, reprimanding, and encouraging them to expend additional efforts. Readers who adopt a historic or cultural perspective on these kinds of findings will be quick to see how bound by time and space such attempts at influence are. That is, no supervisors mentioned physically striking their employees, as would have been done prior to the twentieth century, and no supervisors mentioned using appeals based upon family and company loyalty, as is still done in some Japanese industries.

One of the strongest findings that emerged from these studies was the discovery that there was a "treatment of choice" rule associated with the selection of means of influence. That is, the kinds of influence invoked by the supervisors were found to vary systematically with the nature of the subordinate's problem as diagnosed by the supervisor. Without any particular instruction in the use of power, most of the supervisors converged on the selection of a given means of influence for a given type of problem. These findings are summarized in table 3.3.

Table 3.3 Diagnosis of Subordinate Resistance and the Means
of Influence Used to Overcome It

	Diagnosed Cause of Poor Work			
	Simple Problems			Complex Problems
Means of Influence	Employee Lacks Motivation	Employee Lacks Ability	Employee Lacks Discipline	Combinations of Poor Attitudes, Discipline and/or Lack of Ability
Discussion	Yes	No	Yes	Yes
Extra training (expert power)	No	Yes	No	Yes
Ecological control	No	No	No	Yes
Legitimate power	Yes	Yes	Yes	Yes
Coercion	Yes	No	Yes	Yes

It can be seen that, as the supervisor's diagnosis of what was causing the subordinate's poor performance changed, so too did the means of influence that were used. For instance, when the supervisor believed that the employee's problem was due to poor attitudes, the supervisor used persuasion and informational modes of influence. The supervisor's concern was to find out the reasons for the subordinate's poor attitudes and, if possible, to persuade him to change. If, however, the supervisor attributed the subordinate's poor performance to a lack of ability, then persuasion was rarely mentioned. Rather, the supervisor invoked his expert powers and devoted time to retraining his subordinate.

If the problem shown by a subordinate was complex, with elements of lack of ability and discipline, and poor attitudes, then supervisors increased the number of different means of influence directed toward the subordinate. Apparently, when the supervisors believed that several factors were causing the employee's poor performance ("He could never learn to do the simplest jobs, and on top of that he was always shooting off his mouth"), then the problem was considered more difficult to deal with. Accordingly, more powers were invoked to overcome this added resistance. For instance, 76 percent of a sample of Navy supervisors invoked two or more means of influence (e.g., increased training and change of jobs) when their subordinates manifested complex problems. When the subordinate evidenced a simple problem, however, only 41 percent of the Navy supervisors invoked two or more means of influence. This difference was statistically reliable beyond the .01 level.

A further finding was that, when faced with complex problems, supervisors exercised power by ecological control. That is, significantly more workers were moved to a new job or work shift when their problems were complex rather than simple. The supervisors apparently reasoned: "If he's causing so much fuss on this job, let's try him somewhere else." A moment's reflection will convince the reader that this means of exercising power is not limited to harassed supervisors facing strong resistance. In schools, pupils who are considered intractable by teachers are transferred out of class, while ecological control is exerted over criminals by sending them to prison. In all instances the diagnosis of being hard to influence leads to the temptation to shift the person to a new environment considered more likely to overcome these resistances.

Here we have evidence that powerholders adjusted the kinds of influence they brought to bear to fit what they believed to be the reason for the target's resistance. If the target's resistance was seen as caused by poor attitudes, then persuasion was one of the favored means (coercion was also favored in such cases). If the resistance was seen as caused by a lack of ability, then expert power was used and little time was wasted trying to persuade the target to improve his performance. If the target was seen as manifesting a variety of problems simultaneously, then the powerholder increased the pressure for change by invoking several different kinds of influence. Simply put, as resistance increased, additional means of influence were brought to bear on the target person. And among these was an attempt to move the target person from his present environment.

These findings are consistent with the notion that the use of power involves an active cognitive search which consists of two stages. First, we see that the powerholder diagnoses the causes of the resistance. He says to himself, "The reason X is acting so badly is that. . . ." Second, the powerholder searches for the best means of influence available to him for dealing with this resistance. That is, he says, "Well, if that's why he is doing so poorly, then I'd better do this."

While this process has been illustrated in terms of work settings, it is not difficult to see how a similar search pattern might operate elsewhere. Thus, a parent whose child gets into continual mischief during the summer vacation must decide whether to promise him some benefit for good behavior, sit down and reason with him, send him to summer camp, appeal to his love for his parents, or threaten some kind of punishment. The process of choice will be actively guided by what the parent decides is causing the mischief in the first place.

Limitations to Rational Calculations

There are several reasons why powerholders may not be able to select the best means of influencing a target person. Most obviously, the powerholder may not have available the proper means of influence. For example, a supervisor may not have the authority to promise a pay raise, despite his recognition that he will be able to influence his employees to produce more if such means are used. Related to this reason is the problem that arises when the use of one means of influence may prevent the powerholder from using a second means, despite the powerholder's recognition that the use of the second means would be more appropriate. Thus for example, if one uses coercion on occasion, it becomes difficult then to switch to the use of persuasion. Researchers who have studied the use of power in penal systems point out that therapy programs in prison tend to be unsuccessful because the prisoners tend to be coerced into entering such programs.

The inhibiting effect that the use of one means of influence has upon the use of a second means is also illustrated in the complaints of social caseworkers that their control of the power to grant or withhold welfare money tends to weaken their ability to provide counseling and guidance to their poverty clients. In effect the poor are unwilling to communicate socioemotional problems to a caseworker because of the possibility that some careless revelation about themselves may cause the caseworker to withdraw funds. While many caseworkers would prefer to influence their clients through counseling, they are unable to do so because they also influence the same clients through the use of money. Similar problems have been noted by supervisors in industry who are expected to influence both task attitudes and socioemotional attitudes of their employees. It has been reported (Reed 1962) that subordinates are not willing to openly communicate problems to the supervisors because of the employees' fears that revealing negative information about themselves will reduce their chances for promotion. In both of these instances, the possession of strong economic means prevents the powerholder from using other means despite his recognition of their usefulness for exercising influence.

A second limitation to choosing the appropriate means of influence occurs when a powerholder simply misdiagnoses the causes of the target's resistance and applies the wrong means of influence. Thus, a teacher might threaten to discipline an inattentive student unless the student's behavior improved. The same teacher would rapidly change tactics if it were discovered that the cause of the student's inattention was a hearing loss. Then, perhaps, the student would be moved to the front of the class as a means of improving his attention.

Still another limitation occurs when the powerholder does not consider a particular means of influence as appropriate. For example, open expressions of love as a means of influencing a wife or child are rejected by some men who believe that such expressions are not consistent with their conceived role of manhood. In a different context, Dartmouth College political scientist David Baldwin (1974) has discussed this limitation in terms of the reluctance of government foreign-policy planners to seriously consider other nations in any terms but coercive military power. He points out that:

> students of international politics are so preoccupied with negative sanctions, threat systems, and military force that they have painted themselves into a conceptual corner which has little room for non-military factors, positive sanctions and promise

systems. It is not surprising, therefore, that the recent *International Encyclopedia of the Social Sciences* included an article on military power potential but none on economic power potential. At a time when military power is losing utility in international politics and economic power is gaining utility, this omission is especially unfortunate. [p. 395]

Lack of Ability or Lack of Motivation?

Powerholders usually diagnose the causes of a target person's resistance into one of two groupings. Either the resistance is attributed to the fact that the target person is inept and lacks ability, or to the fact that the target person has deliberately chosen to refuse to comply. In this second instance, the label of "poor attitude" or "lack of motivation" is used. Thus resistance is attributed by powerholders to either the fact that external forces are controlling the target person ("He wants to help but simply doesn't know how") or to internal forces within the target person ("That s.o.b. could do it if he wanted to help out"). The distinction between internal or external forces tends to be critical for understanding the powerholder's choice of influence tactics. In subsequent chapters we will provide data which show that if the powerholder attributes the target person's resistance to internal factors (choosing to resist) then the powerholder will decide to invoke stronger means of influence to overcome this resistance than if the powerholder attributes the target person's resistance to external causes.

Here I wish to consider briefly the question of what kinds of information powerholders use when deciding that the target's resistance is due to either internal or external forces.

University of Wisconsin social psychologist H. Andrew Michener and his colleagues (John Fleishman, Gregory Elliot, and Joel Skolnick [in press, 1975]) have used concepts derived from attribution theory to help explain this decision. Michener et al. have proposed that the powerholder's judgment is based upon four bits of information: (*a*) the difficulty of the demands placed upon the target person; (*b*) the known ability of the target person; (*c*) the extent to which the target person seems to be trying; and (*d*) whether the target person's performance improves or not. In a test of this proposal, Michener found that powerholders attributed a target person's poor performance on an experimental task (solving anagrams) to external forces or, lack of ability, when the task was known to be difficult for most people, when the target person had a prior history of ineptness in solving anagrams, when the target person signaled that he was trying as hard as he could, and when the target person's performance improved over time, even though it never quite reached the level expected by the powerholder. Powerholders attributed the target person's poor performance to a lack of motivation when the opposite of the above four bits of information were communicated to the powerholder.

In short, the process by which powerholders diagnose the causes of a target person's resistance to influence has its own logic. Basically the powerholder attempts to reach a diagnosis by comparing the target person's current behavior with past behavior. Inconsistencies between current and past behavior are considered due to deliberate resistance when the powerholder knows that what has been requested is within the capabilities of the target person. Under these circumstances it is not unusual to hear powerholders justifying their selection of influence tactics in terms of the target person's poor attitude, hostility, or lack of motivation.

Summary

This chapter has examined how powerholders convert inert resources into actual influence. The basic proposal is that the decision to convert resources into influence is guided by an active cognitive search for the best means of making this conversion. This search involves two distinct stages. In the first the reasons for the target person's refusal to comply are diagnosed. The second stage involves selecting that means of influence considered by the powerholder as most likely to overcome the diagnosed causes of resistance.

It has also been suggested that there are stable linkages between the diagnosed causes of a target person's resistance and the particular means of influence that are chosen. If powerholders attribute the target person's resistance to external forces over which the target person has no control ("I'm trying, but I just can't seem to do it"), then the influence techniques chosen involve training and expert knowledge. In essence these techniques serve to restore self-control to the target person so that he can comply in future interactions.

When powerholders attribute the target person's resistance to internal forces under the control of the target person ("I refuse"), then the influence techniques chosen involve discussion and persuasion, at least initially. If, however, discussion fails, then power-holders are tempted to invoke stronger means of influence to over-come what they believe to be deliberate resistance. These stronger means of influence involve the use of both rewards and punish-ments. Chapters 4 and 6 will examine in more detail the circum-stances under which these last two means of influence are used.

Finally the chapter has briefly surveyed sources that restrict the powerholder's selection of the appropriate means of influence. These sources include the fact that often influence tactics are not available to a given powerholder because of his position in an organization, because he does not recognize that it is legitimate to use some influence tactic, or because he has misdiagnosed the rea-sons for the target person's refusal and simply has chosen the wrong means of influence.

4

The Decision
to Use Rewards

If powerholders use rational calculations when invoking such bases of power as persuasion, expertise, and ecological control, it surely is to be expected that careful thought will be used when considering promises and rewards. This can be traced to the fact that there are costs associated with the successful use of rewards that are not associated with, for example, the use of expert knowledge or persuasion. Promises obligate the powerholder to respond with a reward if the target complies; the powerholder must pay up if he is to retain his credibility.

It is a commonplace observation that, despite the costs involved, rewards and promises are continually used in day-to-day social relations. Aside from their use to increase the benefits to persons who have shown exemplary and meritorious behavior in the past, rewards and promises are mainly used to change the behavior of target persons who are unwilling to comply with simple requests from the powerholder. From Skinnerean psychology to managerial pay policies it has been found that the judicious use of small rewards frequently produces large returns to the powerholder. Behavior is shaped by rewards, and motivations are increased in anticipation of being reinforced. One of the strongest findings of experimental psychology is that target persons respond with compliance when rewards are used. Given the strength of rewards for influencing others, a question that remains to be answered is, why aren't rewards used more often?

Let us begin our search for an answer by asking whether there are identifiable circumstances under which powerholders decide to use rewards. Stated in terms of the idea of "treatment of choice," we ask what kinds of diagnoses of the causes of target resistance lead to the conclusion that rewards should be used.

David Baldwin (1971) has proposed one answer to this question by theorizing that the decision to use rewards is reserved for instances in which the target person's resistance is seen as strong and the powerholder doubts his ability to overcome this resistance. We can restate Baldwin's proposal in terms of the powerholder's subjective expectations of being able to influence a target person: *Rewards are most likely to be used when the powerholder has low expectations that simple persuasion will overcome a target person's resistance.*

If the calculations of the powerholder reveal that only a little urging is needed to overcome the target person's resistance, then the powerholder will be unlikely to couple this urging with some offer of a tangible reward. Thus, politicians will promise very little to the voters in districts that always vote for him but will promise anything in exchange for votes in districts that are not "in his pocket." Similarly, the history of international aid programs suggests that more aid tends to be given to countries that were former enemies than to those that were former allies. In both instances, the use of rewards appears associated with low expectations of successful influence through simple persuasion.

In the following sections of this chapter we will review published instances of the use of reward power and examine whether the "expectancy rule" (rewards are used when powerholders hold low expectations that simple persuasion will cause compliance) is consistent with these published reports.

Before proceeding with this review, however, it is necessary to distinguish between the use of rewards for purposes of philanthropy and the use of rewards as a means of exercising power. If this distinction is not made, then it will be possible to find many instances in which rewards are distributed on bases other than expectations of successful influence.

Philanthropy, altruism, generosity, and charity, as Shopler and Bateson (1965) point out, describe situations in which a typically powerful person, often at some sacrifice to himself, helps someone else who is relatively weak. I believe it makes little sense to describe these acts of charity as power acts, despite the fact that in them powerholders give rewards to target persons. What is missing in them is the fact of the more powerful person wanting something from the person receiving the charity. In its purest form, the act of charity involves no power needs, nor are there any target resistances to be overcome by it. As a result, one may expect that forces other than rational calculations (e.g., norms of social responsibility) are involved in the decisions to distribute rewards for charitable purposes. This distinction should be kept in mind in the discussion that follows on the use of reward power. The discussion will be limited to those instances in which the powerholder: (*a*) has access to rewards that the target person desires, (*b*) and wants the target person to carry out some behavior (*c*) that the target person normally does not want to do.

Perceived Similarity and the Use of Rewards

There is a widespread folk saying that suggests one should reward friends and punish enemies. If these recommendations were applied to power relations, it would follow that rewards should be used more frequently with target persons who were liked than with those who were disliked.

A moment's reflection, however, suggests that this use of influence is not consistent with the general rule that rewards are used when expectations of successful influence are lowest. We surely should be more optimistic about our chances of influencing friends than about our chances of influencing enemies. Accordingly, we expect that, when power is involved, rewards will be used more with disliked than with liked persons. Further, we expect that rewards will be used more with dissimilar than with similar persons. This is because we tend to assume that persons who are similar to ourselves will be cooperative and moved by the same forces that move us. To the extent persons differ from us, however, we have no way of understanding their motives. And the intuitive conclusion is that we have to work harder to make them cooperate.

There are relatively few studies, unfortunately, that have directly examined the frequency with which rewards are used among liked and disliked (or similar-dissimilar) target persons. Furthermore, of the few studies in this area most are based upon the use of bargaining games, in which two opponents of relatively equal power bargain with each other using promises and threats. Tedeschi, Schlenker, and Bonoma (1973) have reviewed the various research studies that have been done in this area and concluded that there is good evidence that liked target persons are seen as more cooperative than disliked persons in bargaining games. However, a study in this series by Schlenker and Tedeschi (1972) found no support pro or con for our belief that disliked persons would be offered more rewards in exchange for cooperation than would liked persons.

Positive support for the prediction, however, has been reported in several studies where superior-subordinate relations were involved.

In a study by Baker, Demarco, and Scott (1975), volunteers were asked to act as supervisors of workers who were either sighted or blind. Actually, the workers, by agreement, did equal amounts of work, whether they were sighted or blind. The supervisors were told that the project was funded by a company which used both sighted and blind workers. The work involved filling bags of marbles in front of TV cameras so that the workers' performance could be monitored by the supervisors.

As supervisors, the volunteers were given the power to award ten-cent pay raises every two minutes to any worker, if they chose to do so. The question that was examined in the study was whether more rewards were given to blind than to sighted workers. The results were that the supervisors awarded three times as many pay raises to the blind workers as to the sighted workers, although both sighted and blind workers did equally good work. These results support the idea that rewards would be invoked more frequently to influence dissimilar others. While there are many other possible explanations for this outcome (for example, feeling sorry for the blind workers), we favor the interpretation that the supervisors held lower expectations of successfully influencing these blind workers because of their handicap. As a result more rewards were promised and used as a means of encouraging them to expend extra effort and so to keep up with the sighted workers.

While the Baker et al. study revealed the predicted relation between the use of rewards and similarity of target person and powerholder, it can be argued that liking for the target person may not have been directly involved. A study by Banks (1974), however, directly investigated the use of rewards among liked and disliked target persons. Liking was experimentally created through a variation of the attitude similarity-dissimilarity technique (cf. Byrne 1961) in which subjects are told they share a similar outlook on life with the person they are to be paired with. As in the Baker et al. study, volunteers were assigned to the role of supervisor, with the job of monitoring the performance of trainees. Power to reward was provided the supervisors in the form of money that could be allotted to the trainees in order to encourage good work.

The findings were that significantly more rewards were given to dissimilar trainees than to similar trainees. Instead of rewarding those they liked, the supervisors gave more rewards to those they disliked. This finding can be interpreted to mean that the supervisors had low expectations that the dissimilar target persons would continue to perform at a satisfactory level if the supervisors relied upon simple persuasion. Thus, rewards were more frequently invoked to prevent performance from falling off.

What is needed at this time is research that directly examines a powerholder's expectations of successful influence in relation to the use of rewards with similar and dissimilar target persons. While the above-cited studies by Banks and by Baker et al. are consistent with our "expectations rule," there are still alternate explanations for the findings that need to be ruled out. Until such additional studies are done, the speculations present in this section should be labeled as interesting but untested hypotheses.

Status, Reputation, and Ingratiation

A continuous theme in the literature of Western civilization is that of a hero seeking to define himself through his relations with other people. To be an outcast is tragedy. To lose one's reputation is sufficient cause for war. To win love is divine. We cannot fail to respond with intense interest to accounts of a hero's journey through life with its tragic, noble, and often funny encounters.

In the social sciences, as in literature, there is an intense interest in trying to account for people's persistent urge to be liked and accepted by others. This urge has been studied from many vantage points. We ask, What determines romantic love? Why do persons comply with the opinions of someone they like? Why the necessity to win affection and love?

For some social scientists, the gaining of love and admiration from others is not only seen as a desired end in itself but represents a way to increase one's power over others. Power, says Mott (1970), is access to the pooled energy of many, and Hobbes has written, "to have friends is Power: for they are strengths united." Thus, it is possible to view the urge to relate in positive ways to other persons as one manifestation of a drive for power. Indeed, Tedeschi et al. (1971) recently argued that an important element in understanding interpersonal relations is the assumption that people seek to be consistent in their behavior so that they will be liked and trusted and, accordingly, so that they can exert influence more easily.

If power is involved in the pursuit of friendship, then our expectancy rule should hold concerning when rewards will be used. As a powerholder perceives that the target person views him with indifference or worse, one should expect an increased reliance upon rewards by the powerholder as a means of overcoming this resistance.

While no direct evidence is available on this point, there is considerable biographical material detailing the behavior of persons attempting to rise in society which supports this view. In general, persons desiring to gain new and more prestigious friends spend large amounts of money for parties, presents, and gifts to charity regardless of the objective costs involved. Cleveland Amory (1960) and other observers of society in this country have described in detail the lavish parties given by persons with newly obtained wealth who wish to be admitted to equal standing with those already high in society. In these instances, the spending of large amounts is done solely to change for the better the indifferent or negative attitudes of persons considered of higher status. In line with the arguments presented in this chapter, it is assumed that our social climber does not believe that he will be freely welcomed as an intimate friend. His expectation is that simply asking for friendship will not be enough to overcome the indifference of the higher-status target persons. Hence, stronger means of influence must be used.

Of course, we do not need to examine the drama of attempts to rise in society among the very rich to find instances of this kind of use of rewarding power. At a day-to-day level, presents are frequently given by persons attempting to win the affections of another. Candy, flowers, jewelry, and expensive and inexpensive knicknacks are continually used by lovers who doubt their affection is reciprocated and who wish to influence for the better the opinions of their heart's object.

One concern of powerholders when rewards are invoked for this purpose has to do with the permanence of the social relations that are established. Despite the cynical observation that money can buy anything, observers in the social sciences continue to advance compelling reasons to doubt this belief. For instance, Raven and Kruglanski (1970) argue that the use of sanctions such as rewards are not likely to produce permanent changes in the attitude structure of target persons, at least immediately. Rather, when rewards cease to be applied, there is a high probability that the target person may revert to his original attitudes and behavior.

Similar arguments concerning the lack of permanent social change produced by using rewards can be derived from the resource exchange theory of Foa and Foa (1975). Using this theory, one might argue that the exchange of a material resource, such as money, for an affectional resource, such as love and friendship, is psychologically out of balance and, hence, not likely to endure. Centuries earlier, Machiavelli similarly warned the Prince that the use of reward powers, or "liberality" as he called it, would not guarantee that the Prince would be perpetually held in high regard by his followers. After first warning the Prince that attempts to gain the affection of others through "liberality" might over time exhaust his resources, Machiavelli went on to cite the temporary effects of gaining status through the use of rewards and concludes:

it is much safer to be feared than loved, if one of the two has to be wanting. For it may be said of men in general that they are ungrateful, voluble, dissemblers, anxious to avoid danger, and covetous of gain. *As long as you benefit them, they are entirely yours*; they offer you their blood, their goods, their life and their children . . . when the necessity [for making sacrifices] is remote, but when it approaches they revolt. And the Prince . . . is ruined; for friendship which is gained by purchase, and not through grandeur or nobility of spirit, is bought but not secured. . . . And men have less scruple in offending one who makes himself loved [in this way] than one who makes himself feared.

For love is held by a chain of obligations which, men being selfish, is broken whenever it serves their purposes; but fear is maintained by a dread of punishment which never fails. [p. 90]

Despite such warnings, there is continual documentation from books, public media, research, and everyday observation that persons are willing to dispense rewards in order to change a target person's appraisal from indifference to avowed admiration. While not direct evidence, this kind of use of material rewards is consistent with our "expectancy rule."

So far we have talked about conscious efforts by powerholders to influence the opinions of target persons by using material rewards. There is another variant of this use in which the powerholder is made the victim of his desire for admiration. In this variation, powerholders are influenced to dispense rewards in exchange for flattery from subordinates. The decision to dispense rewards in this instance is based, not on a deliberate effort to win another's affection, but upon needs that powerholders tend to be unaware of. For instance Rogow and Lasswell (1965) have described one type of political leader who willingly exchanged the material resources of his office for flattery. Similarly, in business organizations, it has long been recognized that "buttering up the boss" is a royal road to organizational advancement and success. In exchange for flattery, managers seem willing to grant promotions and higher pay. In these kinds of instances it is doubted that the expectancy rule operates. If asked, managers would claim that they were seeking no ego gratification from their subordinates and that any added pay that was given out was awarded on the basis of the subordinate's loyalty to the company. In short, ingratiation tactics can be viewed as part of the tactical behaviors of those who have few resources.

In summary, to the extent that a powerholder's aim is to increase his social standing, or to improve his reputation, or to make friends of those who are indifferent to his existence, he will be tempted to dispense rewards. If the expectancy rule is correct, the decisions to use rewards in these instances should be accompanied by the belief that the target persons would not change their evaluations for the better by simply talking to the powerholder. The problem here is that the powerholder's sense of worth may be built on shifting sands. As Machiavelli warns the Prince, the powerholder can exhaust his resources in exerting this kind of influence and subsequently lose the friendships he sought in the first place.

Rewards at Work

In his book *Pay and Organizational Effectiveness*, Lawler (1971) listed the many kinds of valued outcomes that employees associate with their pay. Most obviously, money is instrumental in satisfying needs for security and physical well-being. In addition, pay may provide the person with bench marks for evaluating his own worth. Lawler reports that a broad spectrum of psychological motives including esteem, autonomy, and self-actualization have at one time or another been found to be correlated with the amount of pay the person receives. For a fair majority of persons, what one "gets" represents what one is worth.

Despite the central relevance of pay and other material rewards in our society, there have been surprisingly few attempts to examine what influences managers to grant or withhold pay increases. Perhaps the lack of interest in this question arises from the textbook idea that rational managers distribute pay in proportion to the employee's productive contribution to the business establishment. Simple reflection should tell us, however, that these rational considerations are not the whole story. There are many social and psychological forces acting on the manager to lead him to ignore the productivity of the employee. These forces range from the number of persons available for hire, to the financial state of the business, to such subtle psychological forces as the presence of ingratiating employees who exchange flattery for money.

In the next three sections of this chapter we will examine the social-psychological conditions that have been associated with a manager's decision to award higher pay as a means of influencing the behavior of his employees. It will be argued that money is used by managers when they anticipate that at some future time an employee may be unwilling to comply. *Money as reward is used to prevent the occurrence of resistance rather than to eliminate present resistance.* Thus, we modify the expectancy rule to read: rewards are most likely to be used at work when the powerholder has low expectations that the target person will continue to comply in future interactions. The following sections will examine this expectancy rule in terms of the organizational climate in which pay is given, employee motivation, and the social context in which performance is judged.

Organizational Climate

Cartwright (1965) has observed that the organizational climate in which pay is administered will affect a manager's decision about the use of pay. Basically, the organizational climate operates in this way by influencing the manager's assumptions about what motivates employees to work hard. In an *autocratic* organizational climate there exists a general belief system that employees require surveillance and cannot be trusted to work independently. The very fact that there are strict rules and regulations, a continual surveillance of the employees, and a strict hierarchical control of behavior produce the belief among managers that their employees are motivated by outside forces, that is, the managers' orders and influence. Since this is the assumption, it follows that managers will not place too much reliance upon means of influence such as discussion. Use of this form of influence assumes that employees are in charge of their own behavior and that rational discussions are enough to produce compliance. Given these low expectations of successful influence through discussion, there is a great emphasis placed in autocratic climates upon the establishment of strong sanction systems. Most faith is placed in "objectively based pay systems that tie pay to hard criteria such as quantity of output, profits, or sales, and thus require a minimum of trust" (Lawler, 1972, p. 277).

In democratically run business organizations there is a deemphasis upon surveillance, supervisory control, and upon rules and regulations. Rather, the emphasis is on shared decision-making activities in which employees are given the power to make decisions about their own work loads and effort. One consequence of this kind of democratic climate is that managers come to believe that their orders will be carried out willingly and at the discretion of the employee. The employee is seen as freely choosing to do the work properly rather than being compelled to do so by the manager's promises and threats. An interesting observation of Lawler is that democratically run organizations tend to place less emphasis on money and more on psychological forms of return to employees. These psychological forms of return tend to focus on allowing employees more autonomy and opportunities to do meaningful and creative work.

This kind of emphasis is consistent with the expectancy rule derived from Baldwin's hypothesis of an inverse relation between expectations of successful influence and the use of rewards. This rule asserts that reward power is most likely to be used when the powerholder assumes that the target person is actively opposed to accepting influence. As expectations of successful influence go down, the probabilities of a decision to use rewards go up. Since managers in democratically run organizations tend to believe that employees are self-motivated and do not have to be forced to work with either a carrot or a stick, their expectations of being able to exert influence successfully through discussion should be higher.

While I know of no data on this point, what has been said here suggests the curious prediction that pay should be lower in democratically than autocratically run organizations. This is because managers should rely less on such means in the former than the latter organizations. In any case, my point is that one can expect variations in the use of pay within business organizations that can be traced to the kinds of assumptions managers make about employees' motivations. In turn, these assumptions can be traced to the collective values of management which form a part of the organization's psychological climate.

Employee Performance and the Decision to Reward

From Baldwin's proposal we might expect that managers would reward employees doing unsatisfactory work. This is because in these instances expectations of successful influence are lowest. In the previously cited field studies by the present writer (Kipnis and Lane 1962; Kipnis and Cosentino 1969) concerned with supervisors' attempts to elevate subordinates' poor performances, no mention of rewards was made by supervisors as a means of influencing their employees to do better work. Indeed, it would be difficult to locate many managers who attempt to correct incompetence with pay raises. Organizations do not encourage the use of rewards as a means of changing the performance of noncompliant workers. Such a use of power might be viewed as a "bribe" and, hence, as being illicit. Furthermore, having to honor a promise to reward a worker who has previously annoyed a supervisor by his poor work may in fact be personally distasteful, and would certainly anger satisfactory workers.

We have found generally that pay raises, promotions, favorable performance reviews, and the like are used either to maintain a target at some acceptable level of performance or to encourage the target to exceed this level. For instance, in a laboratory simulation of work (Kipnis and Vanderveer 1971), subjects in their role as managers were provided with the power to reward their workers with pay increases if they so chose. It was found that most rewards were given to superior performers, next most to average workers, and the fewest rewards were given to inferior workers. This finding is hardly surprising and merely confirms the commonplace observation that good work is usually rewarded more than bad work.

Exchange theorists might also view this finding as support for the belief that notions of equity regulate human exchanges, since management tends to match the employees' input of effort with appropriate outcome levels of money. From the perspective of power relations, however, one might suspect that the added money awarded the superior worker was not used by the managers merely to reward past performance. Rather, I suggest that the managers had one eye to the future and used rewards to insure that the output of the superior workers would continue at high levels. As a general rule, rewards serve in the mind of the powerholder as a means of preventing entropy, that is, of preventing the performance of well-motivated workers from decaying to some unacceptable level. Thus, promises and rewards are used by managers to overcome *anticipated* resistances, rather than *actual* resistances, by workers.

It follows from this conclusion that superior work per se is not likely to be often rewarded if management is confident that the employee is programmed to remain at this high level without interference from outsiders. Praise and encouragement tend to be substituted for money in these instances. It is only when uncertainty is associated with the employee's performances, when management suspects for example that the employee's high level of performance may soon fall off (the employee may hint of taking another job), that serious consideration is given to awarding higher salary.

The Rewards of Loyalty When Rebellion Is Near

In our research in work settings we have found that the use of pay as reward was sharply influenced by the amount and kind of resistance managers were experiencing from their employees. When employees were all performing satisfactorily, rewards were doled out sparingly. When some employees expressed poor attitudes about the work and reduced their output, then managers increased the number of pay raises given to the remaining satisfactory employees. Presumably these raises were given to prevent their satisfactory employees from joining the ranks of the malcontents.

This conclusion is based upon several industrial simulation studies (Goodstadt and Kipnis 1970; Kipnis and Vanderveer 1971; Fodor 1974), which found that the presence of noncompliant employees, who deliberately refused to obey a manager's orders, increased the number of pay raises given by managers to workers who did accept orders. In the absence of these noncompliant employees, the number of pay raises given out to employees was significantly reduced.

We may illustrate this process with the findings from the Kipnis and Vanderveer study. In this particular study, business majors were appointed as managers of a simulated business and required to direct the work of four employees. The managers were delegated the power to give pay raises if they chose to do so. In one condition (labeled "poor attitude"), one of the four workers deliberately refused to follow orders, while the remaining three workers did satisfactory work. In a second condition (labeled "control condition"), all of the workers did satisfactory work. Table 4 shows the average number of pay raises given by managers to the three compliant workers in these two conditions. Table 4 also shows the managers' evaluation of the three compliant workers' performances at the end of the work sessions. These evaluations were based upon the managers' rating of each worker or four 11-point scales that were summed into an overall evaluation score. Since the amount of work in this study was regulated by the experiments, the reader should understand that the performances of the three compliant workers in both the Poor Attitude Condition and the Control Condition were exactly the same. Hence, any difference in managers' use of rewards toward these three compliant workers could be safely attributed to the presence or absence of the defiant fourth worker.

It can be seen that the same compliant performance evoked more pay raises and higher performance evaluations when the manager experienced resistance from the fourth worker than when no resistance was shown. These differences in pay raises and perform-

ance evaluations were statistically significant. The explanation offered by Vanderveer and myself was that the presence of noncompliant workers provided the managers with new standards for judging
the worth of compliant workers. The managers were suddenly re-
minded of how bad things could be if all the workers, rather than
just one, decided not to comply. The presence of a militant who
challenged authority provided a new baseline for evaluating the
behavior of the loyal workers.

Table 4.1 Evaluation and Average Number of Pay Raises Awarded by
Managers to Three Compliant Workers

Condition	Number of Pay Raises Given to Three Compliant Workers	Performance Evaluations of Three Compliant Workers
Fourth worker expressed defiiance	4.0	32.0
Fourth worker expressed *no* defiance	2.1	26.9

It should not be thought that these findings are restricted to
simple, contrived laboratory situations. A recent doctoral dissertation by my student Ronald J. Grey (1975) provided strong evidence that supervisors in "real life" similarly increase the number
of rewards they give to compliant workers as the number of noncompliant workers they direct increases.

Grey's research was carried out among supervisors of clerical
workers in a large insurance company. Fifty-nine supervisors were
asked to evaluate each of their employees. The supervisors directed
units of varying size, ranging from three to twenty-six female employees, with a median of eleven employees. The data collected
consisted of the supervisor's summed evaluation of each of their
employee's performance on six factors: quality of work, quantity of
work, consistency of performance, ability to follow instructions,
ability to learn unit procedures, and a rating of the employee's
overall worth to the company. In addition the supervisors were
asked whether they would recommend the employee for promotion
and for a pay increase. Finally records of actual pay increases for
the previous year were obtained from company files. This last bit
of reward data was incomplete for many of the employees, and

the actual amount of the pay increase was only partially controlled by the supervisor, thus rendering actual pay raises somewhat suspect. Nevertheless, this information, coded in terms of the percentage of salary increase for the prior year, was included because of our interest in the distribution of rewards.

The major problem for Grey was to obtain information on the number of compliant and noncompliant employees working for each supervisor. In the prior experiments it had been possible to program workers to act in a compliant or noncompliant manner. Thus there was no problem of how to measure the existence of compliance. It had been put there or taken away by the experimenter. Grey measured the number of compliant and noncompliant employees working for each supervisor by including the following question on each employee's evaluation form that the supervisor filled out:

If this individual has a basic weakness, is it due to:
(check one answer)
—Lack of ability
—Poor attitude
—Both a lack of ability and poor attitude
—This individual has no basic weakness

The proportion of inept subordinates working for a supervisor was calculated from the above form by first determining the number of employees working for each supervisor who were rated as lacking ability. This number was then divided by the total number of employees in the supervisor's unit. In like manner the proportions of poor-attitude employees and complex-problem employees were computed. Finally the total proportion of noncompliant employees was obtained by summing the above three indices of noncompliance (% inept + % poor attitude + % complex). Through this procedure, information was obtained about the proportions of employees who resisted their supervisors' orders due to external reasons (lack of ability) or due to internal reasons (poor attitudes). In addition, information was available on the total numbers of employees who resisted their supervisors' orders, regardless of the reasons involved. Supervisors reported, on the average, that about one-third of their employees resisted their orders for reasons of attitude or ability. This figure ranged from a high of 70 percent for one supervisor to a low 0 percent for nine supervisors who said that none of their employees had any weaknesses.

In short, through this method of measurement Grey had a count on the number of noncompliant employees and the number of compliant employees working for each supervisor. Compliant employees were all those employees whom the supervisor said had "no basic weaknesses."

At this point the reader may object that the measures of noncompliance used in the study were subjective and were based solely upon the biased judgment of the supervisor. In part, the objection is correct. Whether or not a given employee was in fact inept or held poor attitudes, as measured by objective standards, was not known. However, such information is not relevant in terms of the objectives of the research. Supervisors' perceptions of these conditions are, for all intents and purposes, their reality. Since they use these perceptions of their employees to decide upon the distribution of rewards and punishments, we must, like the employees, accept these judgments as having some claim to validity in their own right.

The basic question was the extent to which supervisors would distribute rewards equally or unequally to their *compliant* workers. Grey's hypothesis was that the distribution would be unequal; that compliant employees working for a supervisor who had many noncompliant employees would receive more rewards than compliant employees who worked in units that contained few or no noncompliant employees.

Table 4.2 shows the data to test the hypothesis in the form of correlations between the proportion of noncompliant employees working for a given supervisor and the supervisor's average evaluations of the remaining compliant employees. Positive correlations mean that the larger the proportion of noncompliant employees in a given unit, the more favorable the evaluations given by that unit's supervisor to compliant employees.

As examination of table 4.2 reveals that one can predict quite well a supervisor's evaluations of compliant employees by simply knowing the proportion of noncompliant employees in the supervisor's work unit. In particular, the greater the proportion of employees seen by a supervisor as manifesting poor attitudes, the more likely was the supervisor to recommend compliant employees for promotion and pay raises, as well as to give them higher performance-evaluation ratings. The proportion of inept employees appears to have less influence on the supervisor's judgments, although this proportion does carry some slight weight.

Table 4.2 Correlations between the Proportion of NonCompliant Employees
in a Work Unit and Evaluations of Compliant Employees

% Noncompliant employees in the work unit	Evaluations of Compliant Employees			
	Performance Evaluations	Recommended Promotions	Recommended Pay Raise	Actual Pay Raise
1. % Poor-attitude employees	.30**	.32**	.33*	.25*
2. % Inept employees	.23*	.15	.09	−.02
3. % Complex problems[a]	—	—	—	—
4. % Total non-compliance (1 + 2 + 3)	.50**	.48**	.32**	.21*

NOTE: All correlations are partial r's, adjusted for the number of non-compliant employees in the unit, and tenure, sex, and age of the rater and ratee.
[a]Only 2 percent of the employees were rated as complex problems—hence correlations were not computed for this group.
**significant beyond .01 level; *significant beyond the .05 level.

If one disregards the reason for the noncompliance and simply adds up the total proportion of noncompliant employees in a given unit, the findings become even stronger. I am tempted to suggest from these findings that if one wishes to curry favor with the boss, a sure means is to plant several truculent, hostile employees in the unit (the more the better), and then hasten to assure the boss of one's loyalty. One should be deluged with riches.

Returning to the original argument of this section, the data from these several studies are seen as consistent with our expectancy rule. In this instance it would appear that the presence of large numbers of employees who resist a manager's influence serve to lower the manager's expectations that the remaining employees can be counted on to maintain satisfactory performance. Increasing the amounts of rewards, in the form of recommendations for promotion and so on, is seen as a way of helping to guarantee the future loyalty of those who still remain compliant.

By analogy, if a father has all dutiful and compliant sons, his evaluations of their worth might tend to be less favorable than if one of his sons has proved to be a continued disgrace. Under these circumstances his remaining sons would be appreciated far more intensely. Indeed, the father might increase the amount of benefits given to the remaining sons as a means of preventing them from following the example of the disgraced son. Or, to give another example, in the late 1960s, when political dissent was most active, the silent majority was most praised by supporters of the Vietnam War. Thus, the powerholder can be expected to actively use his available resources to promise rewards to his supporters when peril threatens from without or within. As mentioned before, rewards tend to be used by powerholders to prevent the decay of satisfactory performance. Any forces that arouse suspicion that loyal followers are soon to be subverted also serve to increase the powerholder's attraction to invoking rewards.

Summary

In this chapter we have examined the powerholder's decisions to use rewards in relation to his beliefs concerning the amount of resistance liable to be shown by the target person. Following Baldwin's view of when rewards are used, we have suggested that, as expectations for successful influence decrease, the powerholder is tempted to use stronger means of influence. These stronger means tend to take the form of rewards or punishments.

One conclusion reached in this chapter is that rewards are used when the powerholder wishes to secure the good will of the target person or when the powerholder has some doubts that existing compliance by the target person will continue. The implications of this expectancy view need to be worked out in considerably more detail, however, than has been provided here. In particular, study must be given to the situational forces that help shape the powerholder's expectancies, as well as to the personal characteristics of the powerholder, as these also influence expectations of successful influence. Chapter 6 provides considerably more detail concerning the forces shaping decisions to use coercive power. The paucity of research dealing with this issue in relation to the use of rewards, however, precludes discussion of that aspect of the subject at this time.

5   Coercive Power

Of all the bases of power available to man, the power to hurt others is possibly most often used, most often condemned, and most difficult to control. The absence of coercive power creates insecurities, but its presence terrifies. Our feelings about coercion are mixed, similar to those of a ten-year-old looking under his bed for "spooks." He hopes they're not there, but suppose they were! Fascination with coercion is reflected in such disparate events as the enormous popularity of films depicting violence and aggression to the reading of the Old Testament, with its focus on the horrific forms of coercive power used to punish transgressions. Many persons receive great comfort from reading that God used plagues, famines, diseases, and death to crush his enemies. Indeed, I think that the ambivalent feeling held by many toward Christ can be traced to his message to renounce coercion and love those who do you harm. To this day those who truly accept this message are considered naive, if not half-witted.

While the art of coercion has not advanced much since Christ's time, its use is perhaps more widespread today and its expression takes more forms than in past times. Let us briefly consider the many ways in which coercive power may be expressed. First, the state relies on its military and legal resources to intimidate nations, or even its own citizens. Businesses rely upon the control of economic resources. Schools and universities rely upon their right to deny students formal education, while the church threatens individuals with loss of grace. At the personal level, individuals exercise coercive power through a reliance upon physical strength, verbal facility, or the ability to grant or withhold emotional support from others. These bases provide the individual with the means to physically harm, bully, humiliate, or deny love to others.

In this chapter, we will discuss some reasons why people may be tempted to invoke coercive power. As with other bases of power, the use of coercion can be viewed as being a complex function of (1) an aroused need, (2) access to resources which have the potential to be used coercively, and (3) restraining or inhibitory forces acting on the powerholder. Within this framework we will also discuss the possibility that, as the reasons for invoking coercion change, so too will the ways in which the powerholder views himself and his target.

While these reasons can be viewed in terms of the expectancy rule that was discussed in Chapter 4, we shall delay discussion of coercion from this vantage point until Chapter 6. It suffices to say here that the picture of the rationally calculating powerholder fits all of the various reasons for choosing coercion described in this chapter except that of anger. In this instance one frequently finds that little thought has been given to the act of doing harm.

Definition of Coercive Power

Tedeschi, Smith, and Brown (1972) define coercive power as the use of threats and punishments to gain compliance with the powerholder's demands. This definition is consistent with our more general definition of power motivation, but here the means of influence used to induce compliance are considered noxious. While Tedeschi et al. do not state from whose point of view the threats and punishments are considered noxious—that is, the powerholder's, the target's, or an outside observer's—we will consider the point of view of the powerholder. That is, if he *thinks* he is invoking a threat or a punishment, we will call the means of influence coercive.

Because of this emphasis on the powerholder, little will be said about the effectiveness of the use of coercive power in securing a target's compliance. This is because we must know what the target feels about the threatened sanctions before we can tell if the threats and punishments will produce their intended effect. For example, a banker's threat of foreclosure may be viewed as rewarding by a homeowner whose house is in complete disrepair and who is looking for an excuse to move into an apartment. In this instance the banker's threat only strengthens the homeowner's resolve not to pay. There is general agreement that the motivations of the target, and how much weight he gives the powerholder's resources, need to be understood before statements can be made concerning the likelihood of successful use of coercion (French and Raven 1959; Thibaut and Kelley 1959).

The burden of attempting to predict when threats and punishments will achieve intended consequences is a task that may be beyond the ability of social science, except in very limited and contrived situations. This is because the use of coercive power tends to have both immediate and long-range effects. While the immediate effects are predictable, if one has sufficient information about the target, the long-range effects of the use of coercion appear almost unknowable because the use of coercive power generates resistances in the target (Brehm 1966; French and Raven 1959) that may be far stronger than any present initially. Frequently, the perception of threat generates aid from bystanders, who, out of sympathy and moral outrage, join ranks with the target to help thwart the powerholder (Stotland 1959). A good example of this inability to predict the outcomes of the use of coercive power may be found in the *Pentagon Papers,* which documented the early stages of America's entry into the Vietnam War. Repeatedly, steps were taken by military planners to increase military pressure on North Vietnam as a means of causing the early collapse of its efforts in the South. Projects such as Operation Rolling Thunder were devised in which American use of force, including bombing, would periodically escalate until the North Vietnamese gave up. Despite optimistic predictions about the outcome of this use of force, the war actually escalated and intensified—the exact opposite of what had been predicted. The bombing may have strengthened, rather than weakened, the enemy's resolve to resist.

Alfred Adler (1956), in an article written in 1918-19, commenting on the Russian Revolution, made similar observations on the uncontrollable and unpredictable effects of the reliance on coercive power:

The struggle for power has a psychological aspect. Even where the welfare of the subjugated is intended, the use of even moderate power (of a punitive kind) stimulates opposition everywhere, as far as we can see. Human nature generally answers external coercion with a countercoercion. It seeks its satisfaction not in rewards for obedience and docility, but aims to prove that its own means of power are the stronger. The results of the application of power are apt to be disappointing to both parties. . . . Those who are excluded from power lie in wait for the revolt and are receptive to any argument [P. 456].

It is, thus, more manageable and perhaps more important to understand what tempts the powerholder to use threats and punishments than to understand when these threats and punishments will achieve their intended effects. We will describe some of the more important reasons for the use of threats and punishments, ranging from the angry aggressor seeking revenge, to the analytic government policy-maker calculating the costs and benefits of engaging in war. The reader may note that in only one of the instances that we shall describe does the desire to inflict harm figure as a major reason for invoking coercive power. We see no reason to assume that aggressive and malicious intent are always associated with the use of coercive power. In most instances the use of coercive power, when viewed from the vantage of the powerholder, represents an attempt to increase chances for obtaining some desired effect, one which less harsh means of influence are considered unlikely to achieve.

The Use of Coercion for Aggressive Purposes

The first reason why individuals seek out and use coercive power is that they have a desire to punish and harm others for real and imagined wrongs. In this case the power need of the powerholder is oriented toward forcing the target into a negatively valued region so that the target will experience pain and suffering. Of all the various reasons why coercive power is employed, this one has received the most attention from psychologists.

Many observers of human behavior have argued that underlying aggressive behavior of this kind is an instinctual apparatus that propels humans into violent encounters with other (Lorenz 1966; Freud 1957). Furthermore, recent physiological research dealing with the brain's functioning has uncovered findings that are not inconsistent with this contention; it has been shown that older areas of the brain contain regions that control the expression of aggression. Both in animals and humans, electrical or chemical stimulation of the hypothalamus and associated regions of the brain elicit aggressive responses, which appear to be coordinated in humans with thoughts of inflicting harm to others (Moyer 1971).

To think of doing injury, however, is not the same as actually to deliver noxious stimuli to another person. In terms of our model of power usage, the inclination to do harm is only the first step in this process. Before this inclination may be translated into behavior it must first be determined if the angered individual possesses appropriate resources that can be converted into coercive means of influence. Does he possess weapons such as guns or knives? Is he physically stronger than the target, so that he may assault him? Does he possess a "poisoned" tongue to belittle and insult him? Can he withdraw emotional support as a means of doing harm? Lacking such resources, the individual may be forced to "turn the other cheek" and swallow his anger, or he may perhaps secretly turn his efforts to developing appropriate resources and thus eventually be in a position to openly aggress (Gurr 1970). But in any case, the expression of aggression must be contingent upon the availability of appropriate resources.

As an aside it should be noted that psychologists concerned with the study of aggression have paid little attention to how persons without resources react to provocation. Most of the experimental studies in this area have provided subjects with appropriate resources (for example, the power to administer electric shock to the target) and have examined the circumstances under which subjects will convert this resource into coercive power. Thus we lack information about the cognitive transformations that must occur within angered subjects when they do not have the resources to act coercively. Dollard et al. (1939) have suggested that organisms displace their anger onto weaker targets in these instances, but this suggestion has not been the central focus of present-day research. Studies of poverty cultures by modern anthropologists suggest that one common reaction among those lacking resources is the development of forbearance and patience in the face of provocation and the adoption of an "Uncle Tom" orientation toward power. Animal studies also support this suggestion. For example, studies of apes in their natural habitat (Washburn and Hamburg

1968) reveal that weaker apes, when provoked by the more dominant and stronger members of the group, respond with a repertory
of placating acts (fondling the scrotum of the stronger ape) rather
than with aggression. A lack of means, in this case superior physical strength, serves to inhibit an ape's open aggression.

Institutional Power Used for Aggressive Purposes

Attempts to use coercive power to satisfy aggressive needs are
not limited to personal actions, such as physical assaults and the
like. To the extent the angered party has access to *institutional*
resources, such as political patronage or the right to hire and fire
employees, he will be tempted to use these instead of personal resources. A good example of this is found in Swanberg's study
(1961) of the life of William Randolph Hearst, the influential
newspaper publisher. Swanberg reports that Hearst frequently invoked his institutional powers to avenge personal affronts. From
about the years 1917 through 1930, Hearst very much wanted to
be nominated by the Democratic party for the presidency of the
United States, and, if not that, for the governorship of New York
State. These ambitions were continually blocked by Alfred E. Smith,
one of the heads of the Democratic party, who had similar ambitions and publicly charged that Hearst was a liar and worse. In
anger and retribution, Hearst ordered his many newspaper editors
to print only information that would damage the reputation of
Smith. Thus Smith was described in all Hearst papers as a "corrupt
lackey" of various business interests. At one time, a story charged
that Smith was personally responsible for the starvation deaths of
young children in New York City because, as a servant of the milk
lobby, he refused to lower the price of milk. Pictures of wan, starving children were featured prominently. Similar virulent newspaper
articles continued to appear from the 1920s to the 1930s, none of
them particularly true. According to Swanberg, Smith was on
Hearst's "sh-t list" and was to be treated accordingly.

Other instances in which angered individuals have invoked their
institutional resources for purposes of retaliation can easily be
found. Albert Speer (1970), a close associate of Adolph Hitler
before World War II, reported in his memoirs that a night club
comedian, Werner Fink, made fun of Hitler's passion for architecture. Hitler, who was particularly sensitive to any personal criti-

cisms, was infuriated and immediately retaliated by ordering Fink sent to a concentration camp.

In these instances, we have accounts of individuals invoking their institutional powers to seek retribution because of anger over personal insults. The process is difficult to detect because it is covered over with justifications that make it seem as if the individual were only attempting to further the goals of the institution by his coercive actions. Yet the same physiological processes may be involved in the decorticated cat angrily clawing and hissing at an imagined enemy as in the case of the offended publisher printing tales about his enemy. The availability of institutional resources in combination with this anger, however, can produce more destructive and long-lasting consequences.

Security and the Perception of Danger

Little needs to be said about this second reason for seeking and using coercive power. Enormous amounts of time and energy are spent by individuals, businesses, and nations in developing means to protect themselves from dangers, real or imagined. The arousal of fear tends to take priority over any of man's contemplated enterprises.

When fear is aroused, one of the first strategies of most persons is to attempt to mobilize greater force than the potential attacker. Unfortunately, the successful mobilization of means of defense does not necessarily alleviate fears, and often may intensify them. This is because, once armed, individuals become overly sensitized to danger signals. The very presence of means of defense continually signals how unsafe the environment is.

An interesting study by Mulder and Stemerding (1963) illustrates this tendency of people to mobilize resources when faced with threat. In this particular study independent shopkeepers in small Dutch villages were informed of the possibility that a large American-type supermarket was to move into their village, with the strong likelihood of wiping out the smaller shops. The reaction of the shopkeepers was to organize into militant groups, who collectively would possess the resources needed to block the threat. Further, the shopkeepers elected as leader the most militant person among them, suggesting that given sufficient resources the shopkeepers might move from a purely defensive posture to what is called, in military terms, "a defensive first strike," in which safety is secured by eliminating the sources of fear.

It is important to note that, unlike in the first reason offered for seeking coercive power, fear rather than anger is the main emotion involved here. The power need involved is to eliminate through the use of threats and punishments the danger signal originating from the target.

Ego Needs and Sense of Strength

A third reason why people seek to control and use coercive power is to satisfy ego needs related to a sense of worth. In our culture weakness is a pejorative term. It is a feminine trait, perhaps not even valued nowadays by many women. Strength on the other hand is a positively valued male attribute. The young boy is admonished by his parents to fight back and not to be a sissy. The desire to build up one's personal sense of worth by increasing one's physical strength is catered to by a whole industry. Beginning some time in the 1920s and continuing to this day is an enormously successful magazine campaign offering young boys a series of lessons in "dynamic tension," as a means of increasing their physical strength. The burden of the argument is that "97-pound weaklings are ashamed of themselves, tend to be humiliated by bullies, and usually must settle for second best."

Thus we see that, as the result of this cultural linking of strength with self-esteem, individuals come to seek the potential to harm others or actually to harm others as a means of reaffirming their own sense of worth. The envious Iago appears to have had no other motivation for his destruction of Othello than an inner rage that the Moor was more respected than himself; thus, to destroy Othello was to reaffirm the worth of Iago. While I know of no direct evidence on this issue, it appears that paradoxically, self-esteem and perhaps mental health are improved to the extent that the individual believes himself to be stronger than those of higher status.

Raven and Kruglanski (1970) have extended this argument in a discussion of the views of Frantz Fanon, the black psychiatrist and implacable enemy of colonialism. Fanon argued that only the use of coercion and violence would free the colonized from their ingrained feelings of inferiority. In essence, the use of violence becomes a cleansing force, ridding the colonized of their habitual deference and bent knees.

Why should the use of violence produce these beneficial effects among the downtrodden? Raven and Kruglanski argue that only through the use of violence can an individual be sure that he, rather than others, is in control of the situation. These authors point out that if an individual attempts to influence others through gentle means, such as persuasion and pleading, one cannot be sure that any subsequent changes in the target were in fact due to the individual's personal influence. Change accomplished through coercion, on the other hand, can clearly be attributed to the action and the power of the influencing agent. The influencing agent knows that he is effective, that his threats caused people to respect and to listen to what he has to say. In an experimental study on this point Kite (1965) found that when a powerholder used threats to change another's behavior he attributed these changes to his personal influence, whereas when rewards were used to change behavior, changes were attributed to the personal motivations of the target of influence. Similar findings have been reported by Kipnis (1972) and Berger (1973), who both contrasted a variety of "strong" means of influence (pay raises or pay decreases) with persuasion and found that, when the powerholders used "strong" means of influence, they were more likely to believe that they had caused the target's subsequent behavior. In short, persons who have doubts about their own effectiveness appear to be drawn to the use of force to compensate for their feelings of weakness. An unlikely kind of psychotherapy, to say the least!

An Illustration from the State Department

It should not be thought that the association of coercion and self-esteem can only be detected in personal relations. The use of force as a way of affirming a nation's self-esteem has been a constant theme in history. The German people prior to World War II responded readily to Hitler's arguments that the country must rearm as a way of erasing the past humiliations of World War I. In a long, revealing article dealing with policy-makers during John F. Kennedy's time as president, Richard Barnet pointed out that esteem was accorded to those who advocated the direct use of violence. According to Barnet:

Some of the national security managers of the Kennedy-Johnson era, looking back on their experience, talk about the "hairy chest" syndrome. The man who is ready to recommend using violence against foreigners, even where he is overruled, does not damage his reputation . . . but the man who recommends putting an issue to the U.N., seeking negotiations, or "doing nothing," quickly became known as "soft." To be soft, that is, unbelligerent, compassionate . . . is to be irresponsible.

Bureaucratic *machismo* is cultivated in hundreds of little ways. . . . The most important way . . . [it] manifests itself is in attitudes toward violence. Those who are in the business of defining the national interest are fascinated by lethal technology. . . .

To demonstrate toughness, a national security manager must accept the use of violence as routine. . . . The man who agonizes about taking human life is regarded by his colleagues at the very least as "woolly" and probably something of an idealistic "slob." Thus the critics of the Vietnam escalation never raised the issue that "taking out" great areas of Vietnam, a euphemism for killing large numbers of Vietnamese, was wrong. Their arguments were invariably pragmatic—bombing doesn't work, don't get bogged down in a land war in Asia—or they relied on the torturer's idiom: keep the victim alive for later. When we asked one of the most strategically placed doves in the State Department why the moral issue was never raised, he replied that such a discussion "would be as if from another world." [P. 55]

Elsewhere in the article Barnet assumes that the policy-makers' stress on violence in order to prove their own "toughness" may have been a unique occurrence due to the fact that only power-hungry men seek high government positions; hence the "hairy-chested" syndrome found among the policy-makers probably reflected their unique inner drives. The implication of Barnet's remarks is that ordinary men on the street might be less ferocious in that situation. On the contrary, we suggest that the attitudes of the government security managers reflect the shared cultural values of most people in this country. Thus when asked to make decisions which ultimately reduce to winning or losing, letting others "push" one around or not, the culturally acceptable decision is clear: "Don't be a sissy, act like a man."

Material Gain

So far we have been discussing reasons for using coercive power which arise out of emotionally based needs such as anger, fear, and envy. In these instances heightened emotionality of a negative sort appears to impel individuals to seek out and use violent means. Here we consider a reason why people use coercion that has much less to do with emotionality. This reason is concerned with using coercive power as a means of obtaining a greater share of the good life. Doing harm to a target, protecting oneself, or raising one's self-esteem are secondary in this case to the desire of the power-holder to enrich himself by inducing the target to give up some valued commodity. Buss (1971), speaking from the framework of aggression theory, has labeled this reason for using coercive power "instrumental aggression."

The importance of this motivation for using coercive power is suggested by Walster, Berscheid, and Walster (1973), who observe:

> A basic aim of most persons is to seek maximum rewards at a minimum cost for themselves. Theories in a wide variety of disciplines rest on the assumption that "Man is selfish." Psychologists believe that behavior can be shaped by the careful application of reinforcements. Economists assume that individuals will purchase products at the lowest available price . . . [and] politicians contend that "Every man has his price." [P. 151]

Where does power fit into this view of man as attempting to minimize costs? Quite obviously the answer is that with power the individual can force a target to give up a valued commodity with a minimum of cost to the powerholder. The robber with a gun can force people to "stand and deliver" and the business manager with a large financial reserve can cut prices until his local competitors are driven from business. Thus, even if a person is without malice, fear, or envy of his fellows, we might still expect him to seek and use coercive power as a means of satisfying this basic need of minimizing costs. One should note that, considered in this way, our view of power is similar to that of Hobbes's definition of power as "one's present means to obtain some future apparent Good." Lacking present means implies the absence of future benefits, an outcome, according to Walster and her colleagues, that would be distasteful for "selfish" man. Centuries ago Xenophon clearly saw the relation between access to resources, in his case military force, and the ability to maximize gain, when he attempted to persuade his army of ten thousand not to disband but to march back together to Athens from their wars in Asia Minor. Xenophon argued:

"One of the results of our power is the ability to *take* what belongs to the weak." To disband was to lose this base of power and as a result pay dearly for any food, clothing, or shelter that was obtained while returning home individually.

Institutional Use of Coercive Power for Gain

An interesting illustration of the use of coercive power for material gain is provided by Ida M. Tarbell's (1904) account of the early history of the Standard Oil Company and its founder, John D. Rockefeller. Although perhaps dated by now, since the process of economic consolidation among the major industries has been completed for several decades, her account is of interest since it reveals how motivation for gain and the availability of coercive means of influence combined to favor Rockefeller and Standard Oil's growth. It is clear from the story that Rockefeller, far from experiencing regret for what he did, felt fully justified in his behavior, at best perhaps viewing his vanquished business opponents as somewhat stupid.

The story begins with the availability of unexploited resources in the United States that could provide the basis for wealth, if one could figure out how to use them. In the northeastern region of the country, from Pennsylvania through Ohio, a thick oily substance variously labeled "rock oil," "seneca oil," and "petroleum" oozed from the earth. It was a curiosity and something of a nuisance to those who sank wells for water and for salt-water layers from which salt might be distilled. By 1850 a few enterprising souls were bottling the oil as a medicine. Kier's Rock Oil was sold in eight-ounce bottles and was advertised as both a liniment and also as a cure for cholera, liver complaints, bronchitis, and consumption when taken internally. Then George Bissell, a graduate of Dartmouth College, was told that this oil just might·be better than coal oil or whale oil for use in lamps. The enterprising Bissell leased a farm in Pennsylvania near Titusville, where the oil collected in pools, and sent a sample to Professor Silliman of Yale University for analysis. Basically the question was, Could money be made from this stuff? Professor Silliman slowly heated the rock oil, and with each increment of heat new and commercially profitable products were refined out of the crude oil—illuminating oil, which provided more light than the best whale or coal oil available, paraffin for candles, grease and lubricating oil for machinery, gasoline and kerosene. Perhaps 10 percent of the rock oil was waste product.

The good professor concluded his report: "In short your company have in their possession a raw material from which by simple and not expensive processes they may manufacture very valuable products. Nearly the whole of the raw product may be manufactured without waste."

And so the race was on. Edwin L. Drake, a railroad agent, was sent out by Bissell to drill for oil on Bissell's property. After some preliminary misfortunes due to the weather and hauling heavy equipment over wilderness trails, Drake successfully brought in the first well in 1859. By 1869 over a thousand wells were successfully producing. Refineries were set up both in the oil regions and in the cities of Cleveland, Philadelphia, Pittsburgh and Newark. Buyers, both in America and abroad, eagerly bought the refined oil for lighting and lubrication. Prices reached as high as twenty dollars a barrel, as Professor Silliman predicted. The problem was that the enormous flow of oil reduced the price in a short time to less than a dollar a barrel.

By the early 1870s, several oil refinery owners, including John D. Rockefeller (who owned a medium-sized refinery in Cleveland), saw the answer to the problem of price. The refining of oil must be limited to only a few refiners, acting as a single company. In turn production could be controlled and prices maintained at a high level. The key was the railroads. If they could be convinced to give secret and substantial rebates to one company when transporting the oil to New York, then that company would be in a position to undersell all others and drive them from the market.

In 1872, only twelve years after the industry began, Rockefeller and the Standard Oil Company, in conjunction with several other oil refineries, signed a secret agreement with Thomas A. Scott of the Pennsylvania Railroad, and Jay Gould of the Erie Railroad, which provided substantial rebates on all oil shipped by the company. Not only that, the railroads agreed to give Rockefeller a rebate on all oil shipped by independents. From the railroads' point of view, the agreement would provide them with continuous traffic in oil, with a guaranteed price that would not fluctuate with variations in supply and demand. For Rockefeller the agreement allowed his company to sell oil at a price far lower than that of any other oil refiner in Cleveland. Here, then, Rockefeller had developed a base of power which he was not long in using coercively.

Once armed with his ability to sell cheaply, yet with enormous profit, Rockefeller approached other refiners and asked them to turn their refineries over to his appraisers. In his rather dry style he advised his competitors: "I will give you Standard Oil stock or cash as you prefer for the *value we put on your refinery.*" Initially many refiners objected, since the price placed on their businesses by Rockefeller's appraisers was low. Mr. Rockefeller was regretful but firm. "It was useless to resist—if they persisted they would certainly be crushed."

Miss Tarbell relates that these tactics reached a point where a proposal from Mr. Rockefeller was certainly regarded popularly as a little better than a command to "stand and deliver." "The oil business belongs to us," Mr. Rockefeller said. "We have facilities; we must have it. Any business concern that starts in business, we have sufficient money laid aside to wipe him out." And people believed him.

Under the combined threat and persuasion almost the entire independent oil interests of Cleveland collapsed in three months time. Of the twenty-six refineries, at least twenty-one sold out. From a capacity of 1,500 barrels of crude oil a day, Standard Oil rose in three months to 10,000 barrels.

This illustration contains many of the elements of our description of the power act. Mr. Rockefeller's goal was the control of the oil refinery business. Not unnaturally, this goal met resistance from other refiners that initially blocked his plans. Once Mr. Rockefeller had secured an agreement with the railroads, however, he rapidly accrued a base of power, in the form of excess capital, which could then be used to intimidate his rivals. Note that what is missing in this picture is restraining force. Simply put, there was none of any consequence. The main restraint in this instance would have been government laws regulating interstate commerce. As these had not yet been enacted by Congress, what was left was the potential restraint exerted in the form of moral indignation by those forced from business, or Mr. Rockefeller's own personal values against doing business in this way. Neither served—leaving Mr. Rockefeller free to invoke threats and sanctions to satisfy his wants.

Role Involvement

Perhaps the most perplexing and pervasive reason why coercive power is used in our society originates in the involvement of persons in their organizational role. Instances of this use of coercion are easily cited and cover a wide range of institutional experiences. Teachers assigning failing grades to students, supervisors firing or demoting their employees, mortgage bankers ordering the foreclosure of homes or businesses for nonpayment of debts, mothers hitting their children because they have been "naughty," soldiers obeying the order "Fire!" German civil servants assiduously working to develop the means of carrying out the order to "finally settle the Jewish question" in Nazi Germany—all these are examples of the use of coercive power by individuals acting as agents for a larger institution. And in all instances, if you ask "Why?" the answer is the same—a bland or apologetic "I had little choice. It's part of my job."

It is important to note here that the needs of the person invoking coercive power are based neither upon emotionality nor upon the need to gain materially from the act. While emotion might be present, and the individual might stand to gain from his act, basically the motivations arise from the desire of the individual to further the goals of the institution by doing his job properly. Thus if his job involves the potential of doing harm to others, the more dedicated and involved the individual is in his work, the more likely he will be eventually to do harm to others.

There are several points to be made in conjunction with this reason for the use of coercive power. The first is that there are demand characteristics associated with institutional roles that appear to deprive the involved individual of voluntary will. The role occupant justifies his behavior in terms of such words as "should," "obliged," "ought," "required," and other imperatives. In a sense the individual is trapped by his own loyalties to legitimate authority, so that he finds it almost impossible to ignore its demands. Adolph Berle (1967), in speaking of the demands placed upon individuals given access to institutional powers, puts the surrender of voluntary action in this way:

> One of the first impacts [upon assuming office] is realization that the obligations of power take precedence over other obli-

gations formerly held nearest and dearest. A man in power can have no friends, in the sense that he must refuse to the friend considerations, that power aside, he would have accorded.

This form of compliance presents complex problems to the outside observer, when the compliance leads the individual to carry out acts which the larger society would consider illegal or immoral. For instance, in the early 1960s, managers of leading American corporations were convicted of entering into illegal trade agreements to limit competition in the sale of electrical generating equipment. Those who suffered from this act were of course the citizens of the communities that purchased this equipment, who had paid a higher price. What is of interest was that managers of these corporations were not acting to increase their personal wealth by committing this illegal and coercive act but apparently felt compelled to act in this manner to further the goals of their companies (Fuller 1962). In their view the requirement that each company should compete for contracts by submitting sealed bids interfered with one of the key elements of their jobs, the development of stable pricing procedures needed for long-term planning. Far better for the managers of the various companies to agree to take turns in submitting low bids, so that a safe level of return could be assured for all companies.

Involvement in one's role, then, appears to be a partial key to understanding the use of institutional power for coercive purposes. The well-socialized employee does what he must to further the aims of his organization, despite the fact that these actions may involve doing harm to others. What leads to such involvement? Cyert and MacCrimmon (1968) have proposed that involvement in organizational roles occurs where there is a high degree of compatibility between the person's self-image and the role requirement of his job. Further, according to these authors it is necessary for the person to experience a high degree of need fulfillment. In other words, when "what I want to be" and "what I am doing" are congruent and satisfying, then the individual becomes absorbed in his institutional role and willingly carries out those behaviors that will forward the aims of the organization, despite the fact that these behaviors may involve coercion.

An illustration of this process is provided in a *Harper's Magazine* interview with Daniel Ellsberg (Terkel 1972), who discussed how a congruence between self-concept and role requirements controlled the behavior of policy-makers in the Pentagon and the State Department during the Vietnam War. "It was like electricity coursing through their veins," Ellsberg stated in describing how these officials enjoyed their work. "In fact, the speed of decision-making, flickering from one part of the world to another—a weapons system to be decided upon, or one set of decisions about force levels, or big wars, or little wars—from moment to moment gave their lives an electric excitement to which they were clearly addicted and which they could not imagine living without."

Ellsberg then wisely comments on how these satisfactions could only be obtained by an unquestioning "knuckling under" to all decisions. He says, "The course of power however could only be theirs if they stayed in line, if they toed the mark and remained [unquestioning]. An [adverse] judgement by their bosses could lose them access to that flow of information in minutes, if they made the wrong move. They would not be invited to the next White House meeting. They would no longer be in it, be part of it." Further commenting on this role involvement, Ellsberg speaks of the dilemma of George Ball, undersecretary of state, the number-two man in the State Department, who privately opposed American involvement in the war in Vietnam but publicly testified in its favor in front of Congress. Ball, in justifying this behavior years later, stated, "After all, we're just hired hands of the president." Ellsberg concludes by observing, "These men have a self-image of powerlessness except as loyal servants, not of the Constitution, not of their countrymen, not of humanity, but of the men who hired them."

This of course is the dilemma that persons of conscience experience in carrying out their role obligations. To admit that one has the freedom to obey or disobey jeopardizes the rewards and satisfactions obtained at work. Better to assume that one does not have a choice and either ignore private doubts or transform them into convictions as to the correctness of the institution's course of action.

There are, however, complexities here which are not completely explained by invoking the concept of role involvement. There are many instances in which there is little compatibility between the individual's self-image and his institutional role-requirements, as for example the drafted army infantryman, and yet these role occupants still feel obliged to carry out what are perceived to be legitimate role demands.

Milgram (1963), in his well-known studies of obedience, has most extensively treated this problem in psychology and provided some insight into the feelings of those involved in carrying out distasteful role activities. In its most general form, the problem according to Milgram may be defined thus: if x tells y to hurt z, under what conditions will y carry out the command of x and under what conditions will he refuse? Basically what Milgram found was that most persons in the role of y carried out the orders of x to harm z, despite their complete abhorrence of this activity. Obedience to the demands of legitimate authority, the experimenter in this case, in conjunction with their acceptance of their role, compelled persons to act in ways they considered personally distasteful. As Milgram says, "With numbing regularity, good people were seen to knuckle under to the demands of authority and perform actions that were callous and severe. Men who are in everyday life responsible and decent were seduced by the trappings of authority, by the control of their perceptions, and by the uncritical acceptance of the experimenter's definition of the situation into performance of harsh acts."

Basically what is implicated here is the influence of the early socialization process which stresses above all else obedience to parental and school authority and, as Milgram suggests, produces a national character structure which experiences *greater* difficulty in defying authority than in harming others. Support for Milgram's suggestion that compliance to authority is a well learned trait for many of us is found in a nation-wide opinion survey conducted by Kelman and Lawrence (1972). In response to the question, "What would most people do if ordered to shoot all the inhabitants of a Vietnamese village suspected of aiding the enemy, including old men, women, and children," 67 percent of a cross section of the American public said that most people would "follow orders and shoot." Half of those interviewed said that they would do so themselves.

In addition to dramatically showing us how the demands of a given role may override personal convictions and morality, Milgram has also identified in his research some circumstances under which the role occupant may defy orders and refuse to invoke coercive power. These circumstances included: (*a*) distance from the target—the more remote the target was from the role occupant, the more willing was the role occupant to harm the target; (*b*) the arousal of a norm of responsibility through observing others in similar roles refusing to inflict harm; and (*c*) the closeness of authority to the role occupant. As surveillance of the role occupant by an authority figure decreased, obedience also sharply dropped. This finding appears to distinguish between those who Cyert and MacCrimmon have labeled as either role-involved or not. While both may carry out the orders of their superiors to inflict harm on others while their superiors are present, noninvolved persons are more likely to desist in the absence of surveillance.

Absolution and Role Behavior

Let us turn to another problem related to the use of coercion as part of the job. One may ask what are the mechanisms involved that allow people in their institutional roles to carry out behaviors that they would personally condemn if performed by others outside the institution. We have already suggested the answer to this problem in Chapter 2 by pointing out that most people believe that the institution grants them absolution for their acts. Since the individual believes that he has no choice but to obey, he also sees himself as not responsible for the suffering he has caused. Edgar Wallace, in a short story called *The Treasure Hunt*, expresses this view when the hero—a Mr. Reeder—a diligent and relentless police officer, finds himself the target of anger and hatred by those he has caught and sent to prison. "Mr. Reeder in so far as he could resent anything, resented the injustice of being made personally responsible for the performance of a public duty," wrote Wallace.

It is important to note that not only does the individual absolve himself of blame, but society in general does not condemn an individual who uses coercive power in the service of a legitimate institution. Even when the role occupant exceeds or abuses his authority and uses excessive coercive means of influence, most persons are willing to absolve the role occupant of any personal guilt. For instance, in the previously cited national survey by Kelman and Lawrence, most Americans considered the conviction of Lieutenant Calley, commander of the American troops at My Lai, to be too harsh. Almost two-thirds believed it was unfair to hold Calley *personally* responsible for what occurred in the line of duty.

Thinking about Coercion

Except in the case of accidental infliction of harm, the use of coercive power for all the reasons given in the previous pages involves anticipatory planning and reflection. We have to decide why we want to deliver noxious stimuli to the target person. Not only that, our reasons must be justifiable. To inflict harm on another person is not a matter of indifference to the harmdoer, the target person, or to society. Ordinarily the justifications involve some statement about one's own intentions and some statements about the behavior of the target person.

It has been suggested by several social psychologists (Lerner and Simmons 1966; Walster and Berscheid 1967) that harmdoers tend to justify their acts by placing the blame for the acts upon the victim. That is, in cases where the harmdoer does nothing to provide restitution, he will describe the victim as "stupid," "deserving punishment," and so on. And in this way the harmdoer absolves himself of responsibility for the victim's suffering. Memmi (1965) has observed a similar rationalizing process among French colonizers in explaining their treatment of the Tunisians.

This section will amplify on these views and attempt to show how the powerholder's justifications for his acts of coercion may vary as the reason for using coercion varies. I have attempted to describe the powerholder's thoughts prior to the use of coercive power and after the coercion has been successfully used. The reader should be aware that there is little direct evidence to support the validity of these presumed thought processes. What is written here is given as a means of sketching in the range of questions one should ask about coercive power rather than definitive answers.

Table 5.1 provides an analysis of the reasons and thoughts involved in the decision to use coercion. These reasons have been broken down into statements of: (*a*) the initial emotions experienced by the powerholder, (*b*) his justifications for the proposed coercive act, (*c*) a statement as to whether the powerholder desired to harm the target person or had some other rea-

Table 5.1 Thoughts Prior to the Use of Coercion

Powerholder's Thoughts and Feelings	Reasons for the Use of Coercive Power				
	Aggression	Security	Self-esteem	Material	Role Behavior
a. Initial emotion	Anger and rage	Fear	Envy	Greed	Annoyance to anger (?)
b. Personal justification	The target made me suffer.	The target is a source of danger.	I have to show I am better.	The target has something I want.	The target violates role hebavior.
c. Desire to harm target person	Yes	Secondary to desire to protect self	Little or none	Little or none	Little or none
d. Evaluation of target person	Personality, abilities, and character of target are devalued.	Fear will exaggerate target person's potential for harm-doing.	Perhaps grudging respect	Target seen objectively but as a depersonalized object.	Perception varies with role involvement

son in mind for using coercion and, (*d*) how the powerholder saw the target person prior to the use of coercion.

It can be seen in table 5.1 that the profile of hypothesized thoughts varies considerably according to the powerholder's reasons for using coercion. That is, the intensity of the emotions involved, the concern for the target's well-being, and the perceptions of the target all are seen to vary according to the reasons that are involved in the initial decision to use coercion. Thus, for example, if aggression is the reason for using coercion, it is suspected that the worth of the target person is devalued considerably. If the desire for material gain is the reason for using coercion, however, then the powerholder should evaluate the target person as objectively as possible in order to understand his strengths and weaknesses. At the same time, the powerholder should view the target person as a depersonalized object, since any positive feelings might interfere with the use of coercion.

In table 5.2 we have charted the thoughts of the powerholder after he has successfully used coercion. Now he has achieved his goal by force, and in some way must justify to himself the consequences of his acts. We have charted the dimensions of the powerholder's thoughts in terms of his: (*a*) feelings and emotions after successfully using coercion, (*b*) his concern for the target person's discomfort, (*c*) the extent to which the powerholder is willing to state that he was responsible for his acts (did the powerholder believe that he was forced by outside agents to inflict harm, or did he believe that the use of coercion was based upon his own decision?), and (*d*) how the self-esteem of the powerholder may be raised or depressed by the successful use of coercion—that is, does the powerholder like himself better, or worse, or just the same as a result of causing harm.

Here again we see that the powerholder's thoughts about himself and the target person will vary as a function of the reasons for using coercion in the first place. For example, we speculate that the powerholder's self-esteem may be raised after having revenged himself on a disliked target person but be depressed after using coercion as part of his role obligations. Thus Milgram (1963) reported that participants in his forced compliance studies were depressed after being required by their role to inflict harm, whereas Berkowitz (1971) suggested that persons enjoyed committing ag-

Table 5.2 Thoughts after the Successful Use of Coercive Power

Powerholder's Thoughts and Feelings	Reasons for the Use of Coercive Power				
	Aggression	Security	Self-esteem	Material	Role Behavior
a. Subsequent emotions	Satisfaction	Relief	Satisfaction	Satisfaction	Relief to depression (?)
b. Concern for target's suffering	Enjoyment of his pain and suffering	Little or no concern (?)	Sympathy for target (?)	Contempt to sympathy (?) for target	Sympathy (?)
c. Does the powerholder feel responsible for his acts?	Yes	No, use of coercion attributed to outside forces. "I had to protect myself."	Yes	Yes	No, powerholder feels obliged to invoke coercion.
d. Self-esteem	Elevated	Perhaps lowered	Elevated	No change (?)	Depressed

gressive acts, although he has not presented clear evidence on this point. Finally, some support for the speculation that powerholders devalue the worth of a target person after using coercion for material gain is given by a laboratory study done by T. P. Cafferty and S. Streufert (1974). In this study, the authors examined the attitudes of group members after they engaged in competitive actions. It was found that group members who chose to aggress against the opposing group members, and were the victors, rated their opponents less favorably than equally victorious group members who did not choose to aggress in order to win.

We close this final section by noting that the relation between coercive power and the reactions of the powerholder to his own acts is not yet entirely clear. Thus the reader should view the suggestions given here as tentative. Additional research and study is needed to understand just what happens to a powerholder's views of himself and his target when he is continually involved in the use of coercive power.

Summary

In this chapter we have reviewed five reasons why people seek out and use coercive power. The first three are based mainly upon emotional feelings of the powerholder, in that what is primarily sought from the target is relief from unpleasant feelings, whether of anger, fear, or envy. Thus, the powerholder does not gain in any material sense from successfully using power. The fourth reason that has been reviewed, however, is based upon the aim of extracting some desired commodity from the target which the target is unwilling to give freely. Finally, the last reason discussed is concerned with how an individual's involvement with an organization may oblige him to inflict harm on others who appear to be interfering with the proper functioning of the powerholder's institution.

While we have discussed each of these potential reasons for using coercive power as if they were independent of each other, in practice a powerholder may have several overlapping reasons for deciding to use coercion. From Barnet's description of the behavior of national security managers, one could infer that, if asked why coercion was used, the reply would be that it was done in the interests of national security, not, as Barnet implies, because of a desire to maximize one's manliness.

It has also been suggested in this chapter that differing psychological processes relating to the powerholder's own emotions, as well as his perceptions of the target, can be used to distinguish among the five reasons for using coercion. Much research, however, remains to be done to verify our tentative statements concerning these processes.

6　　On the Use of Coercive Power

The previous chapter described various reasons why people seek out and use coercive power—anger, safety, self-esteem, material gain, and institutional involvement. We have described some of the circumstances which arouse these reasons, as when insults provoke anger. This chapter considers in greater detail the calculations of a powerholder when deciding whether to invoke his resources in a coercive manner. In some instances it will be found that strong emotions are associated with the powerholder's judgments, and in other instances rational judgments will have the upper hand and there will be little evidence of emotionality. Of course, from the point of view of the target person, this distinction may not be particularly enlightening since his pain and suffering will be the same in either instance. Nevertheless, from the viewpoint of understanding and perhaps controlling coercion, the distinction is critical.

The major topic to be encountered in this chapter will center on the role played by thought in the decision to harm others. The reason for this emphasis is that discussions of emotional versus cognitive control of coercion in psychology have been particularly one-sided in favor of emotional causes. Books concerned with the problem of angry aggression (our first reason for using coercive power) continue to appear in large numbers. As a result, the implication for many is that being angry, upset, or frustrated are the critical factors. As we shall see, the use of coercive power is frequently guided by rational calculations, with little or no emotion involved.

Kaufmann in his book *Aggression and Altrusism* (1970), presents somewhat similar views concerning the importance of cognitive factors as determinants of aggression. In Kaufman's view, cognitive factors enter the scene at several points. First, the individual learns from his culture when it is proper openly to aggress. Second, the individual learns who are the target persons one can attack in safety; that is, one may attack weaker persons, those of equal or lower social status, but not children, those who are stronger, old people, and so on. Third, citing the research of Schachter and Singer (1962) on the cognitive labeling of emotions, Kaufmann argues that the same feelings of physiological upset may be equally interpreted as anger, happiness, or relief, depending on the label attached to these body feelings. If a person attaches the label "I am angry" to these bodily feelings, then aggression may occur. However, if he interprets the same bodily feelings as due to heightened feelings of euphoria, then aggression will not occur. Thus, the cognitive labels attached by the person to his own bodily feelings help to determine whether or not he will openly aggress.

Cognitive Factors in the Use of Coercive Power

We begin by noting that in most institutional settings powerholders possess a range of means of influencing a target. Hence, they are not limited to punishment only. Managers at work, for instance, can do many things to change their subordinates' work behavior. They can use persuasion, offer rewards, provide extra training, or even shift their employees to new jobs or new work shifts. Thus many options exist for powerholders at work in addition to forcing employees into negatively valued regions by threatening suspension, poor performance evaluations, pay deductions, and firing. If a range of means of influence is available, questions may be raised about the point at which each powerholder decides that more gentle means are not sufficient and that harsher means must be invoked.

In Chapter 3 it was suggested that the powerholder's decisions concerning power were based upon a twofold process of first diagnosing the causes of the target's resistances and then selecting the means of influence that, in his view, was most likely to overcome this resistance. It is reasonable to suggest that the same process occurs in the decision to invoke coercion. Furthermore, it is suggested that expectations of successful influence are closely allied to this decision in a way that parallels the decision to use reward.

Raven and Kruglanski (1970) have offered the generalization that the powerholder anticipates the possible effectiveness of each of his bases of power and avoids using those which he believes will be ineffective. How, then, are variations in anticipations associated with the use of coercion? One answer provided by psychologists Barry Goodstadt and Lawrence Hjelle (1973) is that, as the powerholder's expectations of successful influence are lowered, he is increasingly tempted to exert more pressure upon the target person by invoking coercive means of influence. Milder forms of influence are used when the powerholder believes that the target person is not completely resistant to change.

The reader will, of course, recognize the above statement as our expectancy rule stated in slightly different form. Goodstadt and Hjelle's generalization about coercive power and its use, though independently derived, is remarkably similar to David Baldwin's already cited views on the use of reward power. In both instances, promises and threats are seen as used when expectations of succesful influence are lowest. *Combining the two views, then, leads to the generalization that sanctions, whether positive or negative, are most likely to be invoked when expectations of successful influence are lowest.* Positive sanctions appear to be preferred when the powerholder wishes to retain the good will of the target person or when the powerholder anticipates that compliance is likely to drop in the future. Negative sanctions appear to be preferred when the good will of the target person is less involved and the influence attempts are directed at changing some behavior rather than maintaining it.

If we accept this analysis as it pertains to coercion, then the question becomes: What causes the powerholder to become gloomy and doubt his ability to effect change in the target? Here we will review evidence suggesting that the behavior of the target, the social setting in which the influence is attempted, and the personal characteristics of the powerholder all contribute significantly to lowered expectations of successful influence and to the subsequent decision to use coercion.

The Behavior of the Target

Whenever coercive power is deliberately used, it is almost inevitable that this usage is justified by blaming the behavior of the target. As Kaufmann points out in his book *Aggression and Altruism* (1970): "The target or stimulus has been shown to be of considerable importance in the elicitation of aggressive behavior. We know from everyday experience that some people just seem to be asking to be punched in the nose, whereas others elicit meekness from even the most notorious bully" (p. 55). Recently, a new area of inquiry, victimology, suggests that it is possible to predict who will be a target of violence, based upon the earlier behavior of the victim. It has been reported that a fair majority of homicide victims have as violent an earlier background as their murderers. Thus, as Kaufmann suggests, some people seem to invite nastiness.

Clearly, the attitude and behaviors of the target person toward the powerholder are implicated in the use of coercion. The question is, Just what does the target do that provokes these assaults? Or, in the language of this book, what does the target do to lower the powerholder's expectations of successful influence? Goodstadt and Hjelle (1973) offer the answer that, *when a target's resistance to inflence is attributed to motivational causes ("I refuse") rather than to a lack of ability ("I can't"), powerholder's expectations of successful influence are lowest, and their reliance on coercion is greatest.*

This distinction returns us to the issue of the powerholder's diagnosis of the causes of the target person's noncompliance. It was suggested in Chapter 3 that if the powerholder attributed the target person's resistance to internal causes, or a lack of motivation, then he also believed that the resistance shown was deliberate: that is, that the target person had freely decided not to comply with the wishes of the powerholder. If, however, the target's resistance was attributed to a lack of ability, then the powerholder was more likely to believe that the target person was not in charge of his own behavior and, consequently, was not deliberately resisting.

It was also reported in Chapter 3 that the powerholder was more likely to *discuss* change with the target person if it was believed that resistance was deliberate. Suppose, however, that such discussion fails and the target person persists in his deliberate resistance. It seems clear that the powerholder's expectations for successful influence must drop considerably. Stronger means of influence must now be tried. In contrast, when considering involuntary resistance, I would argue that powerholders remain optimistic for far longer periods of time. In these instances, if one form of training does not work, the powerholder will invoke other forms rather than immediately considering harsh means of influence.

Several studies have tested the implication of this expectancy view of when coercive power is invoked. In one study I asked 103 managers employed in state government and in private industry to read eight case histories of employees doing substandard work. In four of these case histories, the cause of this substandard work was attributed to a lack of ability; in the other four, it was due to motivational causes. For instance, in one of the case histories, an employee was described as "being uneven in performance following a promotion. He had a series of minor accidents with his new equipment, the quality of his work was low, and he appeared tense and nervous." In a second instance, an employee's job performance was also described as uneven. "At quitting time he sometimes tried to leave early, he laughed off mistakes, and if you asked him what the problem was, he said that people were picking on him."

Managers were asked to assess the probability of their being personally able to correct each of these subordinate's performances. In addition, managers rated how desirable it would be to invoke coercive means of disciplining the employee (bawling out the employee, threat of suspension, letter of warning, firing).

It was found that managers, at a statistically reliable level ($p < .01$), consistently rated at lower odds the chance of their being able successfully to influence the employee's behavior when the employee lacked motivation to work than when he lacked the ability to work. That is, the managers said that they personally would have a good chance of improving the performance of an employee who was inept in his work. Managers did not think their chances were very good, however, if the employee had a "chip on his shoulder" or generally lacked motivation to work.

It was also found that the managers recommended the use of coercion far more often among employees who lacked motivation than among those who lacked ability. Here again these differences in recommendations were statistically reliable beyond the .01 level. Threats and actual use of force in the form of firings were reserved for the employee who *would* not perform, rather than for the employee who *could* not perform.

Finally, of interest in the present context was the finding that regardless of the reason for the employee's poor performance, if managers rated themselves as having low expectations of being able to correct the worker's performance, then the managers endorsed the use of coercion. The correlation between the managers' rating of their expectations of being able to improve the employee's performance summed over all incidents and the managers' endorsing the use of coercion summed over all incidents was −.41. The lower the expectations, the more coercion was recommended.

In a laboratory simulation of work, Barry Goodstadt and myself (1970) also demonstrated, via experimentation, that more coercion was invoked when the target person was seen as deliberately resisting the orders of a powerholder. In this simulation study, college business majors were appointed as managers of a manufacturing organization and asked to direct the performance of a group of workers. The managers were provided with a range of institutional means of influence (power to grant pay raises, to shift workers to a new job, to train, to deduct pay, or to fire). It was left to the managers to decide which, if any, of these means would be used. The experimental manipulation involved the programming of one of the workers to perform at substandard levels. In one condition, the reason for this poor performance was ascribed to the ineptness of the worker, who passed notes to the manager saying such things as: "I'm trying, but I can't seem to get it." In a second condition, the same poor performance was ascribed by means of the worker's notes to a lack of motivation, e.g., ("this job is horrible"). It was found that more managers threatened to deduct pay, or actually deducted pay, or fired the worker, when the worker's poor work was due to a lack of motivation than when the poor work was due to ineptness. Similar findings from experimental studies have been reported by Rothbart (1968) and by Michener and Burt (1974).

Finally, in the previously mentioned field study among first-line supervisors (Kipnis and Cosentino, 1969), it was found that 63 percent of the supervisors who attributed their worker's unsatisfactory performances to a lack of motivation, poor attitudes, or discipline used coercive means in attempts to alter this behavior. Among supervisors who attributed their worker's unsatisfactory performance to a lack of ability, only 26 percent invoked coercion. It appears to be a safe generalization that more workers are fired for poor attitudes and lack of discipline than for a lack of ability.

Police tactics and expectations of successful influence. So far we have examined in business settings the generalization that low expectations of successful influence determine the decision to invoke coercion. As we have seen, the perception that the target person is deliberately refusing to comply is far more likely to cause low expectations than the perception that the target person's resistance is involuntary. A final illustration of this linkage can be found in a study of factors causing police officers to arrest offenders for disorderly conduct (Kipnis and Misner 1974). This is a violation that allows police enormous discretionary powers for deciding how to respond, since the laws defining what behaviors constitute public disorder are vague. For instance, a boisterous drunk in a quiet residential street is likely to be approached very quickly by a police officer. The same behavior in a night club district would probably be ignored. In short, the police officer must use his own judgment by assessing the extent of the disturbance and whether or not passersby are being sufficiently disturbed for him to take action. Aside from ignoring the situation, the police officer may attempt to persuade the offender to stop acting in a disorderly manner by making his presence known, by using physical force, or by actually making an arrest.

To examine what guided police officers' decisions to make an arrest, thirty police officers of a large city were asked to describe the most recent incident in which they arrested a male offender for disorderly conduct, that is, an incident in which coercive power was actually used. Another twenty-eight police officers described a similar incident, but one in which they decided not to arrest the citizens. In addition to describing the incident, the police officers described its background in terms of the number of passersby, whether the officer was alone or with a partner, time of day, whether the offender was drinking, and whether women were present. These questions were asked since informal discussions with police officers suggested that these circumstances could influence the officers' decisions. In fact, many of these background factors did influence whether or not an arrest was made. It was found that a citizen was more likely to be arrested for disorderly conduct if he had been drinking heavily, if there were women watching, and if there were at least eleven or more passersby. Assigning a score of 1 to each of these three context factors if they were present, and a score of 0 if they were absent, resulted in a biserial correlation of .59 with the decision as to whether or not to make an arrest. In short, the decision to use coercive police power was highly predictable from certain background information.

The next question examined was in what way these background factors influenced the decision to make an arrest. Why should the presence of women, for instance, influence the police officers' judgments? To examine this question, the actual nature of each of the fifty-eight incidents was examined by means of content analysis. This analysis found that neither the kind of incident (domestic fights, traffic violation, street corner disturbance), nor the presence of initial violence differentiated when an arrest would be made. What clearly determined this decision was whether the offender continued to resist the police officer's orders to stop being disorderly. As resistance and concurrent threat of violence grew, the probabilities of an arrest increased sharply. If the citizen quieted down, and in some form complied with the police officer's persuasions, then the incident terminated without arrest. In short, as the police officer's expectations of successful influence were lowered by the willful resistance of the citizen, the officer was increasingly likely to increase the amount of pressure placed upon the target by the use of harsh means of influence.

Let me illustrate by presenting, verbatim, two of the police accounts, the first ending in an arrest when the citizen refused to comply, and the second in no arrest when compliance was obtained. In both instances, it may be noted that the police officer was faced with personal threat. Wilson (1968) has stated in *Varieties of Police Behavior* that the maintenance of public order exposes the police officer to physical danger and that his reactions to this potential danger need to be taken into account in understanding his "working personality." This would suggest that when the police officer believed that his personal safety was involved, he would be more likely to arrest the citizen than when no such perceptions were involved.

Incident of Arrest: My last arrest for disorderly conduct occurred about three weeks ago in which a male became loud and boisterous on the corner of a very busy street. The people waiting for the bus became very uneasy at the male's behavior. He entered a restaurant, causing several patrons to leave. I identified myself as a policeman, at which time I observed a razor in his hand. I asked him to drop the razor and he refused. I had to disarm him and place him under arrest. I felt as though I couldn't talk or reason with him.

In the next incident, although the potential for danger was equally present, the citizen finally complied, thus ending the incident. The reader should note the police officer's tactical use of threats, that is, using a public address system, and his attempts to "cool off" the situation by simply waiting, rather than continuing the confrontation.

Incident of No Arrest. "I was writing a traffic summons for an illegally parked vehicle, when a man came out of a bar in front of my location and asked me if it was for him. When I told him yes, he began to give me a hard time, and said that the Police Department stinks, that when you need a cop they're never around, said that he would tear the summons up, and that giving him a ticket made me feel good. I told him that I was working on a complaint, that he should stop causing a camotion [sic], and go back into the bar. After this he became louder and said he wouldn't leave. I then notified radio for a wagon over the P.A. system, so he could hear it, and waited outside of my vehicle. He then at this time walked back into the bar."

Toch (1970) has reported similar findings in his analysis of police assaults. In 266 out of 444 incidents of such assaults, violence occurred after the assaulter had expressed verbal resistance to the policeman's orders and the officer had continued to press his case. Toch summarized his findings by stating that "the most frequent sequence we encountered begins with an order or request by the officer, which elicits a contemptuous response from the citizen. The sequence repeats itself and ends [with violence] a number of steps later, in some instances, after a notification of arrest, in others, without it."

How do these findings on resistance fit with the observation that the presence of women, bystanders, and excessive drinking were associated with the decision to arrest? Presumably, women, drinking, and an audience served as disinhibiting forces (Berkowitz 1971) which encouraged the continued expression of hostility and defiance. Brown (1968), for instance, has reported that restraints against the expression of aggression are lowered when previously angered persons are made aware that others have witnessed their humiliation. Issues of "machismo" then complicate the situation for both police officer and the citizen. To give in while an audience, and especially women, are watching would be inconsistent with the citizen's and perhaps the police officer's conceived role of manhood. Both parties are unwilling to "lose face," and antagonisms escalate as the target of arrest refuses to stop what he is doing. The forces acting on the police officer are even more complicated. In addition to concerns about his public image, he is obliged by his role to maintain public order. This he must do through a process of applying increasing pressure on the citizen for compliance with his request to cease being disorderly. If resistance continues, he must in fact make the arrest.

Taken together, the findings from these various studies are consistent in showing that an appointed leader's choice of coercive means of influence is based upon the belief that the target's resistance is willful and voluntary. In turn, this perception reduces expectations of successful influence and generates the conviction that harsh means of influence are necessary to obtain compliance. We have illustrated this process in terms of research studies at places of work and among the police. It is to be expected that similar findings would obtain in such disparate settings as international relations and family quarrels. It is not surprising that the most frequent explanation given by the parents of "battered" children for hitting the child is that the child would not listen to reason and do as he was told. As we shall go on to show, these lowered expectations of successful influence are frequently not based upon reality but upon extraneous social influences which distort the powerholder's evaluations of the intentions of his target. Let us turn now to a second condition that will influence a powerholder's expectations of successful influence—the setting in which influence is exerted.

The Social Setting

Many will argue that there is nothing surprising in being told that powerholders use coercion when they believe that strong and deliberate resistance has been encountered. What is of interest, however, is that the powerholder's expectations can also be shaped by a wide variety of social influences that have nothing to do with the target's behavior. Under stress, for instance, the powerholder may miscalculate the amount of resistance that is being shown by a target. A worker's misunderstanding of a poorly communicated order may be taken as evidence of calculated insolence by an overworked executive. A teacher who has been told that a new student is hostile is far more likely to perceive deliberate resistance in any mistakes made by the student.

In short, the target's behavior is only one factor that may affect the powerholder's expectations of successful influence. Three major environmental sources have to date been identified as influencing expectations of successful influence. These are the extent to which persons control the potential to harm each other; the setting in which power is exercised; and the number of persons to be influenced.

The possession of coercive means. It has already been mentioned that the possession of resources serves to arouse new needs within the powerholder. The possession of excess amounts of money, for instance, expands the range of experiences the individual wants to encounter. Travel, gifts to others, the development of rich tastes in food and clothing become new goals as money becomes available. Little real thought may be given to these experiences in the absence of money.

Access to resources that can be used coercively also appears to arouse an "itch" within the individual to actually punish others. The writer, on occasion, has listened to conversations between gun owners speculating on the amount of human tissue damage that could be caused by the use of various kinds of bullets in their guns. I have also spoken with owners of large, violent dogs who were looking forward to the day when they would be sufficiently provoked to unleash their dogs, with instructions to attack. Throughout history, the development of military weapons is associated with pressures to act aggressively. While those who lack such means may "turn the other cheek," this conciliatory gesture is far less likely to happen when powers of a coercive kind are possessed. Recognition of this fact has been recorded throughout history. Thucydides reported, for instance, that the Athenian generals justified their invasion of the neighboring island of Melos in 416 B.C. by arguing that a rule of nature is that "those with power should rule where they can"—that is, power demands to be used.

Deutsch and Krauss (1960) have provided evidence that the possession of power to harm others transforms what was essentially a benevolent relation into a hostile one. In their research, it was found that persons with the advantage in terms of the control of coercive power became tempted to demand more than an equal share of the available outcomes. Such demands inevitably produced resistance and counterattacks from targets, who resented being subjected to exploitation. Other studies (Tedeschi, Lindskold, Horai, and Gahagan 1969) suggest that, even when the weaker party agrees to compromise, those who possess the capability to inflict harm tend to ignore these peaceful overtures. Why compromise, asks the strong party, when small threats can bring in a larger share?

A field study within industry by Kipnis, Silverman, and Copeland (1973) provides further evidence on how the control by two parties of coercive means served to escalate conflict and the use of coercion. This study compared the influence modes used by supervisors in unionized and nonunionized companies. The presence or absence of a union in an industrial organization can be viewed as a measure of the relative power held by management and labor. In the absence of a union, the balance of power is held by management since it can deal with each employee separately. The presence of a union, however, tends to equalize power between the two parties. Hence, it is of interest to see how management uses power in these two settings—one in which an employee's potential for resistance was low and one in which this potential was high. From what has been said so far, it might be expected that management would use more coercion on a day-to-day level in situations where the potential for resistance was high.

To test this idea, supervisors working in both union and nonunion plants described incidents in which they corrected the performance of their employees. The analysis of the incidents focused on what was done to correct the employee's performance in each of these two settings.

Two findings emerged that are of interest with reference to the use of coercive power. First, supervisors of union employees reported that they encountered more instances of poor attitudes and an unwillingness to work by their workers than did supervisors of nonunion employees. Second, supervisors in union plants reported using more coercive power than those in nonunion plants. That is, supervisors of union workers reported a greater frequency of using threats and reprimands, reducing the employee's privileges, and evoking administrative punishment such as written warnings and suspensions. Seemingly, the presence of unions approaches a situation of bilateral power in which subordinates can actively resist the demands of their supervisors by reason of union support. From the supervisor's point of view, however, this resistance is viewed as reflecting deliberate attempts by subordinates to defy their authority. Hence, the reports of more poor attitudes on the part of work ers in union companies. In this climate, the supervisors may come to doubt that even simple suggestions will be freely carried out. As a result, they are rapidly drawn to threats and actual punishments as a means to back up their orders. Their threats replace simple persuasion as the preferred power tactic.

Many will argue, of course, that the possession of coercive means does not necessarily lead to exploitative and aggressive behaviors and that what has been said so far is too pessimistic. The power-holder, it is argued, may act in all innocence as "the peacekeeper" of the world, stockpiling weapons in order to prevent aggressive actions by others. The problem as I understand it is that while each peacekeeper, or several peacekeepers acting together to establish a balance of power, may have no intent to do harm, the very fact that they possess coercive means makes them objects of distrust. Sooner or later, the possessors of coercive power will fiind themselves drawn into confrontation with others, if for no other reason than that the weaker parties are anxious to eliminate the advantage the peaceholders have over them.

To the extent that these attitudes of mistrust are communicated to the powerholder, he in turn will soon view others with caution. Both the local bully lording it over the neighborhood and the policeman patrolling the neighborhood to maintain public order can never be sure that they will not be subjected to a defensive "first strike." As of the writing of this chapter, for instance, the newspapers have reported that India has developed its own nuclear bomb. And so now the major powers must lower ever so slightly their expectations that India can be easily influenced in international relations.

A final reason why the possession of coercive means of influence makes it difficult to maintain harmonious relations is that the powerholder frequently suspects that others dislike him. Such beliefs were found by Berger (1973), who provided some persons with power to reward and others with power to punish. Those who controlled coercive means felt that target persons disliked them, regardless of whether or not they actually used their coercive means. It is obviously difficult to hold friendly feelings toward persons one suspects of disliking oneself.

In short, providing powerholders with coercive means of influence escalates conflict. For one thing, the possession of coercive means tempts powerholders to use such means in order to maximize outcome for the self. Furthermore, the possession of coercive means encourages the belief that others are unfriendly and will not freely comply with one's persuasions. These beliefs, in turn, further encourage the actual use of coercion by lowering expectations that persuasions will successfully change the target person's behavior.

Competition. The manner in which rewards are distributed in a given social setting can also be expected to affect decisions concerning coercion. Quite simply, to the extent persons must compete for valued outcomes, reliance upon coercion should increase. Karl Marx, for instance, viewed the emerging capitalist system of the nineteenth century as forcing different strata of society into open conflict. Because the economic system was subject to periodic collapse, Marx foresaw that increasing numbers of workers would be unemployed, that these workers would be forced to compete with each other for scarce jobs, and that they eventually would have to fight owners for an equitable division of the wealth. Thus, the very nature of the capitalistic system, in Marx's view, would foster revolution by the workers. The critical factor that distinguishes this form of conflict is that persons are forced to invoke coercion by a social system that determines the form in which required goods and services are distributed. Personal predilections to harm others are not particularly important in this context.

Deutsch (1969) has focused attention among psychologists upon the consequences of this struggle for scarce resources. In Deutsch's view, competition between persons occurs under two circumstances. The first is when individuals cannot agree on the *means* to achieve some agreed-upon goal. Both parents may want their son to obtain good grades in school, but the husband wants an hour of study set aside each day, while the wife argues that the son should decide for himself when to study. Here the competition is in terms of ideas which allow for compromise and accommodation of each to the other. Thus, disagreement does not necessarily have to involve power relations of a harsher kind. Both parties can, if they have respect and affection for each other, reach an agreement without either party experiencing loss.

A more fundamental conflict occurs when the goal region is in dispute, as, for example, when the husband wants the son to concentrate on sports and the wife wants him to concentrate on grades. More formally, Deutsch has stated that competition occurs when the movement of person A into the goal region blocks the movement of person B into this region. If the Acme Company is awarded a contract for $1 million, then the Bolt Company does not get the contract. If students are in a class where grades are based upon a normal curve, then Jane's grade of A lessens Mary's chances for an A. These zero-sum social settings clearly encourage the use of coercive means of influence. The powerholder knows that simple discussion will not convince the target person to let the powerholder be the first to enter the goal region. Of course, this does not mean that relations will always be overtly hostile. Everyday observations suggest otherwise. Rather, a competitive social structure discourages community interests and feelings that allow people to stand together in times of stress. Hence, when persons strive for the same valued outcome, a competitive structure encourages the belief that a solution can only be of the type imposed by superior force.

Such a readiness to use force becomes all the more evident in situations that have not developed strong restraints governing the use of power. This may be particularly true in international relations, or in certain businesses which have typically been guided by a "dog-eat-dog" philosophy. Underlying this process of overt use of power is the gradual transformation of emotional attitudes toward the other, brought on by competition. Further, at a cognitive level, competition generates a firm conviction that the other party will not willingly compromise or accept influence. Thus, the joint action of emotional antipathy and lower expectation of successful influences set the stage for the introduction of harsh means of influence.

Number of target persons. So far, we have suggested that the possession of coercive means of influence and the setting in which power is exercised may both change a powerholder's expectations for successful influence, independently of the actual behavior of the target person. A third aspect of the social setting that can influence the use of coercion has to do with the number of target persons subjected to influence at the same time.

Typically, this problem is referred to in personnel management literature as the problem of "span of control." While top-level business managers may have from three to five persons directly under their control, one encounters instances in which a first-line foreman may have as many as two hundred employees working for him. A consequence of this large number of subordinates is that the appointed leader has very little time to spend with any one employee. Further, the appointed leader may have only the slightest idea of what each person is doing. Thus, he is placed in a position where good work may go unrewarded and poor work may not be corrected. Not too surprisingly, under these circumstances one finds that appointed leaders are attracted to the use of a strict system of controls. Among the features most favored are those that allow continuous monitoring of each individual's performance and that rely heavily on threats of punishment for rule infractions. Evidence for this process has been reported in several studies (Goodstadt and Kipnis 1970; Kipnis, Silverman, and Copeland 1973). In these studies it was found that more coercive means of influence were used by supervisors who were overburdened by the requirement that they supervise large numbers of men. As a supervisor's span of control increased, so too did his reliance on rules and punishments for controlling the behavior of subordinates. Although no direct evidence is available, I suggest that appointed leaders who are required to direct the behavior of large-sized groups would, if asked, express more doubts about their ability to control subordinates through simple persuasion than would leaders given only a few persons to influence.

The paradox involved here is that, from a design point of view, it is economically desirable to organize large numbers of persons into single units; whereas, in terms of psychological comfort, such organization is disastrous. This point tends to be recognized most immediately by appointed leaders who view their work in terms of socioemotional goals. Such leaders resent being forced by the situation to impose coercive rules on those they must direct. Thus, we find teachers continually agitating to reduce the size of the classes they teach and social caseworkers similarly arguing for a reduction in their case load. These persons recognize that, if they cannot give individual attention to their charges, then their very goals of encouraging individual growth will be blunted. Harshness and disciplinary emphasis will replace more gentle means of influence.

To summarize, there are numerous *situational* circumstances that decrease the powerholder's expectations that his influence attempts will be successful. Here we have mentioned some of the more important of these, ranging from the possession of coercive means which tempt the powerholder to demand more and also convince him of others' dislike, to the kinds of social structures in which power is exercised. In competitive structures where rewards are distributed in such a manner that sharing is precluded and a "winner takes all" philosophy prevails, individual powerholders come to believe that others will not freely give way to the powerholder. Under these circumstances, the powerholder may view his alternatives as either using force or not competing at all.

Individual Differences in Expectations of Successful Influence

Even casual observation will convince most observers that there are individual differences associated with the use of coercive power. People who doubt their own competence as a source of influence may be more likely to see others as resisting their influence when, in fact, such resistance may not exist at all. Thus, expectations of successful influence can be changed by not only the behavior of the target or by the social setting in which power is exercised, but also by the powerholder's past history. Recall, for instance, Webster's wonderful cartoon portraits of the Timid Soul, who in one sequence suffered in silence when a fellow passenger on a crowded bus stepped on his toes. The Timid Soul was both afraid to complain and afraid to ask the fellow passenger to move. Psychological studies have provided evidence that, in situations in which it is only possible to influence others by relying on personal powers of persuasion, persons low in self-esteem and self-confidence do not attempt to influence others (French and Snyder 1959; Hochbaum 1954). These timid persons' needs remain unsatisfied because they are not willing to forcefully argue for what they want.

What happens, however, when these same timid persons are given access to a range of institutional means of influence? Do they remain passive? Do they do the work themselves rather than order others to do it? We have not found this to be the case. While still not relying on persuasion, less confident powerholders remain active by relying extensively on their institutional means of influence. Moreover, less confident officeholders are rather rapidly attracted toward harsher means of influence, involving administrative punishments. Kipnis and Lane (1962), for instance, asked Navy noncommissioned officers to indicate to what extent they would use each of five different means of influence to correct the behavior of a troublesome subordinate. These means ranged from discussing the problem with the subordinate to placing the subordinate on "report." Placing a subordinate on report is a first step in the Navy's official disciplinary proceedings. Each noncommissioned officer also indicated the extent to which he was confident he could carry out his leadership duties in seven areas dealing with the technical and human-relations aspects of leadership. It was found that noncommissioned officers who stated they had little confidence in their leadership abilities recommended placing troublesome subordinates on official "report" more often than did confident noncommissioned officers. Furthermore, less confident leaders stated they were less willing to hold face-to-face discussions with the subordinate.

Similar findings have been obtained by Goodstadt and Hjelle (1973) in a laboratory study in which persons who perceived themselves to be either subjectively powerless or powerful (using Rotter's locus-of-control measure) were given access to a range of means of influencing a target. This range of means included the power to reward, to shift persons to new work environments, to persuade, to use expert power, and to punish. Those who saw themselves as weak and powerless chose to invoke punishing means of influence far more frequently than persons who perceived themselves to be powerful. Persons who believed they were powerful attempted to produce change in the target person through persuasion.

Thus, we see that when a person feels of little worth, he or she will be strongly attracted to harsh means of influence, if they are available. Underneath this behavior is the belief that gentle means of influence will not work since no one "respects me enough to do what I say if I only ask."

This conclusion is of considerable interest in extending existing writings on the relation between subjective feelings of powerlessness and violence. That is, it has generally been recognized that persons without resources are most prone to participate in violence. Ransford (1968), for instance, in interviews about the Watts riots found that subjective feelings of powerlessness were related to a willingness to participate in further riots. In these interviews, 41 percent of the respondents who scored high on a scale of power-lessness expressed a willingness to engage in riots, compared to 16 percent of those with low powerlessness scores. In a similar manner, the Kerner Report on civil disorders (1968) stated that "the frustration of powerlessness has led some Negroes to the con-viction that there is no effective alternative to violence as a means of achieving redress of grievances." What is of interest in Goodstadt and Hjelle's research is the conclusion that, even if given a range of means for influencing other persons and thereby having their objective powerlessness reduced, persons who have a long history of experiencing a lack of power will still choose destructive forms of influence.

The explanation for these findings appears to be that chronically low self-confidence, or feelings of powerlessness, reduces a person's expectations that he can influence others through persuasion or other more gentle means of influence. Subjectively, the odds of being able to influence others appear to shift to the difficult end of the scale as feelings of self-worth decrease.

Thus, the suggested relationship is that low self-confidence pro-duces low expectations of successful influence, which in turn lead to a greater reliance upon the use of coercion. Some correlational evidence in support of this chain of relations was found by myself in a questionnaire study of power usage, completed by 103 man-agers in state government and private industries. This study was described at the beginning of this chapter and involved managers' reading descriptions of ineffective employee performance, rating the probable odds that they could personally correct the problem and also rating the extent to which they would use coercion as a means of dealing with the ineffective performance. In addition, managers completed a scale that measured their own self-confi-dence in their abilities as managers.

It was found that managers who had low self-confidence also said that the odds were poor that they personally could correct the ineffective performances described in the questionnaire. The correlation was .39 between ratings of self-confidence and ratings of expectations of successful influence.

The question may now be examined as to the relative importance of both confidence and expectations in determining the use
of coercion. The model proposed here suggests that confidence
should affect expectations of successful influence, which in turn
should affect the decision to use coercion. In support of the model,
the correlation between confidence and endorsement of the use
of coercion was $-.27$ (p $< .01$), while the correlation between
expectations and coercion was $-.41$. Clearly, expectations were
more directly related to the use of coercion than was self-confidence. This pattern of correlations is consistent with the belief that
cognitive evaluations play a central role in the use of coercion.

One implication of these findings is that people who are passive
and timid in day-to-day life tend to be transformed into the most
severe of taskmasters when given access to institutional means of
influence. They bring to their work a history of failure to influence
others through persuasion and other gentle means of influence.
Once armed with the authority to invoke coercion, however, and
now required to influence others who work for them, passive persons very soon learn to use authority harshly. Interestingly enough,
Raser (1966) reached somewhat similar conclusions in a biographical analysis of the personalities of totalitarian and democratic political leaders. Totalitarian leaders were more insecure in
private life and lower in self-esteem. Certainly, Albert Speer's
(1970) portrait of his relations with Hitler fits very well with
Raser's description. Speer describes many incidents in which Hitler
avoided personal confrontations with his close associates and, if
in conflict with them, overcame their resistance through harsh and
punishing means rather than through discussion. Force, then, as
the psychiatrist Fanon suggested, seems the main means by which
the power needs of those who, by nature or by circumstances, are
passive can be satisfied.

Liking for the target person. Another individual-difference factor
affecting a powerholder's decision to use coercion is whether the
target person is liked or disliked. There is a growing body of evidence which shows, not surprisingly, that harsh means of influence
are invoked in attempts to influence a disliked or distrusted target
person (Banks 1974; Michener and Burt 1974; Michener and
Schwertfeger 1972). One immediate explanation that comes to
mind for this finding is that powerholders use threats and punishments because they enjoy seeing the target person suffer. Because

they dislike the target person, they may wish to hurt him as well as to make him comply. Further, as Michener suggests, since powerholders do not wish to maintain affectionate relations with people they don't like, the choice of coercion tends to guarantee that the relationship will not be preserved.

In line with the main argument of this chapter, I would suggest that another explanation for the use of coercion with disliked targets is that powerholders doubt their ability to persuade under these circumstances. Powerholders may assume that their dislike is reciprocated and as a result expect the target person to resist their influence. Thus the desire to punish may not be the only reason for using coercion with those whom we dislike. Instead, lowered expectations of successful influence may be an important instigator. Banks (1974) has amplified this argument by stating that when we dislike somebody we tend to assume that any resistance shown by the disliked other is a deliberate act of free will, while similar resistance from someone we like is attributed to uncontrollable forces in the environment. And as was pointed out earlier in this chapter, the perception of deliberate resistance to our requests produces lowered expectations of successful influence and increases our attraction toward coercive forms of influence.

Prejudice against minority groups illustrates very well this process of power use. While no direct test of the relation between prejudice, expectations, and the use of coercion has been done, one study (Kipnis, Silverman, and Copeland 1973) did investigate whether more coercive power would be used by white supervisors among black employees than among white employees. This possibility was suggested by the congressional hearings held in 1972 concerning race riots on Navy ships. A charge raised at this hearing was that black sailors received harsher punishments than white sailors for the same offense. Similar charges have been made concerning punishments meted out to black and white convicts (Levy and Miller 1970). White guards, it has been reported, were more punitive with black convicts than with white convicts.

The results of the Kipnis et al. study were similar in that coercive means were found to be used more often to influence black than white employees. That is, black workers were suspended or fired more often than white workers for the same infractions. When this information was reported to the company at the end of the study, the supervisors involved denied any malicious intent. Rather, they justified their behavior by arguing that black workers were less dependable. Since the analysis of the incidents reported by the supervisors revealed that the problems attributed to black subordinates were no different in kind or severity from those attributed to white subordinates, it seems probable that prejudice acted in this instance by affecting the supervisors' expectations of successful influence. The same problem manifested by a black subordinate was perceived as more difficult to correct than when manifested by a white subordinate.

Similarity and the use of coercion. Related to the concept of prejudice, but not necessarily sharing the strong emotional antipathy of prejudice, is the perception that someone differs from us in some important way such as religion or political beliefs. It was already mentioned in Chapter 4 that when dissimilar target persons *complied* with a powerholder's demands, they were given more rewards than similar target persons. The proposed explanation for these added rewards was that powerholders doubted that dissimilar target persons would continue to voluntarily comply without being provided with added incentives.

Consider now what happens when dissimilar target persons do not comply. Clearly, powerholders should be very pessimistic that any simple requests they make will be enough to overcome the target person's resistance. "They are not like me at all," thinks the powerholder, "why should they care about me or do what I want them to do?" With these kinds of thoughts, especially when it is not important to the goodwill of the target person, it is but a small step to decide that coercion must be used to overcome resistance.

The hypothesized tie-in between perceived dissimilarity, noncompliance, and the choice of coercive means of influence can be illustrated by findings of the present writer concerning power relations between men and women at work. In this investigation, the decisions by male and female managers to use coercive power with employees of the opposite sex were examined. Even in today's climate of changing sex-role attitudes, most women see themselves as different in important ways from men, and vice versa. Given these assumptions of differences, it seems likely that in situations in which men and women must continually influence each other there should be more reliance upon strong means of influence when resistance does occur. At work then, one might expect managers to use coercion more often with employees of the opposite sex than with employees of the same sex when resistance to the manager's orders is expressed by the employee.

The data to test this hypothesis were drawn from the previously mentioned questionnaire study in which 103 managers in state government and private industry read case histories of employee noncompliance and rated the extent to which they would use coercion as a means of changing for the better an employee's ineffective performance. What has not been mentioned before is that there were two forms of the questionnaire. In one form the ineffective employee was described as a woman and in the second as a man. The questionnaire contained eight incidents of ineffective performance, so that it was possible to have, in counterbalanced form, half the incidents describe female employees and half male employees. Of the 103 managers completing the questionnaire, 32 were female and 71 were male. Thus it was possible to examine whether the manager recommended more coercion when the ineffective employee was of the same sex or of the opposite sex.

Table 6.1 shows the average endorsement of coercion made by male and female managers when dealing with same sex or the opposite sex employees. The higher the score the greater the endorsement of coercion.

Table 6.1 Endorsement of the Use of Coercion by Male and Female Managers

	Male Managers (N = 71)	Female Managers (N = 32)
Male employees	11.98	13.36
Female employees	13.73	12.87

While the differences in ratings appear small, they follow the predicted pattern. Male managers endorsed more coercion with female employees, and female managers endorsed more coercion with male employees.

The statistical analysis (of variance) of these findings revealed a significant relation between the sex of the manager and the sex of the employee ($p < .01$). Male managers endorsed significantly more coercion for females than for male employees (means of 13.73 vs. 11.98). While the female managers endorsed more coercion for the opposite sex (means of 13.36 vs. 12.87), this difference was not statistically reliable.

The next question that was asked was whether managers had lower expectations of successful influence when required to change the behavior of a problem employee of the opposite sex. Subjective expectations were measured by asking each manager to rate the probable odds that they could personally correct the problem being shown by the employee. An analysis of these ratings revealed that male managers rated the odds as poorer when attempting to influence female employees than when attempting to influence male employees. The reverse of these findings were true for female managers. However, the statistical analysis of these ratings of subjective expectations yielded only marginally significant results ($p < .10$), thus leaving unproven, in this instance, the mediating role of expectations of successful influence.

Drawing back from the data, we can ask whether the findings of more reliance upon coercion when attempting to influence the opposite sex tell us anything of interest about relations in general between men and women. One suggestion is that the greater the emphasis on differences between the sexes, the more likely are both parties to assume that the other is irrational. That is, each assumes that the other must be cajoled and pushed and forced into compliance. "I am reasonable, but he or she is stubborn. Talking will do no good." With these assumptions of differences between the sexes, simple discussions tend to be avoided and stronger means are sought. Perhaps Professor Henry Higgins best illustrates these lowered expectations of other sex's reasonableness when he sings in *My Fair Lady*:

> Why can't a woman be more like a man?
> Women are irrational, that's all there is to that
> Their heads are full of cotton, hay, and rags,
> They're nothing but exasperating . . . vacillating
> . . . maddening . . . hags.
> Why can't a woman be more like a man?
> Men are so honest, so thoroughly square. . . .
> Oh, why can't a woman be more like a man?

With these thoughts in mind, it is not surprising that Professor Higgins spends so little time in quiet discussion with his "fair lady."

Sequential Use of Coercion

The concluding section of this chapter now turns to another issue in the use of coercion. This is the temporal sequence to be followed by the powerholder when he is deciding which to use first: coercive means or milder forms of influence.

Throughout this chapter it has been emphasized that anger and hostility do not have to be considered the primary instigators of the use of coercion. Rather, the decision to invoke coercion frequently arises from the powerholder's calculations concerning the best means of inducing compliance. The distinction here has to do with the timing of the delivery of coercive stimuli to a target. When angry and seeking revenge, the powerholder may immediately seek to invoke whatever harsh means are available in order to punish the target. The sequence has been described by Berkowitz (1971) as one of arousal, followed by disinhibition and the immediate evoking of coercive means. Despite the fine old Elizabethan observation that "revenge is a dish that is best eaten cold," most angered persons prefer immediate retaliation. In contrast, most officeholders whose power needs originate in their institutional roles prefer to use coercion as a last, rather than first, resort. The goal of the institutional powerholder is not, strictly speaking, to punish the target but to make him change his behavior in order to further institutional objectives. In the absence of emotional arousal, the decision to use coercion arises from calculations concerning the best means to induce compliance. Since there are far less costs involved in the use of persuasion, training, or ecological changes, as compared with threats, these less costly means will almost invariably be tried first. Exceptions to this generalization exist, of course, such as the previously mentioned less confident or prejudiced officeholders, who were drawn rather rapidly to harsher means.

Some evidence that evoking harsher means of influence will be deferred until more gentle means have been exhausted is available from the previously cited experimental study of Goodstadt and Kipnis (1970). In this study, the focus was on how subjects acting as managers used various power tactics to influence the performance of a worker who had been programmed to perform poorly. This study had six work periods during which the output of the workers was brought in to the managers. Thus, it was possible to examine the means of influence invoked by managers during the first three work periods and the last three work periods.

During the first half of the experiment, the preferred means used to influence the performance of the below-average worker were:

(*a*) ecological control (assigning new jobs), (*b*) expert powers, and (*c*) threatening to deduct pay from the worker's salary. During the last half of the experiment the preferred means of influence involved: (*a*) actually deducting pay from the worker's salary, (*b*) threatening to fire the worker, and (*c*) actually firing the worker. This progressive trend toward reliance on harsher means was less for the worker who was inept than for the worker whose poor performance was based upon poor attitudes. However, since the outputs of both types of worker had been programmed to stay below average, an increasing reliance upon coercion was apparent for both types.

Thus, given the availability of a range of means of influence, I suggest that there will be a progressive scaling of means from less harsh to most severe. University instructors will usually first discuss and give extra instruction to a failing student before assigning a failing grade; managers will assign new jobs, counsel, and train before recommending suspension; and diplomats prefer to "jaw, jaw, jaw" before proceeding to "war, war, war." Underlying this progression, presumably, will be declining expectations of successful influence and the concurrent attraction to strong means of influence.

Summary

The basic assumption that has been examined in this chapter is that all forces that reduce an individual's belief in his own effectiveness also serve to increase the individual's attraction to coercive means of influence. Among the forces that may reduce the powerholder's belief in his own effectiveness are:

a) The perception that the target person is deliberately, rather than involuntarily, resisting influence.

b) Environmental forces such as the kinds of influence means available to the powerholder, the structural arrangements for reward allocation, and the number of target persons to be influenced at the same time.

c) The temperamental and characterological makeup of powerholders, as these determine powerholders' beliefs about their own personal effectiveness and the kinds of people that they see as similar or different than themselves.

7   Inhibition of the Power Act

It was suggested in Chapter 2 that there was a region of inhibition that the powerholder must successfully navigate before he could exercise influence. The necessity for assuming the existence of this region of inhibition arises from the fact that we could not otherwise explain the many instances in which the powerholder appears in complete control of events and individuals and yet takes no further action.

Understanding the forces leading to the inhibition of behavior is one of the two fundamental tasks that have engaged the attention of behavioral scientists, the other being the understanding of the forces leading to the arousal of behavior. Inescapably, the stance one takes in regard to the question of restraint has political overtones. The laboratory finding, for instance, that punishments will deter aggressive behavior so long as the punishments are feared cannot fail to cause speculation as to how to use this information to control behavior on a larger scale.

The humanist, the radical, and the romantic have the fixed idea that the individual must be free to realize his own potential, that the human spirit is distorted by repressive institutions and laws. At all levels of society a continual acrimonious dialogue goes on between those representing the forces for individual freedom and those representing the forces for restraint. Sometimes the debating parties change sides, as when the strong "law and order" representative argues that there should be no laws restraining the conduct of businesses. Despite these occasional role changes, however, the issue of how much restraint and how much freedom society can afford to allow its members is a source of continual debate. Hence the input of research findings from the social sciences is bound to add fuel to any ongoing controversies.

Basically the issue pivots around a set of assumptions made about human nature. If it is assumed that each person has the potential to develop to God-like dimensions, if nurtured properly by society, then freedom from restraints which distort this growth seems the answer to the debate. If one believes, however, that humans left to regulate their own behavior would soon destroy themselves in frantic efforts to maximize their own outcomes, then social restraint is the answer.

Freud in particular saw little possibility of man being able to control urges to use power for selfish goals. In a long letter written in response to a question from Albert Einstein concerning the possibility of ending war, Freud stated his view that the instinctive impulses of man were almost impossible to control. Even when man banded together into a community and established laws to regulate the excesses of violence, sooner or later inequities entered into the law, as one person gained an advantage in power over his fellows, and thus excesses of behavior continued to occur. Toward the end of his letter Freud pessimistically concluded:

> The upshot of these observations . . . is that there is no likelihood of being able to suppress humanity's aggressive tendencies. In some happy corners of the earth, they say, where human nature brings forth abundantly whatever man desires, there flourish races whose lives go gently by, unknowing of aggression or constraint. This I can hardly credit. I would like further details about these happy folk. The Bolshevists, too, aspire to do away with human aggressiveness by ensuring the satisfaction of material needs and enforcing equality between man and man. To me this hope seems vain. Meanwhile they perfect their armaments, and their hatred of outsiders is not the least of the factors of cohesion among them. [1964, p. 77]

It should be noted that Freud, despite his deep pessimism concerning man's fate, acknowledged the possibility that limits could be placed on man's aggressive nature through the development of culture and correlated changes in man's genetic makeup. On the cultural side he foresaw the slow growth and strengthening of the intellect, which would eventually master instinctual life. Freud included in the role of intellect the growth of ethical values which would allow humans to realize the unworthiness of aggression. On the genetic side, Freud assumed that, through a process of evolution, aggressiveness as an inherited trait would become less dominant. Aggression, that is, would have less survival value for the individual as man's technology began to produce enough for all.

These are changes in man's nature that Freud saw as happening in some distant future. When the world of power is considered today, however, many observers would favor the view that curbs should be placed upon behavior rather than more freedom should be granted. Everyday events seem to point to the fact that we are surrounded by power usages that are insufficiently restrained. To our great despair the values of "take" appear far stronger than the values of "wait."

Nevertheless, there *are* forces that strengthen the value of "wait" even if at times they appear very weak. These forces, I believe, operate in one of two ways in limiting the use of power. The first is by reducing the individual's need to seek goals that require the use of power. The second is by requiring the powerholder to use different means of influence than he would have chosen in the absence of restraining forces. Each of these two methods of restraint will be illustrated in the following pages.

Physiological Inhibition of Aggressive Power

People vary greatly in the extent to which they are willing to invoke coercive forms of power against others. Some retain an innate gentleness that restrains their actions, despite the fact that they encounter many provocations. For these people the idea of doing harm invokes feelings of anxiety and guilt (Hare 1968). The very thought of hurting others is troublesome. Some have argued (Clark 1971) that, if one could inject this spirit of pacifism into our political and military leaders, a personal distaste of hurting others would then cause them to trip the decision in favor of peace when faced with a choice between war or peace. Strangely enough, there is some evidence that the spirit of restraint and gentleness in man is at least in part a function of complex biochemical and neurological factors. Further, there is emerging a psychotechnology concerned with learning how to control biological impulses to do harm to others.

There are several sources of research supporting this contention. It has been known for some time that persons characterized by aggressive and violent acts have abnormal EEG brain patterns, in terms of spiking and excessive slow-wave patterns (Knott and Gottlieb, 1944; Gottlieb, Ashby, and Knott 1946). These findings extend to children. In 1938, Jasper, Solomon, and Bradley, for instance, found that there were definite abnormalities in the EEG patterns of children who since infancy were irritable, hyperactive, and aggressive, or who had a short attention-span, and whose behavior and mood varied unexplainably from time to time.

Studies of brain functioning have confirmed these early findings and have also revealed that there are neural systems which when active appear to be directly associated with aggressive behavior. Thus one possible control of aggressive behavior that has been suggested is by interfering with the function of these neural centers. And as is fairly well known at this time, many studies among animals, and occasionally in man, reveal that surgical ablations or incisions in the temporal lobes and posterior hypothalamus will in fact produce reductions in aggressive behaviors.

In addition to evidence of areas that arouse aggressive behavior, there is also evidence, according to Moyer (1971), that there are suppressor systems in the brain serving to inhibit aggressive behavior. These suppressor regions can apparently be activated through direct electrical and chemical stimulation, as well as indirectly through drugs that act on the central nervous system. Delgado (1969) has shown that normally vicious animals can be tamed by the activation of the aggression-suppressor region in the brain by means of radio signals. Bulls raised for fighting have halted their attack at the very last moment in response to a signal from an implanted electrode.

Besides through electrical stimulation or brain extirpation, control over aggressive behavior may be gained through altering the chemical and hormonal factors in the blood stream. It has been known for centuries, for instance, that castration reduces aggressive tendencies in bulls. Blocking the action of the male sex hormone, androgen, through such agents as the injection of the female hormone, estrogen, has been recently suggested as a means of controlling aggressive behavior.

Along the same line, hyperactive and impulsive children can be treated through the use of various forms of amphetamine. These drugs have a calming effect on children such that they become less aggressive and less loud; in general, they become much more acceptable members of the community (Bradley 1942). Moyer has suggested that a wide variety of additional drugs have a calming effect upon man. These range from dilantin, a drug originally used to control epileptic seizures, to various forms of tranquilizing agents. Moyer has somewhat facetiously suggested that some form of calming drug may be routinely added to our milk, or to our water supply, to make people suppress their aggressive power needs.

Kenneth B. Clark, in a presidential address to the American Psychological Association (1972), took note of these possibilities of using drugs to control powerholders. Man, he warned, is easily tempted to use social power for self-serving and selfish ends. Out of existential feelings of fear, weakness, and moral emptiness, originate irrational drives to dominate, destroy, and do harm. In our time, such irrational drives, combined with the access of political leaders to great destructive sources of power, has left the world on the verge of a new age of barbarism. What must be done, according to Clark, is to control and redirect the powerholder in more peaceful directions.

> Given the urgency of this immediate survival problem, the psychological and social sciences must enable us to control the animalistic, barbaric and primitive propensities in man and subordinate these negatives to the uniquely human moral and ethical characteristics of love, kindness, and empathy.

But how is this to be done? Clark argues against traditional methods of moral education as being too slow and uncertain to control powerful leaders. He says:

> We can no longer afford to rely solely on the traditional prescientific attempts to contain human cruelty and destructiveness. The techniques and appeals of religion, moral philosophy, law and education seemed appropriate and civilized approaches to the control of man's primitive and egocentric behavior in a pre-

nuclear age. They are in themselves no longer appropriate because they permit too wide a margin of error and a degree of unpredictability that is rationally inconsistent with the present survival urgency. Furthermore, moral verbalizations of the past have been prostituted by the pathos of power; they have been perverted by the pretenses of rationality in the service of inhumanity if not barbarity.

After briefly noting the advances being made in biochemical investigations, Clark points out that we are on the threshold of that "type of scientific biochemical intervention which could stabilize and make dominant the moral and ethical propensities of man and subordinate, if not eliminate, his negative and primitive behavioral tendencies." Clark sees it as a logical requirement imposed on all power-controlling leaders that they accept and use these biochemical pacifiers, once they are developed, so as to block the leaders' own inclinations to make warlike and aggressive decisions. In short, through chemical means, leaders and nations would be internally disarmed.

Space has been devoted to Clark's proposal because it appears to be technically possible in the not too distant future. In our discussion of power usage it was pointed out that the availability of a means of influencing others tempts the powerholder to use this means. Thus it should come as no surprise that the availability of a new technology for controlling behavior through physiological means should immediately lead to a consideration of its use. Further, Clark's proposal illustrates the dilemma for society created by research in the social sciences. Applications of control technology inevitably involve political and ethical concerns of the most fundamental kind. One must clearly work out whether it is in the best interests of society to interfere with the functioning of the central nervous system as a means of controlling the misuse of power—whether the misuse is by violent criminals lashing out with their fists or knives, or by political leaders corruptly using their offices. Recent law suits by civil libertarians attempting to block researchers from experimentally implanting electrodes in the brains of imprisoned criminals, or to carry out actual brain surgery in the limbic region to reduce violent behavior, suggest the immediacy of these concerns. Chorover (1973) has most recently explored the issues involved here and concludes that society stands to lose more than it will gain by these kinds of efforts.

Deindividuation

Restraint of power usage is frequently justified on the assumption that without restraint the powerholder would take more and more for himself, leaving less and less for others. Thus man's tendency to maximize his outcomes is considered a compelling reason for the necessity of restraints.

Still another reason for justifying restraints, to be considered in this section, is that many people appear to experience great pleasure from controlling the lives of others. That is, power seems to unleash in many persons cruel motives to manipulate others, motives the persons had not suspected of existing prior to their control of power. Aside from the explanation that we harbor within us small demons waiting for the right moment to emerge, we must seek an explanation for these tendencies in the range of experiences that humans are potentially capable of enjoying.

In this regard Stanford University psychologist Phillip Zimbardo (1970) has written that there exists within most people "dark forces" that seek to gratify immediately any desire; forces that seek to live for the here and now and to enjoy any action, no matter how antisocial, that provides emotional release and gratification. These forces are most likely to be manifested when the person has lost the restraints produced by self-awareness and is experiencing what Zimbardo and others (Festinger, Pepitone, and Newcomb 1952) have called a state of deindividuation. It is these particular motivational forces produced by deindividuation that appear to be involved when persons experience great pleasure in exercising personal dominance over others. Awareness of self, then, can be designated as a second restraint in power usage. Apparently to lose his sense of identity encourages the powerholder to influence others in ways that society would ordinarily condemn.

One of the key questions for Zimbardo is to identify the circumstances leading to an individual's experiencing deindividuation, or to a lowering of threshold for normally restrained behavior. Zimbardo has theorized that to the extent the individual believes he is not likely to be identified, or that he is in a large group, or that he experiences altered states of consciousness, restraints may be lowered against carrying out acts normally inhibited by various mechanisms of self-control.

Our interest in Zimbardo's analysis comes from its implications for understanding when an individual may be tempted to use resources to satisfy power needs which violate personal or societal taboos. To the extent power may be exercised under conditions of anonymity, for instance, one would predict that the individual powerholder would be increasingly tempted to use his resources in ways condemned by society.

Zimbardo presents an interesting study of this possibility in an investigation of when coercive means are directed against an innocent target. In this particular study, coeds were provided with a machine that could deliver an electric shock (the resource) to a sister coed, located in another room. The rationale for delivering shock was that the experimenters were studying conditioning processes by means of electric shock. *However the decision as to the number of shocks to give over a series of trials, as well as the intensity of shock, was left up to the individual coeds.* Thus, the coeds were in the role of powerholder, with resources in the form of electric shock that they could use to influence the target if they chose to do so.

Zimbardo's prediction was that the coeds would be more willing to exercise coercive power if they were in a state of deindividuation. To establish the conditions of deindividuation, groups of four coeds participated at a time. Half of these groups put on very large lab coats, hoods over their heads, and their names were never used. In contrast, each coed assigned to the individuation condition was greeted by name and given a big name tag to wear, while the importance of her unique reaction was emphasized by the instructions of the experimenter.

The results of this study revealed that deindividuating the coeds had a significant influence on their willingness to invoke electric shock. The total duration of shock was twice as much for the deindividuated coeds as for the individuated coeds. Zimbardo concluded that "under conditions specified as deindividuating, normally mild-mannered college girls shocked another girl almost every time they had an opportunity to do so, sometimes for as long as they were allowed, and it didn't matter whether or not the fellow student was a nice girl who didn't deserve to be hurt" (p. 270).

Zimbardo's theorizing suggests something that perhaps we have known all along; namely, that when power can be exercised without the surveillance of the public, the powerholder will experience fewer restraints against invoking resources than when such surveillance is present. The control of unchallenged power, in itself, probably serves to deindividuate the powerholder. With power the person can protect himself from public scrutiny and from the necessity of justifying his acts. A study by Zimbardo and his colleagues (1974) of prison guards who were given almost unrestrained power over their prisoners clearly suggests that such a process of deindividuation can occur under these circumstances. The prison guards acted in an increasingly brutal manner and, perhaps more disturbing, reported that they enjoyed the master-slave relationships that were evolving.

Costs as a Restraining Influence on the Exercise of Power

It was mentioned in Chapter 1 that theories which view human interactions as the exchange of benefits have been particularly useful for examining problems of conflict and bargaining. An assumption underlying these theories, that may be traced to economics and to reinforcement psychology, is that each of the parties in these exchanges acts to maximize gains and to minimize costs.

From this assumption, one can conclude that a strong restraint upon an individual's decision to invoke resources has to do with the costs that are involved. As Cartwright (1965) points out: "When an agent is deciding whether to exercise influence, it must be assumed that he calculates in some sense the net advantage to him of making an influence attempt" (p. 8). If the results of the agent's calculation indicate that he will lose more than he will gain, presumably the individual does not attempt to influence others. The young lover may be eager to seduce the maiden, but will look elsewhere if the cost of seduction is marriage. Sorenson (1965), in discussing how decisions were reached concerning the Cuban missile crisis during the early 1960s, stated that the overriding constraint in the situation against invoking military power to eliminate the nuclear missiles in Cuba was the possibility that Russia might be forced into war with the United States. Even the decision to impose a blockade around Cuba was viewed by President Kennedy as clearly likely to incur costs to this country in terms of possible increments in Russian countertactics in Germany and the Near East,

In the above instances we have the idea that the powerholder exercises deliberate restraints on his behavior while calculating the net advantage of action or inaction. The seeming rationality of this behavior has persuaded several theorists to explicitly introduce the idea of costs into their discussions of the use of power. Harsanyi (1962) has argued that, without information about what he calls "opportunity costs," the power of various persons cannot be evaluated, nor can it be predicted when they will use power. Costs for Harsanyi, who leans toward the analysis of power in economic terms, are measured in relatively objective ways such as money expended and commitments that the powerholder must make in exchange for compliance.

In psychology, Thibaut and Kelley (1959) have also made the idea of costs and gains a central component of their views of power. Power for these writers is defined in exchange theory terms as the capability of one person to affect another's outcomes. Once again the major restraint upon the decision to exercise influence is the costs that the powerholder may incur. Police, for example, have the power to arrest others, and hence may be considered to have the ability to affect others' outcomes. However there are limitations on the extent to which the police will use this power, which in Thibaut and Kelley's view are a function of the costs involved in making the arrest. To arrest a wandering hobo may incur few costs for the policeman. To arrest the mayor's son for reckless driving is another matter, since the costs for exerting power may leave the officer without a job.

The exercise of power for the rational man, then, becomes a function of costs and benefits. If the results indicate that he will lose more than he will gain, presumably resources are not invoked and power is not exerted. What seems to happen is that concern over costs convinces the powerholder to give up trying for whatever it was that he wanted.

Within the context of laboratory experimentation, several studies have provided support for the notion that, as costs of exercising power increase, the powerholder restrains himself (Tedeschi, Horai, Lindskold, and Faley 1970; Tedeschi, Bonomo, and Novinson 1970; Thibaut and Faucheux 1965; Bedell and Sistrunk 1973). In these studies subjects are given full information about both the gains and the costs of exercising influence. The focus of interest is in noting whether the participants with power do behave rationally, that is, in a way to maximize gains and minimize costs. The answer is that they do, within reasonable limits. Apparently if the powerholder is fully aware of the costs involved in exercising power, he will use a hedonic calculus to determine his actions. If the results are negative he will limit his use of resources.

The reader can easily contrast this source of restraint, which emphasizes the rational and cognitive components of behavior, with the sources previously discussed. In these earlier sources, the individual is propelled unwittingly into postures of attack, withdrawal, or restraint as the result of the activation of neural and hormonal systems, or being provided with anonymity.

Limitations to the Concept of Costs

There can be no doubt that most persons at most times engage in a form of hedonic calculus before taking any unusual action. Knowledge of this calculus is of importance for understanding the acts that a powerholder has taken. Without it we would not be able to understand why some people leap into action and others hesitate. However, there are limits to the usefulness of the concept of costs for predicting some future behavior of a powerholder or for using the projected ratio of costs and benefits in order to determine precisely whether or not to invoke power.

For one thing, emotionality may influence the calculation of costs, as when the powerholder is angry at the target and is determined to do him injury, regardless of the consequences for himself. Brown (1970) found that when outside observers humiliated a subject by criticizing his behavior in a bargaining game, the subject acted more aggressively against his opponent regardless of the fact that such aggression resulted in a loss of profits. Captain Ahab's furious determination to destroy the white whale, Moby Dick, despite the fact that the whale's destruction would cause his own death, is a deeply moving illustration of how emotions and unbounded determination can override a prudent calculation of costs.

Again, the generalizations concerning costs may not hold because the powerholders are simply not in a position to take into account the costs they are liable to incur. In this connection Berle (1967) observed that it is almost impossible to predict the long-term consequences of invoking power. While the immediate costs involved can frequently be computed, the waves generated by power acts tend to take unpredictable courses. Before World War I began, for example, the leaders of the conflicting countries had not the slightest idea of the costs that their countries would incur over the four years of the war. The tremendous destruction of property in France or Russia was not considered much of a possibility, while the loss of lives in the trenches was considered even less likely.

Finally, the generalization concerning costs may be further weakened by the eternal optimism of persons who are highly motivated to achieve some goal. Real costs that may have served as a deterrent are falsified in the mind in order to make the odds of success more attractive. In the mid 1960s when the stock market was expanding, many companies with excess capital became "conglomerates" by buying up the stock of companies in fields unrelated to those of their products (Brooks 1973). The eventual bankruptcy of many of these conglomerates in the late 1960s and early 1970s could be directly traced to the failure of managers to accurately assess the risks involved in these takeovers. Sustained by previous success and driving ambition, these managers simply ignored warning signs indicating that the resources of their own companies should not be used to expand into areas not directly related to their own kinds of business.

The principal conclusion concerning anticipated costs as an inhibitor of the power act is that people do consider costs and benefits when deciding to take action, and this information is most useful in situations when (*a*) full knowledge of the costs are available; (*b*) emotions are not strongly involved, and (*c*) the immediate consequences of the use of power are all that is considered.

Values and Attitudes

Still other social scientists view the problem of inhibition of power in terms of subjective values and attitudes (Berkowitz and Daniels 1963; Leventhal and Lane 1970; Pepitone 1971; Staub 1971; Walster, Berscheid, and Walster 1973). Despite the fact that the individual may gain substantial advantage by invoking his resources, it frequently happens that he inhibits the invoking of resources because he questions the propriety of the act. The need to act in a just manner overrides the temptation to maximize gain.

Frequently persons in power must decide whether to guide their actions by normative values or by a utilitarian estimate of the costs involved in taking some action. Clashes are deep, frequently emotional, and inevitable when persons holding these two views must jointly decide what to do. One side crisply argues for action because the cost/benefit ratio is favorable, and the other side righteously argues for inaction because the power act is unethical. Neither side can understand the other, and an impasse is reached. When Chester Bowles was assistant secretary of state in the Kennedy administration, he found himself almost alone in his opposition to the government-supported invasion of Cuba at the Bay of Pigs. His opposition was based upon deep convictions about the propriety of such acts. His views, of course, conflicted with the more utilitarian values of the majority of Kennedy's staff, who were committed to a tough-minded exercise of power. During this period he entered the following observation in his diary (reported in Halberstam [1973]):

> The question which concerns me about the new administration is whether it lacks a genuine conviction about what is right and what is wrong.
> Anyone in public life who has strong convictions about the right and wrong of public morality, both domestic and international has a very great advantage in times of strain since his instincts on what to do are clear and immediate. Lacking such a framework of moral conviction of what is right and what is wrong, he is forced to lean almost entirely upon his mental processes. He adds up the pluses and minuses of any question and comes up with a conclusion. Under normal conditions when he is not tired or frustrated this pragmatic approach should successfully bring him on the right side of the question.
> What worries me are the conclusions that such an individual may reach when he is tired, angry, frustrated, or emotionally affected. The Cuban fiasco demonstrates how far astray a man as brilliant and well intentioned as Kennedy can go who lacks a basic moral reference point.

Shortly after Bowles made this diary entry he was forced to resign from his position in the State Department.

Some researchers prefer to include the inhibiting effects of personal values as simply another cost factor. In my opinion, this approach is not useful. If all sources of inhibition are labeled "costs," then this concept loses explanatory value. Values and attitudes serve to restrain behavior for very precise reasons; transgressions invoke guilt, shame, and anxiety. These are not the logical and cognitive variables traditionally associated with the calculations of costs.

How Ideas about Justice Restrain the Use of Power

Ethical restraints on the use of power can be related to at least two views of justice. The first view is derived in modern-day form from exchange theory. The emphasis, however, is not on the cost/benefit ratios each party derives from the exchange but upon the perceived fairness of the exchange. The question of fair or equitable exchanges was first described systematically in psychology by Adams (1963) and modified somewhat by Walster, Berscheid, and Walster (1973). The equitable-exchange model proposes that most people accept the norm that the rewards gained by each person in an exchange should be proportional to his contributions. Thus an equitable relationship is one in which a person's outcomes are based upon his inputs. If person A works harder than Person B (their inputs), then A should receive more rewards than B (their outcomes), if they are doing the same work. Simple justice occurs, in Adam's view, when inputs and outcomes are in balance. This view of justice can be summed up by saying, "You get what you deserve."

Many studies have found that people tend to order their lives and judge how fair situations are in terms of their equity standard. Thus persons who get less than others of similar skills have been found to "slack off" (reduce inputs) in order to compensate for being under-rewarded (Adams, 1963; Adams and Rosenbaum 1962). Other studies of persons in positions to allocate rewards to both themselves and others show that these powerholders do not take everything for themselves despite the fact that they are in a position to do so. (Leventhal and Lane 1970; Pepitone 1971). Rather, the rewards are distributed in proportion to each person's contribution. Pepitone (1971) found that college students who were initially awarded more than they deserved in a two-person bargaining game with fellow students, subsequently made bargaining decisions designed to redistribute the available rewards more evenly. In so doing the students reduced the amount of rewards they received themselves. Despite being in a position of power, these students exercised restraints that would be difficult to predict from the simple notion that persons are motivated to maximize their own gains.

A second view of justice that may restrain the use of power can be called the "equality" model. Most recently this view of justice has been examined in psychology by Lerner (1974). The equality view argues that rewards should be distributed to all persons in a collective equally rather than proportionally to each member's inputs. For example, on many collective settlements in Israel all persons share outcomes equally—the same living quarters, the same food, the same vacations and pay—despite the fact that some do the work of skilled engineers and managers while others do simple, unskilled manual work. Clearly, the individual's inputs in this system are not proportional to his outcomes. While there has been little research in psychology dealing with the ideal of equality as compared to equity, both models could serve to inhibit a power-holder from using resources simply to maximize his own outcomes. In one instance inhibition could originate in the value judgment that "I have not done enough to deserve these outcomes," and in the second instance inhibition would originate in the value judgment "share and share alike."

What evidence is there that either or both of these ethical concepts are taken into account by powerholders? The answer suggested by the available research is that persons in positions of power are most likely to be guided by notions of *equity* rather than *equality*. Apparently this is because the powerholder can allocate more desired outcomes to himself under the first system than the second, but he is still restrained from taking all. Let us examine the basis for this conclusion.

The first set of evidence comes from studies of interpersonal bargaining. These studies provide reasonably strong evidence to support the generalization that, as an individual's resources increase in comparison to others, those controlling greater resources depart from equality by allocating more of the available resources for themselves and accordingly provide the less powerful with a smaller share (Tedeschi, Lindskold, Horai, and Gahagan 1969; Shure, Meeker, and Hansford 1965). In a two-person bargaining study by Tedeschi et al. one group of subjects was given strong power over their opponents and so could determine the amount of money each could earn. In a second condition subjects and opponents had equal power. The not too surprising finding was that subjects in the strong-power condition shared money with their opponents 18 percent of the time, while subjects in the equal-power condition shared 36 percent of the time. In short, the control of superior power tempted the actors to allocate more for themselves.

Departures from equality should not, however, be seen simply as greedy actions by those in power. If this were the simple case, then in the above-cited Tedeschi et al. study those with strong power would not have shared at all. Rather, it is suggested that the powerholder convinces himself that his inputs into a situation, as represented by his superior power, are greater than those of the less powerful, and accordingly he deserves a larger share of the outcomes.

A second bit of evidence suggesting that powerholders prefer equity over equality may be found in studies of pay and morale within industry. University of Michigan sociologist E. Yuchtman (personal communication) asked male and female employees ranging from blue-collar workers to executives whether they would prefer a pay system that gave equal pay to all workers at the same level in the organization, regardless of each worker's ability (equality), or a system of pay that rewarded persons at the same level on the basis of their skills and abilities (equity). The findings were that more executives than blue-collar workers preferred to be paid on the basis of equity. Further, male workers preferred an equitable pay system and female workers preferred an equalitarian system. Quite clearly, persons in positions of power or dominance preferred a system that allowed them to maximize their outcomes by using their skills and abilities. Those with less power (blue-collar workers, women) preferred a system that distributed rewards equally. An explanation of these findings, offered by Yuchtman, is that people in power can get more by relying on an equitable distribution of rewards, while people without power can get more by relying upon an equalitarian distribution of rewards.

We started out this section by asking how ethical ideas might restrain the use of power. The reader, however, may complain that from what has been said so far, ethicality is apparently used to rationalize a lack of restraint. I would not subscribe to this conclusion. My conclusion is that, when given a choice between the two fundamental systems of justice that exist in Western society, persons in positions of power would opt for the belief that "each person should get what he deserves" rather than that "all should share alike." This is because, when power is considered an input, those with power can claim more as a simple matter of justice. Thus "share and share alike" tends to be a value system of the have-nots rather than the haves. A matter of some interest which requires exploration in the social sciences is the process by which persons who initially call for equality subsequently adopt a system of justice based upon equity. Studies among children by Lerner (1974) suggest that a lack of cooperative relationship promotes a preference for equity rather than equality. How the control of resources may also promote this shift would contribute further to our understanding of these differing conceptions of justice.

Cultural Climate and Normative Values

Now we may turn to the last source of restraint that will be examined in this chapter. This source originates in the norms of groups, institutions, and society. Without exception, all cultures take pains to teach young children the propriety of using various resources. Through direct and indirect means the child is taught the general range of situations in which it is permissible, even expected, to use power. In a fighting culture such as that of the Sioux Indian, the young child is encouraged to view a wide range of situations as requiring the use of violence and cruelty (Erikson 1950). In sharp contrast, the children of the Saulteaux Indians, people with a peaceful trapping and fishing culture, are taught to react with indifference and gentleness to the same stimuli that arouse the Sioux child to anger. The child then appears to store the information taught by his society, and include it in a repertory of responses that are available for later use. At the appropriate time he may match the situation with the range of responses he has learned, selecting that response which he views as most appropriate. Included here, of course, is the decision as to whether or not it is appropriate to invoke any given resource.

Societies not only teach the young how to deal with power in a direct fashion but teach them indirectly as well in terms of the values and goals that are considered important. Social goals are ordered for the child in terms of their relative importance. When conflicts occur, the child and subsequently the adult will attempt to satisfy those goals considered to have the highest importance. In our society children are taught to value achievement, the accumulation of material wealth, the need to respect others, to be loyal to friends, and to be of help to others if needed. Of all of these values, the one on which middle-class parents place overwhelming emphasis is the importance of individual achievement and accomplishment. In terms of the rewards and punishments, praises and blames, doled out to the child, the vast majority center around success of the child in mastering his environment.

Given this emphasis, it is not surprising that the drive to achieve may place the person in a competitive relation with his fellows. This is because most achievement type situations are defined in this society as those in which one does better than one's peers, whether at school, at play, in business. Thus, when faced with a decision of using resources to achieve, even if such a use might do injury to others, our cultural values would affirm the invoking of these resources as a proper action.

What I am saying is that a cultural emphasis on achievement is quite likely to lead to a lowering of restraints against using power tactics to satisfy this need. The noted sociologist Seymour Lipset (1974) puts the matter this way in discussing the consequences of failure to achieve: "In America what counts is whether you have won the game, not how you have played it" (p. 60). David McClelland, in his book *The Achieving Society* (1961), has reached similar conclusions, I believe, in his analysis of attributes of the Greek god Hermes, whom he compares to the present day high-achievement motivated businessman. One problem with Hermes was that he was dishonest and unethical at the same time as he was highly motivated to achieve. The key question examined by McClelland is whether a high need for achievement tends of itself to encourage humans to use any means available to satisfy this need.

While not answering this question directly, McClelland provides an indirect answer in his conclusion that the driving force of a strong need for achievement underlies the economic growth of nations. The countries mentioned by McClelland as given impetus for growth through the attempts of their citizens to satisfy their achievement needs—the city states of early Greece, Spain during the fifteenth century, and England—all achieved their greatness not only by commerce but also by wars and the cruel exploitation of their weaker neighbors.

While not directly encouraging the use of power for exploitative purposes, societies that give priority to maximizing individual achievement goals apparently invite their citizens to use whatever resources may be available to satisfy this need.

Penalties for Norm Violation

We may conclude that norms, laws, traditions, and values give powerful guidance to when and where resources will be used. While not absolute, these written and unwritten norms serve to form a climate which serves to encourage or restrain the use of resources, even though their use would have been considered completely appropriate in a different moral climate.

A careful reading of history suggests that, when individuals and nations possess a range of resources, they will forgo the use of several of them for no other reason than that the climate of their time prohibits the use of these resources. The decision of President Truman to use the atomic bomb at Hiroshima could only have been made against the background of continuous killing and destruction of World War II. Without this climate of death, the reasons that were offered for this decision (it would save American lives, or a negotiated peace allowing the Japanese emperor tradition to survive would be unacceptable to most Americans) would not have been sufficient to allow Truman to reach a positive decision. Similar attempts to use far less destructive forms of thermonuclear weapons in Vietnam and Korea have been continually restrained, partly, I believe, because of the overwhelming rejection of such means by most Americans.

Not only do moral climate and norms guide the powerholder's choice of means of influence, but they also include the prescription of penalties when they are violated. Michener and Burt (1974) have written that norms serve to limit the use of power if for no other reason than that continued violation of norms by powerholders would serve to provoke revolts against them.

The importance of penalties associated with a powerholder's violations of norms has also been emphasized by Adolph Berle (1967) in contrasting the American attitudes towards war in the 1840s with those held in the late 1960s. The belief in the American destiny in the 1840s encouraged President James K. Polk to provoke a war with Mexico. Polk had a strong desire to secure California, then Mexican territory, for the United States. After an attempt to negotiate a purchase failed, Polk sent General Zachary Taylor to cross the Rio Grande, causing Mexican forces to retaliate. Two weeks later Polk asked for a declaration of war. At the conclusion of the war, by the Treaty of Guadalupe Hidalgo, the United States acquired the territory that is now Utah, Nevada, Upper California, Arizona, New Mexico, and parts of Colorado and Wyoming. As Berle points out: "Power was never more obviously personal than in President Polk's use of it in the Mexican affair. His aim was aggressive, acquisitive, expansionist, and imperialist. *The reader can imagine the editorials, demonstrations, teach-ins, outpourings of wrath had a comparable decision been taken in the year 1969.*" (Italics mine.)

And Berle is right. Military actions in Vietnam, rather than being cheered by the American public as a fulfillment of the American dream of expansion and manifest destiny, cost Lyndon Johnson a second term in office.

Summary

Inhibitions against invoking resources may act in either of two ways. First, they may diminish the individual's power motivations. Thus, taking of the "power pill" (to paraphrase Clark [1971]) may eliminate the ruler's desire to dominate and manipulate others. Second, the individual may have to use different resources than those initially preferred in order to satisfy his needs, as is true in the case of thermonuclear weapons. In this instance, the need remains but the individual must shift to a reliance upon different resources to induce behavior in the target. Both of these inhibitory functions can be observed to be in operation in guiding the powerholder's decisions concerning whether or not to invoke resources. We have perhaps overemphasized this issue in these pages to sensitize the reader to its importance in understanding the use of power. Too frequently in conducting research on power, experimenters design studies which arouse some power need, provide subjects with resources to satisfy this need if they so choose, but do not include any restraints against the use of these resources, which in fact exist in the real world. Thus, the ease with which persons exercise power, particularly of an aggressive, coercive kind, in the laboratory may, in part, be a function of the fact that no inhibitions against using resources were included in the study.

8　Motivation for Power

The problem of man's strivings for power, as Veroff and Veroff (1972) have written, has held a perpetual and pervasive fascination for students of the human race. We are continually perplexed by the vigor of this motivation as it seeks expression in myriads of encounters and transactions. We are troubled at the ease with which forces striving for power seem to overcome so easily the forces striving for community, harmony, and love. Despite the centrality of this issue, and its intrinsic interest, less has been said in psychology about the origins and consequences of power motivations than has been said about, say, the origins of the motive to achieve, or to affiliate, or to avoid anxiety. It may well be that this omission stems from the fact, as Rollo May (1972) hints, that striving for power is in fact striving for self-assertion, self-development, and growth and that there is very little to be said about power motives, per se, except in the context of discussion of striving for competence. From this view, perhaps one can argue that human beings need power as they need air to breathe and that there are no real mysteries to be solved in this area.

The previous chapters provided the reader with various reasons why powerholders might be motivated to use influence or to restrain themselves from using it. Basically these reasons were concerned with motivations that arise out of the situation in which the individual finds himself, such as his role expectations, or the existence of threats to his own safety, and so on. The purpose of this chapter is to examine the more enduring aspects of human strivings for power. The reader should not be surprised to learn that explanations for power motivation overlap and even at times are contradictory. Power has many faces, some ugly, some bland, and some that are considered admirable by all (McClelland, 1969). According to which face the particular theorist chooses, the reasons for striving for power will be viewed approvingly or disapprovingly—as manifestations of man's inborn urge to overcome odds and create new worlds, or as a sick manifestation of childhood traumas that seek expression years afterward.

Power Striving as Neurotic Behavior—"Sick People Seek Power"

McClelland (1969) has made the observation that persons tend to derive great satisfaction in being told that they have high drives to achieve, or to affiliate, but experience guilt if they are told they have a high drive to achieve power. These emotions occur because of the many negative meanings associated with power motives in our culture. To be told that you are highly motivated for power tends to mean, in the everyday view, that you are a sadistic person who derives great enjoyment from controlling the fate of others. Indeed several psychoanalytic theories see power strivings as representing sick, neurotic behavior. The sickness is based upon the fact that the individual seeks power not as a means of achieving goals that require the services of others but simply as a means of controlling others. By controlling others, various psychological needs of which the person is not aware may be satisfied.

Neo-Freudians were among the first to be concerned with the question of power strivings as a manifestation of neuroses. In particular, psychoanalysts such as Alfred Adler, Karen Horney, and Eric Fromm have seen a direct link between the early social development of the child and subsequent strivings for power. In the psychoanalytic view the initial goals of persons with high needs for power are to use this power as a defense against feelings of low esteem and worthlessness. Neurotic strivings for power, as Horney notes, are born of anxiety, hatred, and feelings of inferiority. The normal person's striving for power is born of strength, the neurotic's of weakness.

While the psychoanalytic school has been in agreement in identifying the early socialization process with subsequent adult power strivings, there has been less agreement concerning the specific causes for such strivings to arise in the first place. In Adler's view (1956), power strivings arise out of childhood feelings of weakness. Adler points out that, from the point of view of nature, humans alone are inferior organisms. They are weak and defenseless. These feelings of inferiority and insecurity serve as basic motivational forces that goad people to discover better ways of adapting to their world. At the positive pole, this pressure to survive leads to the development of speech, intelligence, and communal activities. At the negative pole, it leads to strivings for superiority and dominance over others.

Children are particularly vulnerable to feelings of helplessness and dependency. If this general helplessness is burdened by rejecting or brutal parents, or if the child suffers from some physical disability, then in Adler's view the world tends to be seen by the child as enemy country. In fact Adler says that children with physical disability become particularly involved in a struggle for existence that strangles their social feelings. Instead of adjusting to their fellows, they are preoccupied with themselves, their survival, and with the impressions they make on others. One mode of adjustment is for the child to overcompensate for his weakness by striving for superiority. Through this exaggerated compensatory mechanism he attempts to reduce his feelings of inferiority and loss of self-esteem. Here, then, the process of character development begins in the child's attempts to better his chances for survival.

As an adult, this neurotic striving for power manifests itself in continual attempts to prove one's own superiority by outdoing and controlling others. When the world is viewed as the enemy, Adler states, there is a good deal of hostility associated with attempts to outdo and control. The power-striving individual tends to experience satisfaction rather than sorrow and pity if he finds that his actions have caused target persons to suffer.

This early description of the origin of power strivings was correct as far as it went, but it did not cover all the dynamic forces with which the helpless child must cope. Much more than compensatory strivings over physical weaknesses may be involved in the adult's neurotic striving for power. The incompleteness of the statement was one of the reasons for Karen Horney's (1950) more explicit considerations of the meaning of early childhood feelings of rage and hostility in the development of adult behavior. Once again we begin with the defenseless child. Only, in Horney's view, it is not physical disability which serves as the overwhelming threat but the absence of parental love and protection. Her assumption was that the child who does not receive unconditional love and affection develops feelings of anger and hostility which cannot be openly expressed for fear of further antagonizing its parents. Thus the child is faced with the "double bind" of being angry and yet being afraid of being abandoned. Unable to cope with this kind of conflict, the child experiences deep fears and anxieties. And it is the child's efforts to reduce these noxious feelings that produce neurotic life-styles, including the striving for power.

In Horney's thinking, power is sought when the person's anxiety is coupled with the belief that the world is out to take advantage of the person. Here the strivings for power can serve two purposes. First, to be powerful is an assurance against the nagging fears of being helpless and abandoned. No longer does the person have to beg for help—rather, it is up to him to decide whether to help others. Rather than seek advice, which is a form of weakness, he gives advice. Other manifestations of this seeking to appear strong and dominant, according to Horney, are the neurotic person's incessant attempts to make others admire and love him for his beauty, or his intelligence, or his force of character. In short, by one means or another, he seeks to be the master and so bolster his self-esteem and repress the suspicion that he is not worthy.

A second purpose that is served by these neurotic forms of power striving is to allow the adult to express repressed hostility. Hostility takes the form of attempting to dominate others through insults and sharp criticisms. Horney has observed in her clinical practice that, when a patient's conscious motives were to dominate and control others, the patient had continued difficulties in maintaining affectionate relations with others. This is because the goal of power over others leads to a rejection of equality. Loving relations become especially difficult to maintain, unless the person finds a partner who actively enjoys the submissive role.

In practice, the neurotic strivings for power are seen in the person's incessant demands that others obey him, that he receive a greater share than others, and that others restrain from criticizing him. These strivings can be detected in the unhappiness of others who are required to bear the brunt of the neurotic power-striving person's anger, manipulations, and unconscious cruelties.

In the next chapter I will suggest that similar outcomes may occur in interpersonal relations through the continued exercise of power that is not resisted. However, the distinction between the metamorphic effects of power described in the next chapter and those effects described by Horney is that in the second instance the powerholder unconsciously seeks dominance and devaluation of others as a means of reducing feelings of basic anxiety and helplessness. *Rather than being a consequence of exercising power,* dominance and belittlement of others are the very reasons why power is sought by such neurotic persons in the first place.

Political Power and Childhood Deprivations

If we accept the idea that one origin of striving for power is in childhood deprivations, then it is possible to ask how such strivings manifest themselves in adult behavior. A particularly informative illustration can be found in the studies of political leaders by Harold Lasswell. Since this research is consistent with the idea of a continuity between early childhood experiences and subsequent power-seeking in adults, we will examine one of Lasswell's studies (Rogow and Lasswell 1963) in some detail.

The basic question asked by Lasswell is how political power is used and abused once it has been gained. Further, he asks whether there is a relation between the ego needs of political leaders and the tendency to abuse the power of elected office. To provide answers, Rogow and Lasswell analyzed the careers of thirty elected political leaders who in various ways had been involved in political scandal. Of interest was Lasswell's finding that early material poverty, as well as psychological poverty, could produce an adult character structure obsessed with power-seeking. That is, a politician's misuse of power associated with his office could be traced to early childhood deprivations of either a psychological or material kind.

Lasswell divided the thirty politicians into two types according to their early childhood experiences. The first type was called the "game politician." These officeholders tended to come from wealthy families in which they, as children, were either weak or fragile or had fathers who were strict disciplinarians. The image presented here is of children made to feel helpless and unloved by reason of either physical disabilities or tyrannical parents. Striving for political power, then, was seen as a means of compensating for low self-esteem. These politicians saw politics as a "game" that allowed them the self-expression and self-realization they had been denied as children.

Power was sought by game politicians as a means of obtaining prestige, adulation, and a sense of importance. However, game politicians showed no inclination to make money from illicit use of their power. While corruption surrounded their tenure in office, this corruption was tolerated not for personal gain but to win friends by being a party to deals which involved buying and selling political favors. Game politicians regarded the uses and abuses of money in politics as legitimate so long as they promoted the financial interests of their friends. What they received in return was the flattery and admiration of their special friends—ego needs that had been denied them as children.

A second type of politician was labeled by Rogow and Lasswell as the "gain politician." Generally these persons came from poor, immigrant families that struggled continuously for money and food. However, these families did provide the child with love and emotional security. As adults, gain politicians fought their way to power in their neighborhoods, using physical force if necessary, until finally they controlled a local political machine. Rather than prestige, the dominant motive of gain politicians was to make money for themselves and their families. To this end they engaged in payoffs, deals, and provided inside information to the highest bidders. Unlike the game politicians, they cared little for what others thought of them so long as it did not interfere with their moneymaking.

Rogow and Lasswell in summarizing their findings offered the following observations concerning the importance of early childhood experience for the motivations of these politicians.

1. Severe early deprivation may encourage the striving for power and the use of it in corrupt forms as a means of controlling one's environment.

2. The nature of the early deprivation affects the purposes for which power is employed.

3. If deprivation mainly affects the need for love and ego needs, power will be used in corrupt forms for self-aggrandizement.

4. If the early deprivation mainly affects welfare values, power will be used in corrupt forms for material advantages.

Power Striving as a Substitute for Affection

Some people experience strong pleasure in being able to control the fate of others. Haroutunian (1949) has described the pleasure of exercising power as follows:

> To lord it over others is a means of security, freedom, goods, and so on. But it is also a good in itself. A good which can overwhelm every other good dictated by reason and conscience alike. It is strangely gratifying to make people come and go at our bidding, to overrule their minds and their wills, to take away their power, and virtually annihilate them. . . . There is a soul fulfillment in mastery over human beings. There is no pleasure quite like it, and for its sake men have risked every good and done every conceivable evil. It is well to remember these facts and take them seriously. [p. 9]

This enjoyment seems particularly important to people identified in the psychological literature as high in need for dominance (Watson 1972) or as Machiavellians (Christie and Geis 1970). The question to be considered here is whether those who enjoy exercising power for its own sake are in fact the same persons identified by Adler and by Horney as suffering from early childhood deprivations, or is "something more" involved? Several writers suggest that "something more" is in fact involved and that childhood experiences are not enough to account for the subsequent enjoyment of manipulating the lives of others.

This "something more" involves the simple truth that human beings are unable to live in isolation from their fellows. Not only do we need others as a means of evaluating ourselves, in the manner suggested by George Herbert Mead and by Charles Cooley, but also we need others to provide us with emotional support. Human beings alone, deprived of friendship, social relations, and love, yet always aware of their own mortality, may seek power in order to gain by force the love and esteem from others that they cannot obtain freely.

As a result of this need to make contact with one's fellow humans, the striving for mastery over others for the sake of mastery itself may paradoxically originate in man's fear of being estranged from his fellows (Haroutunian 1949).

In its more modest forms this need may be expressed in using the power to reward (as was suggested in Chapter 4) as a means of binding the affection of indifferent target persons. As its extreme this motive expresses itself in such sentiments as the sadistic desire to kill and torment others and in this perverted way, paradoxically, to express one's linkages with others (Fromm 1959).

Thus another source goading human beings to seek power over others originates in feelings of aloneness and emotional emptiness rather than in childhood experiences. The awful chaos that threatens a person who has no emotional ties, who is the perpetual stranger, can be warded off by forcing others, through power, to give that person the love he craves. Further, the very act of forcing others tends to be seen as an affirmation of one's existence. It is no accident that the principal character in Albert Camus's *The Stranger* resorts to senseless violence as a means of affirming his emotional existence, after having remained for a long period emotionally isolated from others. Here and in other works such as his *Caligula* Camus recognized the link between aloneness and subsequent explosions of sadism and violence. Through these acts of domination one affirms one's own existence and one's emotional ties to others. An important derivation from this view of power striving, which we may now examine, is that any arrangement of society that isolates human beings from each other will encourage the development of power motives whose goal is the domination of others.

The extensive writings of Eric Fromm perhaps best express the interdependency between societal arrangements and man's strivings for mastery over others. Human beings have a basic need to receive love, comfort, and companionship, Fromm argues, and it is how these basic wants are met that determines the structure of motives. From a historical perspective Fromm sees man's relations with others as having been drastically altered by the advent of the industrial revolution and the growth of capitalism. In earlier times the individual was "locked" into relations with his primary family from birth to death. The primary ties of family and work provided each person with a sure sense of personal identity and emotional support. The advent of capitalism freed man from these static primary ties. Man's position in society was no longer predestined by birth and family name. Yet paradoxically this very freedom carried with it an enormous price. Now each person by his own efforts had to establish loving relations with others. No longer were these needs to be automatically satisfied by the structure of society.

To make an emotional connection with someone else is difficult to achieve in a modern society in which the emphasis is on "doing better" than others, in which the enormous concentrations of wealth and technology leave each individual with a profound sense of insignificance and lack of control, and in which the concentrations of people in large cities increase each person's sense of isolation from his neighbor. What then? How is the person to satisfy this basic need of relations with others? How is the person to escape from the unbearable position of aloneness and powerlessness?

One solution, among several examined by Fromm, is to force others to provide one with companionship. This solution may be expressed in sadistic behavior, in which the person desires to have absolute and unrestricted power over others. As Fromm says, the individual's feelings of strength are rooted in the fact that he is master of someone else, and this realization may satisfy his desire to commune with others. The pleasure in his complete domination over another person springs paradoxically from the individual's inability to bear aloneness. One can see a striking parallel between Fromm's views of the consequences of social isolation and Zimbardo's description of the consequences of deindividuation. In both instances isolation of self increases the urge to dominate and control others.

Men isolated from their fellows by the norms, customs, and arrangements of society may develop enormous cravings for power as the best means to establish relations with others. They hope to do with power what they have been unable to accomplish with love. And in part they are correct. I have already pointed out that people will flock around a person with power, flatter him, offer him love and admiration, deference and respect, which he so badly wants.

The problem with this solution is that the more power one seeks and obtains, the more one tends, paradoxically, to isolate oneself from others. The powerholder frequently suspects that the respect and admiration he is given is not for his own self but is given in recognition of the power he controls. As a result he may find himself holding in contempt those persons who surround him, considering them as lackeys or worse. The affection received from such persons, rather than satisfying his basic need for love, may in fact make the craving more unbearable. Thus in one sense power may increase suspicion and distrust of others, the very opposite of the original hopes of the person striving for power. Rather than decrease the "abhorrent void within," to use Kenneth B. Clark's (1971) phrase, the isolation of power may increase it, forcing the person, in anger over his failure to make the desired contacts with others, to ever greater attempts to dominate them.

All People Seek Power

So far the reasons offered for striving for power have been entirely negative. In terms of the description of the power act offered in Chapter 2, the individual's motives for wanting to exercise control are concerned with domination for its own sake. McClelland (1969) has suggested that there is another face of power that is not concerned with these dark motives. This face of power focuses on the beneficial reasons why power motives may arise, reasons in which there is no intent to harm or psychologically diminish the other person.

The intent, rather, is to have the means to control one's world. From this perspective survival is seen as the basic motive underlying universal strivings for power. The sociologist Robert A. Nisbet (1970) writes in this regard that control is the conscious or unconscious aim of all human behavior; and that every element of the individual's socialization process is designed to help the individual acquire control over the environment.

People seek power, then, to survive and to control their worlds. This section will examine the origins of this explanation of power motivation. The reader will see that the explanation for a universal tendency to strive for power centers around the fact that human beings seek not only to survive, but to maximize their own outcomes, and in so doing come into conflict with fellow human beings likewise so engaged. As a result power is sought not for its own sake but for aid in the competitive struggle with others. If this conclusion is valid, it further suggests that strivings for power do not originate in an instinctive desire to control and dominate others, as has been suggested by Freud, but as Hobbes suggests, in a pervasive tendency in mankind to satisfy one's appetites. Out of this need comes the pursuit of power.

An interesting derivation of this view is that the more the developing individual is socialized to achieve, to strive, to maintain the uniqueness of his identity, the more likely it is that he will, as an adult, pursue power. In this connection Skinner has argued, in his book *Beyond Freedom and Dignity* (1971), that a society that stresses the importance of self-realization rather than communal goals is bound in the final analysis to force its members into power strivings, since uniqueness tends to be defined in terms of "doing better" than others.

Rollo May (1972), in discussing human growth, also reflects this view: "Power is essential for all living things. To survive, man must use his powers and confront opposing forces at every point in his struggle" (p. 1). To survive, to grow, to create, all persons must pursue power, since without it these positive goals cannot be achieved. In fact May argues that persons who deliberately avoid using power, glorifying in what they consider their own innocence, tend to be the best candidates for mental illness. Such innocence, May contends, manifests itself eventually in depression and self-hatred as the person's own psychological growth is thwarted by his unwillingness to exert influence and in this way affirm his own worth.

The point of May's argument is, of course, that all persons seek and use power for instrumental reasons rather than because they enjoy controlling others. To deny the importance of power, May argues, is to commit onself to continued helplessness. Yet one may ask, why should this be? Given the multitude of technological advances that have made the distribution of food, shelter, and clothing widespread, why is it necessary for humans to evoke their resources and force others to carry out some act? Seemingly, if there is enough for all, enlightened self-interest would suggest that a reliance on "innocence," in May's term, is surely better than a reliance on power. Furthermore, if there is abundance, why doesn't the motive to strive for power wither away in mankind?

Thomas Hobbes in the seventeenth century, writing in *Leviathan*, explained the universal striving of man for power as the logical result of self-interest. Human beings, according to Hobbes, are motivated by appetites, some inborn but most learned from experience. These appetites are incessant and continually change.

Most important, appetites steer man's behavior because, as Hobbes states, "Men desire 'felicity'—that is men desire continual success in satisfying their appetites." Thus in terms of human behavior Hobbes gives us the image of human beings seeking to satisfy a never-ending stream of wants and desires. When one appetite is satisfied, new ones press for "felicity."

Of course the problem is how man shall satisfy these never-ceasing appetites. To answer this question Hobbes turned his attention to an analysis of power. According to Hobbes, "The power of man is his present means to obtain some future apparent good." That is, man satisfies his appetites and achieves "felicity" through his access to power. Power in Hobbes usage, appears to be equivalent to our definition of the control of resources. Power resides in those resources that are needed or feared by others because they are in short supply. Thus power is seen by Hobbes as the extent to which one person's means exceeds those of his fellows:

> The Value or worth of a man is as of all other things, his price, that is to say, so much as would be given for the use of his power; and therefore is not absolute, *but a thing dependent on the need and judgement of another*. An able conductor of soldiers is of great price in time of war, ongoing or imminent, but in Peace not so. A learned and uncorrupt judge is much worth in time of peace, but not so much in war. And as in other things, so in man, not the seller, but the buyer determines the price. For let a man (as most men do,) rate themselves as the highest value they can; yet their true value is no more than it is esteemed by others. [Pp. 151–52; emphasis added]

In other words Hobbes is telling us that the judgment by others of our skills, abilities, and possessions determines the power we possess. In the 1950s, when there were relatively few engineers to service an expanding American economy, engineers had great prestige and power. They could force employers to provide them with large salaries and benefits, by threatening to withhold their services. By the early 1970s, however, many persons had become engineers and consequently the bargaining power of engineers with employers was practically nil. In short, resources can be invoked to achieve intended effects so long as there is a buyer, to use Hobbes's terms. Intelligence provides no special advantage to the individual, when all are equally gifted and bright. Similarly, beauty is no longer a base of power when all are beautiful, and money loses its special advantage for purchasing goods and services when everyone is equally rich.

What determines an individual's potential power? The answer supplied by Hobbes has a particularly modern ring and covers both personal resources (natural power, in Hobbes's terms) and resources originating from society and institutions. Here is a brief excerpt from *Leviathan* which lists some of the many bases of power that can be used to provide satisfaction of man's incessant appetites.

> Natural Power is the eminence of the facilities of body or mind: as extraordinary strength, form, eloquence, and nobility. To have friends is power, for they are strength united. Also riches joined with liberality is power; because it procures friends and servants. Reputation of power is power; because it attracts with it the adherence of those that need protection. Also what quality soever maketh a man beloved or feared of many; or the reputation of such quality is power because it is a means to have the assistance and services of many. [P. 150]

The timelessness of Hobbes's definition of power is shown in a recent discussion in the *New York Times* Magazine (October 7, 1973) on the reason why the American Bar Association can have a major effect on state legislatures. "Its greatest source of power, and the way it is exercised," explained a staff member, "comes from the standing of the lawyers in the community and the state bar association. They are the pillars of the community. They know their Congressmen and Senators personally." In short, the lawyer's "reputation of power is power," as Hobbes said. Power, then, is ultimately whatever gives the person access to the "pooled energy of many" (Mott 1970), so that the powerholder can cause others to carry out acts that will bring him "felicity."

Hobbes's system of assumptions leads to the inevitable conclusion that all persons must continuously strive for power, without ceasing. The reason for this may be traced in propositional form as follows: (1) human beings are driven by a never-ending stream of appetites that must be satisfied; (2) the possession of power is the means by which these appetites are satisfied; (3) power always resides in the possession of commodities or resources that are in short supply; (4) because power resides in those commodities that are in short supply, all persons must continually strive for power if they are to satisfy their wants. If everybody possesses a resource in equal amounts it is no longer in scarce supply and hence cannot be used to satisfy one's appetites; thus one must continually scramble for new resources to keep ahead of others likewise striving for scarce resources; (5) an inevitable byproduct of this power striving is that human beings are forced into conflict with each other in order to obtain effective bases of power. Hobbes states most eloquently these sobering conclusions:

> So that in the first place I put for a general inclination of all mankind, a perpetual and restless desire of Power after power, that ceaseth only in death. And the cause of this is not always that a man hopes for a more intensive delight than he has attained already, or that he cannot be content with a moderate power, but because he cannot assure the power and means to live well which he has present without the acquisition of more.

Thus every one is necessarily pulled into a competitive struggle for resources, or at least to resist the efforts of others to command their resources (Macpherson 1968). Since by definition there can never be enough scarce resources, and all persons have the same wish for happiness, they must necessarily struggle with each other in order to gain power to secure for themselves the future. In answer to our question then as to why technology cannot reduce power strivings, Hobbes would answer that needs are incessant and continually changing. Technology cannot keep up with the continual stream of "appetites" that humans invent and for which they need power to find "felicity." One might conclude from Hobbes's analysis that, to avoid the continual chase after power, one must give up one's appetites, since more power leads to more appetites, which require more power, and so on—a never-ending circle.

We have given this attention to Hobbes's views because they serve as the basis for most modern-day conceptions of the idea that power strivings may be a universal phenomenon, not one limited to the psychologically sick person. However, the basic goal of Hobbes's writings was not to provide a psychological analysis of power striving but to give a political justification of the need for a strong monarchical system. As a result, Hobbes's ideas are at best a combination of psychological observations of man's nature (all persons are driven by appetites) combined with an economic analysis of the problem attendant on the fact that resources become less valuable as they become more common.

Various modern psychologists have adopted aspects of the Hobbesian analysis, although with less emphasis on the pessimistic aspects of power strivings that pertain to the continual struggle to obtain more than one's fellows. For instance, Tedeschi and his colleagues (Tedeschi, Schlenker, and Bonoma 1971) have assumed a universal drive for power in proposing an alternate explanation to dissonance theory.

Basically, the explanation of Tedeschi et al. originates in the finding that the dissonance effect is most likely to occur when people believe that their behaviors are engaged in freely and are not under the experimenter's control. Tedeschi et al. ask why perceived freedom should have this effect. The answer proposed by these writers is that all persons are concerned with the impression they make on others. That is, consistency of words and deeds enhances the individual's own credibility and *enables him to be more successful in influencing others.* For a person to state, for instance, that he likes apples on one day and to say that he hates apples on the next would cause others to be uncertain as to what statements by the person to believe. Hence the impression they have of him might be less favorable. It is this state of affairs that each person wishes to avoid, since everyone intuitively realizes that people trust others who act rationally. If we are distrusted, our goal of exercising power and influence is blocked.

The motive to avoid doing contradictory things, in Tedeschi et al.'s view, can be seen as not arising from an internal experience of psychological tension, as proposed by dissonance theory, but from a calculated desire by the individual to be in the best position to exert influence and power, by presenting a public stance of rationality and consistency. While Tedeschi et al. do not explicitly propose that all persons seek power, their related hypothesis that all persons seek to maintain a consistent public image so as to influence others is clearly in the Hobbesian tradition.

Effectiveness and Power Motivation

Hobbes in his discussion of human appetites makes no distinction between the drives of individuals to secure wealth and material possessions and the drive to obtain self-knowledge and self-growth. Many psychologists, however, view the individual in terms of his strivings to become a mature adult. Less attention is paid to his attempts to gain material wealth. As could be expected, there appears to be a definite relation between the development of power motives and the striving for psychological growth and effectiveness. May, in *Power and Innocence* (1972), explicitly traces this relation. "Man's basic psychological reason for living," he states, "is to affirm himself, to struggle for self-esteem, to say I am, to do this in the face of nature's magnificent indifference." To do this all people must seek power, if only because, without power to command attention, the individual is basically helpless to realize these goals.

May's view of power strivings as a necessary correlate of attempts to achieve psychological well-being is a valuable addition to the literature on this subject. This is because he provides a view of power motives as a potentially positive rather than negative force in life. He stresses the idea that the reasons for seeking power do not have to center around the goal of dominating and exploiting others but can spring from the assertion of one's own individuality. Of course what is missing from May's writings is a consideration of what may happen when all people simultaneously strive to assert their own individuality. In what ways will they come into conflict with each other?

A Hobbesian analysis of such strivings for maturity suggests inevitable conflict as all strive to assert their will against the indifference of nature and human beings. On the other hand, such conflict may promote the attempts by mature persons to learn how to compromise and to turn competition into cooperation.

Some People Seek Power

So far this chapter has contained little empirical data that pertain to individual differences in power striving. Perhaps the strongest contribution to the empirical literature on individual and group differences is based upon the analysis of power imagery in stories, speeches, and fantasy (Veroff and Veroff 1972; Winter 1973). This research is based on the assumption that the greater the amount of power imagery in the verbal and written expressions of people, the greater their need to control and exercise influence.

Before we can examine the research on power imagery, it is necessary to point out that there are two methods of measuring power imagery in use, each yielding very different findings. The first measure, developed by Veroff (1957), can be labeled *fear of power*, and measures a person's desire to be free from the control of others. This motive is most likely to be aroused when freedom of choice is threatened. The second measure, developed by Winter (1973), involves a positive attraction to the use of power. This second measure closely approximates everyday ideas about "power cravings," in that persons with high scores on Winter's measure are described as deriving satisfaction from influencing other persons.

Through the use of these two measures, an impressive variety of empirical relations have been uncovered concerning how power motives are expressed in day-to-day life. With reference to the *fear of power* measure, the findings indicate, as I mentioned, that this motive is most likely to be aroused when self-assertion is threatened. Veroff and Veroff (1972) report that high *fear of power* scores have been found more often, for instance, among black respondents than among white respondents, among educated women more than among educated men—in general among status groups concerned with overcoming their own weaknesses.

These findings can be interpreted as meaning that, when persons are without power, when their goals of achieving psychological growth or material well-being have been blocked, then their conscious motive structure will center around thoughts of power. To have power under these circumstances will allow the individual, at a minimum, as Veroff and Veroff suggest, to be free from the control of others. These empirical findings are consistent with the idea of Alfred Adler that power motives arise as compensations for physical or psychological weaknesses and threats.

Using the Winter measure of power needs, the findings appear more complex for persons who hold high motives to influence others. Basically, however, such persons have been found by Winter to be attracted to situations and things that enhance the possibility of exercising power. Winter has reported that persons scoring high on his measure of need for power tended to buy prestige objects that would cause envy in others, were attracted to occupations where they could exercise influence (teaching, sales), were more likely to run for political office, tried to dominate others in group discussions, and at times drank too much as a means of fantasizing about power. This is, in many ways, a not very attractive portrait of an individual's single-minded pursuit of power. While Winter does not provide us with the early developmental history of those who scored high on his measure of power motive, the picture that is presented appears consistent with the description of neurotic power-seekers provided by Alfred Adler, Karen Horney, and Eric Fromm.

The research of Winter has so far not been concerned with an analysis of the process by which power is exercised, nor does it tell us what persons with a high need for power think of themselves or others as a result of continually seeking to exercise power.

Suppose, for example, that persons with high scores on the Winter measure of power striving were given access to a range of means of influence (expert power, reward power, coercive power, and so on). If these power bases could be freely used to influence targets without costs to these persons, would those with high power-needs enjoy themselves? Would they be more adept at selecting the appropriate influence mode to overcome various kinds of target resistances than persons with low power-needs?

Some answers to these questions are suggested by turning to the results of studies that have employed the Machiavellian scale developed by two psychologists, Richard Christe and Florence Geis (1970). This scale was specifically constructed to measure the tendency of some persons to take advantage of other persons. While a full description of the scale and its uses is beyond the scope of this book, it suffices to point out that Winter's description of persons with high need for power and the description of persons scoring high on the Machiavellian scale appear to overlap considerably. Thus it seems reasonable to extrapolate the findings from the latter area of research to the former. Studies of persons classified as Machiavellian personalities have found that when they were placed in positions of influence over peers (but given no formal means of influence) they invented a variety of verbal influence modes to use with their targets and enjoyed the chance to fool and deceive others. Further, those with high Machiavellianism scores were found to be more exploitive in situations involving the opportunity to gain resources at another's expense. Studies by Banks (1974) and by Berger (1973) have also found that high scorers on the Machiavellian scale were less credible in their use of power and more adept in its use. Thus the available data point to the conclusion that persons who enjoy exercising control over people use different power tactics than those who do not enjoy exercising such influence.

One further point concerning Winter's measure of power motivation. There is still, I believe, a good deal to be learned about what happens when "power-driven" persons are in situations that allow a full range of power to be exercised. The research described above only indirectly touches on the potential explosiveness of such combinations. Studies of the presence of power imagery in the speeches of American presidents (Winter 1973), for instance, suggest that conflict may be an inevitable outcome of this combination. This is because the demands of leaders with strong power motives are never-ending when they have access to unlimited resources. Conflict arises because sooner or later these demands produce stronger and stronger resistances among target persons or target nations.

So far we have speculated about how persons scoring high on the Winter measure of power motivation would actually use different means of influence. Similar speculations can be raised concerning the Veroff measure of fear of power. The most likely answer is that persons with high fear of power needs would be attracted to the use of threats and punishments as the preferred power tactic. This suggestion is made because many of the characteristics associated with persons with high fear-of-power scores (that is, persons deprived of material or psychological resources) appear similar to those of persons discussed in Chapter 6 who stated that they lacked self-confidence or who believed that they were not in control of their own behavior. It would appear that what links these variously described individuals are low expectations of successful influence and the associated belief that only strong means of influence will cause others to comply.

Summary

The general conclusion to be drawn from this chapter is that all forces that reduce the individual's feelings of competence, or that serve to promote new wants and aspirations, increase the individual's motives to gain power. Feelings of weakness in any form, as Veroff and Veroff note (1972) are associated with high power-motivations. We have attempted to distinguish in this chapter when such feelings of weakness attract the individual to seek power for its own sake and when such feelings do not establish a bond between power and the desire to control and dominate. It has been suggested that if these feelings of weakness originate from psychological traumas of early childhood or from present alienation from others, then the goal of power motives is most likely to be to dominate and control others for the sake of the control itself. If the feelings of weakness originate from a need to obtain commodities, or to further goals of growth and maturity, then it appears that the goal of power motives will not include the dream of manipulation of others as an end in itself. Rather power will be used as a means of obtaining services or objects that are controlled by other people. Once these services or objects have been obtained, the powerholder's concern with the exercise of influence tends to cease.

9   The Metamorphic Effects of Power

Typically, power acts begin with the presence of needs that are satisfied by convincing somebody else to do something. These acts are commonplace features of day-to-day encounters with friends, loved ones, and strangers. The powerholder may wish to give a party but his spouse refuses, or he may want to buy a new car from a car agency with no down payment, or he may be a supervisor trying to improve an employee's performance, or he may be a parent attempting to influence his child's behavior. These are not dramatic moments in history, but they contain the same elements of the power act that can be found in the attempts of great political leaders to obtain certain rights from other countries. In all instances, the powerholder anticipates, or has found, that a simple request for compliance will be refused. Therefore, he has to decide what additional force he can use in order to get what he wants.

In this chapter we turn to the question of how the taking of action by the powerholder may influence his opinions about the target person and about himself. Suppose he is successful in getting the target to carry out some desired act. Will he like the target better or worse for showing compliance? And will he like himself better or worse for being able to cause behaviors in others? It is clear from the existing literature that one can expect some kind of changes to occur as a result of successfully influencing others (Sampson 1965; Sorokin and Lundin 1959). As was mentioned earlier, these changes can be called the metamorphic effects of power, a term that indicates how the use of resources to influence others can transform the powerholder's views of both the less powerful and of himself.

The major argument of this chapter is that the continual exercise of *successful* influence changes the powerholder's views of others and of himself, regardless of whether the actors involved are, say, a husband who continually dominates his wife or a great political leader who is responsible for the well-being of an entire nation. The transformations are the same in both instances. They are brought about, in my opinion, as the result of ordinary psychological processes that relate to how we perceive and interpret events. Hence, the transformations produced by the successful use of power are not restricted to remote actors holding high office in distant lands.

The existence of metamorphic effects have been recognized from almost the earliest writings of man concerning the use of power. The Greek dramatists were particularly sensitive to the fate of persons who were at the high tide of their power and status. In the plays of Sophocles, for instance, the viewer is confronted with the image of great and powerful rulers transformed by their prior successes so that they are filled with a sense of their own worth and importance—with "hubris"—impatient of the advice of others and unwilling to listen to opinions that disagree with their own. Yet, in the end they are destroyed by events, which they discover, to their anguish, that they cannot control. Oedipus is destroyed soon after the crowds say (and he believes) that "he is almost like a God"; King Creon, at the zenith of his political and military power, is brought down as a result of his unjust and unfeeling belief in the infallibility of his judgments. Sophocles warns us never to be envious of the powerful until we see the nature of their endings. Too often arrogance, bred of power, finally causes its own defeat and unhappy ending.

Thucydides describes this process of transformation quite accurately in his assessment of the state of mind of the Athenians after six years of success in the Peloponnesian Wars:

So thoroughly did their present power persuade the citizens that nothing could withstand them, and that they could achieve what was possible and impractical alike, with ample means, or inadequate, it mattered not. The secret of this was their general extraordinary success, *which made them confuse their strength with their hopes.* [Emphasis added]

Soon after, of course, the Athenian city-state suffered an irreversible decline by voting to continue its wars of expansion.

While it is true that writers of different times have not always seen a powerful leader destroyed, a persistent image in literature and political science, from the earliest times until now, has been that of an individual, virtuous and innocent at the time he assumes power, soon transformed by his own success into, at worst, a tyrant or, at best, an insensitive and immoral person. In the twentieth century, we have seen political leaders (for example, Stalin) who as young men were fired with the idea of bringing freedom and equality to all but who in the end were transformed into the most inhuman of leaders, devoid of feelings for those who originally started them on their march.

It is not necessary to assume that these transformations are restricted to persons exercising political influence. The exercise of power that is only weakly resisted has similar consequences in all domains of human behavior. In their classic account of life in the Indian village of Karimpur during the 1920s, the Wisers (1967) observed the same transformations occurring among agents of absentee landlords—agents who, once appointed to their positions, exploited their fellow villagers. What is of interest is the Wisers' argument that the behavior of these agents was not due to preexisting character defects but to their control of power and just as important, the *villagers' servility.* The Wisers state this argument as follows:

If you were to take one of the most harmless men in the village and put him in the watchman's place, he would be a rascal within six months. . . . The sense of power and sudden popularity which a man experiences on finding himself an agent of some outside authority is in itself a danger. If he tests the new power and finds that he does not inspire fear, he may be content to perform his duties without further ventures. But if he finds his neighbors easily intimidated, and if his personal ambitions urge him on, he repeats his assertions of power until he becomes a hardened tyrant. [P. 113]

The well-known observation of Lord Acton that "power tends to corrupt and absolute power corrupts absolutely" reflects the idea of these almost abrupt changes in the humanitarian impulses of the powerholder. In this chapter we will attempt to account for these transformations by presenting in propositional form the steps by which power may change the powerholder. First, however, we will examine more closely Lord Acton's concept of corruption in relation to power in order to understand the kinds of changes our model focuses upon. This examination is based in part upon Lasswell's analysis of the various meanings assigned to the term "corruption."

Pursuit of Power as a Life Goal

The first meaning assigned to the observation "power corrupts" refers to the belief that those who gain power tend to value it above all other values and restlessly pursue additional power throughout their lives. This Hobbesian view suggests that the individual is driven by the fear that others may achieve equality with him in power and so deprive the individual of his own power. Ida Tarbell's (1904) study of John D. Rockefeller suggests that Rockefeller could not stop extending his domination over all aspects of business that touched on oil, despite the fact that he was among the most powerful of American businessmen. During the early 1970s, President Nixon seemed to have charted a similar goal for the United States of America in his insistence that the country could not rest until it was "number one" among nations.

The corrupting influence of power, in this view, is that power becomes an end in itself and replaces the Christian value of love, charity, compassion for the weak, and the like. The urge to be "number one" becomes the exclusive preoccupation of the powerholder. When faced with a choice between giving up power or maintaining it by less than moral or legal methods, those with a taste for power choose the second option.

Cartwright and Zander (1968) have suggested that this view of the corrupting influence of power can be placed in the context of modern learning theory by assuming that the control of power allows the individual to gratify appetitive needs more readily. This is because control of power allows the individual to allot to himself more of those things that do indeed provide satisfaction. Because of these need-reduction properties inherent in the control of power, it follows that individuals learn to value power and seek it.

Power as a Means to an End

A second meaning of the statement "power corrupts" refers to behavior of the powerholder that is motivated by a desire for personal gain. When this form of corruption is under examination, one usually finds the powerholder in a position of trust, where he has access to institutional resources or the resources of another person. What seems to happen is that access to these resources tempts the powerholder to line his own pocket. Power is corrupting in this context because it encourages the individual to deviate from the formal duties of a public role as a means of enriching himself or others to whom he owes favors (Scott 1972). In a sense, striving for power in this second usage is only a means to an end, rather than an end in itself. Studies by Rogow and Lasswell (1963) of the gain politician that were discussed in Chapter 8 serve to illustrate these kinds of temptations that are associated with access to power.

Power, Self-Concepts, and Morality

Corruption can also refer to the way in which the control of power changes the powerholder's self-perceptions and his perceptions of others. Sorokin and Lundin (1959), in a review of the behavior and attributes of individuals controlling political and economic power, stated that persons holding great power develop an exalted and vain view of their own worth which inhibits compassion for others. Furthermore, Sorokin and Lundin suggested that powerful persons evolve new codes of ethics that serve to justify their use of power. Throughout history, we find that a special divinity is assumed to surround the powerful, so that they are excused from gross acts such as murder, terrorism, and intimidation. This view has come down through history in several forms. Machiavelli, for instance, argues that it is necessary for a prince to learn how not to be good. That is, the prince must do those things, whether good or evil, that will perpetuate his own power. Likewise, Sorokin and Lundin cite studies of business executives who led double lives morally, with one set of moral values for the office and a second for the home. Sorokin and Lundin, echoing the beliefs of Sophocles two thousand years earlier, assert that the very possession of vast power tends to demoralize the powerholder.

Why should we continually find reference in the literature to the twin themes that powerful leaders develop exalted views of their own worth and that they believe they are exempt from common moral standards? Do these attitudes develop as the inevitable long-term consequence of successfully exercising power? I believe this may be the case.

Examine, first, one possible route by which the control of power may cause changes in how a powerholder sees himself and others. Two related processes are involved. First of all, the powerholder may find himself the recipient of flattery and well-wishing from the less powerful, who are anxious to keep in his good graces. It is quite common for powerholders to receive positive feedback, both true and false, concerning their own worth from persons eager to continue receiving benefits. Anything will do, from simple compliments about style of dress to elaborate testimonial dinners.

In addition, because of the resources they control, powerholders may find that their ideas and opinions are readily agreed with. There is nothing particularly complex in this observation. Common sense tells followers that it will be costly to continually disagree with a powerholder. From fear of power, followers have been known to accept any suggestions from powerholders, no matter how foolish they seem to be. This public compliance may lead the powerholders to believe that their ideas and views are superior to those held by others, when in fact compliance was not based upon the superiority of their ideas but on the superiority of their power. As a result of this deference and flattery, the possibility cannot fail to be raised in the minds of the powerholders that they may be something special.

Indeed, as a result of this continuous stream of positive feedback, it would be strange if changes did not occur in the powerholder's beliefs about himself. He may come to believe that he is an effective and insightful person, whose ideas are superior to others'. In part, this impression of self may be correct, and in part it may be erroneously derived from a continual association with servile followers.

One sign that ideas of personal superiority have become firmly established is that powerholders begin to express irritation if their ideas are challenged. Berle (1967) has suggested that a false assumption of superiority is one of the early causes of a powerholder's decline. The decline occurs because followers hesitate to present true facts that are counter to the powerholder's beliefs. Followers tend to survive by acting as "yes-men." Thus, decisions are made that tend to underestimate the true nature of the opposing forces. The assumption that "I am number one" makes it very difficult to accommodate information that says otherwise. Among recent American presidents, few have included as personal advisors individuals whose opinions diverged in fundamental ways from their own.

That is, American presidents tend to select personal advisors who do not continually challenge policy. Thus corrective feedback is frequently lacking. David Halberstam points out in *The Best and the Brightest* (1974) that the personal advisors of President John F. Kennedy, for instance, had no use for persons such as Adlai Stevenson and Chester Bowles, who might have effectively blocked the decision to escalate the war in Vietnam. Stevenson and Bowles were generally considered too "soft" to be allowed to advise on policy concerned with international relations. Similarly, business executives exclude from their advisors those whose views are "irritating" because they disagree too often with the executives' ideas and decisions.

Perhaps the most extreme example in modern times of this predilection of the powerful to reject information that challenges beliefs in their own infallibility was Adolf Hitler. He refused to use any information that did not agree with his beliefs of the moment. And, worse still, his advisors were fearful to provide him with news that might contradict his beliefs. The military ruin that overwhelmed the German army following its initial successes in Russia arose in strong part from the unwillingness of Hitler's generals to "speak out." Imprisonment and worse awaited those who disagreed with Hitler's judgments.

Changes in Morality

Since unchallenged power brings psychic as well as material rewards, it is not too surprising that those in power wish to maintain this state of affairs. As a result, changes in values and normative beliefs appear to occur as part of the powerholder's attempts to preserve and extend his influence and power. It is a strong person who can willfully decide not to "bend the law just a bit" so as to maintain or extend his own influence.

The kinds of power one controls may determine which commonly held social values will be changed. When Antigone invoked the universal laws of the gods as justification for the need to give her brother a proper burial, King Creon countered with a new set of laws the chief of which was reverence for the city of Thebes and the king's laws and orders. And if newer secular law conflicts with the ancient customs of the gods, then these latter customs must be suspended. Otherwise, there remains the possibility that King Creon's rule may be challenged. Hence, the old values must give way to the new, and the powerholder adopts a moral code consistent with the kinds of power he controls or serves.

In a different context, Galbraith (1967) has said that managers in large corporations are practically forced to make decisions which minimize risk to corporate investment, despite the fact that these decisions violate laws and the general welfare of the public. For businessmen, the morality that develops is designed to protect and extend corporate power and resources.

Albert Memmi (1965) has described a similar process underlying changes in the moral values of French colonists in Algeria during the late 1940s and the 1950s. Faced with a choice of either relinquishing the rich life of the colonist because of moral doubts about the exploitation of the native Algerians or in some way minimizing the issues of morality, French colonists who stayed chose the latter course. Memmi writes:

> For it was not just a case of intellectualizing, but the choice of an entire way of life. This man [the colonizer], perhaps a warm friend and affectionate father, who in his native country could have been a democrat will surely be transformed into a conservative, reactionary, or even a colonial fascist. He cannot help but approve discrimination and the codification of injustice, he will be delighted at police tortures and, if the necessity arises, will become convinced of the necessity of massacres. Everything will lead him to these new beliefs: his new interests, his professional relations, his family ties, and bonds of friendship formed in the colony. The colonial situation manufactures colonists, just as it manufactures the colonized. [P. 56]

In essence, the corruption of power in this usage refers to the fact that commonly held norms and values are ignored by powerholders when such norms and values appear to threaten or restrict the powerholder's use of his resources. Basically, the norms that are changed are those that interfere with the exercise of power.

Power and Perception of Others

A fourth meaning assigned to the idea that power corrupts refers to the belief that powerholders devalue the worth of the less powerful and act to increase social distance from them. Here, then, in my opinion, is the most destructive psychological consequence of one-sided power relationships—the transformation that occurs in how the more powerful see the less powerful. From individuals with both strengths and weaknesses, the less powerful become objects of manipulation with a lesser claim on human rights than is claimed by the powerholder. In Martin Buber's terms, it is the transformation of one person's perception of another from "thou" to "it," from individual to object.

Considering these tendencies to devalue others and to maintain psychological distance, many writers believe that the control of power precludes the possibility of harmonious interpersonal relations. According to Sampson (1965), inequity in power inevitably produces dominance, manipulation and precludes the possibility of establishing truly loving relations. He further states that it is impossible for any human relationship to avoid distortion to the extent that power enters into it. "At minimum," according to Sampson," the deference and compliance shown by the less powerful is seen as a sign of weakness, if not servility" (p. 233).

Why do these transformations occur? What in the power relation suppresses genuine concern for another person's well-being and leads to the development of contemptuous attitudes? There appear to be two possible explanations.

The first reason for the process of devaluation of the target person has been hinted at in the discussion of changes in moral values. It originates in the fact that it is easier to influence others if psychological distance is maintained and emotional involvement is kept to a minimum. This is especially true if the powerholder believes it likely that he will order the less powerful to carry out behaviors that are distasteful. To the extent that the powerholder feels sympathy for the position of the less powerful, he may not want to issue these orders. It is psychologically more comfortable to assume that the target person is not as worthy as oneself. The powerholder can, then, with good conscience, make the target person do things that he would not be willing to do himself. For instance, Memmi records the following accusations directed by the French at the colonized Algerians, all calculated to minimize the Algerians' worth:

> An old physician told me in confidence, with a mixture of surliness and solemnity that the "colonized do not know how to breathe"; a professor explained to me pedantically that "the people here don't know how to walk; they make tiny little steps which don't get them ahead." [P. 67]

Self-interest, then, according to Memmi, is well served by devaluation of the target person and helps explain the variety of wild accusations directed by the French toward the Algerians.

A second reason why devaluation of the target person occurs is more subtle, less dramatic, and yet of greater interest for psychologists. This has to do with the possibility that the very act of successfully influencing causes devaluation of the target person. This possibility appears to be particularly true when the powerholder invokes controlling or strong means of influence that are seen by the powerholder to deprive the target person of freedom of choice. I suggest here that when these strong means of influence are invoked, the powerholder believes that the target person is not in control of his own behavior. Rather, the target person's behavior is seen as caused by the powerholder's orders and suggestions. In essence, the locus of control is seen to reside in the powerholder, who attributes causality for change to himself. "There is no need to make a fuss over his accomplishments," says the powerholder, "he simply did what I told him to do, step by step."

If what has been said here is correct, then the frequency of devaluation of target persons may be far more pervasive than has been thought. Rather than being limited to master-slave relations, it is possible that devaluations occur in any power relationship—teacher-student, dominant husband-subordinate wife—where the powerholder uses influence means that demand compliance, and the target person obeys. The very act of compliance under these circumstances diminishes the worth of any product achieved by the target person in the eyes of the powerholder.

In the following sections I will amplify how the use of power may transform the powerholder's view of himself and others. First, to summarize, I have pointed out that the corrupting influence of power can refer to the fact that:

a) persons acquire a "taste for power" and restlessly pursue more power as an end in itself; or

b) access to power tempts the individual to illegally use institutional resources as a means of enriching himself; or

c) with the control of power persons are provided with false feedback concerning their own worth and develop new values designed to protect their power;

d) at the same time they devalue the worth of the less powerful and prefer to avoid close social contacts with them.

The model of power usage to be presented next will account more systematically for the changes described in (c) and (d), since such changes in intra- and interpersonal perceptions are of direct interest to psychologists.

The Metamorphic Effects of Power—A Model of Change

The model of the metamorphic effects of power contains six elements. These are (1) the resources possessed by the powerholder, (2) the frequency and kinds of influence attempts made by the powerholder, (3) the attributions by the powerholder concerned with who is in charge of the target person's behavior, (4) the evaluation of the target person, (5) the preferred social distance from the target person, and (6) the powerholder's evaluation of self.

In the following sections, each of these components will be examined in terms of the kinds of evidence available to support its inclusion in the model. As an overview, the metamorphic model assumes that the control of resources, in conjunction with a strong power need, triggers a train of events that goes like this: (a) with the control of resources goes increased temptation to influence others' behavior to satisfy personal wants; (b) if powerholders use strong and controlling means of influence to satisfy these personal wants, and compliance follows, (c) there arises the belief that the behavior of the target person is not self-controlled but has been caused by the powerholder; as a result (d) there is a devaluation of the target person's abilities, and (e) a preference to maintain social and psychological distance from the target person; (f) simultaneously the powerholder's evaluation of himself changes so that he views himself more favorably than the target person.

Several points of clarification need to be made concerning the model.

Successful influence and changes in perceptions. First, success moderates the metamorphic effects of power. That is, the metamorphic effects are seen to occur when power relations have been stabilized and the powerholder has generally had his way, as is true, say, in many teacher-student relations, marriage relations, superior-subordinate relations at work, physician-patient relations, and so on. The model is less likely to provide understanding in circumstances where the contending parties are of relatively equal power or where the weaker party is continually and actively resisting the powerholder's influence, as in the case of individuals in the present women's movement or the civil rights movement of the 1960s. Continued resistance forces the powerholder to reexamine more objectively the target person and, as a result, diminishes stereotypes.

Cause and effect—a reciprocal process. The second point is that the metamorphic model is described in this chapter as a unidirectional cause and effect model. For instance, it will be stated that because a powerholder uses strong means of influence he will devalue the worth of the target person. It is equally plausible, however, to expect that there are many situations in which the direction of causality is reversed. In these situations, the powerholder's prior evaluation of the target person determines his choice of means of influence. Chapter 6 contains descriptions of the research of Banks (1974), and of Michener and Burt (1974), which reported that powerholders used stronger means of influence with disliked rather than liked target persons. Gamson (1968) has similarly discussed a reciprocal linkage between a powerholder's trust for a target person and the decision to use coercive power. He has argued that distrust causes the powerholder to use coercion and also that the use of coercion will cause a powerholder to distrust a target person.

In short, there are both logical grounds and some laboratory evidence to support the belief that there are reciprocal processes between the use of influence and the powerholder's conscious representation of himself and those around him. Over time powerholders build up images of target persons in terms of how much resistance to influence these target persons are likely to show and what means of influence are most likely to overcome this resistance and cause compliance. Such continuous exchange of influence and evaluation make it very complicated to unravel the direction of cause and effect, except in those special instances were we have knowledge of the kinds of means of influence available to the powerholders prior to their meetings with target persons, or where we know how much a powerholder likes a target person prior to influence being exerted.

Actually reciprocal interactions between variables are likely to occur in all areas of the social sciences, although they are usually ignored by social scientists. For example, Fleishman, Harris, and Burt (1955) have proposed that managers who are both task-oriented and considerate of their employees are likely to have productive work groups. It is equally plausible to suppose that in many instances managers behave in both a task-oriented and a considerate manner simply because their work groups are already productive. Thus the productivity of the work group can alter the leader's behavior. Similarly, in studies of parent-child interactions, the general focus is on the ways in which the parent causes behavior in the child. Yet it is also recognized that the parent's behavior can be changed in profound ways by the child's influence. For instance, the child can make the parent aggressive, and vice versa. Or, again, it is argued by social psychologists that similarity between two people causes attraction; yet it is equally true that attraction causes people to see themselves as similar.

Unidirectional causality, then, is not a necessary assumption for the metamorphic model. I believe, however, that the more interesting features of the model are revealed by stressing the directionality of events (the successful use of strong influence, for example, causes devaluation of the target person). For this reason I will begin with the decision of the powerholder to exercise influence and end with the powerholder's evaluation of self and the target person. The reader should recognize however that I view the linkages between the elements of the model as reciprocal in terms of cause and effect.

Control of Resources

The metamorphic model begins by attempting to specify when a powerholder will attempt to influence a target person in order to gain satisfaction. I propose that such influence is more likely to be tried when the powerholder possesses resources needed by the target person. The relationship between resources and influence attempts can be stated as follows.

Control of resources needed by the target person increases the probability that the powerholder will attempt to influence the target person.

The assessment of the resources controlled by the powerholder is the starting point for the metamorphic model. This assessment may be relatively objective in terms of an independent cataloguing of the powerholder's resources (wealth, beauty, intelligence, charm, strength, and so forth) or it may be done subjectively by the powerholder himself. Over the long run, we expect that the objective and subjective accounts will tend to agree with each other, although we realize that, in the short run, mistakes will be made. For example, a person may assume that he is far more charming and desirable than he is found to be by most persons he is trying to influence. In this instance, corrective feedback will be quickly forthcoming as the person fails to convince others to carry out some action by simply relying on his charm.

Why does the possession of appropriate resources increase the probabilities that the powerholder will take action? I suggest that the possession of appropriate resources raises the powerholder's expectations that he will gain compliance if he exerts influence. That is, the possession of appropriate resources convinces the powerholder that he is likely to succeed if he makes some attempt to overcome resistance. He knows that the target cannot fail to be moved if he invokes that which the target wants. The individual who wants a new car is likely to approach the car salesman and make an offer only if he has money; the therapist who wants to change his client's behavior will do so by invoking his (the therapist's) specialized knowledge; and the love-stricken suitor will gain the love of his lady by invoking his charm and persuasive powers. Lacking the appropriate resources, each of the above actors must remain mute. In short, the combination of some want that requires the services of others and the possession of resources that will be given weight by these others can be expected to produce action, while the absence of either the aroused need or appropriate resources will lead to inaction.

Of course, the relation between the possession of resources and attempts to influence others is not inevitable. Studies of community power, for example, have reported many instances in which the power elite refrained from influencing community issues, despite their personal interest in the outcome (Hawley and Wirt 1968). However, there does appear to be at least a moderate relation between the possession of resources and their use, if for no other reason than that those without resources are less likely to attempt to influence others (Deutsch and Krauss 1960; Lippitt, Polansky, Redl and Rosen 1952; Zander, Cohen and Stotland, 1957).

To illustrate how the possession of resources influences the taking of action, we will describe a recent study by the present writer (Kipnis 1972) in which college students acted as managers of a simulated manufacturing company. The managers were to make sure that the company's products were manufactured efficiently by their workers. In one condition—the power condition—the managers were given a broad range of institutional powers to influence their subordinates' behavior (power to give raises, to deduct pay, to train the workers, to transfer workers to a new task, and to fire the workers); in a second condition—the no-power condition—the managers were given no means of influencing their subordinates beyond telling them that they were the managers. As a result, in this latter condition, the managers could only rely on two bases of power when attempting to influence subordinates—their legitimate powers as managers and their personal powers of persuasion.

The procedure involved having four workers (confederates of the experimenter), who were in a separate room from the manager, work for six three-minute periods. At the end of each three-minute period, each worker's output, appropriately identified, was brought into the manager for checking. All workers were performing satisfactorily, although some were doing better than others. The manager was given an intercom system in order to give direction and advice to each worker, *if he chose to do so*. The power-needs involved in this instance arose from the manager's role, which required that he obtain high production from his employees.

Table 9.1 shows the average number of times that the managers contacted their workers to give them orders and direction. Inspection of this table shows that managers in the power condition made twice as many attempts to influence their workers as did managers with no power (p. $< .05$). Moreover, it can be seen that the difference in amount of influence attempted by managers with and without power steadily widened. During the first two trials, the difference in number of influence attempts between those with and without power was 1.0; but by the last block of trials this difference had risen to 4.6 influence attempts. In short, the control of a broad range of powers that could be invoked without costs to the managers encouraged the exertion of influence.

Table 9.1 Mean Frequency of Influence Attempts

Managers	Blocks of Trials			Total Number of Attempts to Influence Workers
	1–2	3–4	5–6	
With power	2.1	4.0	8.2	14.3
Without power	1.1	2.3	3.6	7.0

One may ask how influence was transmitted via the intercom. What did the managers have to say to their workers in order to keep production going? As can be imagined, the communications of managers without powers were limited to their persuasive or legitimate powers (praising performance, ordering workers to speed up, goal-setting, and urging workers to try harder). Of interest was the finding that very few managers with power relied on personal persuasion. Out of 198 separate influence attempts made by managers with power via the intercom, only 32 (or 16 percent) relied solely on persuasion. The remainder all included reliance on their delegated powers (promises of raises, threats of deductions, arranging contests between workers for money). Previously in the experimental literature, it had been reported by Deutsch and his associates (Deutsch 1969; Deutsch and Krauss 1960) that the availability of coercive power encourages the powerholder to use it in order to influence a target person. The results shown above suggest that other bases of power in addition to coercion also tempt the powerholder to exert influence.

The Effects of Influence

So far, it has been proposed that the control of resources increases the probability that the powerholder will attempt to influence others. Consider now the next step in the sequence; that is, how the act of influencing can shape the powerholder's views of the target person. We begin by examining the problem of "Who's in charge?"

Let us suppose that a target person complies with a request by the powerholder. One issue to be examined is whether we can determine when a powerholder will believe that his influence, rather than the free will of the target person, was the direct cause of the target person's compliance. In terms of attribution theory (Kelley 1967) the question is whether the powerholder locates the cause of compliance within himself or within the target person.

I suggest that the powerholder decides who is in charge of the target person's behavior by examining the means of influence he has invoked. When the powerholder uses strong and controlling means of influence, such as threats and promises, he is more likely to believe that he has caused the target person's subsequent compliance. If he uses weak means of influence, such as suggestions and simple requests, the powerholder is more likely to believe that the target person decided on his own to comply. Both Cartwright (1959) and Raven and Kruglanski (1970) have discussed this possibility in their examination of the strength of the power used and the amount of freedom various power bases allow a target person.

These ideas can be stated in more formal terms as follows.

The more a powerholder attempts to influence a target person's behavior using directive and controlling means of influence, and this influence, is followed by compliance, the more likely the powerholder is to believe that the target's behavior is not self-controlled, but controlled by the powerholder.

Assume, for instance, that a mother says to her thirteen-year-old son: "Go to the store and buy a half-gallon of milk." Perhaps the child ignores the first request but goes when it has been repeated several times. Then the mother will conclude, quite naturally, that the son's trip to the store was caused by her requests. Furthermore, this belief is likely to be reinforced even more if the mother decides to offer to pay her son for the errand. On the other hand, the mother's belief that she has directly caused her son's behavior is liable to be weakened if she only says: "Do me a favor, if you have the time, and go to the store for me" Under these circumstances, the mother is likely to be uncertain as to whether she exercised complete control over her son. Perhaps it was the son's good nature which made him decide to do the errand?

Raven and Kruglanski (1970) have suggested in this regard that reliance on certain forms of persuasion alone allows the target person a good deal of latitude to decide whether or not to obey. For example, if a powerholder merely says to a target: "Here are the facts; you decide for yourself," the powerholder cannot be certain that his influence per se caused any subsequent changes, since the target has a good deal of freedom to weigh alternatives and choose for himself. Hence, the target's actions could be viewed as relatively autonomous, influenced at best by the powerholder's providing new information.

Restricting the target's freedom of choice, however, by promising to increase his pay in exchange for compliance or, as was done in the film *The Godfather,* making the target "an offer he couldn't refuse" is more likely to convince the powerholder that any subsequent compliance was due to his influence.

More generally, it is suggested *that the strength of any means of influence can be inferred from the dependency of the target on the resources that are invoked.* The greater the target's dependency, the more likely it is that the powerholder will believe the target's subsequent compliance was due to the powerholder's request. Offering food to a starving man in exchange for compliance is a stronger act of influence than offering this food to a man who has just eaten. Furthermore, we believe that powerholders subjectively assign weights to the means of influence that they bring to bear on targets, so that they have a good idea of how much pressure they are exerting. When the powerholder believes that he has brought strong means to bear, then he believes that he is in control. This is especially true if the target changes his behavior in ways that are not consistent with his day-to-day style of life, and the changes parallel those suggested by the powerholder (Kruglanski and Cohen 1973).

Let us now examine several research studies that provide evidence to support the view that reliance on strong means of influence affects attribution of causality. These studies range from those concerned with persuasion and attitude change to studies of attempts to control behavior in marriage relations.

Attribution and Attitude Change

The first study we wish to examine was reported by the psychologist D. G. Dutton (1973) and was an attempt to examine the consequences of using "high-powered" and "low-powered" arguments to change a target's convictions. In the high-powered condition, Dutton instructed college students on how to construct persuasive arguments based upon "scientific findings" (for example, by attributing the source of the argument to a high-status person, using two-sided arguments, rational appeals, and so on). In the low-powered condition, students were informed of these principles of persuasion *but were asked to construct arguments that deliberately violated the principles.* Thus, there was one group of students who believed that they were to use arguments based upon scientific principles of persuasion and a second group of students who believed they were using arguments, perhaps equally good in content, but which directly violated these scientific principles.

Once having constructed his arguments, the student used them in attempts to convince a target person, who had initially disagreed with the student's position (government control of ecology). After hearing the student's arguments, the target person always changed his views to agree with that of the student. Thus, all students were successful in converting the target person to a new position.

The question is, did the students view the target person's conversion as being due to their own persuasiveness? The answer is mixed. When asked why the target person had changed his attitudes, students in the low-powered condition attributed the change to the target's "basic agreement on the issue once he was exposed to it." In short, the students believed that the target person made up his own mind. This belief arose, I think, because the students could not logically attribute change to the strength of their persuasive arguments. The students knew in advance that their arguments were poor and violated scientific procedures of persuasion. Yet the target person shifted his beliefs. How to account for this yielding? The answer is to assume that the persuasive arguments encouraged the target person to rethink his own position on ecology. Thus, the subsequent changes were controlled by the target person—helped, perhaps, by the student's clumsy presentation of additional facts.

Students in the "high-powered" condition attributed the changes in the target person's belief to the strength of their own arguments.

They had overwhelmed these "doubting Thomases" with precisely prepared scientific arguments.

Thus, we find that when persons believe that they have used strong and decisive arguments, then they also believe that any subsequent changes in the target's belief systems were caused by the force of their arguments, against which the target person's resistances crumbled. Contrarily, using forms of persuasion that are known to be weak, results in the belief that any subsequent changes were due to the fact that the target person made up his own mind.

Attribution and use of strong means of influence at work. At work, managers have available both strong and weak means of influence. Thus, a manager may "dangle" the promise of a promotion or pay raise in front of an employee if he improves even more than he has so far. At other times, the manager may try to influence an employee through casual conversation in which simple suggestions are offered without further mention of sanctions. Under these differing circumstances, one could expect that the manager's explanation for any subsequent compliance by his employees would differ. Changes associated with the use of sanctions would be explained in terms of the manager's own use of power. Changes associated with simple suggestions would be viewed as originating in the employee's own decision to change his behavior.

In the previously mentioned industrial-simulation study by the present writer, in which some managers were given a broad range of power to influence their workers and other managers were not given such power, evidence in support of this expectation was found.

It may be recalled that, in this study, one group of managers was delegated a range of powers to influence their employees (power to raise pay, to deduct pay or to fire, to train, and to change the employee's job). These managers had what I would call "strong" means of influence in comparison to a second group of managers who were given no delegated powers beyond telling them that they were in charge.

At the completion of the actual work, the managers were asked to evaluate their workers' performances. One set of questions asked the managers to estimate what had caused their workers to perform effectively. There were three alternatives, and each was evaluated as to its importance: "the workers' own motivations to do well";

my orders and suggestions"; and "the workers' desire for money."

More managers *without* power than *with* power attributed their workers' performances to the "workers' own motivations to do well." Thus, managers without power saw their workers as self-motivated and as determining for themselves how hard they should work. Conversely, more managers with power than without power assumed that the workers' performances were due to their desire to earn money; that is, the workers' performances were attributed to the power controlled by the managers. Thus, in terms of attribution process, managers who possessed "strong means of influence" believed that their employees were not in control of their own performances but regulated by powers controlled by the managers.

Another way of looking at the determinants of attribution is in terms of whether a relation existed between the number of actual influence attempts made by managers and their subsequent beliefs about who was in charge of the employee's performance—the employee himself or the manager.

It may be recalled that influence attempts in this study were measured by the number of times the managers talked to their employees over an intercom system. Further, it may be recalled that most of the communications made by managers with power contained explicit references to formal sanctions, whereas the communications of managers without power could only rely on persuasion or legitimacy as power bases. Within the condition in which managers controlled a range of institutional powers, a correlation of $+.65$ was found between the frequency with which managers spoke on the intercom to their employees and the manager's endorsement of the statement "my orders and influence caused the workers to perform effectively." The more managers invoked strong means of influencing their workers, the more they believed they had caused their performances. In the no-power condition, in which managers could only invoke their persuasive powers, the correlation between the frequency of speaking to employees and the endorsement of the above statement was a much lower .39. As was noted before, since the workers' performances in this study were preprogrammed, managers had no actual influence on their workers' performances. Thus, it appears that the very use of strong means induced the beliefs in managers that they controlled their employees' performances.

Similar findings have been reported by Berger (1973) in a study which used the same basic industrial-simulation design. In this study, influence attempts by the manager were dichotomized into those in which managers made explicit reference to direct and controlling means of influence through reliance upon company sanctions ("If you increase production by ten units, I'll give you a pay raise") and those influence attempts that relied on persuasion ("Try harder next time, we need more production"). The correlation between frequency of use of sanctions and the manager's belief that he was the cause of his workers' satisfactory performance was .40 (p < .01). A similar correlation, between frequency of persuasion and the manager's beliefs, was .24 (p ns) —again, much lower. What these findings suggest is that reliance on persuasion leaves lingering doubts in the manager's mind as to how influential he actually was. Relying on more controlling means such as threats of pay loss or promises of pay raises, however, produces greater certitude that the cause of behavior in the target person was the powerholder's commands.

Attribution and marriage. The distribution of power and decision-making within families is a topic of interest to both social scientists and to husbands and wives groping for ways to influence each other without anger and rancor. Here I wish to discuss the results of a study of decision-making in marriage as it pertains to the metamorphic effects of power. More particularly, the study will be discussed as it provides evidence of the relation between strong and weak means of influence and beliefs concerning "Who's in charge?"

The data of the study were gathered by myself, M. Gergen, and P. Castell through questionnaires given to married men and women. Only one partner from each family answered the questionnaire, without discussing his or her answers with the other partner. The method for obtaining respondents was simple, but probably not precise in terms of random-sampling procedures. Undergraduate students in several of my classes distributed the questionnaire to all the married persons they knew, most of whom were living in the Philadelphia area. The questionnaire explained that we were seeking information on decision-making in marriages. A stamped return envelope was also included so that each respondent could answer in privacy. Of the 180 questionnaires that were distributed, 76 usable ones were returned. These had been completed by 51 married women and 25 married men. The group covered the full range of married life from less than a year to well over fifteen years of marriage. While the low rate of returns prevents us from drawing conclusions about the distribution of decision-making in families living in the Philadelphia area, we can still use the data to examine the relationship between the respondents' beliefs concerning who was in charge of the marriage and the strength of means of influencing their spouse that they used.

One part of the questionnaire listed seventeen ways in which the respondent could change his or her spouse's mind. Each of the seventeen ways or means of influence was rated on a nine-point scale (ranging from "never" to "very often") to indicate how often that particular form of influence had been used during the last six months. The respondents were cautioned not to answer in terms of what they would like to do. Examples of the means of influence included: (1) Make my spouse realize that I know more about the matter—that I have expert knowledge; (2) argue until my spouse changes his/her mind; (3) present the facts as I see them, and let my spouse decide; (4) give up quickly since there is very little I can do to change my spouse's mind once it is made up.

The seventeen means of influence were factor-analyzed, and five factors emerged. These five factors are taken to represent the different forms of influence that husbands and wives use when attempting to convince the other party to comply. The factor names and the items defining each factor are shown in Table 9.2.

Of particular interest in terms of the present discussion were the factors labelled Authoritative Means of Influence and Accommodative Means of Influence. From what has been said so far, it could be expected that husbands or wives with high scores on the Authoritative factor or low scores on the Accommodative factor would believe that they were dominant in the marriage and controlled the spouse's behavior.

Our measure of control in the marriage was based upon the frequency with which respondents stated that they made the final decisions on a series of family matters. There were thirteen issues listed in the questionnaire: (1) handling of family finance, (2) recreation, (3) religious matters, (4) demonstration of affection, (5) friends, (6) table manners, (7) having company and parties, (8) philosophy of life, (9) ways of dealing with family, (10) wife's working, (11) intimate relations, (12) sharing household tasks, (13) politics. The instructions read as follows: "When you and your husband or wife do have a disagreement, would you say for each of these items who has the final say in a decision." The alternatives that were provided for each item were "I almost always decide," "I usually decide," "Husband-wife equal," "My spouse usually decides," "My spouse almost always decides." This measure of decision-making power in families has been used extensively in marriage research since its development by Wolfe (1959).

Table 9.2 Questionnaire Items Defining Various Dimensions of Influence Used to Change Spouse's Mind

---

Factor 1. Last Resort
1. Get angry and demand that he/she give in (.740)
2. Threaten to use physical force if my spouse does not agree (.703)

Factor 2. Accommodative Means
1. Offer to compromise, in which I give up a little if he/she gives up a little (.706)
2. Hold mutual talks in which both persons' points of view are objectively discussed without arguments (.675)

Factor 3. Authoritative Means
1. Make my spouse realize that I know more about the matter—that I have expert knowledge (.628)
2. Make my spouse realize that I have a legitimate right to demand that he/she agree with me (.600)

Factor 4. Dependency Appeals
1. Appeal to the person's love and affection for me (.717)
2. Show how much his/her stand hurts me (by crying, pouting, sulking) (.556)

Factor 5. Giving Up
1. Give up quickly since there is very little I can do to change my spouse's mind once it is made up (.463)
2. Give in on other issues so that my spouse will agree with me (.410)

NOTE: Numbers in parentheses are factor loadings.

The measure of the extent to which the respondent believed that he or she controlled the spouse's behavior consisted of the number of times the respondent answered on the thirteen items that "I almost always" or "I usually decide" when disagreements occurred. This score could range from 0 to 13. The more the respondent answered "I decide," the more he or she was considered to control the behavior of his or her spouse.

The correlation between the frequency of using Authoritative means of influence and Decision-making power was $+.27$ ($p <$

.05). Similarly, the correlation between the use of accommodative means of influence and decision-making power was $-.35$ (p $<$ .01). The multiple correlation of these combined means of influence with the measure of decision-making was .45. In short the study demonstrated that, in marriage, persons who stated that they were in charge also stated that they relied upon controlling means of influence and avoided using means of influence that gave the other party the freedom to decide. Thus as in prior studies a link between the strength of influence and the powerholder's attributions of causality has been demonstrated. We hasten to add that since the findings are based upon survey data there is no way of knowing whether the use of strong means of influence caused respondents to believe that they were in charge of the marriage.

Attribution and coercion. The successful use of coercive power leaves little doubt in the mind of the powerholder that he has caused a target's behavior. It is perhaps one of the strongest means of influence available for causing compliance, although, as we shall suggest subsequently, it has great costs associated with its use. Nevertheless, there can be little doubt in the mind of the powerholder that the use of threats and force, if followed by compliance, is due to his influence. Thus, the aide employed in a psychiatric ward who says to a patient: "Stop throwing your food around or I'll tie you to this chair" is pretty sure that, if the patient complies, it was because of this threat.

A provocative prison-simulation study by Zimbardo and his associates (1974) provides evidence of how the use of coercion convinces the powerholder that he controls the target person. In this study, normal volunteers agreed to play the role of either prison guard or prisoner for an extended period of time—in fact, for almost a week. While not instructed on how to act, the guards mainly attempted to influence prisoners by commands, verbal insults, threats, and extreme disciplinary tactics. Very little use was made by the guards of simple requests. In post-interviews, the comments of these guards left little doubt that they believed they controlled the prisoners' behavior. One guard said, "I was tired of seeing the prisoners in their rags. . . . I watched them tear at each other *on orders given by us*" (italics mine), while a second guard said, "but we were always there to show them just who was the boss."

In short, the use of threats followed by compliance almost invariably convinces the powerholder that he is in command of the target person's behavior. Even a simple conversation may take on the force of a direct command, in the powerholder's view, when coercion is the only means of influence that is typically used. We have already mentioned a study by Berger (1973) in which business students served as the managers of a simulated manufacturing establishment. Findings from this study illustrate how even simple conversations can be seen by the powerholder as controlling, when coercion is his main means of influencing others. In this study, one group of managers was provided with only coercive power to influence their employees (that is, the power to deduct pay). In this condition Berger found that a reliance upon persuasion ("Try to do better next time") was just as likely to make managers believe that they had "caused" their employee's performance, as a reliance upon coercion ("If you don't work faster, I will deduct pay"). When coercion was the only formal means of influence available, the correlation between the frequency with which threats of pay deduction were used and the managers' beliefs that they had "caused" their employees to work hard was .50; while the correlation between the managers' reliance upon frequency of persuasion and the managers' beliefs was also .50. This latter correlation represents the only instance I have found in which the use of persuasion affected attributional processes to the same extent as stronger means of influence. Apparently, when powerholders can only invoke coercion, they view even informal suggestions as having the force of a formal threat.

Housewives and housemaids. The final illustration of the relation between the strength of means of influence and attributional processes is taken from a study of housewives' use of influence on their housemaids by Donna Mauch and the present writer. Our interest in this area arose from hearing many remarks about housemaids that emphasized the difficulties involved in finding satisfactory employees and in directing their work. The focus of these remarks was clearly concerned with means of influence and evaluation—both elements of the metamorphic model. The method for gathering data was to distribute questionnaires to all persons known by Mauch to employ housemaids. Of the seventy questionnaires that were distributed, twenty-five were returned. This low rate of return prevents us from making general statements concerning housewife-housemaid relations, but it does allow an examination of the correlation between influence tactics and the attributions of the housewives as to who was in charge of the maids' work behavior—housewife or housemaid.

One part of the questionnaire listed five means of influence, and respondents were asked how frequently they had used each of these means in the past few months when they found their employee's work performance needed to be improved or was unsatisfactory. Five direct means of influence were listed: (1) ask her to redo the work or to improve; (2) Admonish her; (3) Show her the correct way; (4) offer incentives for improvement; (5) discuss with her the reasons why I am dissatisfied with her work. Each of these means of influence was rated on a 4-point scale: fairly often, often, occasionally, rarely.

An analysis of the intercorrelations among these items revealed, with two exceptions, positive high correlations ranging from .36 to .61. This suggested that for all practical purposes the items were reflecting various forms of strong and directive means of influence. Therefore the responses to each of the five items were summed to form an index that was labeled "frequency of direct influence." High scores indicated that the respondents used controlling means of influence fairly often.

Our measure of attribution of causality read: "When your worker performs her work in a satisfactory manner, how important would you estimate each of these reasons is for explaining her good work? (Rate each person on a scale ranging from 1 to 7, where $1 = $ of no importance and $7 = $ very important)." Three reasons attributed the housemaid's good work to forces controlled by the housewife: "pay," "the instructions I give," and "the fact that I check up on her work." One reason attributed the good work to the free choice of the maid: "her own motivations to do well." Table 3 gives the correlations between the extent to which the housewives in this sample relied upon direct and controlling means of influence and their beliefs concerning who controlled their maids' performance—themselves or the maids.

Once again we find a relationship between the strength of the influence tactics that were selected by the powerholder and beliefs about who was in charge of the target person's behavior. Table 9.3 shows a moderately strong correlation of .56 between the

housewives' use of directive means of influence and their beliefs
that their "check-ups" were the cause of their maids' good work.
Conversely, the absence of such use of directive means of influence
was correlated at a reasonably high level ($-.69$), with the housewives' beliefs that the maids' good work was based upon the maids'
own decisions to do such work.

Table 9.3 Relation between the use of Directive Means of Influence and
Attributions of Control (N = 25)

Cause of maid's good work	Frequency of Use of Directive Influence
1. Pay offered caused maid's good work	.19
2. My instructions caused maid's good work	.14
3. My check-ups caused maid's good work	.56**
4. My maid's own motivations to do well caused her good work	$-.69$**

**p < .01

Of course these survey findings do not prove that the use of
strong means of influence "caused" the attributions of the housewives. In fact the reverse is probably true. Simple logic would suggest that, because they felt that they could not trust their maids to
work on their own, the housewives felt obligated to "check-up"
on their maids. The same lack of trust also led to the use of directive and controlling means of influence. It has already been stated
that cause-and-effect relations can go in both directions when power
is examined. The previously cited experimental studies appear sufficient to document the point that the strength of influence tactics
can guide attributions; and the reverse of this relation has probably
been shown by this last study.

Evaluation of Target

The reader may question why we have dwelt for such great
lengths on the development of beliefs concerning whether or not
one person thinks he controls another person's behavior. The reason for taking time here is that I propose that these cognitions
mediate a powerholder's subsequent relations with the target. This
relation can be expressed as follows.

To the extent that powerholders believe that they have caused a target's behavior, powerholders are likely to devalue the target's worth.

If you believe you have caused someone else to do something, the suggestion made here is that you will minimize the other's worth. For example, teachers are frequently heard to "put down" the talents of a student by implying that the student did no more than carry out the detailed instructions of a teacher. And parents reserve their fondest boasts for the times when their young child spontaneously shows some early development, such as walking, without help. The child who is slow in development—a euphemism for having to be guided by others—is viewed with affectionate concern and dismay by the parents.

Sampson (1965), in his examination of power and marriage relations, discusses at length how the acceptance of power inequality in marriage during the Victorian age was buttressed by the belief of the husband (and, frequently, of the wife as well) that women were incapable of assuming the range of responsibilities of men. The accepted relation between man and wife was one of subordination, of authority and obedience. In theory, and frequently in practice, it was the husband who "caused" the wife's behavior. And these beliefs and practices were accepted not only as right and inevitable by men but also by a vast majority of women. Sampson provides a revealing statement on the pervasiveness of the belief in the inability of women to cope from a Mrs. Norton, who advocated equality under nineteenth-century British law for women but not equality in relations with men: "The wild and stupid theories advanced by a few women . . . of equal intelligence [with men] are not the opinion of the majority of their sex. I for one believe in the natural superiority of men as I do in the existence of God. The natural position of women is inferiority to man" (p. 54).

In this instance, all parties involved subscribed to the self-fulfilling belief that, if the man guides the woman's behavior, it is only because the woman is incapable of independent action.

Findings from the questionnaire survey on decision-making power in marriage that I described earlier in this chapter echoed these Victorian attitudes. It may be recalled that one set of questions measured who was in charge of decision-making when disagreements occurred. A second group of questions that was also included asked the respondents to evaluate the capabilities of their spouses. We found that if one party to the marriage believed that he or she controlled the decision-making power in the family (as indicated by a high number of "I decide" answers), this party also believed the spouse incapable of independent action. Our research found equal numbers of men and women claiming that they made most of the final decisions in their family. And, further, there were no sexist biases associated with the outcomes of controlling power; both men and women who stated that they controlled the decision-making power in the family devalued the worth of their dependent spouses.

Let me describe in more detail the data that was used to reach the above conclusions. One section of the decision-making questionnaire asked each respondent to evaluate on a five-point scale (ranging from below-average to superior) how their spouses compared with people in general on each of ten characteristics. The characteristics were (1) capable of solving problems, (2) skilled at his/her work, (3) socially adept, (4) common sense, (5) independent, (6) reliable, (7) organized, (8) intelligent, (9) physically able, and (10) persuasive. A total evaluation score for each spouse was obtained by summing the ratings over the ten characteristics. Thus, high scores meant that the respondent judged his or her spouse to be superior to people in general and low scores indicated a negative appraisal. This total was found to correlate $-.42$ with the number of times the respondent stated he or she made the final decision when disagreements arose with the spouse. The more respondents perceived that they controlled their partner's behavior, the less favorably they evaluated their spouses.

This finding is, of course, very consistent with the explanation that, if you believe you control another's behavior, then you cannot give him full credit for any actions he takes or for any products he may produce. Thus, the husband or wife who continually decides what the spouse should do is forced to conclude, ever so unwillingly perhaps, that the spouse does not measure up as a capable, skilled, and intelligent person. Every day that they conflict and that the dependent spouse agrees to do what the partner has decided, can only confirm the dominant partner's judgment that the spouse is inept.

However, because these findings are based upon survey data, alternate interpretations of them can be offered. To deal with these ambiguities, we will next turn to experimental studies within organizational settings which also examine the relation between attributional processes and evaluation of the target person.

Organizational setting and the devaluation of the target. A good part of our adult lives is spent in hierarchical organizations in which those with higher positions are given the authority to influence the behavior of those with less status. Since these hierarchical power-relations basically rely on strong means of influence, it should come as no surprise to learn that those in dominant positions at work tend to express slighting attitudes about the competence of those whose behavior they direct. Thus, for example, a study by Strickland (1958) found that when supervisors were experimentally assigned to monitor one worker but not an equally competent second worker, the very act of continually supervising the worker resulted in the supervisor distrusting the worker he had under surveillance.

A field survey by Zander, Cohen, and Stotland (1959) among staff employed in mental hospitals also showed the same tendency for those in a position of power to express slighting attitudes about the less powerful. In this survey, psychiatrists were asked to appraise the psychologists they supervised. The psychologists were also asked to evaluate themselves. The results were that the psychiatrists believed that the psychologists were only competent to test patients, not to treat them. Psychologists thought far more of their own worth and saw themselves as not only competent to test patients but to provide a variety of therapeutic, diagnostic, and research services. In this instance, then, devaluation of psychologists by psychiatrists was expressed in terms of denying that psychologists had the potential to do more demanding and responsible work.

The relation between power and evaluation of a target was also examined in a previously described industrial-simulation study of mine (Kipnis 1972) in which some managers were given a broad range of powers (rewards, coercion, ecological control, training) to influence their employees, and other managers were given no power beyond telling them that they were the bosses. At the end of this study we asked the managers to evaluate their employees' work on scales measuring quality of work, quantity of work, and willingness to promote and rehire the workers. Despite the fact that the simulated employees had turned out the same amount of work in all instances, managers *with power* evaluated their workers' performances as much poorer than did managers *without power*.

Those with power saw their employees as less competent and less deserving of promotion or rehire than managers without power. We would argue that the reason for these lower evaluations among managers with power was the managers' belief that they had "caused" their workers' performance. Hence, they discounted the worth of their workers' own contributions to the work that was achieved.

Further support for our view is found in the comments of the managers after the study was over, when they were asked what they had to do in order to be successful in their roles as managers. Managers *without power* continually stressed the importance of allowing the worker freedom to do work on his own; by being allowed this freedom, they said, the worker would be motivated to perform at high levels. For example, one manager without power said: "You must have control, but not to the point where you would dominate the worker. You must also have gentleness so you won't offend the worker." Another manager without power said: "You should have ability to show confidence in the worker, encouragement, and allow them freedom to perform their jobs in their own way."

Managers who had been given power stressed the necessity of manipulating workers as a means of raising production. One manager with power said: "You have to know how to influence the men to do more and do it better." And another manager with power said: "You have to know how to motivate the workers, even when they may not want to be motivated." Independent raters who examined these statements found that managers with power were significantly more concerned with manipulating workers than managers without power. Seventy-six percent of managers with power and 21 percent of managers without power expressed manipulatory attitudes about their workers. Thus, in this instance, the control and use of strong means of influence created what may be termed a Theory X organization, to use McGregor's term: that is, managers came to view workers as objects of control, unlikely to work unless forced to do so by the managers' orders and influence. One correlate of this unhappy state of affairs, as we have seen, was that the workers' abilities were devalued.

Similar findings were obtained by Berger (1973) using the same industrial-simulation design as mine. Berger reported a correlation of $-.31$ (p $<$ .01) between managers' evaluations of their workers and managers' attributions of causality for their workers' performances. Lower evaluations of workers were given when the managers believed that the main reason for the effort shown by the employees was the managers' orders and influence.

Of further interest in Berger's findings was that the attribution-devaluation relationship was greatest when managers were highly involved in running the simulated business. That is, in one condition Berger told the managers that their own pay was contingent on how well they ran the business, while in a second condition no such involving instructions were given. Indeed, the managers were told that they would receive a flat salary for their time. In the former condition the correlation between attribution and evaluation was $-.40$ (p $<$ .01), while in the latter the correlation was $-.21$ (p ns). A similar finding has been reported by Dutton (1973), who found that a powerholder's degree of involvement in the outcome influenced attributional processes.

We suggest, then, that the more involved an individual is in the act of influencing others, the more likely he is to assume that he is responsible for changes in the others' behavior, when strong means of influence are used. This assumption, in turn, intensifies subsequent devaluation of the target.

The final set of findings pertaining to the relationship between attribution and evaluation of the target person is taken from our survey study of housewives' use of influence among housemaids. It may be recalled that in this study twenty-five housewives described on a questionnaire the frequency with which they used controlling means of influence with their housemaids and the extent to which they believed that they controlled the behavior of the housemaids. In addition to this information, the housewives also evaluated their maids. The measure of evaluation in this instance was a summed rating of the maid's ability in five areas of housework. These were: (1) planning of work time, (2) ability to do work without supervision, (3) completeness and neatness of work, (4) inniative; and (5) the amount of work completed. The measure of attribution of control of the maid's behavior, it may be recalled, was the extent to which the housewife believed that any good work done by the maid was due either to the maid's "own motivations to do well" or to forces controlled by the housewife, such as the degree to which the housewife checked up on the maid. The correlation between the housewife's evaluations of the housemaid and the extent to which the housewife believed that her "check-ups" caused the maid's good performance was −.60. That is, the more the good work was attributed to the housewife's surveillance of the housemaid, the more the maid's abilities were devalued. The more the housewife attributed the maid's good work to the maid's "own motivations to do well," the more she was appreciated—the correlation in this instance between evaluations and attribution being +.80.

To summarize, then, various field and laboratory investigations have been cited in this section whose findings support the idea that a powerholder's evaluations of a target person pivots on whether or not the target person is seen to be complying freely or has been forced to comply. In the next two sections we wish to consider briefly two issues that may mediate the relationship between attributions of control and evaluation.

Distinguishing between affection for a person and evaluation of his capabilities. Up to this point, it has been stated that, if a powerholder uses strong means of influence successfully, then he will feel contempt for the target of influence. Yet even a cursory reflection would suggest that we frequently like a person who is compliant and accommodating (Dutton 1973). A husband who makes all the decisions in the family may be very fond of his wife. However, devaluation of the wife may occur because at the same time the husband assumes that she is incapable of taking care of important family matters. In Henrik Ibsen's play *A Doll's House*, we find the noble person of Nora facing this dilemma in that her husband regards her as somewhat less than a child, someone to be loved and protected but never to do anything of meaning. Archie Bunker, in the popular TV series "All in the Family, continually expresses contempt for his wife's ability to cope but seemingly has a grudging admiration for her at times. Here, then, we have instances in which the target is liked as a person but full credit is not given for any outcomes he or she may achieve, since these outcomes are but extensions of the powerholder's ideas.

In other instances, however, we find that the individual who uses strong means of influence may express great contempt for the target. During the Vietnamese War, it was commonplace to hear

American soldiers talking about "nuking the gooks," that is, using nuclear weapons to wipe out the inferior Vietnamese. Similarly, in the prison-simulation study conducted by Zimbardo and his colleagues (1974) the prison guards viewed the compliant prisoners with the greatest of contempt. Zimbardo reported that, over the five days of the experiment, guards increased significantly in the use of deindividuating references ("Hey, you slob, come here!") and in the use of depreciation-insults when talking to the prisoners. In this situation, as the guards increased in their ability to control the behavior of their prisoners, rather than the guards' liking for the prisoners increasing, because they were so compliant, the reverse occurred. The literature that deals with the consequence of causing other persons to experience pain and suffering (Davis and Jones 1960; Lerner and Simmons 1966) also indicates that the harmdoer tends to derogate the worth of the target, presumably as a means of protecting the harmdoer from feeling guilt.

How, then, are we to understand more precisely what determines the scope of derogation? Why in one instance is a compliant target seen as likable, but not talented, and in another instance seen as generally unworthy and contemptible?

One explanation has to do with the nature of the means of influence that are brought to bear on the target. As I mentioned in Chapter 6, it is necessary to justify to oneself and to society the uses of strong means of influence. This process of justification of the use of strong means appears implicated, I believe, as a reason for devaluing the worth of a target person. For example, a powerholder may promise food to a hungry man in exchange for compliance, or he may threaten to take the food away in retaliation for noncompliance. In the first instance, the powerholder may see himself as a benefactor contributing to the target's welfare. In the second instance, the powerholder may view his threat to deprive the hungry man of food less favorably. In fact, he may be downright depressed to find himself using threats and force in order to get what he wants. As several writers have pointed out (Walster, Berscheid, and Walster 1973; Lagent and Mettee 1973), this predicament may be minimized by in some way rationalizing one's own actions. Among these ways is the simple notion that the target is a scoundrel and deserves this kind of harsh treatment. Wayne Karlin and fellow writers (1973), in an introduction to their book of stories about American soldiers in Vietnam, *Free*

Fire Zone, described how these soldiers viewed their own acts: "The agent of suffering must believe that the victim and his world are outside of humanity. *Free Fire Zone* is about men dehumanizing themselves by imagining the Indochinese as less than human, who victimized their own precious humanity by warring on the 'gooks'."

The very act of using coercion, then, may convince the power-holder that the target person is untrustworthy and a person who requires continuous surveillance (Strickland 1958). The power-holder cannot allow himself the luxury of feeling compassion for the target, for then he would have no one to blame for his acts but himself. In short, it is suggested that, when the powerholder freely chooses to use strong and harsh means of influence that are successful, he will express complete derogation of his target. On the other hand, if a powerholder uses strong but nonharsh means of influence, then it is more likely that the powerholder will derogate the target's abilities but will still retain positive feelings for him. This is because using nonharsh means still allows the power-holder to retain positive feelings about himself.

Methodological note. In studying the relation between attribution and evaluation of a target person, the researcher must be prepared for three kinds of responses. The first response—called Type A—occurs when the target person does what the power-holder wants but without the use of strong means of influence. This anticipation of a powerholder's intentions and desires has been described by several theorists (e.g., Baldwin 1971), who call attention to its role in maintaining organizational effectiveness. To the extent that a target person is willing to anticipate a leader's desires, this anticipation allows for interactions without the overt use of strong means of influence. Needless to say, when a target person does what a powerholder wants without even being asked, such acts usually are most appreciated.

The second response—called Type B—occurs when the target person does what the powerholder wants but only after strong means of influence have been brought to bear. The research described in the previous pages has mostly involved comparisons of target persons who have made Type A and Type B responses.

There is, however, a third kind of response—Type C—that the researcher must be prepared to encounter in field settings. In a Type C response the target person does not comply even after strong means of influence have been used. Thus, a child may continue to be rebellious even after the strongest threats by his parents; there seems to be simply no way in which one can make him obey the simple dictates of parents and society.

Table 9.4 shows the powerholder's reactions to each of these three types of responses to power tactics.

Table 9.4 Evaluation of Target Person as a Function of Target Compliance

	Type A	Type B	Type C
	Target Person Complies without Use of Strong Means of Influence	Target Person Complies after Strong Means of Influence Are Used	Target Person Does Not Comply Despite the Use of Strong Means of Influence
Who does the powerholder see as causing the target's behavior?	The target person's own motivations to do well	The powerholder's orders and demands	The target person's free choice, viewed by the powerholder as stubbornness
Evaluation of target person by the powerholder	High	Intermediate	Low, but perhaps grudging respect (?)

The reader may see that, if the comparison involves a comparison between Type B and Type C target persons, then we should expect to find a positive rather than negative relation between attributions of causality and evaluations of a target. This result should follow because in this instance the powerholder evaluates more favorably a person who complies with his influence attempts than one who continues to resist. However. as can also be seen, the powerholder's highest evaluations are reserved for the target person who does what the powerholder wants without any strong urgings from the powerholder, that is, does it spontaneously.

Increased Social Distance

The widespread observation (Jackson 1964; Sorokin and Lundin 1959; Zander, Cohen, and Stotland 1959) has been that those in positions of power "move away" from social contacts with the less powerful. That is, there is a preference among powerholders for social exchanges with those of equal or higher status and a tendency to avoid social "chitchat" or contact with those of lesser rank. In the previously mentioned study by Zander, Cohen, and Stotland (1959) among psychiatrists and psychologists, psychiatrists expressed much less interest in having leisure-time contacts with psychologists than psychologists did for contacts with psychiatrists. Similarly, in the industrial-simulation study by the present writer (Kipnis 1972), managers with power said they were much less willing "to have a cup of coffee or a coke with their employees now that the simulation exercise was over" than did managers without power. Finally, in our survey of decision-making power in marriage, the dominant spouse was dissatisfied with his or her marriage and with the amount of sexual satisfaction found in the marriage. The correlation between the extent to which respondents controlled the decision-making powers in the family ("I decide") and the respondent's satisfaction with his or her marriage was −.45. The correlation between decision-making power and enjoyment of sexual relations was −.29. Thus, those who controlled power in the marriage expressed the wish to "move away" from the submissive spouse, both emotionally and physically.

On the basis of these data, a fourth generalization can now be given.

Control over a target person's behavior is associated with a preference to increase social distance and psychological distance from the target person.

We do not have to look to psychological experiments to define the existence of these preferences to "move away" from the less powerful. In everyday life one finds continued instances of this drive toward segregation, ranging from executive bathrooms to the now illegal doctrine of "separate but equal facilities" espoused by Southerners as a means of maintaining separation of whites from blacks in the public school system. In general, one can expect that the more complete the control exercised by the powerholder over the target, the less the powerholder will be interested in spending time with the target.

Several explanations have been offered for this tendency of those in positions of power to move away from those without power. Zander, Cohen, and Stotland suggest that those with high power can afford to be indifferent toward those of lesser power since the less powerful are neither a threat to their security or in a position to offer any insights of interest. Mulder (1963) has argued that the movement of the more powerful away from the less powerful reflects "power gradient" motivations; that is, individuals are continually attracted to regions containing greater resources than their own and away from regions containing fewer resources. Distrust of the motives of the less powerful has also been suggested as another explanation of this movement "away" from the less powerful. Sampson (1965) has observed that some persons in positions of power are repelled by the obsequiousness of the less powerful, their lack of candor, and their penchant for flattery. There is a suspicion that whatever is said by the less powerful is designed to win favor. One can never be sure that there are not ulterior motives in any positive regard expressed by the less powerful. These suspicions may also contribute to a preference for social distance.

A final possible explanation for this preference for social distance is suggested by B. F Skinner, who points out that Western man balks at information which sets limits on his conception of himself as an agent of free will. By extension, we may also desire to avoid these persons who appear not to be in control of their own behavior but in fact are controlled by us. Fundamentally, then, it may be the target's lack of freedom of choice that provides this "movement away" from his company. To be controlled by another person robs one of those very qualities of dignity and self-worth that attract one person to another.

Power and Self-Esteem

Let us next examine how the powerholder's view of himself may vary as a function of the power he controls and uses. As Clark (1971) has pointed out, "power cannot be exercised without inducing some form of reaction." While Clark's observations were directed toward the target, it is equally true that one can expect reactions in the powerholder. While it seems reasonable to expect such variations, there has been very little published that has systematically examined this issue. Furthermore, the available literature presents contradictory findings on how the successful use of power may change the powerholder's views of himself. In some instances, favorable self-evaluations occur, and in other instances unfavorable self-evaluations occur. These latter changes appear to be particularly likely to happen if the powerholder's only means of influencing a target are coercive means.

Despite these occasional downturns in self-evaluations, as a general rule the control and use of power appears most often to increase self-esteem, if only by comparison with the self-esteem of those who possess few or no resources. Let us pursue this argument by imagining a person who has few resources that others around him give weight. He may be an unskilled, illiterate worker whose only claim on his fellow man is the fact that he is poor and helpless; or he may be an old man living alone, without relatives, in a small room in a large city. such individuals tend to act passively and believe that luck or chance controls their fate. Lacking resources, these individuals are likely to have few of their wants satisfied. Their options are limited to giving up all their wants or remaining dependent on the whims of passersby for the satisfaction of their wants.

Resources, then, enhance feelings of well-being in several ways. Most obviously, they allow the individual to live a more comfortable life. If the resources are of a material kind, then the individual can exchange his wealth for good food, good clothing, and a certain inner elegance which, in the opinion of society, marks the contented man. It should come as no surprise to learn that public opinion surveys almost always find that satisfaction with the quality of one's life is directly associated with the possession of material wealth.

Beyond the material comforts that accrue to the powerholder are the wide range of psychic comforts that also accrue. We have previously suggested that those with access to valued resources are more likely to receive flattering feedback from the less powerful. Even the most foolish of suggestions may be carried out by a target who wants to keep in the good graces of the powerholder. To the extent that one's definition of self is defined by the attitudes of others (Mead 1934), the control of valued resources heavily tips the scales in favor of a positive self-regard. The potential mental health benefits accruing to those with valued resources is suggested in a recent review by Porter and Lawler (1965) on factors influencing the satisfaction and performance of persons at work. It was found that the higher the executive level of the employee, the more likely were important psychological need systems to be satisfied. Top executives were far more fulfilled in terms of needs for esteem, autonomy, and self-actualization. Clearly, then, in comparison to the individual with few resources, those with many resources appear happier, more fulfilled, and, no doubt, more satisfied with themselves.

It is not, however, argued that the control and use of power is always associated with the development of a positive self-image. Power appears to be a necessary, but not sufficient, condition for this development to occur. Beyond the fact that the absence of resources is associated with a negative view of the self, additional information appears to be needed to predict just when the presence of power will elevate self-esteem.

Suggestions as to the kind of information that is needed can be obtained from the writings of Charles H. Cooley (1922) and George H. Mead (1934) on role-taking and the development of the self-concept. These social scientists proposed that the development of a sense of self occurs in terms of how significant others view one's own actions and behaviors. To the extent we believe that "others" disapprove of our behavior, we may come to define who we are in unfavorable terms. If we believe that others approve our behavior, then we may hold positive feelings about ourselves.

In this connection it is clear that there are shared societal expectations concerning the merit attached to using various forms of power. Society views with admiration power usage based on the distribution of rewards or the use of expert knowledge; it views with indifference and forbearance the use of legitimacy as a means of influence; but it regards with suspicion persons who use threats, force, and coercion.

It is not unreasonable to believe that those who use these various means of influence also share society's views. To use power for beneficial purposes establishes one's good name in society. In the early decades of this century, public relations advisors convinced John D. Rockefeller and others of equally great wealth to provide millions for public projects in order to overcome the negative image held of them by the general public.

On the other hand, persons who mainly use coercive power may view themselves more negatively than persons who do not have to use such power in order to influence others. Accepting society's views of one's actions leaves a person but little choice in the matter of self-appraisal. If hurting others is the main means one has of satisfying power needs, then the self will soon be seen in a negative way.

In short, it is the "price" society puts on one's use of power that may determine self-regard. In Chapter 5 I pointed out that there are instances in which society applauds the use of coercion as, for example, a means of demonstrating courage and manhood. Nevertheless, the use of coercive forms of influence is generally disapproved of by a large segment of society and, hence, may cause the powerholder to lower his sense of self-worth.

What evidence is there that the kinds of powers we use can shape our self-image? Unfortunately, there is little evidence from controlled laboratory studies that have directly examined this idea. Further, the available studies provide only contradictory results. A negative relation between the successful use of power and changes in self-regard was reported by Zimbardo and his colleagues (1974) in the previously cited prison-simulation study. It may be recalled that, in this study, volunteers served as prisoners or as prison guards for a period of five days. Twice during the progress of the simulation, each participant was asked to complete a self-description scale. The prisoners expressed increasing negative feelings as the simulation proceeded, not a particularly surprising finding since they were the targets of intensely coercive treatment. What was surprising, however, was that the wielders of coercive power, the prison guards, also increased in feelings of emotional distress, although not as much as the prisoners. Despite some of the guards' remarks that might indicate they enjoyed using power ("Acting authoritatively can be fun," "Power can be a great pleasure"), Zimbardo reported that, as a group, prison guards' self-esteem was reduced. Apparently, the experience of punishing others had severe negative consequences. Parallel findings have been reported by Milgram (1963) in his well-known studies of obedience.

Balancing these findings, however, Berger (1973) reported that the self-evaluations of powerholders became more positive when they used a broad spectrum of powers but showed no changes when only coercive power was used. In this laboratory simulation of work, one group of managers was only allowed to use coercion to influence their workers (threats of pay loss or firings); a second group was only allowed to use rewards (promise of pay raises); and a third group was allowed to use both rewards and coercion. At the end of the simulation, Berger asked his managers to evaluate their own performances on a semantic-differential scale. It was found that the more the managers used their institutional powers to influence their workers, the more favorably they evaluated their own performance. This finding, however, was mainly restricted to only one group of managers who controlled both the power to reward and to punish. Among managers who controlled only the power to reward, the results were less strong; while among managers who were given only coercive power, there was no relation between self-evaluations and the use of power.

Thus, the results appear complex. Berger's findings demonstrated in a laboratory setting that self-concepts can be influenced by the use of power. However, in this particular instance, the use of coercion did not lower self-esteem, as has been proposed here. Rather, the use of a broad spectrum of powers produced a favorable change in self-esteem.

To further cloud the issue, in two additional studies carried out by the present writer and collaborators, no relationship was found between the use of power and appraisals of the self. In the first study, involving the simulation of a business (Kipnis 1972), I found that managers who were given a broad range of institutional powers to influence their employees did not evaluate their own performance at the end of the simulation as better than that of managers who were given no institutional powers. Both groups of managers saw their own performances in equally favorable ways despite the fact that the managers with power made many more attempts to influence their workers' performances.

The second bit of negative evidence was found in the survey on decision-making powers in marriage done by the present writer, M. Gergen, and P. Castell. In this survey, each respondent evaluated himself or herself on ten characteristics (problem-solving ability, skill at work, common sense, and and so on). The ten characteristics were exactly the same as those that had previously been used to describe their spouses (p. 197). The total self-description score derived from the evaluations did not correlate with our measure of decision-making power. Respondents who stated they controlled decision-making in the marriage and respondents who said they hardly ever made the final decision described themselves in equally favorable terms. This latter finding is particularly disappointing since it was expected that persons in positions of power within the family structure would receive more favorable feedback from their spouses than those who said they did not control power.

What is most needed at this point to untangle the complex relations between power and self-evaluation are more empirical studies and a conceptualization of the problem that takes into account the basis of power, the means of power, the scope of power, and the amount of power available to the powerholder (Dahl 1957), as these contribute to the powerholder's conception of himself. At a minimum, I believe that such research will find that *the successful wielder of power will view himself in more favorable terms than he views the target of influence.* Thus, rather than stating that self-perceptions rise or fall on some absolute scale as a result of the successful use of power, I suspect these perceptions rise or fall in relation to the esteem accorded the target person. More formally, this relationship can be stated as follows:

> *Powerholders will evaluate themselves more favorably than they evaluate the target of power.*

The only evidence I am aware of to support this generalization is provided by our study of decision-making in marriage. Since each respondent evaluated himself or herself on ten characteristics and also evaluated the spouse on these same characteristics, it was possible to determine whether the respondents evaluated themselves more favorably or less favorably than their spouses. The findings showed that if respondents stated that they controlled the decision-making power in the family, they also described themselves in more flattering terms than they described their spouses. The correlation between the extent to which respondents stated that they controlled decision-making in the marriage and the degree to which they described themselves in more favorable terms than they described their spouses was $+.29$ ($p < .01$).

If further investigations confirm this finding that powerholders evaluate themselves more favorably than their targets, we may begin to understand how actual changes in self-evaluation can occur as a result of the successful use of power. That is, in addition to seeing changes that may occur through favorable feedback, flattery, and deference, we should also find that the self is viewed with increasing favor as the status of the target person rises. If the target person is respected and admired, then the act of successful influence should elevate the powerholder's self-evaluations considerably. This is because successful influence implies that the power-holder is superior to the target person.

Summary

This chapter started with the observation that the successful exercise of influence may bring about profound changes in the powerholder's views of himself and of the target person. The process through which change is believed to occur has as its central focus the attributions of the powerholder concerning "who is in charge" of the target persons behavior. To the extent that the powerholder assumes that he is in charge, then the metamorphic effects described herein are assumed to occur. Much of the chapter, then, has been devoted to examining the circumstances under which the powerholder comes to believe that he, rather than the target person, has been responsible for the eventual compliance of the target person.

The strongest available evidence centers on the likelihood of the powerholder devaluing the target person following the use of strong means of influence. It is difficult to imagine incidents in which influence tactics that allow the target person freely to choose to comply can lead to devaluation. Indeed if we fully understand how our esteem for the target person is related to the strength of the influence that we use, then we can understand seemingly paradoxical relationships, such as occur in folk myths that tell us Satan insinuates himself with soft words and persuasions rather than with outright force, which custom also says is available to him. Of what worth is a soul that was forced to choose evil as compared to one who freely chose to sin?

At this time the most equivocal evidence concerns changes in the powerholder's views of himself as a result of the successful exercise of power. The main conclusion is that powerholders who believe they control the behavior of target persons see themselves as more worthy than the target person. New techniques of studying the interactions between the powerholder and the target person that allow, for instance, for the possibility of flattering feedback from the target person over long periods of time, and that also allow for variations in the bases of power, are needed before additional statements about changes in the powerholder's self-esteem can be made.

10 Conclusion

One purpose of the social sciences is to point out new perspectives for viewing events in the world. When such a perspective is tried, it encourages a person to adjust his vantage point by a trifle, so that he may see something that had been obscured until then—although it was always there.

A goal of this book has been to sensitize psychologists to the issue of the control and use of power, and to the need of psychology to be able to account for the actions of the powerholder. The eventual usefulness of the kind of thinking presented in this book depends upon whether other social scientists accept the particular frame of reference for viewing power that has been presented here.

Chapter 9 focused attention upon the complex changes in a person's perceptions and evaluations of self and others that could result from the exercise of power. I have sketched out in the metamorphic model some of the elements that appear to be needed if one is to conceptualize these changes in any systematic fashion. Earlier chapters attempted to point out some of the environmental forces that affect the powerholder's choice of means of influence and to propose that these forces act by directly affecting the powerholder's expectations of successful influence.

What remains to be done is to tie together the reasoning on means of influence with the reasoning on the metamorphic model.

For instance it has been suggested that persons who lacked self-confidence, when placed in roles that required the exercise of influence, were rapidly attracted to the use of harsh means of influence. Since the metamorphic model proposes that persons who use harsh means of influence devalue the targets of power, does it follow necessarily that persons lacking self-confidence will typically denigrate those persons their roles require them to influence? This question can be raised, but unfortunately the empirical data needed to answer it have not been collected. Thus a future stage in the examination of the powerholder must examine the links between the powerholder's motives and expectations of successful influence, his choice of means of influence, and his perceptions of self and others following the target's compliance.

Despite the fact that there are gaps in the chain connecting power motives with the perception of the target person, and despite the lack of a broad empirical base for my ideas, I believe that the usefulness of the approach described in this book is shown by the fact that similar findings concerning the links between the powerholder's attributions, his expectations of successful influence, and his choice of strong or weak means of influence have been found in both laboratory and field settings. Similarly, the fact that one could detect the same kinds of changes among powerholders in such varied and common settings as marriage, among employers of housemaids, and in work situations suggests the usefulness of the metamorphic model. The findings are consistent with the suggestions made in Chapter 1 that the inclinations of powerholders to devalue the target of influence are not restricted to remote actors holding high office in distant lands. Rather, these inclinations may be an everyday result of the successful use of power and are due to the way humans make inferences and reach conclusions about "cause and effect" in the world around them.

In *Walden Two*, B. F. Skinner inadvertently reaches similar conclusions, I believe, but draws back from a serious consideration of them in his portrayal of Frazier, the director and founder of the novel's utopian community. The problem, of course, as critics of Skinner have often noted, is to decide who will give out the rewards. Frazier frequently discusses this problem in his conversations with Burris, a visitor from the outside world. In all of these talks Frazier denies that power has the potential to corrupt in his community. Safeguards have been developed, in the sense that managers rotate their duties and those without power continue to have the freedom to challenge. Indeed the very goal of the community is to produce autonomous persons who control their own outcomes and rewards.

Still, at the very end of the book, one is left with the strong suspicion that the exercise of power has left its mark on Frazier, who seems to consider himself superior to the rest. This is clearly revealed when he and his visitor have climbed to a high hill overlooking Walden Two.

"Then he [Frazier] flung his hand loosely in a sweeping gesture which embraced all of Walden II. 'These are my children, Burris', he said."

It would have been more convincing if Frazier had said (and believed): "These are my equals" or, better yet, "These are my superiors." Skinner, however, is too insightful a psychologist to believe that the administrator of rewards could state such humble beliefs. The transformations are there, but their consequences are minimized by Skinner.

Unopposed Power

As a final point I want to stress again that what has been said about the use of power, and particularly the metamorphic effects of power, is limited to instances in which the use of power has been relatively unchallenged for a period of time. It has long been recognized that the ultimate solution to the self-aggrandizing tendencies that potentially exist when individuals are given complete control is to institutionalize formal means of resistance. The development of formal structures that allow employees to participate in decision-making within industry, as well as the separation of powers between the executive, legislative, and judicial departments contained in the American constitution, reflect these attempts to curb the debasing effects of unresisted power. I would disagree with Professor David McClelland, who has written that checks on power in America are too often excessive and that the "American's concern about the possible misuse of power verges at times on a neurotic obsession" (1969, p. 152). He is correct in saying that such checks make the leadership role unnecessarily difficult. Yet once that is acknowledged, even a cursory examination of the modern-day world suggests that the cost of unchecked power is a world in disarray. Indeed the unchecked use of power in the second Nixon administration that eventually led to Nixon's resignation from office can be directly traced to the fact that since the early 1930s Congress has delegated to the executive department powers that had been traditionally reserved by the Constitution for the legislative branch. The argument in each of the instances in which such powers were delegated was that Congress took too long to reach decisions that required instant action. Hence such decision-making powers (e.g., the use of the army for small wars) should be given to the office of the president as a means of making leadership less difficult. The upshot of this continual delegation of powers is too well known to be discussed in this book. My only point is that perhaps we must be willing to pay the costs of delays in management and decision-making, since to allow those in power unlimited freedom eventually leads to far greater costs.

In any case the issues raised in this book can be examined through empirical studies rather than through polemics. We can, if we so choose, examine the consequences for effective leadership of given amounts of freedom and given amounts of control. Social science technology has developed to the point where it is possible to be an "experimenting society" (Campbell 1969). I would suggest that among the questions to be studied and experimented with, in broad outline, are those that pertain to decisions concerning the use of various power tactics, how various forms of restraint modify these tactics, and how power usage under these various conditions affects the powerholder's views of himself and others.

References

Adams, J. S. Toward an understanding of inequity. *Journal of Abnormal and Social Psychology,* 1963, *67,* 422–36.

———, and Rosenbaum, W. B. The relationship of worker productivity to cognitive dissonance about wage inequities. *Journal of Applied Psychology,* 1962, *46,* 161–64.

Adler, A. *Individual psychology of Alfred Adler.* H. L. Ansbacher and R. R. Ansbacher, New York: Harper and Row, 1956.

Amory, C. *Who killed society?* New York: Harper and Row, 1960.

Atkinson, J. W. *Motives in fantasy action and society.* New York: Van Nostrand, 1958.

Bachrach, P., and Baratz, M. S. Decisions and non-decisions: An analytical framework. *American Political Science Review,* 1963, *57,* 632–42.

Baker, L. D., DiMarco, N., and Scott, W. E., Jr. Effects of supervisor's sex and level of authoritarianism on evaluation and reinforcement of blind and sighted workers. *Journal of Applied Psychology,* 1975, *60,* 28–32.

Baldwin, D. A. Internation influence revisited. *Journal of Conflict Resolution,* 1971, *15,* 471–86.

———. Economic power. In J. T. Tedeschi, ed., *Perspectives on Social Power.* Chicago: Aldine, 1974, Chap. 11.

Banks, W. C. The effects of perceived similarity and influencer's personality upon the use of rewards and punishments. Paper presented at the 1974 Eastern Psychological Association Meetings, Philadelphia, Pa.

Barnett, R. L. The game of nations. Harpers, 1971, *November,* pp. 53–59.

Bedell, J., and Sistrunk, F. Power, opportunity cost, and sex in a mixed motive game. *Journal of Personality and Social Psychology,* 1973, *2,* 270-95.

Berger, L. Use of power, Machiavellianism, and involvement in a simulated industrial setting. Ph.D. dissertation, Temple University, Philadelphia, Pa. 1973.

Berkowitz, L. The contagion of violence. In W. J. Arnold, ed., *Nebraska Symposium on Motivation, 1970.* Lincoln, Nebraska: University of Nebraska Press, 1971, pp. 95–135.

————, and Daniels, L. R. Responsibility and dependency. *Journal of Abnormal and Social Psychology,* 1963, *66,* 429–36.

Berle, A. *Power.* New York: Harcourt, Brace, and World, 1967.

Bierstedt, R. An analysis of social power. *American Sociological Review,* 1950, *15,* 730–36.

Blau, P. M. *Exchange and power in social life.* New York: Wiley, 1964.

Bowers, D. G., and Seashore, S. E. Predicting organizational effectiveness with a four factor theory of leadership. *Administrative Science Quarterly,* 1966, *September,* 238–63.

Bradley, C. Problem children: Electroencephalographic diagnosis and pharmacologic treatment. *Connecticut Medical Journal,* 1942, *6,* 773–77.

Brehm, J. W. *A theory of psychological reactance.* New York: Academic Press, 1966.

Brooks, J. *The go-go years.* New York: Ballantine, 1973.

Brown, B. R. Face-saving following experimentally induced embarrassment. *Journal of Experimental Social Psychology,* 1968, *6,* 255–71.

Buss, A. H. Aggression pays. In J. L. Singer, ed., *The control of aggression and violence.* New York: Academic Press, 1971.

Byrne, D. Interpersonal influence and attitude similarity. *Journal of Abnormal and Social Psychology,* 1961, *62,* 713–15.

Cafferty, T. P., and Streufert, S. Conflict and attitude toward the opponent. *Journal of Applied Psychology,* 1974, *59,* 48–53.

Campbell, D. T. Reforms as experiments. *American Psychologist,* 1969, *24,* 409–29.

Caplan, N., and Nelson, S. D. On being useful. *American Psychologist,* 1973, *28,* 199–211.

Cartwright, D. Influence, leadership, control. In J. G. March, ed., *Handbook of organizations.* Chicago: Rand-McNally, 1965, pp. 1–47.

———, and Zander, A. *Group dynamics.* New York: Harper and Row, 1968.

———, ed. *Studies in social power.* Ann Arbor: University of Michigan, Institute for Social Research, 1959.

Chorover, S. L. Big brother and psychotechnology. *Psychology Today,* 1973, *7,* 43–57.

Christie, R., and Geis, F. *Studies in machiavellianism.* New York: Academic Press, 1970.

Clark, K. B. The pathos of power. *American Psychologist,* 1971, *26,* 1047–57.

Cooley, C. H. *Human nature and the social order.* New York: Scribner's, 1902.

Cyert, R. M., and MacCrimmon, K. R. Organizations. In G. Lindzey and E. Aronson, eds., *The handbook of social psychology,* Reading, Mass.: Addison-Wesley, 1968.

Dahl, R. A. The concept of power. *Behavioral Science,* 1957, *2,* 201–18.

Davis, K. E., and Jones, E. E. Changes in interpersonal perception as a means of reducing cognitive dissonance. *Journal of Abnormal and Social Psychology,* 1960, *61,* 402–10.

DeCharms, R. *Personal causation.* New York: Academic Press, 1968.

Delgado, J. M. R. *Physical control of the mind.* New York: Harper and Row, 1969.

Deutsch, M. Conflicts: Productive and destructive. *Journal of Social Issues,* 1969, *25,* 7–41.

———, and Krauss, R. M. The effect of threat upon interpersonal bargaining. *Journal of Abnormal and Social Psychology,* 1960, *61,* 181–89.

Dollard, J. C.; Dobb, L.; Miller, N.; and Sears, R. *Frustration and aggression,* New Haven: Yale University Press, 1939.

Domhoff, G. W. *Who rules America?* Englewood Cliffs, New Jersey: Prentice-Hall, 1967.

Dutton, D. G. Attribution of cause for opinion change and liking for audience members. *Journal of Personality and Social Psychology,* 1973, *26,* 208–16.

Emerson, R. M. Power-defense relations. *American Sociological Review,* 1962, *27,* 31–41.

Elazar, D. *The poltics of American federalism.* Lexington, Mass.: D. C. Heath, 1969.

Erikson, E. H. Childhood and tradition in two American Indian tribes. In C. Kluckhohn & O. H. A. Murray, eds., *Personality in nature, society, and culture.* New York: Knopf, 1950.

Etzioni, A. Organizational dimensions and their interrelationship. In B. Indik and F. K. Berrien, eds., *People, groups and organizations.* New York: Teachers College Press, 1968.

Festinger, L.; Pepitone, A.; and Newcomb, T. Some consequences of de-individuation in a group. *Journal of Abnormal and Social Psychology,* 1952, *47,* 382–89.

Fleishman, E. A.; Harris, E. F.; and Burtt, H. E. *Leadership and supervision in industry.* Columbus, Ohio: Bureau of Educational Research, Ohio State University, 1955.

Foa, U. G., and Foa, E. B. *Societal structures of the mind.* Springfield, Illinois: C. C. Thomas, 1975.

Fodor, E. M. Disparagement by a subordinate as an influence on the use of power. *Journal of Applied Psychology,* 1974, *59,* 652–55.

French, J. R. P., Jr., and Snyder, R. Leadership and interpersonal power. In D. Cartwright, ed., *Studies in social power.* Ann Arbor: University of Michigan, Institute for Social Research, 1959.

French, J. R. P., Jr., and Raven, B. The bases of social power. In D. Cartwright, ed., *Studies in social power.* Ann Arbor: University of Michigan, Institute for Social Research, 1959, pp. 150–67.

Freud, S. Civilization and its discontents. London: Hogarth Press, 1957.

———. Why war? In L. Bramson & G. Goethals, eds., *War.* New York: Basic Books, 1964.

Fromm, E. Individual and social origins of neurosis. In C. Kluckhorn and H. A. Murray, eds., *Personality in nature, society, and culture.* New York: Knopf, 1959.

Fuller, J. G. *The gentlemen conspirators.* New York: Grove Press, 1962.

Galbraith, J. K. *The new industrial state.* Boston: Houghton Mifflin, 1967.

Gamson, W. A. *Power and discontent.* Homewood, Ill.: The Dorsey Press, 1968.

Godfrey, E. P.; Fiedler, F. E.; and Hall, D. M. *Boards, management and company success.* Danville, Ill.: Interstate, 1959.

Goldstein, J.; Davis, R.; and Herman, D. Escalation of aggression: Experimental studies. *Journal of Personality and Social Psychology,* 1975, *31,* 162–67.

Goodstadt, B., and Hjelle, L. A. Power to the powerless. *Journal of Personality and Social Psychology,* 1973, 27, 190–96.

————, & Kipnis, D. Situational influences on the use of power. *Journal of Applied Psychology,* 1970, *54,* 201–07.

Gottlieb, J. S.; Ashby, M. C.; and Knott, J. R. Primary behavior disorders and psychopathic personality. *Archives of Neurology and Psychiatry,* 1946, *56,* 381–400.

Grey, R. J. The influence of organizational context on supervisor's evaluative process. Ph.D. dissertation, Temple University, 1975.

Gurr, T. *Why men rebel.* Princeton, New Jersey: Princeton University Press, 1970.

Halberstam, D. *The best and the brightest.* New York: Fawcett-World, 1973.

Haroutunian, J. *Lust for power.* New York: Scribner's, 1949.

Hare, R. D. Psychopathy, autonomic functioning and the orienting response. *Journal of Abnormal Psychology,* 1968, *73,* 1–24.

Harsanyi, J. C. Measurement of social power, opportunity costs, and the theory of two-person bargaining games. *Behavioral Science,* 1962, *7,* 67–79.

Hawley, D. W., and Wirt, F. *The search for community power.* Englewood Cliffs, New Jersey: Prentice-Hall, 1968.

Hobbes, T. *Leviathan.* England: Penguin Books, 1968.

Hochbaum, G. The relation between group members' self-confidence and their reaction to group pressure to uniformity. *American Sociological Review,* 1954, *19,* 678–87.

Horney, K. *Neurosis and human growth.* New York: Norton, 1950.

Jackson, J. M. The organization and its communication problems. In H. J. Leavitt and L. R. Pondy, eds., *Readings in Managerial Psychology,* Chicago: University of Chicago Press, 1964.

Jasper, H. H.; Solomon, P.; and Bradley, C. Electroencephalographic studies of delinquent boys. *American Journal of Psychiatry,* 1938, *95,* 641–58.

Jones, E. E. *Ingratiation.* New York: Appleton-Century-Crofts, 1964.

Kahn, R. L.; Wolfe, D. M.; Quinn, R. P.; and Snoek, J. D. *Organizational Stress.* New York: Wiley, 1964.

Kaufmann, H. *Aggression and altruism.* New York: Holt, Rinehart, and Winston, 1970.

Kelley, H. H. Attribution theory in social psychology. In David Levine, ed., *Nebraska Symposium on Motivation,* Lincoln, Nebraska: The University of Nebraska Press, 1967.

Kelman, H. C., and Lawrence, L. H. Assignment of responsibility in the case of Lt. Calley. *Journal of Social Issues,* 1972, *28,* 177–212.

Kerner, O., et al. *Report of the National Advisory Commission on civil disorders.* New York: Bantam Books, 1968.

Kipnis, D. Some determinants of supervisory esteem. *Personnel Psychology,* 1960, *13,* 377–91.

Kipnis, D. Does power corrupt? *Journal of Personality and Social Psychology,* 1972, *24,* 33–41.

————. The powerholder. In J. T. Tedeschi, ed., *Perspectives on Social Power.* Chicago: Aldine, 1974, pp. 82–124.

————, and Consentino, J. Use of leadership powers in industry. *Journal of Applied Psychology,* 1969, 53, 460–66.

————, and Lane, W. P. Self-confidence and leadership. *Journal of Applied Psychology,* 1962, *46,* 291–95.

————, and Misner, P. The police officer's decision to arrest. Paper presented to Eastern Psychological Association, Philadelphia, Pa. 1974.

————, Silverman, A., and Copeland, C. The effects of emotional arousal upon the use of coercion among Negro and union employees. *Journal of Applied Psychology,* 1973, *57,* 38–43.

————, and Vanderveer, R. Ingratiation and the use of power. *Journal of Personality and Social Psychology,* 1971, *17,* 280–86.

Kite, W. R. Attribution of causality as a function of the use of reward and punishment. Ph.d. dissertation, Stanford University, 1965.

Kruglanski, A., and Cohen, M. Attributed freedom and personal causation. *Journal of Personality and Social Psychology,* 1973, *26,* 245–50.

Knott, J. R., and Gottlieb, J. S. Electroencephalographic evaluation of psychopathic personality. *Archives of Neurology and Psychiatry,* 1944, *52,* 515–19.

Lagent, P., and Mettee, D. R. Turning the other cheek versus getting even. *Journal of Personality and Social Psychology,* 1973, *2,* 243–53.

Lawler, E. E. *Pay and organizational effectiveness.* New York: McGraw-Hill, 1971.

Lerner, M. J. The justice motive: "Equity" and parity among children. *Journal of Personality and Social Psychology,* 1974, *29,* 539–45.

Lerner, M. J., and Simmons, C. H. Observer's reaction to the "innocent" victim. *Journal of Personality and Social Psychology,* 1966, *4,* 203–10.

Leventhal, G. S., and Lane, D. W. Sex, age and equity behavior. *Journal of Personality and Social Psychology,* 1970, *15,* 312–16.

Levy, H. J., and Miller, D. *Going to jail.* New York: Dell, 1970.

Lippitt, R.; Polansky, N.; Redl, F.; and Rosen, S. The dynamics of power. *Human Relations,* 1952, *5,* 37–64.

Lipset, S. Education and equality. *Society,* 1974, *11,* 56–66.

Lorenz, K. *On aggression.* New York: Harcourt, Brace, and World, 1966.

Machiavelli, N. *The prince.* New York: Mentor Books, 1952.

Macpherson, C. B. Introduction. In T. Hobbes, *Leviathan* England: Penguin, 1968.

Marwell, G., and Schmitt, D. R. Dimensions of compliance-gaining behavior. *Sociometry,* 1967, 350–64.

Maslow, A. Deficiency motivation and growth motivation. In M. R. Jones, ed., *The Nebraska symposium on motivation.* Omaha: University of Nebraska Press, 1955.

Masters, W. H., and Johnson, V. E. *Human sexual response.* Boston: Little, Brown, 1966.

May, Rollo. *Power and innocence.* New York: Norton, 1972.

McClelland, D. C. *The achieving society.* Princeton, New Jersey: Van Nostrand, 1961.

————. The two faces of power. *Journal of International Affairs,* 1969, *24,* 141–54.

Mead, G. H. *Mind, self, and society.* Chicago: University of Chicago Press, 1934.

Magargee, E. L. The role of inhibition in the assessment and understanding of violence. In J. L. Singer, ed., *The control of aggression and violence.* New York: Academic Press, 1971.

Memmi, A. *The colonizer and the colonized.* Boston: Beacon Press, 1965.

Michener, A., and Burt, M. R. Legitimacy as a base of social influence. In J. T. Tedeschi, ed., *Perspectives on social power.* Chicago: Aldine, 1974.

————; Fleishman, J.; Elliot, G.; and Skolnick, J. Influence use and target attributes. *Journal of Personality and Social Psychology,* 1976 (in press).

————, and Schwertfeger, M. Liking as a determinant of power tactic preference. *Sociometry,* 1972, *35,* 190–202.

Milgram, S. Behavioral studies of obedience. *Journal of Abnormal and Social Psychology,* 1963, *67,* 371–78.

Mills, C. W. *The power elite.* New York: Oxford University Press, 1956.

Minton, H. L. Power and personality. In J. T. Tedeschi, ed., *The social influence process,* Chicago: Aldine, 1972.

Mott, P. E. Power, authority and influence. In M. Aiken and P. E. Mott, eds., *The structure of community power.* New York: Random House, 1970, pp. 3–16.

Moyer, K. E. The physiology of aggression and the implications for aggression control. In J. L. Singer, ed., *The control of aggression and violence.* New York: Academic Press, 1971.

Mulder, M. *Group structure, motivation, and group performance.* The Hague: Mouton, 1963.

———, & Stemerding, A. Threat, attraction to group, and need for strong leadership. *Human Relations,* 1963, *16,* 317–34.

Nisbet, Robert A. *The social bond.* New York: Alfred A. Knopf, 1970.

Pelz, D. C. Leadership within a hierarchical organization. *Journal of Social Issues,* 1951, *7,* 49–55.

Pepitone, A. The role of justice in independent decision-making. *Journal of Experimental Social Psychology,* 1971, *7,* 144–56.

Pollard, W. E., and Mitchell, T. R. A decision theory analysis of social power. *Psychological Bulletin,* 1973, *78,* 433–46.

Porter, L., and Lawler, E. Properties of organization structure in relation to job attitude and job structure. *Psychological Bulletin,* 1965, *64,* 23–51.

Ransford, H. E. Isolation, powerlessness and violence. *Journal of Sociology,* 1968, *73,* 581–91.

Raser, J. R. Personal characteristics of political decision makers. Peace research and society. *International Papers,* 1966, *5,* 161–81.

Raven, B. H. The comparative analysis of power and influence. In J. T. Tedeschi, ed., *Perspectives on social power.* Chicago: Aldine, 1974.

———, and Kruglanski, A. W. Conflict and power. In P. Swingle, ed., *The structure of conflict.* New York: Academic Press, 1970.

Reed, W. H. Upward communication in industrial hierarchies. *Human Relations,* 1962, *15,* 3–15.

Rogow, A. A., and Lasswell, H. D. *Power, corruption, and rectitude.* Englewood Cliffs, New Jersey, Prentice-Hall, 1963.

Rothbart, M. Effects of motivation, equity, and compliance on the use of rewards and punishments. *Journal of Personality and Social Psychology,* 1968, *9,* 353–62.

Sampson, R. V. *Equality and power*. London: Heineman, 1965.

Schachter, S., and Singer, J. E. Cognitive, social, and physiological determinants of emotional states. *Psychological Review*, 1962, *69*, 377–99.

Schermerhorn, R. A. *Society and power*. New York: Random House, 1961.

Schlenker, B., and Tedeschi, J. T. Interpersonal attraction and the use of reward and coercive power. *Human Relations*, 1972, *25*, 427–40.

Schopler, J., and Bateson, N. The power of dependence. *Journal of Personality and Social Psychology*, 1965, *2*, 247–54.

Scott, J. G. *Comparative political corruption*. Englewood Cliffs, New Jersey: Prentice-Hall, 1972.

Shure, G. H.; Meeker, R. J.; and Hansford, E. A. The effectiveness of pacifist strategy. *Journal of Conflict Resolution*, 1965, *9*, 106–17.

Skinner, B. F. *Walden two*. New York: Macmillan, 1949.

———. *Beyond freedom and dignity*. New York: Bantam Books, 1971.

Sorenson, T. C. *Kennedy*. New York: Harper, 1965.

Sorokin, P. A., and Lundin, W. A. *Power and morality: Who shall guard the guardians?* Boston: Sargent, 1959.

Speer, A. *Inside the Third Reich*. New York: Avon Books, 1970.

Staub, E. The learning and unlearning of aggression. In J. L. Singer, ed., *The control of aggression and violence*. New York: Academic Press, 1971.

Stotland, E. Peer groups and reaction to power figures. In D. Cartwright, ed., *Studies in social power*. Ann Arbor: University of Michigan, Institute for Social Research, 1959.

Strickland, L. H. Surveillance and trust. *Journal of Personality*, 1958, *26*, 201–15.

Swanberg, W. A. *Citizen Hearst*. New York: Scribner's, 1961.

Swingle, P., ed., *The structure of conflict*. New York: Academic Press, 1970.

Tarbel, I. M. *The history of the Standard Oil Company*. New York: Macmillan, 1904.

Tedeschi, J. T.; Bonoma, T. V.; and Novinson, N. Behavior of a threatener: retaliation vs. fixed opportunity costs. *Journal of Conflict Resolution*, 1970, *14*, 69–76.

———; Horai, J.; Lindskold, S.; and Faley, T. The effects of opportunity costs and target compliance on the behavior of a threatening source. *Journal of Experimental Social Psychology,* 1970, *6,* 205–13.

———; Lindskold, S.; Horai, J.; and Gahagan, J. P. Social power and the credibility of promises. *Journal of Personality and Social Psychology,* 1969, *13,* 253–61.

———; Schlenker, B. R.; and Bonoma, T. V. Cognitive dissonance: Private ratiocination or private spectacle? *American Psychologist,* 1971, *26,* 685–95.

———; Schlenker, B. R.; and Bonoma, T. V., *Conflict, power, and games.* Chicago: Aldine, 1973.

———; Smith, R. B., III.; & Brown, R. C. A reconceptualization of aggression. Manuscript, State University of New York at Albany, 1972.

Terkel, S. Servant of the state, a conversation with Daniel Ellsberg. *Harpers,* 1972, *February,* 52–61.

Thibaut, J. W., and Faucheux, C. The development of contractual norms in a bargaining situation under two types of stress. *Journal of Experimental Social Psychology,* 1965, *1,* 89–102.

———, and Kelley, H. H. *The social psychology of groups.* New York: Wiley, 1959.

Toch, H. The social psychology of violence. In E. L. Megargee and J. Hokanson, eds., *The dynamics of aggression.* New York: Harper and Row, 1970, pp. 160–69.

Veroff, J. Development and validation of a projective measure of power motivation. *Journal of Abnormal and Social Psychology,* 1957, *54,* 1–8.

———, and Veroff, J. Reconsideration of a measure of power motivation. *Psychological Bulletin,* 1972, *78,* 279–91.

Walster, E.; Aronson, V.; Abrahams, D.; and Rottman, L. Importance of physical attraction and attractiveness in dating behavior. *Journal of Personality and Social Psychology,* 1966, *4,* 508–16.

———, and Berscheid, E. When does a harm-doer compensate a victim? *Journal of Personality and Social Psychology,* 1967, *6,* 435–41.

———; Berscheid, E.; and Walster, G. W. New directions in equity research. *Journal of Personality and Social Psychology,* 1973, *25,* 151–76.

Washburn, S. L., and Hamburg, D. A. Aggressive behavior in old world monkeys and apes. In P. C. Jay, ed., *Primates.* New York: Holt, Rinehart, and Winston, 1968.

Watson, D. Reinforcement theory of personality and social system. *Journal of Personality and Social Psychology,* 1972, *22,* 88–94.

Wilson, J. Q. *Varieties of police behavior*. Cambridge, Mass.: Harvard University Press, 1968.

Winter, D. G. *The power motive*. New York: The Free Press, 1973.

Wiser, W., and Wiser, C. *Behind mud walls*. Berkeley, California: University of California Press, 1967.

Wolfe, D. M. Power and authority in the family. In D. Cartwright, ed., *Studies in social power*. Ann Arbor, Michigan: Institute for Social Research, 1959, pp. 99–117.

Zander, A., Cohen, A. R., and Stotland, E. Power and the relations among the professions. In D. Cartwright, ed., *Studies in social power*. Ann Arbor: University of Michigan, Institute for Social Research, 1959.

Zimbardo, P. G. The human choice: Individuation, reason and order versus deindividuation, impulse, and chaos. In W. J. Arnold and D. Levine, eds., *Nebraska Symposium on Motivation, 1969*. Lincoln: University of Nebraska Press, 1970, pp. 237–307.

————; Haney, C.; Banks, W. C.; and Jaffe, D. Psychology of imprisonment, in Z. Rubin, ed., *Doing unto others*. Englewood Cliffs, New Jersey: Prentice-Hall, 1974.

Index

Ability versus attitudes. *See* Attribution of powerholders

Absolution, and power usage, 19, 95–96

Alienation, and power motives, 154–57

Altruism, compared to use of rewards, 61

Antigone, 175

Attribution, by powerholders: and resistance of targets, 49–57, 105–11; and attitude change, 186–95

Bases of power, 9–12

Camus, A., 155

Cause and effect, problems of interpretation, 179–80

Choice of influence tactics, 28; effects of setting, 41–46; powerholder's status and, 46–48; cognitive processes involved, 49–54; perception of target resistance, 52, 56–57; expectations of successful influence versus self-confidence, 120–21

Coercive power, 77–127; illustrated in three settings, 42–44; defined, 78–80; aggression, 80–83; security,

83–84; ego needs, 84–85; material gain, 86–90; role involvement, 91–96; control of superior resources, 112–15; individual differences in use of, 118–23; expectations of successful influence and use, 104

Competition, 115–16

Compliance, request for, 21

Contrast effect, and the use of rewards, 70–76

Dependency, effects on motivation for power, 150–52

"End-run" definition of power, 13–14

Equity versus equality, 141–44

Exchange theory, 12, 70

Friendship, and power usage, 63–67

Hearst, William Randolph, 82

Hedonic calculus, 26, 87

Hierarchical needs, 18

Hitler, Adolph, 82

Hubris, 169

Human nature, assumptions about, 128–30, 158–62